THE GENTLE REFORMERS:
MASSACHUSETTS DEMOCRATS
IN THE CLEVELAND ERA

THE GENTLE REFORMERS:
MASSACHUSETTS DEMOCRATS
IN THE CLEVELAND ERA

BY GEOFFREY BLODGETT

HARVARD UNIVERSITY PRESS
CAMBRIDGE, MASSACHUSETTS · 1966

Publication of this book has been aided
by a grant from the Ford Foundation

Library of Congress Catalog Card Number 66–13178

4402

TO THE MEMORY OF
ROBERT SAMUEL FLETCHER
1900–1959

THIS STUDY got under way a decade ago as a graduate student's excited foray into the politics of Boston in the 1890's. At the outset my attention was drawn to the melodramatic events of 1896. I was struck by the way in which William Jennings Bryan's campaign for the presidency fractured his own party by forcing Democrats of every persuasion either to commit themselves to his cause or somehow oppose it. Clearly the division was not a simple clean sectional split between urban East and agrarian West. In Massachusetts that year Bryan's candidacy splintered the Democratic party into a swarm of hostile groups, each of which assumed a stubborn stance during the campaign and kept it for years thereafter. So bitter was the feeling generated that summer among these angry factions that I wondered how on earth they had ever worked together in earlier years under a common label. My curiosity was whetted when I considered the apparent gulf of mistrust which, then as now, divided the New England populace into native Yankee and immigrant stock. Who were the Democrats of Massachusetts and how had they defined themselves?

Further inquiry suggested that, for Massachusetts and the nation, the seizure of Democratic party machinery by the Bryanites spelled the definitive collapse of an ill-fated political reform movement which had begun in 1884, with the first election of Grover Cleveland to the presidency. Across the twelve-year span between these two elections, Cleveland's substantial bulk and his determined will had served as satisfying emblems for the cause of gentle, conservative, respectable reform among his followers. Centered in the urban East, their movement found eminent protagonists in the states of the Upper South and Old Northwest as well. In Massachusetts as elsewhere they strove to fashion a party and a program which might reinforce and institutionalize the ethic of high-minded propriety in public life—an ethic they believed had been asserted in Cleveland's victory over James G. Blaine in 1884.

They called themselves Cleveland Democrats. In Massachusetts they comprised an odd collection of incongruous groups and individuals: old-line Yankee Democrats whose party loyalty sprang from family preference and commercial interests dating well back into the century; Irish Democrats who had made the party their refuge since the bitter years of the Know-Nothings in the 1850's; righteously independent Mugwumps who could not stomach the tainted Republicanism of Blaine; and a crucial sprinkling of rising young Yankee lawyers pitched into political activism by Cleveland's example and their own ambitions. Ethnic, occupational, and social differences divided them more seriously than they cared to admit. But confrontation with common problems and opportunities bound them together in a consensus of attitudes which justified a common label. What happened to them and their ideas can be called a case study in Cleveland Democracy.

It might be well to summarize, by way of brief introduction, the main chronological drift of this study. Circumstances had thrown Cleveland's supporters together rather suddenly in the campaign of 1884, and in the wake of the election differences among them welled up immediately over the meaning of Cleveland's victory. Was it triumph for reform or for the Democratic party? Demands for patronage from hungry Democratic regulars aggravated the Mugwumps' hostility toward the party system itself and reinforced their demand for further implementation of civil service ideals. Patronage issues intensified the mutual distrust between Irish and Yankee and jeopardized their delicate coalition behind Cleveland. But toward the end of Cleveland's first term, patronage disputes were surmounted when tariff reform replaced civil service reform as the driving issue of Cleveland Democracy. Tariff agitation in Massachusetts helped to unify party factions where civil service agitation had divided them. The drive for lower tariffs also enabled Massachusetts Democrats to regard themselves as reformers while simultaneously giving them a rationale for economic orthodoxy during years of mounting unrest among industrial workers. Despite Cleveland's ouster from the White House in the election of 1888, his various Bay State followers seemed to have forged themselves into a coherent working coalition.

In the early 1890's they achieved varying degrees of success at Boston City Hall, at the golden-domed State House, and on Capitol Hill in Washington. Cleveland Democrats won the Boston mayoralty, the governorship, and a narrow majority of the state's congressional delegation. At each level of government—city, state, and nation—they probed the limits of their commitment to reform while trying to cope with the problems of an urban, industrial society. Their efforts were strenuous; their achievements modest. By the mid-nineties, at all three levels, their definition of reform was apparently exhausted. In the city and the state, as well as in Washington, the onset of depression in 1893 disrupted blithe political calculations and conservative social assumptions, threatening the original terms of cooperation among the diverse groups within the party. In the grimy downtown wards of Boston new Irish leaders rose to challenge the validity of subservient Irish cooperation with Yankee Democrats and Mugwumps. Across the state the traditional Republican majority reasserted its dominance. Simultaneously western agrarians rose to challenge control of the national party by the eastern lieutenants of Grover Cleveland, and tariff reform gave way to the silver issue as the main preoccupation of the party. Weakened locally and nationally, the party was suddenly in dire straits.

In 1896 Bryanism finished the party of Grover Cleveland. The ethic of Cleveland Democracy was no longer viable, either in Massachusetts or the nation. Thereafter Mugwumps retreated into political isolation and impotence, Irish Democrats in Boston fell to cultivating habits of expedient localism, and Yankee Democrats split into radical and antiradical factions—or turned Republican. Despite a valiant effort by some of Cleveland's erstwhile followers to translate their ideals into the cause of anti-imperialism or (in the case of Josiah Quincy) into municipal socialism, the conservative reform of the Cleveland era had suddenly become anachronistic.

The familiar chronology of national political history, as well as the neglected annals of state and local history, can take on fresh meaning when successive crises are analyzed in terms of the configuration of groups they precipitate in a single broad metropolitan community. In the belief that the art of history is not dissection but re-creation, I have tried to understand these groups in their own setting, on their own terms, and in the light of the hopes and anxieties of their articulate leadership. My narrative is sprinkled liberally with forgotten heroes—men such as William E. Russell, the brisk, appealing young Democratic governor of Massachusetts in the early 1890's; the militant, impetuous Mugwump-turned-Bryanite, George Fred Williams; the taciturn but energetic patrician Josiah Quincy (the last to bear that august name); and the powerful, temperamental Irish party leader, Pat Maguire. The thread of their story wanders back and forth across established bounds of local, state, and national history. The federated structure of American politics required them and most of their party colleagues to work and think together on all three of these levels of action in their pursuit of success. By the same token the ideals and assumptions of Cleveland Democracy cannot be understood unless their application is examined at each tier of the federal structure. The preoccupation of urban Irishmen with patronage and political security in the city may have seemed antagonistic or at best irrelevant to Yankee concern for the level of the tariff and political reform in the state, but neither group found it could ignore the interests of the other in practice. Party survival demanded that they search for common ground. How far they succeeded, and why they ultimately failed, is the subject of this book.

If there is a rhythm to events of the American past, the wavering prestige of reform should be a valuable measure of it. Those times in our history when the tempo of public life has run fast have been characteristically years of renovation. Achievement in such times was measured by its contribution to progress, and men's reputations depended on how far they altered the terms of life around them. In between such eras have come slack times, when social inertia and the tangle of politics-as-usual slowed the current of change and deflected its course. Historians seem attracted to the crises in this rhythm between reform and retrenchment. Of course no era wholly fits these tidy rubrics. But the last quarter of the nineteenth century does violence to them both. These were years when reformers made advances toward permanent change, but headway was wobbly and erratic. Reform activity, for all its vigor, rubbed across the grain of politics. "Scratch a reformer and you will find a disappointed politician." This was a shrewd thing to say in Boston in the 1890's. Its truth was apparent in the careers of the men who worked for reform within the American party system of those years.

For Yankee Democrats in particular, the conditions of survival imposed by their environment were increasingly severe. They were a minority within a minority. Their native New England had fallen behind the rest of the nation in population growth and economic expansion, and it was as well rapidly losing its proud claim to the intellectual tutelage of the American people. These setbacks were clearly reflected in New England's declining political power in sectional rivalries over tariff and rail policy. More subtly they were reflected in the rampant materialism of a post-Civil War America which scorned the presumptions of educated gentlemen in politics. New England as a whole had taken on a comprehensive minority status. Moreover, within New England, and particularly in Boston, adherence to the traditional Yankee ethos of politics and society stamped one as a member of an increasingly isolated minority as the local population grew in diversity and autonomy of interests. Native-born and foreign-born, Yankee, Irish, Italian, and Jew, Protestant and Catholic, commerce and college, slum-dweller and suburbanite, employer and employee, rich and poor, genteel, nouveau and dispossessed, Republican and Democrat, Mugwump, trade-unionist, and socialist,—within this broadening mesh of cross-purposes, the Cleveland Democrat was often lonely, the product and the victim of an environment he longed to control.

Perspective would allow us, if we wished, to call these men the early heralds of the Progressive Era. As the Wisconsin followers of Robert LaFollette embodied militant Progressivism at the turn of the century, so the Massachusetts followers of Grover Cleveland epitomized its prototype a decade or so before. But for Cleveland Democrats the horizon of reform grew less—not more—distinct as the new century approached. The tough habits and abrupt reversals of politics thwarted their aspirations, and for most of them the commitment to reform ended in rancor, confusion, and disappointment. Perhaps we should remember them as casualties, not heralds.

For several years I have received the encouragement and taxed the patience of many people in putting this book together. A suggestion of Professor Frederick Merk, that the response of Bostonians to agrarian radicalism in the 1890's might merit a seminar paper, was the beginning of my debts. From the paper grew a doctoral thesis, and from the thesis grew this book. Professor Frank Freidel supervised that process, and his shrewd, clear-eyed guidance as well as the inspiration of his own craftsmanship have been invaluable. Mr. Philip Putnam Chase began almost forty years ago to gather from the cellars, attics, and old barns of metropolitan Boston many of the personal records on which this study is based. The Director of the Massachusetts Historical Society, Dr. Stephen T. Riley, and his assistant, Miss Winifred Collins, were most generous in meeting my recurrent demands for help. I also wish to thank the staffs of Widener Library, Houghton Library, the Manuscript Division of the Library of Congress, the Massachusetts State House Library, the Library of the College of the Holy Cross, and the Oberlin College Library for their aid. Ambassador Henry Cabot Lodge, Mr. Richard M. Russell, Mr. Edmund Quincy, and Mrs. Robert Homans, among the descendants of my protagonists, have kindly given access to family papers. Grants from the Social Science Research Council and the Ford Foundation kept me going at crucial junctures. Professors Richard M. Abrams, Richard M. Brown, Samuel P. Hays, Thomas LeDuc, and my

father, Professor Harold W. Blodgett, read the entire manuscript
at various stages of its development, and to all of them I am
deeply appreciative for valuable criticism. Responsibility for any
remaining errors of fact or eccentricities of judgment remains of
course my own. The substance of Chapter Two appeared originally in *The Mississippi Valley Historical Review;* it is reprinted
here with permission. The substance of Chapter Nine appeared
originally in *The New England Quarterly.* Miss June Wright of
the Oberlin College stenographic office provided typing service
whose quality is proverbial. Meanwhile my wife Jane bore all
the burdens of her calling with remarkable grace, and for that
my gratitude is boundless.

Geoffrey Blodgett

Oberlin, Ohio
August 15, 1965

CONTENTS

THE GENTLE REFORMERS:
MASSACHUSETTS DEMOCRATS
IN THE CLEVELAND ERA

CHAPTER ONE · 1884

ON FRIDAY, June 6, 1884, at about four o'clock in the afternoon, word flashed along Boston's newspaper row that James G. Blaine had been nominated for the presidency by the Republican party in Chicago. The news spread quickly via scampering office-boy through the law offices along State Street, down to the Customs House near the wharfs, among the real estate and insurance firms on Washington Street, across the Charles River by horse-car to Cambridge and Harvard Square, and out to the parlors of suburban towns like Roxbury, Brookline, Newton, Dedham, and Quincy. Many of those who received the news from Chicago had already made preparations for it. By prearrangement, the following afternoon the Massachusetts Reform Club gathered at the Parker House to act on Blaine's nomination. The Yankee gentlemen of the Reform Club, overwhelmingly Republican in persuasion, were almost as unanimous in their distaste for James G. Blaine. Yet oddly Blaine's nomination did not send them into gloom. Young Richard Henry Dana recalled in his private journal, "All was excitement, and everybody was on fire. Not a man in the room wished to support Blaine." Decades later, men who had gone to the Parker House that June day remembered the tight-lipped enthusiasm of the moment when they left their party.[1]

They had sufficient cause to bolt. They believed they faced a simple moral issue. Blaine, they felt, was a dishonest man. They would not cast votes to send a dishonest man to the White House. And they would not support the party that asked them to do it. Yet they rendered their judgment on man and party not with regret but rather with surprising eagerness, almost joy, as if they were experiencing release. Some of these bolters had been among the flushed recruits who helped organize the Republican

party some thirty years before. Some had undergone the futilities
of bolting when President Ulysses Grant sought re-election in
1872, only to return quietly to Republican ranks after Horace
Greeley had made a mockery of their hopes. For many others
this was a first departure, a turning point in young careers. Yet
almost to a man they met to condemn their party with bright
anticipation.

The spirit of the Independents' bolt in 1884 sprang from their
growing sense of denied potency in Massachusetts politics. The
Republican party, the party of virtue and victory in the Civil
War, had become a decreasingly satisfying agent of their aspirations. Each passing year had brought fresh evidence that the
party was becoming primarily a machine for dispensing nominations, patronage offices, and legislative favors as rewards to those
whose loyalty sustained it with money and votes. For these purposes the machine was eminently successful. Since the Civil
War New England had become a sprawling rotten borough of
Republicanism. A lopsided majority of its electoral votes was
assured to Republican presidential candidates. Solid Republican
majorities represented the region in Congress. In Massachusetts
a smoothly functioning state-wide organization returned substantial Republican majorities to the state legislature with systematic regularity. The party dictated terms of political behavior
from the precinct up, determined what men would be rewarded
with political eminence, and fixed close limits on political innovation or independence.

Republican domination in the state had been assured by close
communion between the party and the world of productive commerce. Elected personnel partly reflected this intimate, almost
organic relation. Of the fifty-two men who represented Massachusetts in Congress between 1864 and 1884, forty-two were
Republicans. Of these, twenty-three were lawyers, and seventeen were merchants or manufacturers.[2] Understandably, the
state's cloth, leather, and paper industries were well cared for
by the party through tariff arrangements and other means. Except for an occasional local squabble over liquor or schools or
neglected veterans, the party was habitually rewarded for its

services. The contentment of both prospering men of property and native-born factory laborers, as well as the predictable loyalty of the small towns, provided the party with a broad, stable, voting base.

Meanwhile the range of political options was steadily constricted for those who felt discontented with single-party domination of the two-party system. Rebellion became a plausible alternative to acquiescence in existing arrangements, if only an ennobling pretext could be found. Thus Blaine's nomination broke the Republican party open, releasing those who hungered to assert their independence. Great changes were under way, promising to alter the patterns of the recent past. The bolt of 1884 came as a climax to several years of unusual political tension in state and nation. It would prove to be the impulse for a momentous transformation in the role of the Democratic party.

The Republican party's restless Independents had taken heart from the events of the early 1880's. For years they had rallied to the warning cry of "Spoils," stubbornly protesting the barter of public offices to party hacks. "Snivel Service Reform," as their cause was called by contemptuous foes, was not calculated to win gratitude or esteem for its advocates in party councils. Despite recent efforts at grass-roots organization among the reformers, prospects for sudden success seemed poor. Many reformers felt, as one of them ruefully put it, like "babies in the Independent Orphan Asylum." [3] But in their discouragement they had not reckoned with the vagaries of the popular mood. President Garfield's murder in 1881 by a frustrated office seeker aroused unexpected public concern over circumstances which could so suddenly twist the placid course of history. As suddenly, civil service reform ceased to be a forlorn hope.

Armed with a new militance, the reformers pressed toward their goal. In Massachusetts they were strongest in the suburban cities on the southwestern perimeter of Boston. In the fall of 1882 they helped elect two congressmen pledged to work for a national civil service law. Leopold Morse, a German Jew who had emigrated to America in 1849 and prospered in Boston's clothing trade, won election with reformers' support in the

Cambridge district. In the southern suburbs of Boston Colonel
Theodore Lyman, a cousin of Harvard president Charles Eliot,
won the backing of eminent neighbors and ousted the Republican incumbent by challenging his voting record on spoils bills.
In other states across the country Republican spoilsmen were
dealt comparable defeats. Soon after the congressional elections
of 1882, a lame-duck Congress responded by passing the Pendleton Act. President Arthur signed the bill in January 1883, and at
last an effective civil service system seemed a tangible prospect.
The sequence of victories was encouraging. It showed that civil
service reform could stand the test of the polls and that its
advocacy was no longer a kiss of death in politics.[4]

The reformers promptly set to work framing a law to bring the
merit principle into play in Massachusetts. Richard Henry Dana
and Josiah Quincy, two young Harvard graduates whose names
were as yet their best credentials, worked tirelessly to prepare
a bill for submission to the General Court in January 1884. Then
began an anxious struggle to persuade the Republican majority
in the legislature to pass the bill. Burial seemed more likely, but
through persistent lobbying, Quincy secured a roll-call vote on
the measure late in the session. The strategy worked. A reluctant
majority of party regulars, forced to the issue, voted for state
civil service reform. The bill passed on June 3, 1884. The reformers had scored another major victory, on the eve of Blaine's
nomination for the presidency. Far from confirming their Republican loyalty, success only whetted their appetite for greater
recognition and power in the politics of their state.[5]

Despite the improving fortune of the civil service issue, Republican reformers felt buffeted and constricted within their
party. Their discontent had shown itself most recently during
the gubernatorial campaign of 1883, one of the harshest political
fights in Massachusetts history. That year Republicans marshaled all their strength to defeat brawling Governor Ben Butler
in his try for re-election. Butler was a stench in Republican
nostrils. As a Republican himself during the years of Grant's
presidency, Butler had represented Massachusetts among Grant's
henchmen in Congress, provocation sufficient in itself to Yankee

sensibilities. More recently, as a renegade to radicalism, he had guided the state's Greenback forces into control of the Democratic party machinery and gotten himself elected governor.

Despite his rather mild behavior in the State House, those who could recall his record in the Civil War, his talent for personal notoriety, and the rout of Republican ideals during his years as Grant's confidant, were eager to remove him. One of Butler's fiercest critics was Moorfield Storey. A prominent State Street lawyer, Storey had begun his career as secretary to Massachusetts Senator Charles Sumner in Washington just after the war. From the days when Storey sat in the galleries of Congress and watched Butler's performance in the impeachment of Andrew Johnson, he had harbored a profound distrust of the Massachusetts demagogue. Now, with Butler seeking a second term as governor, Storey itched to expose the past. "I find everywhere I go," he wrote to Henry Cabot Lodge, the newly appointed Republican state chairman, "young men who are entirely ignorant of Butler's previous history and cannot therefore understand the feeling of older men toward him. Such men who know him only by what he has done since January 1, and who cannot interpret his acts and speeches by the light of his past are a little apt to think that he is unjustly abused . . ." Storey urged a campaign of exposure, based on the slogan, "We are opposed to Butler and Butlerism." [6]

But many younger Republicans wanted more to fight for. They felt that Butler's defeat would mean little in itself so long as the Republican party remained in the grip of its own old guard. They wanted to offer the voters a clear choice between radical demagoguery and respectable reform. The Republican platform should be not simply a condemnation of Butler's past, but a manifesto of issues for the future. The young reformers also sought to oppose Butler with a leader who would sympathize with their own struggle for recognition within the Republican party. They were tired of the formalities used to appease them in the past. Josiah Quincy underscored their impatience. "Putting a man like C. F. Adams, Jr., on as chairman of the committee to conduct the president of the convention to the

chair is simply a farce," he wrote to Lodge. "Where we want to
see him is on the committee on resolutions . . . If the Republican
party does not get the votes of the young men who don't know
or care about the issues of the past its days are numbered."
Other men of the same temper wanted to place Charles Francis
Adams, Jr., at the head of the Republican ticket.[7]

Both the platform and the ticket disappointed them. Guided
by Lodge, the Republican convention nominated for governor
Congressman George Robinson, a competent man, but one whose
chest hardly heaved with the air of reform. Second place on the
ticket went to Oliver Ames, a free-spending shovel manufacturer whose candidacy was abhorrent to the young reformers.
Their defeat in party convention, as one reformer put it, was
like "having ice-water poured down our backs." [8]

The Republican ticket attracted both the money and the votes
of the state's aroused Republican majority, and Butler was
beaten. But the party came back into accustomed power in
January 1884 with its reform wing still subservient. The reformers nursed a sense of missed chances, a nagging conviction
that their own careers had been stunted just at a time when
their chief issue, civil service reform, was suddenly blooming.
They felt defeated by the party structure itself and longed for
an opportunity to break out of its fixed hierarchy of men and
issues. Thus Winslow Warren, a lawyer from Dedham, wrote to
William Everett, a Quincy schoolmaster, "I am more than ever
convinced we shall never effect anything within the old party
lines—and yet we are over-weighted with timid spirits tied on
to the old names." [9]

By the spring of 1884 this kind of talk was common in Boston.
Along the law offices of State Street, in the lounges of a dozen
Boston clubs, and among the clustering suburban towns wherever gentlemen gathered to share political views, the notion of a
new political dispensation gathered sympathy. It even sent a
chill through the ranks of established party patrons. One
wealthy Republican, dunned for a contribution to the Republican war chest in May, 1884, sniffed the air and decided to wait.
"I must say," he commented, "that in the present state of parties

. . . it is quite in the cards that I might find myself voting against a candidate whose canvass was being helped by my own contribution."[10]

Republican tension was hardly confined to Massachusetts. Across the country the feeling grew that an end to the long Republican hegemony over national political life was at hand. The prospect of a bitter intraparty fight for the coming presidential nomination between the incumbent Chester Arthur and his rival Blaine fed a sense of party crisis. Independent Republicans in New York and New England were reluctant to support either man as the price of party victory. Hopefully they launched a boom behind the mildly reformist Senator Edmunds of Vermont. But Edmunds was a colorless man and his candidacy never left the ground. By the middle of May Blaine seemed to have the nomination sewed up. Carl Schurz, acknowledged mentor for Republican reformers, and Horace White, editor of the oracular New York *Evening Post*, decided that if Blaine were nominated, and the Democrats offered no suitable alternative, Independent Republicans should meet to endorse a third candidate.[11]

When Massachusetts Independents gathered at the Parker House on June 7 to condemn Blaine's nomination, their action was not, then, a sudden, spontaneous burst of moral outrage. Rather for most of them it signaled escape from an unhappy bondage under Republican discipline. Blaine gave them the chance they had been waiting for—to purge themselves of the stain of party corruption and simultaneously to make a clean, swift break with a history of personal disappointment. Their bolt had a cathartic effect on them which they would not soon forget.

Their rallies were by all odds the most enthusiastic held in Massachusetts during the campaign. Within forty-eight hours of the Parker House bolt, organization work began in the Boston law offices of young Josiah Quincy. Within a week, a public meeting was called at Young's Hotel. The crowd, too big for Young's, moved on to Meionaon Hall. There the roll was called on the Committee of One Hundred, chosen to direct the campaign. Negotiations opened with the New York Independents, resulting in an Independent National Conference in New York in late July. Broadsides, manifestoes, addresses, open letters, and newly discovered Mulligan Letters exposing Blaine's past began to pour forth in astonishing supply from Mugwump headquarters on Washington Street. Under the leadership of a brash and voluble young Dedham lawyer, George Fred Williams, the Committee of One Hundred strove for Blaine's defeat with gusto and self-congratulation.[12] Their feverish activity finally moved the pro-Blaine *Boston Traveller* to comment, upon receipt of the latest Mugwump "Address":

> It is about time, we would suggest, that a conference was held at Young's. It will then be in order to rally at Quincy and Cambridge, and by that time the public would be delighted to have these excellent people write an open letter to themselves, and sign it twice over apiece, in accordance with the pleasing precedent set in that regard early in the campaign. [Blaine's coming victory in Maine] should be met by another vigorous address, to be followed rapidly by a conference at Young's, meetings at Quincy and Cambridge, and another very strong open letter to themselves . . .[13]

The *Traveller* had a point. The Mugwumps' behavior in 1884, for all its frenzy, had a cast of clan ritual about it, noticeable even to contemporaries, which set guidelines for the future. Not the least important relic of that campaign was an unwitting manual of precedents to govern the ideal Mugwump response to political crisis. By the 1890's the code of behavior was well understood and would come automatically to mind when men tried to escape present confusion for the certainties of the past. In retrospect the bolt of 1884 took on the quality of tribal legend, carefully recorded. Attendance at the meetings at Parker's, at Young's, at Meionaon, the trip to New York, and above all membership on the Committee of One Hundred became sources of personal pride in the letters and reminiscences of old men.[14]

But in 1884 the ceremony was in the making. Beneath the brave cheer of combat lay uncertainty about what to do next. The younger bolters particularly—Josiah Quincy, Richard Henry Dana, George Fred Williams—while concentrating their public words on the past sins of Blaine and his party, found their private thoughts turning to their own futures. Their friends tacitly agreed that by bolting such men had advanced their own political fortunes. But stern requirements of politics could not be ignored, least of all by young men on the make. The upheaval they helped initiate did not, after all, mean an end to parties. In some minds rose the hope of a new party made up of men like themselves, not merely as a passing answer to crisis, but as a permanent repository of the best virtues and the best issues. President Eliot of Harvard expressed this hope in his speech at Meionaon:

Political progress is to be made only by a conflict of national parties, and, as a rule, of two national parties. And, therefore, I hope that out of this meeting will grow a new party, as one was grown years ago. I know that the young men of this country are sick to death of the demagoging policy of the parties of today. But we want not an Independent party. An Independent is one balancing between the two parties. We want to found a new party in our country, a party of national principles, and one which can look forward to a national triumph.[15]

Some of the older Mugwumps, with established careers outside of politics, warned against burning every bridge. Accustomed to the dual roles of patron and critic, they viewed with equanimity the prospect of temporary rupture with the Republican party, to be healed in due course as in times past. Thus James Freeman Clarke, the renowned Unitarian divine whose perspective on revolt stretched from a youthful residence at Brook Farm, calmly advised his fellow bolters, "The only hope for the Republican party itself is the defeat of Blaine. Going out of power for a while, it would recover something of its former quality, and return to its better traditions. We do not cease to be Republicans, because we vote for once by the side of our opponents." [16] This was all very well for elders like Clarke, for whom politics was a solemn but occasional duty, to be taken up at the command of conscience. But the younger Mugwumps, while soberly protesting to each other their political disinterest, found it hard to achieve Clarke's Olympian detachment. Part of their problem was solved for them when Republican managers read out of their party caucuses any man who refused to support Blaine. For better or worse, the Mugwumps were no longer Republicans. Charles Francis Adams, Jr., had a point when he warned the Mugwumps they ran the risk of becoming "what the Italians call *forestieri*, or dwellers in the woods." [17]

The Democratic party instantly ended Mugwump thoughts of an Independent ticket by nominating Grover Cleveland for the presidency. Cleveland was thoroughly acceptable to the Mugwumps. A few Boston eyebrows rose when a Buffalo paper exposed the paternity scandal in Cleveland's private life, and the Committee of One Hundred prudently dispatched a lawyer to Buffalo to check the story. However, Cleveland's blunt, candid response to the affair resolved most doubts and if anything enhanced his image in Mugwump eyes.[18] But the thought of embracing Cleveland's party was another matter. New Englanders tended to look upon the Democratic party as a ramshackle and slovenly array, lacking even the sustaining character which the Republican party had gained through its reputation for success. By the 1880's men versed in political realities no longer attached to the Democratic party any live stigma from the Civil War. The party was no longer "dangerous" except for purposes of Republican stump rhetoric. But the bloody shirt had done the work Republicans had intended for it: it prevented Democrats from winning elections. And because the Democratic party in New England was repeatedly buried at the polls in state and national contests, observers made a habit of assuming it lacked the essentials for legitimate party rivalry. Gradually the party name became a byword for incapacity, and a new image replaced that earned in the 1850's and 1860's, one more benign but as damning politically. Fear, distrust, and hatred of the party dried up in the warm sun of Republican supremacy, leaving a pervasive, mild contempt. Thoughtful Republicans came to regard their rivals as a feckless, blundering crew, incapable of combining leadership with principle.

Grover Cleveland's nomination did not erase this image among leading Mugwumps. Their speeches were laced with doubt about the implications of a Cleveland victory. If support for

Cleveland entailed supporting the Democratic party, the venture was distinctly hazardous in the Mugwump view. They spoke of it cautiously as an "experiment," and exposed their apprehension by trying to calm each other down in public. "Don't tell me that ruin awaits us if for four years we have a Democratic President," said Charles Codman, a prominent civil service advocate. "Whatever the past of a party which still retains in its list men like Cleveland and Bayard, of that party we can't afford to speak in contempt," said Thomas Wentworth Higginson, the rugged old Unitarian reformer. Late in the campaign John Murray Forbes, the wealthy Boston capitalist who had helped finance the bolt, added a final consoling word. He expected the Republicans to return to power in due course, "when the Democratic party may have justified the fears of its enemies by maladministration." [19]

The recent history of the Democratic party in Massachusetts gave little encouragement to Mugwumps inclined toward wishful thinking. In the annual state elections since the war the Democrats had elected just two governors, and each was promptly voted out of office the following year. One rode in during a passing storm over prohibition. The other was Ben Butler. Butler's seizure of the Democratic party machinery in 1882 had underscored the party's weakness for free-lance adventurers and erratic causes. Lack of inner coherence made it vulnerable to the likes of Butler. In normal years it was a listless coalition of isolated groups whose interests were sunk in mutual irrelevance. Its voting strength rested in the swarming Irish districts of Boston and the larger mill cities. In the latter—Fall River, Lawrence, Haverhill, Holyoke—party organizations, while tapping substantial voting support, were ridden with petty localism, factional strife among ethnic groups, and leadership vendettas, and only rarely were they able to produce leaders capable of operating effectively or very long in state and national politics. Only in Boston did the party enjoy sufficient strength to accumulate a sense of structural durability. Even here the problem of leadership had defied satisfactory solution. The Irish were pushing out on the limits of their power in the city and had elected their first congressman in 1882, but were not as yet contenders for control of the state party. Party direction came chiefly from a small nucleus of important Bostonians bound together by habit and inheritance, vaguely referred to in later years as "old-line Democrats." A significant number of them (including Peter Butler, F. O. Prince, and C. T. Russell) had begun their public careers as followers of Daniel Webster and had shouldered into Democratic ranks during the dissolution of the Whig party in the mid-fifties. They were augmented after the war by youthful corporation lawyers like Richard Olney (whose father was a Whig) and aspiring capitalists like Henry M. Whitney.[20]

Professional and family ties knit many of these men together in politics and business. For example, Henry M. Whitney of Brookline was the brother of William C. Whitney, the powerful New York financier who later became Cleveland's Secretary of the Navy. Their father, General James S. Whitney, was a maritime shipper who had been picked by the last previous Democratic President—Buchanan—for the collectorship of the port of Boston, the fattest patronage plum in New England. William C. Whitney's legal adviser in New York was Peter B. Olney, brother of Boston's Richard Olney. And Richard Olney's uncle was Peter Butler, a shipper and railroad entrepreneur who had strongly backed the marine freight ventures of General James S. Whitney.[21] This quiet core of Democratic leaders, shunning the limelight, rarely yielded candidates for public office. But it held great power in commercial Boston. Its interest in the Democratic party was incidental to this power. It used the party primarily to advance its shipping and transportation interests through local political arrangements.

The party did not lack a veneer of character and polish. The Leverett Saltonstall of that day was a Democrat. John Quincy Adams, the eldest son of Charles Francis Adams, Sr., had been an active Democrat since the 1860's, reacting against the Radical Republicans' harsh reconstruction policy toward the South. The geologist Nathaniel Shaler gave the party a lonely representation on the Harvard faculty. Moreover, the Democrats had benefited in a modest way from disenchantment with Grant's administration by providing a landing place for occasional rebels from Republican ranks. Often the Democrats tried to attract restless Republican votes by nominating candidates unstained by any previous association with the Democratic party. In 1872, for instance, after a wondrous attempt to persuade Charles Sumner to run for governor as a Democrat, the party settled on Francis W. Bird, a crusty old free-soiler who had just bolted the Republicans for Greeley. Again in 1876 the elder Charles Francis Adams, in the twilight of his distinguished career, was prevailed upon to stand for governor on the ticket with the Democratic presidential nominee, Samuel J. Tilden. In those years when party leaders were forced to nominate a regular Democrat for governor they showed a marked preference for men as little smudged by the party machinery as possible. Elderly judges were in particular demand.[22]

This habit of absorbing its talent from the top left the Democratic party wide open for Ben Butler's aggressions. Butler drove a wedge between the party's traditional Yankee leadership and its voting strength among immigrants and laborers. In 1878 he demoralized the party convention in a violent, unsuccessful bid for the gubernatorial nomination and then drew off the bulk of the Democratic vote by running on his own ticket. The orthodox party leaders, pointedly described by the *Boston Advertiser* as "gray-headed, conservative, American-born citizens . . . , the brains and motive power of the Democratic party," found themselves that year convening in rump session in the wake of Butler's depredations. Much the same thing happened a year later.[23] By 1882 the party was badly unhinged and unable to discover a single issue (other than prohibition) on which it could take a united stand.

In this atmosphere a young Democrat, heir to his father's party, could find little satisfaction in his politics. William E. Russell of Cambridge, son of a Democratic war horse and five years out of Harvard, sat down one day in September 1882, just before the annual party convention, to air his grievance. "I spent yesterday afternoon," he wrote his father, "in the good Sunday

work of attempting to lift the Democratic sheep out of the pit
into which they have fallen—in other words, trying to find and
formulate some respectable principles, which they may declare
to be their political creed . . . I hope whatever resolutions the
convention adopts, they will be plain and outspoken; don't let it
leave us any longer crying in the wilderness, and wondering
why the devil we are Democrats anyway." Russell attached to
the letter his own platform, a careful mixture of Jeffersonian
states rights, tariff reform, and civil service reform.[24]

But within a week Ben Butler captured the Democratic
nomination for governor, the party having confirmed young Russell's fears and bowed to the logic of its past. Butler won the
governorship in 1882 by rooting out the established party leadership of Yankee lawyers and merchants and by fusing his
personal following with urban ward leaders who were Democratic politicians by steady profession. The Boston Irish flocked
to Butler now that he carried authentic Democratic credentials.
John Boyle O'Reilly, editor of the Boston *Pilot* and a man of
broad and dashing radical sympathies, became a Butler partisan.
Congressman Patrick Collins, the political leader of the Boston
Irish and already a person of some prominence in the national
party, supported Butler mostly for the sake of regularity and
without enthusiasm. A self-made man well on his way to personal affluence and the respect of State Street, Collins was
uneasy at the spell Butler cast over his own following.[25]

In 1883, when the Republicans mounted their all-out offensive
against Butler, the Irish remained loyal to him. But their support was not enough. The Yankee Democrats whose party he
had stolen campaigned and voted against him. Richard Olney,
Henry M. Whitney, John Quincy Adams, Leverett Saltonstall,
Professor Shaler, and Francis Bird all contributed to the Republican victory.[26] With Butler's defeat in 1883, radicalism was
banished from two-party politics in Massachusetts. Until the
advent of Bryanism in the 1890's, radical reform activity in the
state lacked political force or relevance. Between 1884 and 1896
the two major parties shared an orientation toward basic social
issues which, set beside the free-wheeling debate of the years

before and after, seems deeply conservative. With the end of
Ben Butler's bawdy career, the range of Boston's political
thought decisively narrowed. The air was cleared for the new
party divisions of 1884 and the arrival of Cleveland Democracy
in Massachusetts.

Butler himself hastened the transition by making an improb-
able bid for the Democratic presidential nomination in 1884.
His friends among the Irish Democratic regulars indulged
Butler in his ambition up to the moment the national convention
made its choice. The Irish voting bloc as a whole certainly preferred Butler to Grover Cleveland. Cleveland's nomination, followed by Butler's decision to run for the presidency on a
Greenback ticket, threw the Irish into turmoil. Butler's defection
drew off thousands of Irish Democratic votes. But he could not
shake the regularity of Boston's Irish Democratic leadership.
Boyle O'Reilly swallowed hard and submitted to his party's
choice. Patrick Collins, glad to be rid of Butler, used all his
prestige to keep the city's Irish in line. A young district leader
in Boston summed up the attitude of Irish party workers toward
Butler: "I never followed him until he came into the party, and
I shall not follow him an inch further than its limits. The party
is greater than any man." [27]

Accepting Grover Cleveland was a sterner test of party loyalty
than abandoning Ben Butler. The Irish leaders disliked the New
York governor mainly because they did not think he could win.
Cleveland's record of constant quarrels with Tammany Hall,
hardly endearing in itself to a good Irishman, seemed to forfeit a
crucial state in the presidential contest. Remembering the
Greeley fiasco of 1872, the Irish regulars felt it was poor strategy
to nominate a maverick simply to attract the protest vote against
Blaine. For every Republican vote gained by Cleveland, Patrick
Collins estimated, twenty Democrats were lost. Moreover, the
feeling would not down that Cleveland was in some vague way
both anti-Irish and anti-labor. There were stories aplenty floating
through the saloons and caucus halls to confirm both fears. They
mingled there with rumors of Cleveland's bastard child and news
of James G. Blaine's secret reverence for his Catholic mother's

beads and scapulars. But for all that, Cleveland was the Democratic party nominee, which settled the question for every
prominent Irish leader in Boston. Patrick Collins won Cleveland's lasting gratitude by announcing his support of the ticket
soon after the convention. The two leading Irish Catholic newspapers in Boston, the *Pilot* and the *Republic,* promptly came
out for Cleveland. Patrick Maguire, editor of the *Republic* and
the most powerful Irish leader in the city after Collins, devoted
long columns to refuting charges against the nominee. The mood
in the Irish wards was heavy with mistrust, but the organization
worked for Cleveland down to the wire.[28]

Meanwhile, Ben Butler's departure left the Democratic state
organization an empty vessel. For a while in mid-summer it
drifted like an abandoned prize while party regulars and the
old anti-Butler Yankee leadership competed to possess it. In the
calculations of both groups loomed the Mugwumps, articulate,
prosperous, without a party. The Boston Irish, apprehensive
over Cleveland's righteous new admirers, did not intend to have
their own loyalty rewarded by being shunted aside in the big
decisions. After the Mugwumps' bolt at the Parker House, Pat
Maguire's *Republic* sputtered, "Because the Republicans have
gone and made fools of themselves is no reason why 'independent cranks,' professing to be reformers, should have a voice
in Democratic deliberations." Yankee Democrats, on the other
hand, were anxious to welcome Mugwump recruits into the
party, to stabilize it socially and financially. But they too intended to govern on their own terms, as senior partners, so to
speak, in a purified Democracy. The Mugwumps for their part
remained torn between admiration for Cleveland and disgust for
his party. Late in July they announced they would take no step
toward outright fusion with the Democrats.[29] Their overriding
object was Blaine's defeat. If they could bring that off, the
question of party would answer itself. Meanwhile they would
straddle their fence, "mug" on one side, "wump" on the other,
the picture of haughty orphanage.

When the time came to choose a candidate for governor, the
Massachusetts Democracy reverted to old form. With the Yan-

kee Democrats in control, the convention nominated State
Supreme Court Judge William C. Endicott, freshly returned
from an extended stay on the continent. Endicott reluctantly
agreed to run, on the condition that he be required to have
nothing whatever to do with the campaign. It seems that a
precocious party neophyte had more to do with Endicott's
nomination than anyone intended. Brooks Adams, the youngest
of the Adams brothers, had been pitched into one of his brief
torrents of political activism by the uprising against Blaine and
convinced himself that the Democratic party in Massachusetts
required his personal management. He apparently succeeded in
bending the state convention to his will. A few days after the
convention had adjourned, Richard Olney wrote apologetically
to Judge Endicott about its action:

I have not the responsibility in the matter that you perhaps
imagine, and have a right to imagine. On receipt of the last of your
two telegrams, I telegraphed Brooks Adams at Worcester that you
declined and that I did not want to go on to the ticket. I am responsible for nothing that happened afterwards. At the same time I agree
with you that what is done cannot be undone, and that although
Brooks Adams has taken most unwarrantable liberties with both of
us, he cannot be disavowed publicly, while nothing prevents you
doing what I have already done, that is, your giving him a piece of
your mind.

Brooks Adams, who subsequently boasted to Carl Schurz, "I
have been, so to speak, the mover of the Democratic policy
here," must have received his reprimand in high glee.[30]
   In any event, with Endicott on their ticket the Democrats
turned their best face toward the Mugwumps. Leaving further
overtures to the future, both groups swung their attention to the
national contest. As election day approached, Cleveland men of
every stripe began to smell victory. "The Mugwumps are too
much wrought up to see clear," Brooks Adams informed Schurz.
"But we are in truth on the very border of victory or I can
read no signs." The Mugwumps were indeed wrought up. Henrietta Dana wrote to Richard Henry Dana that she prayed daily
for Blaine's defeat by reciting the forty-second psalm ("Judge

me, O God, and distinguish my cause from the nation that is unholy; deliver me from the unjust and deceitful man").[31]

Between them, Blaine and Butler prevented Cleveland's followers from delivering Massachusetts. Blaine carried the state by 24,372 votes—almost exactly the number that Butler polled in the state. But Blaine's plurality in Massachusetts was only about half that of Garfield's in 1880, and estimates of Mugwump strength ran up to 40,000. Massachusetts Mugwumps joyously persuaded themselves that their inspiration had swung the election in New York and that they had in fact made Grover Cleveland President. Irish Democratic leaders in Boston, for their part, exulted that Butler had polled only 3724 votes in the city, or about one for every ten cast for Cleveland. In the moment of party victory the Irish leaders would not deny credit to the Mugwumps. Pat Maguire's *Republic* conceded expansively, "They nobly assisted the Massachusetts Democrats, in particular, to bury the traitorous Butler in a grave so deep that the day of his political resurrection in this state will never again dawn. They proved themselves valiant allies, and deserve all the honors that are so generally awarded them." [32]

A Democrat had finally been elected President, and in Massachusetts a bright new era opened up for a rejuvenated party. Much work awaited it: Judge Endicott had gone down to predictable defeat, and Republicans still controlled the state government. The Democrats and their circumspect new allies faced a gingerly future together. The young Mugwump leader George Fred Williams, reporting on the election to Carl Schurz, set a proper tone: "Mr. Pierce and I, the committee on jollification, have prevailed upon the Democrats to forego the torchlight procession and fireworks, in order that we may not excite antipathy among Republicans, and we shall have a sober meeting to look forward to the responsibilities which success has brought." [33]

CHAPTER TWO · THE MUGWUMP MIND

DURING the decade after the election of 1884, the Mugwumps infected Massachusetts and much of the country with their thought. Its peculiar flavor spread out of all proportion to Mugwump numbers, influencing the behavior of the new administration in Washington, enhancing the prestige of reform journals like Godkin's *Nation*, giving fresh hope to those who wanted to improve the moral tone of American politics. In Massachusetts the Mugwumps' influence, while hardly as telling as they would have had it, helped to alter fixed patterns of political behavior by dissipating much of the humdrum apathy which had befogged conservative political thought for a generation. The 1880's were on the whole a placid, congenial time for orthodoxy in America, a fleeting breathing spell in which men of economic and social respectability could reassess their common heritage before the stir of alien radicals, factory laborers, and western farmers captured national concern. The Mugwumps used this interval to bring orthodoxy up to date. They brought to the task their community's best equipment: educated intelligence, the prestige of established wealth, and vigorous if not overly adventurous minds. Their talents were guided by an awesome legacy, the New England of Thoreau and Emerson, of Parker, Whittier, and Sumner. To this inheritance they sought to restore political viability.

It has been fashionable to ascribe the Mugwumps' behavior to their concern for status and for the aggressions of new wealth and new races. They are seen as uprooted gentility, unhappily at bay in a changing world. There is truth in this view. But the evidence for it becomes more persuasive as the Mugwumps aged and lost their early fervor. In the beginning, in 1884 and for a while after, they were enthusiasts. In those years a dominating motive for their behavior was a desire to escape the status fitted for them by indulgent families, an eagerness to break loose from their role as passive heirs. This did not make them rebels against the New England past. The dead hand they felt on their shoulders was their own experience, not that of their fathers. The Civil War inspired in most of them a vague respect as the great event of boyhood. What they resented was the aftermath of war, the sapped idealism of the "brown" years in which they reached maturity. The new American establishment of industrial wealth blocked them from a gloried antebellum past they wanted to share. Many of their friends had left Boston for greener fields, to make money where the money was being made in postwar America. The Mugwumps were in a sense the people who stayed home. They did not regret their choice. But they did not want Boston to become another New England hill town.[1]

They suffered little, socially and professionally, for their restlessness. Leading Boston businessmen applauded their revolt. John Murray Forbes, the most powerful Boston capitalist of his day, supported the Mugwumps from the outset. So did Robert Treat Paine, Boston's leading philanthropist, and Henry L. Pierce, the chocolate magnate. The investment houses of Lee, Higginson & Company and Jackson & Curtis contributed influential champions in Henry Lee, Henry Lee Higginson, and Charles Cabot Jackson. Another patron was Martin Brimmer, about whose person revolved much of the fashion, taste, and genteel wealth of postwar Boston. Among his many philanthropic causes Brimmer included civil service reform, and for years his fabled evening receptions at 47 Beacon Street were de rigueur for bachelor Mugwumps.[2]

The colleges hailed Mugwumpery. Charles Eliot Norton, Francis Child, William James, J. Lawrence Laughlin, James Barr Ames, Barrett Wendell, as well as the presidents of Harvard, Amherst, and Williams, joined the movement. For Harvard's President Charles W. Eliot, Cleveland's first election seemed a chance to advance in politics the bold ideals of efficient public administration which he had cultivated in Harvard Yard. Harvard was a seminal source for the whole cluster of ideals that gave Muwumpery its drive. Most of the important Mugwumps were Harvard men. All shared in some degree a conviction common to the educated mind of their day: a certainty of moral as well as intellectual superiority over the surrounding populace. Among the Mugwumps the conviction bred a sense of equivalent duty. They affected a stewardship of quality. Eliot embodied the bustling rationalism of this stewardship. Charles Eliot Norton was its sage. Son of the Unitarian "pope" Andrews Norton and teacher of fine arts at Harvard, Norton provided the young men passing through the college with a focus for their elitist instincts. In elegant, acerbic language he weighed the American democratic experiment from year to year, balancing blunder against gain from the vantage of quiet Shady Hill. Unlike Eliot he stayed away from crowds at election time. But if the circle of his influence was smaller, his impact on the young Mugwumps who knew him was equally profound.[3]

Those who bore the burden of the Mugwump cause in Massachusetts were generally novices at public affairs. They gained practical guidance from several older men whose reputations rested on broader grounds than financial power or academic distinction. Of these, Charles Francis Adams, Jr., Charles R. Codman, Thomas Wentworth Higginson, and Edward Atkinson were the most influential. The regular appearance of their names on Mugwump addresses and appeals was more than window dressing; they gave a needed stability to the behavior of young recruits. Charles Francis Adams, Jr., was a particularly awesome counselor. He was that ever rarer Boston phenomenon, an Adams who was making a practical go of his own career. After creditable service in the war, Adams had worked for a decade as the controlling member of Massachusetts' new state railroad commission (which was in large part his own creation). Thereafter he took on the problems of the Union Pacific, first as a government watchdog, then as a director, and finally as president of the line. His record in railroading was not an unrelieved success, least so in his own mind. But it cast him as a man of affairs, and this made him a giant to the younger Mugwumps.

In striking contrast to Henry and Brooks (who viewed him with mixed affection and disdain) Charles Francis Adams, Jr., eluded the aura of failure that hung over his family and kept a proud, respected place in the public eye. He lacked the razor brilliance of his younger brothers, but what he said was more often listened to, and certainly won more respect in Boston.[4]

Charles R. Codman cut a smaller figure on his times. A wealthy, gentleman lawyer who lived much of the time at his country place on Cape Cod, Codman had been a Republican of some prestige in Massachusetts before 1884. By bolting his party that year, he ended his career in politics, for Cape Cod did not smile on Mugwumps. In 1885 he turned down Grover Cleveland's offer of a post on the federal civil service commission, but continued to work from the sidelines for civil service reform and other proper causes. Codman's importance to history lies in the transparent honesty of his writing. Highly respected by President Cleveland, Carl Schurz, and his Boston contemporaries, he was a strong link between the Mugwumps of New England and New York. His letters and memoirs, winding in a thin scrawl across their pages, reveal a wisdom about American politicians and reformers not often matched among his friends.[5]

To buoy the judgment of Adams and Codman in Mugwump councils, old Thomas Wentworth Higginson of Cambridge lent his indestructible optimism. A younger contemporary of Thoreau, Parker, and John Brown, nature-lover, transcendentalist, and abolitionist, Higginson was a living monument to the antebellum New England the Mugwumps revered. Through his life he watched Cambridge transform itself from a quiet college town of a few thousand souls into a dirty industrial city, and he never admitted a word of regret. Through the postwar decades he kept an open mind trained on his country's flaws. Woman suffrage caught his fancy, then Bellamy's Nationalism. He fought religious intolerance, Bible-reading in the public schools, poll taxes, liquor, and monopolies, all with equal gusto. To Mugwumpery he brought the fervor of abolitionism undiminished. His cheerful radicalism was like a fresh wind.[6]

Edward Atkinson was sui generis, a self-made product of

entrepreneurial nineteenth-century America. He had worked for a living since he was fifteen, and after years of experience in textile manufacture, had developed a brisk business in factory fire insurance. By the 1880's he had established himself as a successful petty capitalist, an inventor of some ingenuity, an expert in family nutrition, and a savant in political economy. He was one of the great intellectual amateurs of his day and proud of it. To a lady who once addressed him as "Professor," he tartly replied, "I am plain Mr. Atkinson; a businessman and not a scientist." His store of practical economic knowledge was matched only by his enormous ego. Although a late convert to the bolt against Blaine, he was thereafter in the thick of the movement. As the other Mugwumps offered their conscience for the guidance of politicians, Atkinson offered his theories and statistics. He enjoyed a sense of secretly manipulating the minds of public officials. Forwarding a long memorandum to the governor of Massachusetts in 1891, he calmly noted, "You have the opportunity of a lifetime. I place the key in your hands. You will have to alter its shape or form lest the making of the key should be imputed to some one else than yourself . . . No copies kept." If Atkinson's mind was entrapped by the laissez-faire liberalism of the age, this hardly lessened his influence. The politicians on whom he lavished his wisdom often came back for more. His arguments for low tariffs and sound currency gave their speeches a ring of authority. He was a good man to have on one's side.[7]

The men who made Mugwumpery a coherent force in Massachusetts politics were a younger, more homogeneous group. The most active leaders were Moorfield Storey of Brookline, George Fred Williams and Winslow Warren of Dedham, Josiah Quincy and William Everett of Quincy, John F. Andrew of Boston, and Richard Henry Dana of Cambridge. All but Warren and Everett were under forty in 1884. All but Williams were Harvard graduates. All were lawyers. In these respects they accurately reflected the Mugwump rank and file in and around Boston.

Moorfield Storey was the most prominent of the younger Mugwumps in the 1880's. He had returned to Boston from his stint as Senator Sumner's secretary in 1869 to enter the city's leading commercial law firm. Within a decade he was being counted among the first lawyers of Boston. When Charles Francis Adams, Jr., chose him to represent Union Pacific in crucial debt settlement negotiations with the federal government in 1885, Storey's reputation was confirmed. His prowess in law gave him the means to approach politics with disinterest, or, as he might have put it, from above. Yet the record shows a passionate involvement. Active in politics since 1882, he had fought Ben Butler and James G. Blaine with warm hatred. A prolific author of campaign literature, he tended more than other Mugwumps to turn his pen to personal vendettas. Ben Butler and, later on, President McKinley were both denied honorary degrees from Harvard through Storey's intervention, and he enjoyed the added satisfaction of preventing a statue of Butler from being erected on the State House lawn. His refusal to speak to Henry Cabot Lodge became a minor Boston legend. The aging Henry Adams once wrote to Storey, "I am fairly knocked out, but I imagine that you are still in the ring, and as long as you can stand, you will enjoy loathing somebody." But Storey's spleen merely intensified his burning political moralism. He shaped his standards from his parents' precepts (his father was a Conscience Whig, his mother an abolitionist), the tutelage of Charles Sumner, and his own acute, legalistic mind which bristled at the thought of political compromise. While he distrusted any sign of success in politics as prima facie evidence of a moral flaw, Storey believed an educated man had to take a hand in public life—"He must be active for good or he will be counted for evil." Over long years, Storey was active for good, his prickly righteousness a constant menace to organized complacency.[8]

If any Mugwump matched Storey in disdain for expediency, it was William Everett. William Everett was a clear case of the Mugwump as displaced person. As the son of Edward Everett, a Harvard Ph.D., master of a small private school for boys in Quincy, an erudite and eccentric man living on the edge of genteel poverty, he was almost a caricature of the Mugwump type. A slight, nervous man with soaring forehead, sharp nose, sparse gray side whiskers and steel-rimmed spectacles, he had, he once said, been "born bolting into the world and never did anything according to conventional rules—nor ever will." It was he who traced the word "mugwump" to Eliot's Indian Bible and delightedly discovered it meant "noble leader." It was his frequent function as a man of letters to contribute lyric verses for Mugwump banquets. His fellow reformers treated him with the gentle protection one might accord a mascot. Politics abused his sensibilities. Yet politics had been a family calling, and Everett found grim satisfaction in his forays into public prominence. From 1884 on he tried repeatedly to get himself elected to Congress, first as an Independent, later as a Democrat. On the stump, lashing an opponent with sarcasm, epigrams, and puns, he was a surprisingly effective speaker. But in his tries for Congress, he ran up against two of the best campaigners in the Republican stable, John Davis Long and Henry Cabot Lodge. He was beaten in 1884, 1890, and 1892. In a rare confession of discouragement he wrote to Governor William E. Russell in 1893, "It seems to me my position in politics is more honorable than effective . . . If my destiny is to keep school, I can do it better without breaks that break in foam." Then his luck turned. Lodge vacated his seat to become United States Senator. Everett won the special election for his place by sixty-four votes and achieved his ambition. His long drive for public office, against trials that would have stilled a less determined man, reveal with special clarity the nature of the Mugwump revival set off in Massachusetts in 1884.[9]

Richard Henry Dana and John Forrester Andrew were two other sons of famous New Englanders who probed the possibilities of Mugwumpery. Of the two, Andrew took the greater risk by bolting in 1884. A state senator at the time, he was probably the only office-holding Republican in the country to campaign against Blaine after having been a delegate to the convention that nominated him. A prim, quiet, conscientious young man, Andrew regretted leaving the party his father had honored as war governor. Perhaps he agreed with a friend who wrote to him in October, 1884, "I feel that our attitude is a negative and a destructive one, like that of the men who destroy their gods lest they should fall into the hands of scoffers." Yet curiously he switched parties with little difficulty. Re-elected to the state senate in 1884 with Democratic help, he accepted the Democratic nomination for governor two years later (ignoring a fellow Mugwump's plea: "Don't do it on any account . . . You are and can remain free to go where you like—to join the proper side, at the proper time . . ."). In 1889 Andrew entered Congress as a Democrat. He was politician enough to know he could not remain a hostage to Mugwumpery outside the party system. He was an effective congressman, but broken health and an early death halted his career in 1895.[10]

Meanwhile, Richard Henry Dana roved back and forth between parties with abandon, a fair specimen of what his friend Theodore Roosevelt called "those political and literary hermaphrodites the mugwumps." While voting for Cleveland in 1884, Dana remained a Republican in local politics until 1886, when he publicly quit the party to support Andrew for governor. In 1888 he helped Thomas Wentworth Higginson run (unsuccessfully) for Congress as an Independent. In 1890, after voting for a Democratic governor, Dana ran for mayor of Cambridge—as a Republican. He lost and, with some plausibility, blamed his defeat on Republican spite. "They preferred a Democratic mayor to endorsing a mugwump, so bitter was the feeling," he concluded. Dana's party-hopping demanded better powers of calculation than he ever pretended to possess. At bottom he was less interested in his own ambitions than in the civil service and secret ballot laws he nursed through the state legislature in the 1880's. Happily so, for his party inconsistencies brought scorn and smiles from all sides.[11]

Of all the young Mugwumps, George Fred Williams and Josiah Quincy were destined to leave the most lasting marks on the political history of their region. Williams, born in Dedham in 1852, the son of a German immigrant sea captain who was killed in a wreck off Boston Harbor in 1861, had graduated from Dartmouth in 1872. He had spent his sophomore and junior

years in Germany visiting relatives, caring for wounded sur-
vivors of the Franco-Prussian War, and studying metaphysics at
Heidelberg. A romantic, heterodox youth in search of a calling,
he had spent one year after college teaching school on Cape
Cod and another reporting for the *Boston Globe*. Then he took
a law degree at Boston University and opened practice in
Boston. He was among the earliest bolters in 1884 and gained
prominence in the ensuing campaign as executive chairman of
the Boston Committee of One Hundred. A hard-working,
ostentatious man, he threw himself into politics with rash
abandon. Friends differed in their opinions of him. "He is a
thoroughly good fellow," old Francis W. Bird believed, "a radical Independent, thinks for himself, but is also a *teachable*
listener." Yet Williams inspired many quiet resentments among
his reformist colleagues by his restless self-assertion. His passionate sense of personal destiny, clashing with the Mugwump
canon of disinterest, sometimes verged on the mystic. "I shall
retire from active politics at the first possible moment," he wrote
when he was thirty-three, "but so long as I can serve my country
I shall make all else subservient; all my ambitions and hopes
for myself, taken together, cannot stir me as does my ardent
love for our country. I shall live to prove this; I feel the hand
of fate upon me." The striking intensity of Williams' character,
as well as his German ancestry and Dartmouth background,
contributed to his reputation among Harvard-trained Yankee
Mugwumps as a wild duck.[12]

Josiah Quincy, in contrast, carried impeccable credentials.
Quincys had played a robust role in Boston's history since the
first of them arrived in Massachusetts Bay in 1633. The family
had produced among others a revolutionary patriot (Josiah
Quincy, 1744–1775), a Boston mayor and Harvard president
(Josiah Quincy, 1772–1864), another Boston mayor (Josiah
Quincy, 1802–1882), and a prominent abolitionist (Edmund
Quincy, 1808–1877). But the family had thinned in numbers
and fortune by the late nineteenth century. The family homestead in Quincy, where the latest Josiah Quincy was born in
1859, was later sold and turned into a private school for girls.

Quincy's father (Josiah P. Quincy, 1829–1910), had shunned public life. A mildly renowned gentleman of letters, he gave his son a taste for calm, open-minded speculation on the social scene. The son entered Harvard with the class of 1880 and wrote a stunning record. He won the Lee Prize his freshman and sophomore years, the Boylston Prize his junior year, and the Bowdoin Prize his last year. He was elected to Phi Beta Kappa and to the presidency of the *Crimson,* and spoke for his class at Commencement. Quincy's classmates found him a puzzling companion. Reticent, self-contained, and inaccessible, he had many admirers but few friends. A certain stiffness of bearing concealed his unorthodox cast of mind behind a somber, impassive exterior. Graduation found him at loose ends, undecided about a career. He spent a year teaching at William Everett's academy in Quincy and found it a trial. "I have made a more or less faithful effort to do what was given me," he wrote to Everett when the year was over, "but cannot help realizing how many imperfections there were in it. In the speaking, particularly, I am afraid that I have not come up to what you expected." The next three years he spent partly at Harvard Law School and partly in travel abroad. Neither law practice nor business suited his taste. (Throughout his life his negligence with money would agonize his friends and family.) When in 1884 he finally turned to politics for a vocation it was with a sense of emancipation and discovery. Over the next twenty years, this aloof patrician would consume his career in the craft of governing. He had found the family cause.[13]

For both Quincy and Williams Mugwumpery was but a way station on the path to distinctive careers in the Democratic party. But in 1884 neither had yet fully revealed the qualities which would eventually set him apart from his fellow Mugwumps. To all appearances they were merely two more bright and impatient young lawyers on their first venture into public life, possessed by an ambition to do great things. More would be heard from them both.

Winslow Warren rounded out the inner circle of Mugwump leadership. A mild, competent trust lawyer approaching fifty in

1884, Warren enjoyed nearly unanimous respect among a wide range of friends. He was politically unambitious, and until Grover Cleveland appointed him Collector of the Port of Boston in 1894 his highest office was the presidency of the Massachusetts branch of the Society of the Cincinnati. Meanwhile, his fellow Mugwumps gladly exploited his patience for routine chores, and he devoted much of his spare time to his job as corresponding secretary of the Massachusetts Reform Club, the central pivot of Mugwump organization in the state.[14]

Virtually every prominent Boston Mugwump had joined the Reform Club by the late 1880's. Founded in 1882, it was the main forum of independent political opinion in New England. By the end of the decade it had 286 members and an impressive waiting list. In composition it remained small and Yankee, a select circle for respectable debate. "I do not overestimate the influence of the Club," Winslow Warren wrote contentedly to William Everett, "but I know the feeling outside of our limits that we are a very troublesome factor to the spoilsmen and cordially disliked in such quarters." In 1886 New York Mugwumps sent to Boston for a copy of the club's constitution, eager to launch a similar force in their own city.[15]

The Reform Club was only the most renowned of Mugwump haunts. In the 1880's it was said that no two Bostonians could have an idea in common without forming a club around it. The city was overrun with clubs—not only St. Botolph's, the Somerset, the Algonquin, and other sanctuaries of the powerful and well-born—but a club to match every political notion and persuasion. Republicans had the Massachusetts Club, Democrats the Bay State Club. Young Republicans and young Democrats had separate clubs. Nationalists, philanthropists, protectionists, free traders, civil service reformers, and Butlerites all had their particular clubs. Forty years later one of the Mugwumps recalled that "every Saturday afternoon Parker's and Young's Hotel were filled with clubs, dining and talking heavily, smoking and drinking to excess, in order to save the Republic." ("Now they play golf instead," he added.) Perhaps it is possible in the Mugwumps' case to reconstruct patterns in that hot talk, and discover the motives and rationales that shaped their view of politics and reform.[16]

The Mugwumps cannot be understood as aristocratic gentlemen of leisure. Most of them earned their own living. Some had investments, and many lived in comfortable wealth, commuting to the city from their homes in pleasant surburban towns. In summer they disappeared for a month or so to Newport, Campobello, or Mount Desert. Most had had at least a season abroad. But they spent the bulk of their time in Boston at work. For the great majority, freedom from the cares of income was a hope for the future. (Robert Grant, a Mugwump lawyer whose interests were more literary than political, wrote an engaging series for *Scribner's Magazine* in 1895 on the art of living like a gentleman on ten thousand dollars a year. But Grant had to resort to municipal patronage in the 1880's to round out his own purse. Boston's Irish Mayor O'Brien made him a water commissioner before he became, in later years, Judge Grant.)[17] The Mugwumps habitually protested that their interest in politics was costly to their professional obligations. Convinced that public office should be a duty and not a career, they often shrank from running for public office on the grounds that they could not afford the financial sacrifice. Their hesitancy was not all posturing.

What strikes one most emphatically is the Mugwumps' enthusiasm for the taste of public life. Approaching the sources of political power holding their noses, talking steadily of duty and disinterest, they were thoroughly excited. When Carl Schurz advised George Fred Williams after the 1884 campaign to put politics aside until he had made his fortune in law, Williams replied, "My dear mother is grateful to you for the advice; she dreads the hard blows dealt in politics, and has been worried by the abuse which has been showered upon me in the late campaign; but I glory in it." Another young Mugwump lawyer wrote to Schurz in a similar vein, "I know that public spirit may be indulged in too far. In fact, I have already allowed myself to do a great deal of work in church and state that another could have done as well simply because I liked to do it." Later the same man gleefully reported that he had traced his ancestry to a seventeenth-century Boston Antinomian, and had thus accounted for his peculiar enthusiasm.[18]

These sunny views were partly the exuberance of youth. They did not survive many years, and even in the 1880's they could give way to melancholy with startling suddenness. But despite this oscillation, Boston Mugwumps maintained a notably more genial temper than did their contemporaries in New York. The Bostonians looked to New York for leadership; Godkin's *Nation* was their bible, Schurz their father-confessor. For their part the New Yorkers tended to regard the Boston brethren with a certain condescension, as tender newcomers to the good fight, in need of realistic instruction. The historic tension between the two cities was shared in muted form by their reformers. The Boston Mugwumps provided a curious exception to the traditional view of Boston as an introverted, dark-faced sister to Manhattan. Both in their attitudes toward local machine politicians and toward Grover Cleveland's performance as President, they were more tolerant and less stiffly righteous than the Mugwumps in New York. Long years of dismal experience with Grant, Conkling, and Tammany Hall had played out the resilience in the New Yorkers. Tammany's power in New York, even in the interregnum between Tweed and Croker, far surpassed that of the Irish bosses of Boston. Politicians and reformers faced each other with cold intransigence in New York; in Boston the chasm had only begun to open. Thus the Boston Mugwumps enjoyed a livelier sense of potential effectiveness within the political power structure of their city than did Schurz and R. R. Bowker and George William Curtis in New York. They escaped the sense of hopeless isolation that plagued the New Yorkers and other Mugwumps scattered through the East. ("I know the Mugwumps in Princeton," a history professor complained to William Everett, "but could not name another in New Jersey. If I had bushels of Mugwump literature for New Jersey, I should not know to whom to send it.")[19]

But if the Boston Mugwumps maintained better morale than Mugwumps elsewhere, still they approached their tasks with the assumptions of a minority. They regarded themselves as intellectually, socially, and ethnically outnumbered. In a sense this was simply accurate observation. But the elitism it nourished in them fitted badly with the political necessities they faced in Massachusetts. Their departure from the Republican party in 1884, a departure justified by ethical issues of national scope, had thrown them together with a party whose local character sorely tried their minority sensibilities. The Democrats of Boston, strongly Irish Catholic and working-class in their voting strength, practicing in the precincts a brand of politics seasoned with violence and gross manipulation, shaped a hard question for the Mugwumps. Were they democrats themselves? Senator George Frisbie Hoar, a perceptive Republican, once concluded that the Mugwumps had little faith "in the capacity of mankind in general for suffrage anywhere." Most Mugwumps would have quarreled indignantly with Hoar. Yet they spent their lives wrestling with the issue. A few proved by their own careers their belief in the ability of the mass of men to govern themselves. Others quietly acknowledged now and then that they lacked this faith. For a surprising number the returns on universal manhood suffrage were not yet in. As with so much else they judged democracy by the past just beyond their memory. Frederic Jesup Stimson, a Mugwump lawyer, wrote in his autobiography, "I doubt if a more perfect democracy has existed in the world's history than that of New England, especially Massachusetts, between our Revolution and the Civil War." Stimson was born in 1855. Charles Eliot Norton, born in 1827, adjusted his range accordingly. His classic community was "New England during the first thirty years of the century, before the coming in of Jacksonian Democracy, and the invasion of the Irish, and the establishment of the system of Protection . . ." In defining their ideal democracy Stimson and Norton had similar criteria: economic and ethnic homogeneity tempered with respect for family, education, and professional repute. "There were no poor, and no foreigners," Stimson wrote. "Yet though all were recognized to be of the same stock, there were very nice grades of social distinction." Only in such an atmosphere could the cherished machinery of New England democracy, the sedate town meeting, work as intended.[20]

The atmosphere changed swiftly after the Civil War. Norton had accurately assigned the causes. Heavy immigration, urbanized politics, and the rushing growth of protected industry had by the 1880's made town-meeting democracy almost a rural relic. Swelling communities sought municipal charters, and town meetings gave way to mayors, aldermen, common councils, and all their pungent associations. A population of ten thousand qualified a town for municipal status. By 1890 over 60 percent of the people of Massachusetts lived in cities, and nearly 40 percent lived within twelve miles of the State House in Boston. Here and there the old order resisted change. In Quincy, for example, Charles Francis Adams, Jr., and John Quincy Adams clung tenaciously to the forms which had confirmed their family's primacy for over a century. "We both delighted in town meeting," Charles Francis Adams, Jr., recalled in his autobiography. "We were bone of their bone, flesh of their flesh; and the mass of those there knew it and felt it; and, for twenty years, we together practically managed Quincy affairs." But in 1887, a new crowd— Irish-American Knights of Labor, Adams noted—took charge of Quincy's government and secured a municipal charter. Adams moved to another town, and an era closed.[21]

Democracy had broken out of the stable framework in which New England had contained it. Now, to the Mugwump eye, it ran through her cities, crude, impetuous, without a memory. Unbridled democracy seemed to threaten not only private property but personal liberty and all the subtle authority which the town meeting had once assured the educated man of substance. Most Mugwumps retained their faith in democracy with regret for the past and apprehension for what lay ahead. Charles Eliot Norton said it best in a letter to his friend James Russell Lowell in 1884: "I have as strong a conviction as you that 'democracy' will work; but it may work ignobly, ignorantly, brutally; here at least it does not look as if the better elements of social life, of human nature, were growing and flourishing in proportion to the baser."[22]

A veil of public restraint concealed, for the most part, the inner turmoil of the Mugwumps as they watched New England democracy transforming. They strove mightily with their august sense of civic stewardship when confronted by the Irish immigrant. (The more so as the immigrant rarely accepted their stewardship or grasped what it was all about.) The ease with which Irish bosses manipulated the new voters of the cities alarmed them. But—unlike Carl Schurz in New York—they did not seriously believe that Irish votes were controlled by a secret master strategy of the Catholic Church. They took no part in the rabid attacks on the Church fomented by New England Protestant fringe groups at the end of the 1880's. Norton, for one, openly admired the Church as an instrument of charity and social discipline. One of its greatest services, he felt, was the control it exercised over the Irish immigrant. Mugwumps felt more impatience at the periodic waves of Irish nationalism which swept over Boston, compounding ethnic tensions in the community. Unwilling to sort out the complex issues of Irish Home Rule, they resented the intrusion of the question into the local air. ("I give up the Irish question," said Edward Atkinson. "I can neither make head or tail of it. I wonder who can.") They were rankled that the newcomers should look to their homeland rather than to the Yankee past for patriotic inspiration. For the Mugwumps the intensity of Irish nationalism suggested the distance the Irish had to come toward proper assimilation. "Our Irish fellow citizens are too apt to forget that they are Americans, who as such have forsworn all allegiance to foreign powers and with their allegiance should lay aside their active interference in foreign politics," Moorfield Storey wrote. "They are Americans like the rest of us, and should behave as such." [23]

Occasionally a Mugwump was gratified by Irish efforts to meet the Yankee conception of democratic citizenship. Richard Henry Dana went into Boston's North End during the 1884 campaign to explain the tariff to Irish laborers. He came out astonished at their attention, perception, and applause. Edward Atkinson, explaining the glories of his native Brookline to an English friend, noted that the town meeting still worked there, despite

an Irish majority at every meeting. The Irish, he observed, were
economical and even penurious folk. Many owned real estate
in Brookline, and even the servant girls practiced thrift. "It has
been the study of the conditions of this singular town, like
which I suppose there is no other in the world," Atkinson concluded, "which has given me confidence in democracy and in
practical manhood suffrage." [24]

But most Mugwumps found close communion with the lower
classes a hard adjustment outside their own kitchens. As political
circumstance pitched them together with rank-and-file Democrats, references to "micks" and "bummers" and "a hard lot"
cropped up more frequently in their notes to one another. And
not only the Irish could prove offensive. The Democratic party
appealed to both native and immigrant laborers, as well as
Mugwumps, in an effort to achieve a state-wide majority after
1884. In more than one instance, Mugwump involvement in this
effort proved socially embarrassing. In November 1886, the
Chelsea Independent Club, a body of substantial laboring men,
invited the Mugwump William Everett to a banquet in his
honor. The Quincy schoolmaster, taken aback, asked his friend
Winslow Warren what he should do. After thorough study of
the issue, Warren advised Everett to accept the invitation. It
was time, he said, for the Mugwumps to try to counter the
popular impression that they were genteel aristocrats, out of
touch with the working class. "If this labor movement is to be
moulded to good ends and a breach between capital and labor
prevented," Warren soberly argued, "it must be by stimulating
mutual confidence between the thoughtful earnest men on both
sides, by a comparison of views and by useful study and guidance." Warren left his friend with little choice. Everett reluctantly accepted the invitation to dine in Chelsea, but only on
the condition that there be no liquor or cigars at the table. The
club president readily agreed. "I am strongly opposed to both,"
he replied, and added by way of reassurance, "We do not intend
to surprise you in any way . . . We want to enjoy with you a
happy social time." Everett was consoled to learn that his fellow
Mugwumps George Fred Williams and John F. Andrew had also

agreed to attend. As Williams put it to Everett, "I suppose you will find it pleasanter if some of your Independent coadjutors share the agony with you." All participants seem to have survived the ordeal.[25]

The Mugwumps wanted to be as decent as possible to the laboring man. They feared the signs of growing friction in the social structure of the late 1880's. They were even reluctant to talk about the problem. When Warren had finished his letter to Everett about the Chelsea banquet, he added a cautious postscript: "This talk of classes must be confidential but we need not shut our eyes to the fact that they in some measure exist in this country." Barriers in the social structure were hardly new to New England. Still a man could transcend them if he tried and move up the ladder in his quest toward commonly accepted goals. This at least was orthodoxy. But now new blocs were forming, consciously antagonistic to each other in their economic aims, creating loyalties which clashed with the Mugwumps' notion of the public good. Mugwump worry focused on the trade-union and mounted after 1886, the year which marked the crisis and collapse of the Knights of Labor and the beginnings of statewide trade-union organization. The Mugwumps applied little sustained analytical thought to the labor problem. They seemed to dislike thinking about the working man as such, and indulged in truisms and self-deception to ease the effort. "I despise this talk about the rights of labor," said Edward Atkinson. "The poor man has no more rights than the rich man. What you want to think about are the *rights of man,* whether he be rich or poor." The Mugwumps' social thought was littered with contradictions, blind spots, and irresolution—striking evidence of the anxiety the labor question roused in them.[26]

Few Mugwumps condemned the trade-union out of hand. Following the courts, they respected the right of workers to associate and organize among themselves. The sticking point came when the union tried to coerce nonunion workers and prevent them from working on terms the union called unfair. Here was the issue of free contract, the right to work, the scab. The Mugwump approached the issue along a familiar path.

Thus Moorfield Storey invoked the "self-evident truth" that "every man may work for anyone who chooses to hire him, for any wages which he chooses to take, that he may make any legal contract and any legal use of his own hands and his own property." Thus Edward Atkinson told a Knights of Labor Assembly in Boston, "You are trying to tell men how they shall work, when they shall work, where they shall work, and how long they shall work; you call a man a scab who won't submit . . . I tell you right here that the 'scab' is the man who will come out ahead, and you will get left." Atkinson suggested that his audience form a club of scabs, "a liberty club, a mind-your-own-business club"—the Squires of Work. Squires, he noted, had always won out over Knights. A few years later, Harvard's Eliot would have occasion to call the scab "a creditable type of nineteenth century hero," who "values his personal freedom more than the society and approbation of his mates." [27]

Storey, Atkinson, and Eliot shared with their fellow Mugwumps a profound faith in the free play of competitive economic forces. They assumed an evergrowing national income as inevitable, provided always that man-made impediments on the operation of natural economic laws were kept at a bare minimum and did not jar the fundamental harmony between labor and capital. Labor's share in the nation's wealth would increase only as harmony bore fruit in more efficient production. But what of the stark, insistent facts of urban poverty? Only the most callous of men could ignore them. The Mugwumps were not callous men, as the sums they gave to Boston's charities attest. Still, they had no solution for the poor. Many doubted that a solution existed. None had faith in radical cures that promised an end to poverty. The civil service reformer Charles Codman sat down one night to ponder questions raised by Henry George, and then recorded his reply on the pages of his private journal:

it seems a law of our human social existence that a certain amount of poverty always follows as the immediate result of any great progressive step in the power of man over nature. So far as we can see "progress and poverty" must necessarily accompany each other for a time. . . There must always be progress in human affairs. We can set no limit to it, and it would seem then that poverty can never quite be extinguished. In the triumphal progress of man over his physical surroundings he will always more or less though without malice or intention distress his fellow man. . . This social fact which we observe and recognize brings to mind the prediction of our Saviour—"The poor ye have always with you." [28]

In the teeth of the most vivid revelations of economic inequality, most Mugwumps remained stubbornly passive. Even the fertile mind of Edward Atkinson, spurred to inventive genius by the plight of the poor, reached a solution pathetic in its inadequacy. Poverty, he decided, resulted from poor people spending too much money. Most waste came from unwise food consumption. If a worker's family could save each day a nickel per member on its food bill, it might live in comfort. To this end Atkinson proudly offered an invention—his Aladdin oven, a species of pressure cooker which produced huge nutritious meals at allegedly phenomenal savings. ("Political economy is one branch of human knowledge, cookery another," a labor leader commented. "We want the best of each, but not both together.")[29]

Viewing the top of the social structure, the Mugwumps became more indignant. The very rich fired their moral wrath as the very poor chilled it. Much of their anger was spent on millionaires in politics, men like the shovel-maker Oliver Ames who they believed was spending his way to the governor's chair. They felt the root cause of corrupt politics was the purchase of political results by rich and respectable men who shut their eyes to the methods their money bought. Furious at such irresponsibility, the Mugwumps had no patience for that class of men who, unlike themselves, affected not to care. These were Boston's politically apathetic, idle rich, the gentle sons of antebellum merchants, who lived their lives of ease, culture, and impotence within the generous limits of their trust funds. The political torpor of the wealthy was only part of the complaint against them. Many were suspected of being chronic tax evaders. Moreover President Eliot, for one, believed that the increased luxury of life in New England's cultural community had sapped its intellectual vigor. He found the ritual and aestheticism fostered by high living to be one of the most discouraging phenomena of his day. It remained for Edward Atkinson, himself a kind of throwback to an earlier New England, to register the choicest notes of exasperation and contempt:

We are doing very well by the poor, but how we are neglecting the rich! Poor creatures, many of them. I meet them at the club sometimes . . . When a man is so far gone that he is incapable of comprehending the very vacuity of his existence, what can be done for him? I have long since come to the conclusion that all trusts for the protection of spendthrifts ought to be abolished or prohibited by law. Give a man at least a chance to be brought under the healthy stimulus of prospective necessity.[30]

For the Mugwump the sins of the rich lay in their use of money, not the making of it. The surfeit of the wealthy had nothing to do with the plight of the poor. Charity aside, the Mugwump would listen to no proposals for redistributing wealth. If all the wasted money of rich men were divided among the working class, Atkinson assured his labor audience, "it would not give the whole body of the workmen the price of an extra glass of beer a day." [31]

The Mugwumps looked out on the economic and social problems of their time with well-meaning but uncreative conservatism. They absorbed their prime assumptions at second hand, from the texts of Harvard's Francis Bowen, the pages of Godkin's *Nation*, the essays of William Graham Sumner, and a thousand forgotten conversations. Imprecise notions from Adam Smith, John Stuart Mill, and Herbert Spencer mingled in shadowy fashion in their minds. There was more Spencer than Mill in their thought; yet the stock phrases of Social Darwinism rarely cropped up in their writing. The whole orthodoxy they received was fragmented, disconsonant, badly digested. When they came to apply the hard, foursquare shibboleths of Spencerian laissez faire to the real world, plain compassion often softened the impact of dogma. They had been taught, one of them recalled, "to hold the balance even between the powerful and the lowly, the rich and the poor, as the first principle of humane authority." [32] In the 1880's this mediation still seemed a plausible social function. But in calculating an even balance, the Mugwump mind was caught in its most serious contradiction. Wrestling endlessly with its faith in the unfettered individual will was a quiet, implacable fatalism. Given the free use of his abilities, the individual man—no matter where he came from—could do what he set out to do. If he failed, his fellow men could hope to do little for him. The world would get better; the poor would always be with it. Clinging to the fictions of free contract, open opportunity, and inevitable progress, the Mugwump could not comprehend a world in which the maintenance of an even balance between wealth and poverty might make things worse.

The Mugwumps staked little claim to economic authority. Their main concern was with party politics. In the decades after the Civil War, party loomed as large and the loyalties it inspired were as fierce as at any time since the origin of the party system. These were the years when the Republican and Democratic parties fixed themselves in perpetuity on the land as self-justifying, self-sustaining national institutions. Behind the hullabaloo over graft, bribery, and extortion, the routine of party patronage had become the central preoccupation of American politicians. Party patronage, recognized as the primary means by which elected officials confirmed their obligation to those who made their election possible, had defined a new pattern of political responsibility in America. Identification with one party or the other became the stern prerequisite of an active political existence. All the trappings of party—the caucus, the contribution, the brightly tinted party ballots—forced men to line up or admit they could not play the game. In an era when greatness was absent from American public life, the party was truly bigger than any man.

Mugwumpery was above all else an escape from party. By breaking fixed rules of political behavior, the Mugwumps hoped to change them, and so recapture for men some of the potency the party had absorbed for itself. It is a measure of that power that the Mugwumps were ridiculed and despised for their temerity by Republican and Democratic party men alike. To have defied the sway of party seemed to many observers both ludicrous and unforgivable. "I would rather be in the claws of the 'Tammany tiger,'" a Blaine fan wrote to a Democratic friend in Boston, "than in the kidgloved hands of the hypocritical, unprincipled, unscrupulous, vainglorious Republican renegade who goes to another party tooting his gilded trumpet of 'Reform . . .'" Even in Brahmin Boston, where the Mugwumps were better cushioned against abuse than elsewhere, the flick of political revenge could be felt. Thus Richard Henry Dana found his election to the Massachusetts Historical Society (which in that era fancied itself a local House of Peers) blocked for years by a prominent Republican member who disliked Dana's errant politics.[33]

The Mugwumps gave as good as they got. In Massachusetts Henry Cabot Lodge was their prize whipping boy. Lodge's defeat for Congress in 1884, coming on the heels of his decision to support Blaine, was perfect justice to the Mugwumps. "You ought to be in the van of progress—the progress of ideas—parties be d——d [sic]," a Mugwump lectured him in 1886. When Lodge's career began to confirm the shrewdness of his choice, Mugwump hatred for him mounted. Moorfield Storey stopped speaking to him in 1887, and lesser Mugwumps followed Storey's lead. In 1890, when Lodge's career in Congress was well launched, a clique of resentful Mugwumps engineered his defeat for re-election to the Harvard Board of Overseers. "I suppose it is only natural that men who lead lives that are sheltered from the world should display their spite in an essentially feminine way," a Republican friend commented to Lodge.[34]

These petty blows and tempers suggest how hard the Mugwumps found it to rise above the tawdry lines of party and gain the grand perspective of their dreams. Doubly irritating was their recognition in calmer moments that all real difference between the two major parties was fast disappearing. At the very time the parties were becoming invincible as institutions, they seemed to shed whatever distinctive principles had justified their origins. The Democrats had long since cheapened and perverted the republican wisdom of Jefferson with the arbitrary, centralizing influences of Jacksonian spoils politics; and the character of the Republican party by the 1880's made the moral crisis which had forced its birth seem almost irrelevant. When parties ceased to stand for anything but their own aggrandizement, it was time for conscientious men to make political choices without regard to machines, slates, and deals.

The Mugwumps did not relish ties to any specific political loyalties, whether of party, locality, or constituency. They would submit to group discipline only so far as it furthered their own sense of individual importance. Even their unity in the campaign of 1884 was a matter of degree. As the head of the Committee of One Hundred commented, "Should this organization attempt to put upon its chairman the duty of muzzling the opinions of Independent speakers, it must provide a whole battalion of chairmen and a large force of sextons to carry away the numerous and intrepid dead." William Everett was once reported to have remarked, "When I am in a small minority I believe I am right. When I am in a minority of one, I know I am right." Often the Mugwumps' elitist frame of mind estranged them from the people surrounding them within established boundaries of precinct, ward, and district. This was notably true for those who lived in such places as Boston's Ward Ten near the State House, where immigrants had changed the neighborhood, or in suburban towns where Mugwumps faced an overwhelming local Republican majority. ("I could not get the office of fence-viewer today," a Dedham Mugwump wrote, "for the simple reason that I have tried to prevent the election to the presidency of a dishonest man.") Their political isolation forced the Mugwumps through a remarkably swift conversion from the inbred values of intense localism fostered by the town-meeting tradition toward a view of their political responsibilities as essentially detached and universal, toward a concept of representation that placed mind and principle above circumstance and number. Their new bias against geographical political divisions nurtured an admiration for the English tradition of unrestricted representation which allowed a man to stand for any district, regardless of its location. When William Everett contested the Lynn

congressional district against Henry Cabot Lodge while maintaining residence in his native Quincy, fellow Mugwumps hailed
the venture as an excellent new precedent for American politics.
When George Fred Williams lost his own congressional seat in
the election of 1892, he gave the new mood clear expression: "I
have never felt more satisfaction at my own situation; my work
was not done for my district, but for the whole country, and my
district has not full jurisdiction to pronounce judgment upon
me." [35]

The Mugwumps' notion of representation unfettered by local
responsibility was part of a general determination to escape
the confines of party discipline. As James Russell Lowell put it
in 1888, where once the Abolitionists had emancipated the Negro
from slavery, the Mugwumps now sought to "emancipate the
respectable white man." Party discipline seemed fatal to free
judgment. Military analogies repeatedly sprang to mind: discipline came at the cost of conscience; preferment was won by
loyalty and longevity, not talent; departure was tantamount to
desertion. At the bottom of the trouble, the Mugwumps believed, was the local party caucus, at which candidates were
agreed upon, convention delegates chosen, and steering committees selected. Since attendance at the caucus bound a man to
the decisions of the majority, even though he might have come
to protest those decisions, the Mugwumps often found attendance intolerable to their conscience. The caucus, they felt,
destroyed the deliberative tone of town-meeting democracy,
substituted the narrow concept of delegation for that of representation, and degraded the democratic process to the level of
hapless conformity. "Leaders seem to be no more," George Fred
Williams wailed to Grover Cleveland; "men must go to the
caucus first and form their opinions as the wires are pulled.
Policy, Policy, Policy—is the motive of political judgment, and
not the education and guidance of the people." To boycott the
caucus brought no satisfaction. For then caucus control (and
with it the whole machinery of party) fell inevitably into the
sure hands of men who made politics their career. These were a
distinct breed, called "the politicians" or "the managers." For

Moorfield Storey, theirs was not a fit calling for any decent
person: "If he enters the service of a party, and especially if he
is dependent on obtaining and holding office for his living, he
ceases to be a free man." A Mugwump could associate with
"politicians" only at the risk of his personal, political, and professional reputation.[36]

Through the years the Mugwumps wavered erratically trying
to decide how best to cope with the party, the caucus, and the
professional politician. The solution most talked of was, of course,
civil service reform. Throughout the 1880's the driving impetus
toward civil service reform was the Mugwump desire to slash
through the tangle of personal influence and responsibility that
tied public office to the party system. The more exuberant
theorists envisioned an ideal future government run by bloodless
administrative technicians whose only loyalty was an abstract
patriotism. But in practice Mugwumps did not deceive themselves about the limits of civil service. It could, after all, apply
only to appointive office, and there was little Mugwump sentiment in favor of using civil service to narrow the sphere of
elective office-holding. Nor did many Mugwumps desire to
secure civil service posts for themselves. Fearing the consequences of being muzzled by the requirements of political
neutrality imposed on civil servants, they preferred to be advocates of the cause rather than instruments of it. They did not
want to abandon the political arena, but to be heard in it.

Another strategy was to abandon the nether world of local
politics to the crass professionals and try to exert influence only
in state, congressional, and presidential nominations. Even at
these levels the Mugwumps occasionally betrayed a skittish fear
for their political chastity. "An Independent can hardly go to a
Democratic convention *unless he is a Democrat*," Winslow
Warren warned in 1886. "It is one thing to accept a nomination
and another to make it."[37] At times the Mugwumps could
swallow this distinction between the guilt of participation and
the innocence of availability. But their indignation was forever
coming to a boil, and then, despite their disillusionment with
party, they had but one recurring thought—a new party, led by

their own kind. From 1884 to 1900 talk of the disintegration of
the existing two-party system was constantly on the Mugwump
tongue. The more imminent a major reshuffling seemed, the
happier the Mugwumps. Every fresh proof of party stability
pitched them into gloom.

Nothing ever came of the Mugwump hope for a new party. In
the last analysis they did not really want the hope to crystallize.
Anticipation alone was both necessary and sufficient, and their
muddling confirmed them as political amateurs. While they
shrank from admitting it to one another, they knew well enough
that they lacked the time, the capacity, or the desire for sustained
political participation. (In July of 1885 Winslow Warren proposed that the Mugwumps launch a third party in Massachusetts.
But he noted that the summer heat was driving Mugwumps out
of Boston by the scores and wondered if enough remained to
start the work. Warren himself left shortly for his August vacation, and no more was heard of the new party for another
year.)[38] Unlike the Progressives of the succeeding generation,
the Mugwumps made no real effort to break the control of the
elective process enjoyed by party professionals. The direct
primary, woman suffrage, the initiative and recall, the nonpartisan "citizen's ticket"—these had only the most tenuous
antecedents in Mugwumpery. Not only did these reforms require
more (and more lasting) political energy than the Mugwumps
could muster, but they were in essence the weapons of an
aroused majority. In varying degrees they all presupposed a
majority organization. If successful, they would create lines of
active political responsibility as binding as those they replaced.

The Mugwumps cherished their minority privileges. Foremost among these was freedom from practical, specific, political
responsibilities. They acknowledged obligations only to their
public principles and to their personal integrity, and it was a
happy feature of their minority existence that the two never
came into conflict. They had no stomach for the compromises
that responsibility to a majority demanded. Their function as
they saw it was to stand in the teeth of the wind and wait for
the possible to bend to their ideal. They would take their stand

on ground which they deemed critical—the secret ballot, a limit to campaign spending, civil service, a lower tariff—and so, they hoped, change the course of government and history. If they failed, there was pride in failure. Defeat in time acquired a moral grandeur for the Mugwumps, as they repeatedly discovered the public will to be at odds with their ideals. "In a country so constituted as ours," Barrett Wendell wrote in 1896, "there are few deeds more admirable than that of a public man who, devoted to a principle, is willing unflinchingly to face a hostile majority." [39] At one time or another, almost every other Mugwump tried to say the same thing. But as a group they did not really try to change the strength or quality of the American majority. They were resigned to watching the majority and its machinery govern, while they the Mugwumps judged the merit of the results. To participate, to work avidly for change within the party system, would be to implicate themselves, and so lose the right and freedom to judge. The Mugwumps' characteristic response to political crisis was not to man the barricades. It was to bolt.

What finally justified the Mugwump to himself, and justifies an enduring place for him in the history of his era, was his insistence on his own autonomy. Here he was true to his inheritance. Cupped in Mugwump hands, the New England conscience clung to life between the Civil War and the new century. The Mugwump sought always to keep open ground between himself and the freshly organized, swiftly enveloping urban society that threatened to destroy the personal freedom he valued so mightily. He praised liberty where he could find it, whether in the scab laborer, the rare Irishman who defied his boss, or in his own efforts to leap clear of the "juggernaut-car of party." His notion of liberty was flawed, but it was not irrelevant to his world.

Back in the fall of 1870 when young Richard Henry Dana entered Harvard, his father had written him a letter of advice. Warning his son against female entanglements, the father unconsciously echoed the most urgent wisdom of nineteenth-century New England. "Think what you are to do on earth," he wrote. "Man is meant *to be* and *to do,* and not to be tied down. You have four years of college, and then a profession,—through all of which you must be *free,* to do whatever will be best for your future." [40] When the young men of the Mugwump movement faced the sterner tests of the world beyond Harvard Yard, their mood—excited, anxious, virginal—was shaped by words like these.

GROVER CLEVELAND's victory in 1884 forced Mugwumps and Democrats to live together whether they wanted to or not. From election day on, Cleveland's supporters in Massachusetts jousted and parried with each other, covertly, viciously, hopefully, contesting for the upper hand in their fragile alliance. At stake for the Mugwumps—who had entered into this strange entente in revulsion against the discipline of party—was the reputation of the man they thought they had made President by bolting. At stake for regular Democrats— many of whom had supported Cleveland only out of a sense of party loyalty—were thousands of federal offices held by Republicans since the days of Buchanan. At stake for a score of bright young men—Mugwumps, Yankee Democrats, and Irishmen—was a foothold in a blooming political future.

The dull, prosaic record of Grover Cleveland's patronage policy makes a façade for the story of this competition. Behind the façade were dust clouds and clamor aplenty, for patronage was no dull issue in the 1880's. If it was not the most important task to face the new President, most men seemed to agree it was the one above all others that would shape his final reputation. Of some 126,000 federal employees on the rolls in 1884, 110,000 won their jobs by political influence of some sort; only the slim remainder were classified civil servants. According to one estimate, the President himself had 7,828 political appointments to make. These appointments were in many ways the most significant choices open to an American President in the postwar decades. As Lord Bryce noted in answer to his famous question as to why great men were not chosen President, "Four-fifths of his work is the same in kind as that which devolves on the chairman of a commercial company or the manager of a railway, the work of choosing good subordinates, seeing that they attend to their business, and taking a sound practical view of such administrative questions as require his decision." Three quarters of a century later, it is hard to comprehend adequately the corollaries which follow from this statement of priorities. It takes rare perspective to understand, for instance, how in 1885 a rumor that the office of weigher in the New York Customs House was about to go to someone other than the applicant who had passed his civil service exam with the highest grade could lead the Mugwump Charles Codman to announce to the Secretary of War that a national crisis was at hand. Civil service reformers doubtless inflated their issue. But the historian would evade the central meaning of Cleveland's first years as President by neglecting it.[1]

Patronage loomed big for a number of reasons. Cleveland's election gave the Pendleton Act the first stiff test of its young life. Could the newly classified civil servants survive the transfer of executive power from Republicans to Democrats? Were their jobs really beyond the touch of party? Moreover, the election results had placed the jobs of the 110,000 unclassified federal workers in sudden jeopardy. Even if the classified minority remained intact, and the power of party ran roughshod through the rest, the cause of civil service reform would suffer a setback. But there was a more enduring reason for the prominence of the patronage issue. The powers of the federal government were so construed in the postwar years that to most observers what a man did in a federal office was vastly less important than what he did not do. The cry of "spoils" and "corruption" depended for its emotional appeal on a negative, static view of the governmental function. When the entire ethos of conventional political thought denied a creative role to the politician, by default he came to be judged mostly on the basis of his self-restraint. How he sought patronage, or dispensed it, how circumspectly he used a place when he got it for himself—these became criteria of surpassing importance in marking the virtue of a public servant.

The Mugwumps shared such views with most Americans not closely involved in the political process. More than most, perhaps, they looked forward to a steady deflation in the significance of governmental activity. Edward Atkinson, for instance, envisioned a future in which "the functions of the officers of Government will become less important than they now are, and it need not long be necessary for able men to make a great sacrifice in order to take a share in the executive work. Ordinary men will do the ordinary work to be done." The Mugwumps looked to Grover Cleveland to take steps toward implementing this ideal. Yet paradoxically they felt the pull of ambition and chafed at the bonds which kept them from offering their own services to the new President. Self-restraint was dictated to them by Mugwump leaders in New York. Shortly after Cleveland's election the New Yorkers drew up a Mugwump ordinance of self-denial that barred them from seeking office for themselves or even recommending others. Simultaneously the *Nation* pontificated that Mugwumps ought not even to accept offices under Cleveland when they were offered. The Democrats, in the *Nation*'s view, were wholly responsible for their own future, and since Democrats had a reputation for collapsing under pressure, Mugwumps had better stand to one side and await events.[2]

This was hard doctrine for the younger Massachusetts Mugwumps. One of them fired off a hot protest to the *Nation:* "If the Independents brought about the change of administration which has just taken place (and you know perfectly well we did bring it about), we are not only bound to accept our share of the responsibility for the change, but to do what in us lies to make the change a public benefit." George Fred Williams among others believed it was foolish to issue a blanket refusal before any offers were made. A little wistfully he inquired of Carl Schurz whether emergencies might not arise later on, making it the duty of some Mugwumps to accept office. But the New York policy prevailed, and Massachusetts Mugwumps accepted the role of critic with a minimum of grumbling.[3]

A month after his election, in response to demands from New York, Cleveland announced his own patronage rules in a cautious letter to George William Curtis, president of the National Civil Service Reform League. He promised to remove no incumbent officeholders before their appointments expired, unless they conducted themselves as "offensive partisans." When vacancies occurred, Democrats would receive "all proper consideration," provided they were otherwise fit for office. Cleveland's letter was a great success. Mugwumps were remarkably pleased with it. And Democrats everywhere sharpened their knives: any Republican was an "offensive partisan." Evidently Cleveland's true intent would have to be revealed by accumulated instances.[4]

All through Cleveland's first administration the Mugwumps of New York and Boston occupied themselves in vigorous debate over Cleveland's patronage record. His policies marked a substantial improvement on the past, but he conceded more to party than his letter to Curtis had led many to expect. The New York Mugwumps made a harsher estimate than their friends in Boston. Schurz and Curtis, while admitting that progress had been made, preferred to demand the impossible of Cleveland and to lay the gentler appraisals of others to cowardice and irresolution. The Bostonians, on the other hand, were concerned to keep the President as their special hero. Their greater involvement in the politics of their state made them more anxious to score the new administration as a success. If Cleveland failed, they failed. Periodically they pleaded with Schurz for forbearance. "I am firmly persuaded," one wrote in 1885, "that our most pressing duty is not so much to be minutely critical of the acts of the administration and to insist upon the very last application of every principle as to make the reform movement popular, and particularly to make it palatable to the better portion of the Democratic party." Matters worsened as increasing numbers of Republican officeholders were replaced by Democrats at the expiration of their terms. By 1887 the relation between Cleveland and Schurz had grown so cold that Charles Codman, a mutual friend, attempted mediation. Codman journeyed to the Capitol to talk with the President (who insisted he had been faithful to his original assurances) and then tried to explain him to Schurz in a long letter. Codman admitted that perhaps Cleveland had not wholly grasped the task of the presidency, looked too much to detail, and lacked the touch for logical administration. But he was nevertheless "honest and manly and simple and brave." His faults were the faults of his people, Codman concluded; it was the French who demanded perfection, not Anglo-Saxons. Schurz was unmoved. He and Curtis had already decided to part company with the President. When Cleveland sought re-election in 1888, Curtis refused to speak for him, and Schurz spent the campaign season in Europe. "Our weak-kneed idealists kill us every time," Winslow Warren wrote pointedly to William Everett. "Because I can't get *all* I want right off I am not in favor of pitching everything overboard. That's not my way of strengthening a man who tries to do his duty and brace up a rotten party." [5]

The Massachusetts Mugwumps, then, wanted to hold up the President as their own. If they could not serve him openly, they were at least determined not to surrender him to his "rotten party." Their situation was delicate at the outset of Cleveland's first administration. Unable to serve, unable even to recommend, they had to play a devious game. Ferreting out information about local Democratic candidates for patronage, they sent a stream of gossip, innuendo, and conscientious criticism to Washington to influence the final choice. George Fred Williams, the most fervent of the Mugwump sleuths, tried hard to convince himself he had found a noble calling. Styling himself "an invisible snag to unworthy aspirants," he stated grandly to a friend in Washington, "Lest our refusal to join in the recommendation of men for offices and our refusal to accept offices ourselves be taken to indicate a lack of disposition to assist the administration, I wish to repeat that [neither] my professional nor private business shall stand in the way of thorough investigations of men or things, to assist Mr. Cleveland." Williams and others feared that if Cleveland had to rely on the advice of Democrats alone, he would excite Mugwump hostility against his will or intention. [6]

It had been clear for years that Massachusetts Democrats, particularly what one Mugwump called "the Irish or Dynamite wing," did not warm to civil service reform. Schurz had warned within a week of Cleveland's election that trouble was in store if Patrick Collins and the other Irish leaders were not taken in hand and converted. To the Irish Democrats it was axiomatic that civil service was a meddlesome device designed to block rewards which had finally fallen due. Boston's Pat Maguire announced cheerfully through his weekly *Republic* that Democrats anticipated sweeping reforms through rigorous application of the doctrine of the "offensive partisan." But Maguire was whistling up a dark alley. His easy tolerance of Mugwumps evaporated as soon as it became apparent that Cleveland was listening to their advice. For all their posturing, the *Republic* noted early in March 1885, the Mugwumps were obviously as hungry for office as any Irishman. "Not any of your petty offices, be it understood, but a foreign mission or consulate, which would enable them to air their aristocratic manners and show their silk stockings to the wondering gaze of European society." (In one case, at least, Maguire had nailed the truth. Shortly after Cleveland's inauguration, in the midst of the furor over patronage, the Mugwump schoolmaster William Everett had slipped down to Washington and tried to land a European ministry.)[7]

From the outset the patronage issue illuminated the gulf of social and political distrust which divided Irishman from Yankee in Massachusetts. The Mugwumps scored heavily against the Irish Democrats when Cleveland formed his cabinet. More so then than now, a president chose his cabinet with an eye to geography. A New England member was almost protocol. Boston's Irish wanted one of their own kind in Cleveland's cabinet. Intensely self-conscious about their close identification with the Democratic party, they were anxious to dignify their loyalty with recognition. They felt, moreover, that Cleveland's troubles with Tammany Hall gave them a striking chance to put across a Boston Irishman. Of their number, only Patrick Collins came near fitting the specifications for membership in a presidential cabinet.

Patrick Collins was the first authentic Irishman to represent Boston in Congress. Re-elected to his second term in 1884, he had risen easily above the image of the muddy-booted, clannish Irish roughneck that fixed itself in Yankee minds. But he could not forget his climb. Born in 1844 in County Cork, son of an

Irish peasant, he had been brought to Boston by his widowed mother during the massive, famine-propelled emigration of the late 1840's. Growing up in nearby Chelsea in years when Know-Nothing hysteria gripped Massachusetts was a nasty experience for the boy, one he could never erase entirely from his memory. When he was thirteen his mother took him to Ohio where he worked in the coal fields as a manual laborer. Two years later he returned to Boston, determined to learn a craftsman's trade. He became an upholsterer, was foreman of his shop by age nineteen, and joined a union. But Collins was ambitious. Soon he was studying law in a Boston law office and at Harvard, where he won his LL.B. in 1871. All through his early years Collins felt the cross-pull of his origins and his aspirations. His career is a study in clashing motives. Loyalty to race and class—to his craft union, to Irish nationalism, to the Celtic swarm of Boston's North End—was strong in him when he was young. But after he had gotten his start in politics (he served in the state legislature while studying at Harvard), these loyalties became a growing burden. As his private law practice expanded in the 1870's, the resentments of a harsh youth gave way to a profound desire for respectability and Yankee acceptance. The "Paddy" in him had almost disappeared by 1874, when he became the "General Collins" of Governor Gaston's ornamental military staff. Collins had been a Fenian in his youth and remained an Irish nationalist all his life. But he tried to bring a tone of moderation to the cause. When Charles Francis Adams, Sr., the former ambassador to Great Britain, ran for governor as a Democrat in 1876, Collins strenuously urged his fellow Irishmen to vote on "American" issues only and to support Adams despite his poor reputation among Fenians. Adams seemed to Collins an infinitely superior source of party leadership than the likes of Ben Butler. After waiting out the Butler years in Massachusetts politics, Collins helped to swing the Irish Democratic vote decisively to the right in 1884, behind Grover Cleveland. The maneuver satisfied. Though Cleveland had hardly been his first choice for the party nomination, the political realignment which Cleveland's election created in Massachusetts restored the close ties between Collins and the Irish voting bloc in Boston, and made local leaders more responsive to his increasingly conservative temperament.[8]

From 1884 on, Collins' impelling desire was to ease the tension between Irish and Yankee in Boston. His highest political value was to do for his own people what he had done for himself—knit them into the existing fabric of American life. This was his purpose for the Democratic party. Through dutiful loyalty to genteel, native-born Democratic leaders, the Irish, he hoped, might find the security and respect America had so far denied them. Accepting the party's established leadership in state and nation, accepting as his own the Yankee Democratic precepts of little government, economy, and localism, Collins asked only for recognition of the Irish numbers he now commanded. Jobs were a sufficient token of approval. He wanted Cleveland's patronage.

Conscious of the need to tie down the Irish vote for the future, several important Yankee Democrats joined Boston's Irish leaders in an effort to wedge Collins into Cleveland's cabinet. A delegation of New Englanders cornered the President-elect in a New York hotel to plead Collins' case. Boyle O'Reilly made a trip to Washington to talk for Collins, and other Irish editors mustered what influence they could bring to bear. By the middle of February 1885, Collins began to think he would be tapped. But Massachusetts Mugwumps had other ideas. Collins' selection for the cabinet would have been a profound blow to their self-esteem and the New England values they had sustained by bolting. Yankee Democrats John Quincy Adams and Judge William C. Endicott were their candidates. To their relief, the prize finally fell to Judge Endicott. He suited nicely. Descendant of the Bay Colony's first governor and grandson of Jefferson's Secretary of the Navy, Endicott was a true New England patrician. He had forsaken Whiggery in 1860 to become a Democrat and thereafter graced the party's slate as a frequent candidate for state attorney general. His willingness to run for governor in 1884 had done him no harm. When Cleveland chose him for his Secretary of War, Carl Schurz wrote to Boston to inquire into Endicott's character. A Mugwump correspondent replied that

the appointee was "rather a lazy man with good intellectual en-
dowments always surrounded by the best of men and women.
He has as you know been a Justice of our Supreme Court and
is respected by all. He has not been an ardent C[ivil] S[ervice]
reformer nor has he ever taken active part in politics . . ." Endicott's origins outweighed his achievements, but the Mugwumps
were satisfied with him, and found comfort in having thwarted
Collins.[9]

Irish leaders accepted Cleveland's choice with grim grace and
set about trying to force concessions at a less exalted level. Of
some 4,500 federal jobs in Massachusetts, few required more
than a modicum of clerical skill. Many of these places, however,
were protected by the Pendleton Act. For deserving Democrats
to get their fair share, indulgent men were needed to head the
Boston Customs House, the Post Office, and the Office of Internal Revenue. The new administration seemed anxious to do
what it could toward mending fences in Massachusetts in the
wake of Endicott's appointment. To mollify Collins, Cleveland
named one Eben Pillsbury to be Collector of Internal Revenue
in Massachusetts. Pillsbury was a veteran Democrat, scarred by
partisan skirmishes all over northern New England. Mugwumps
learned of his appointment with astonishment and anger. "If
this style of Democrat is to take the place of the Republican
official," George Fred Williams warned Secretary Endicott, "we
must wait four more years as Independents without a party, or
go back to the Republican party, as many now threaten to do."
Williams urged that Pillsbury be recalled, as "a warning to
Collins and his friends and co-workers, that they cannot impose
upon the President such miserable stuff with impunity, and that
they must set up a higher standard." Cleveland ultimately bowed
to Mugwump demands for Pillsbury's removal, but not before
Pillsbury had crowded Boston's Internal Revenue Office with
Irishmen. Mugwumps were sure that the quality of the service
had deteriorated apace. (Williams claimed that one of Pillsbury's appointees brought his son to work so that the boy
might teach the father how to read and write.) The Pillsbury
episode made clear to both Cleveland and local Democrats how

little trifling the Mugwumps would take in matters of patronage. Without more caution, the tense alliance would snap apart.[10]

The battle for the spoils reached a climax late in 1885 when Cleveland wrestled with the choice of a collector for the Boston Customs House. This office was still the juiciest patronage plum in New England, though it was not all it had been. The decline of the port of Boston in its competition with New York over the course of the nineteenth century had taken its toll in diminished receipts. Nor could customs officers share in fancy side profits from the forfeited property of luckless importers now that the notorious moiety system had been abolished. The collectorship was no longer the fulcrum of power it had been in the age of Jackson, when David Henshaw and George Bancroft battled for control of the Democratic party in Massachusetts. But the office in the old stone fort at the foot of State Street remained the center of swirling contention. The Collector now wielded little direct political power, but he still determined access to some 425,000 dollars worth of salaries. The post interested Boston's importers as well as her politicians. The business policies of the Collector—how rigidly he interpreted his duties as administrator of federal tariff regulations—were as crucial to some as his views on patronage were to others.[11]

All the most powerful elements in the Democratic party united on the choice of Peter Butler to be Collector. Butler was one of that small, close group of "commercial Democrats" active in the party since the days of Webster. A popular local merchant prince with a sure understanding of his party's need for jobs and friends, he attracted almost unanimous support from organization Democrats, Yankee and Irish alike. He even satisfied the followers of General Ben Butler, whose influence was dying but still dangerous. Boston's Democratic press, led by Charles H. Taylor of the *Globe*, trumpeted Peter Butler's claim. Boyle O'Reilly added his support from the pages of the *Pilot*. Large, keenly interested importing houses like Jordan, Marsh & Company and Nash, Spaulding wheeled into line. Long petitions appeared supporting Butler, signed, according to Charles H. Taylor, by nine tenths of the merchants who did business at the

Customs House. Butler's campaign for the job was run from the Boston offices of Henry M. Whitney, whose brother sat on Cleveland's cabinet. Finally, Patrick Collins again put Cleveland on the spot by informing him that Butler's selection was a matter of personal and political honor.[12]

Against this awesome array the Mugwumps stood virtually alone, as determined to block Butler as they had been to keep Collins out of the cabinet. Their choice for the post was Leverett Saltonstall. Saltonstall was a man of much the same caliber as Secretary of War Endicott—scion of a distinguished family, trained in law, steeped in dignity. Like Endicott he had entered the Democratic party by way of the ephemeral Constitutional Union cause of 1860, having opposed what he regarded as an unconstitutional assault on the institution of slavery. More active in postwar politics than Endicott, he had been prominent among those Democrats who struggled fitfully against Ben Butler's aggressions on the party. In the words of a Mugwump admirer, Saltonstall was "conservative by tradition and temperament . . . , always disposed to move slowly in the direction of what seemed to many of his fellow-citizens necessary and inevitable progress." No hot reformer, he nevertheless favored the civil service idea and could be trusted to run the Customs House to Mugwump liking. Secretary Endicott favored him, as did Mugwumps of substance like John Murray Forbes and Henry Lee Higginson.[13]

The contest between Butler and Saltonstall lasted over half a year. Once more both factions put their future support in the balance for Cleveland to ponder. Patrick Collins announced repeatedly that he regarded the question as a test whether his services to the party were to be recognized. The Mugwumps stated as flatly that the choice would determine whether "after all the politicians are still to rule." Nathaniel Shaler, who prided himself on being the only true Democrat at Harvard, informed the President that the issue lay between attracting "the more intelligent native people" to the party in Massachusetts or resting its fortunes on "the inconstant foreign vote." For a time it seemed that Cleveland could not act at all without splitting the link between Democrat and reformer in New England.[14]

Then a breach in the ranks of the Democratic organization opened the way for a solution. The phalanx of support for Peter Butler gave way at an unexpected point—the Democratic City Committee of Boston. It was through the city committee that Pat Maguire and his leading lieutenant, Mike Cunniff, were attempting to master the sprawling political organization of the Boston Irish. On the face of it, Maguire's defection was puzzling. Combative and undiplomatic, he did not seem cut out for the job of resolving factional differences through subtle maneuvers. To Mugwumps like George Fred Williams he was just the biggest of a bad lot, "a hard swearing, hard drinking Irish Democratic politician and boss." But Maguire wielded growing power in Boston and he had long since learned to use it to his own advantage. Not only did he speak to a sizable Irish Catholic audience through the *Republic,* his personal weekly newspaper founded in 1882; more importantly, he had warmed a seat on the city committee since 1859 and was by now its strongest member. Maguire had reached the top by gambling well. Back in 1876 he had thrown his weight behind the Yankee Democrat F. O. Prince as candidate for mayor and prevailed in his choice against a skeptical majority on the city committee. Prince had then won the election and Maguire found himself a local kingmaker. As Prince's deputies at the Democratic National Convention in 1884, Maguire and Cunniff had tracked down the New Yorker Daniel Manning before the nominations and promised their support for Manning's candidate, Grover Cleveland. Their commitment was durable. Even more than Patrick Collins, Maguire and Cunniff had risked their claim on Irish votes by abandoning Ben Butler for Cleveland. Like Collins they expected compensation. Like Collins they sought protection from the perils of lingering Butler sentiment in the wards of Boston. They would work with any group which seemed likely to enhance their power in the city. Fearful that the fight for the collectorship might isolate them from the President, they decided to run for cover. The hearty, heavy humor of Maguire's weekly journal pointed the way. In the summer of 1885 the *Republic* announced "a great and boundless love for the inoffensive Mugwump." "A valuable little pigmy he can be, at times, and right valiant withal," the paper continued. "Though somewhat given to pugnacity, and apt to plume himself rather highly on his many virtues, he is thoroughly lovable and single-minded, and no Democrat feels other than kindly disposed to him." [15]

Maguire's politics were more limber than his prose. He switched his support from Peter Butler to Leverett Saltonstall in mid-October 1885. He carried with him those Irish spokesmen whose reputations were least tarnished in Mugwump eyes, including the highly regarded lawyers John E. Fitzgerald and Thomas Gargan. His maneuver revealed the fluidity of Boston politics in the mid-eighties and the limits of ethnic loyalty among her Irish leaders. The tactic would become typical in later years as the Irish fought among themselves for access to Yankee sources of power in the state. At a stroke Maguire had cut Patrick Collins adrift in his efforts to have Peter Butler named Collector and made Saltonstall's appointment possible. Collins resisted fiercely to the last, threatening to quit his post as Democratic State Chairman and close off all patronage discussions with Cleveland if Butler were not chosen. When Cleveland named Saltonstall to the post in November 1885, Collins went into a black sulk. Although he was persuaded not to resign his post as state chairman, after 1885 he took little interest in local politics. The fight for the collectorship ushered in a long period of political apathy in Collins' career. While Cleveland treated him with rare kindness thereafter and saw to it that he presided over the national party convention in 1888, Collins gave up his seat in Congress that year and returned to private law practice. In the critical years of Democratic revival in Massachusetts in the early nineties, Collins responded to the call to the stump, but his role was passive and acquiescent. The swiftly changing complexion of his party—on which he had staked so much in 1884—had made him a local patriarch before he was fifty years old.[16]

Despite Collins' discomfiture, the appointment of Leverett Saltonstall to the collectorship was an important initial step toward accommodation between Democrats and Mugwumps in

Massachusetts. It suggested that political self-interest, in Pat Maguire's case at least, could dictate conciliation as well as enmity. But before the alliance could work, two conditions had to be met. The Mugwumps needed assurance that partnership with the Irish Democrats of Boston would not disgrace them, and some way had to be found for Irish Democrats to live with civil service.

The first condition was satisfied in a manner hardly expected. In December 1884, a month after Cleveland's election, Boston voted into City Hall the first Irish Catholic mayor in its history, and the city's Brahmins braced themselves for the consequences. The bulky, bearded ghost of Mayor Hugh O'Brien looms in the folk memory of the Boston Irish like some minor Moses, who came (prematurely, perhaps) to lead his people from Yankee bondage in the city. The casual notation of the mythic name "O'Brien" on the record has tempted many to assume that Boston's modern history began while he was Mayor. But the real Hugh O'Brien served a different cause. His mayoralty was an effort at conciliation, not defiance. O'Brien had been born in Ireland in 1827 and brought to Boston with his parents five years later. While still a boy he worked as a printer's devil in the composing rooms of the *Boston Courier*. Later he set up as editor of his own paper, a commercial journal for greater Boston. He embarked on a political career in middle age, joining the Boston board of aldermen in 1875. Unterrorized by the partisan thicket of aldermanic politics, he won a reputation for decisive legislative skill. Early in the eighties he engineered the passage of a bill that made two dollars a minimum day's pay for the city's labor force. This law was an important bench mark in the slow progress of the urban manual laborer toward a minimum wage, but it hardly endeared its sponsor to Yankee taxpayers. When O'Brien was elected mayor in 1884, shrewd observers laid his victory to a Republican plot to work revenge on Boston Mugwumps. O'Brien was to be their price for Blaine's defeat. Some shuddered at the vision of an Irishman in City Hall sanctioning the outrages of the past: ". . . the $20.00 dinners eaten by the unwashed members of our city government, the riotous harbor

excursions on the steamer Empire State, the parades of the
Montgomery Guard where the members in uniform have been
carried home afterwards through the streets in carts, drunk,
packed in like herrings . . ." If Democratic rule was what the
Mugwumps wanted, they would now get a strong dose right
at home.[17]

To the astonishment of Republicans and Mugwumps alike,
O'Brien ran City Hall with circumspection and economy. He
displayed a rugged resistance to pressures in the city council
toward using the city's treasury for the greater benefit of her
public servants. He cooperated with municipal reformers in
pushing through the state legislature a revision of Boston's city
charter in order to narrow the powers of the council, and his
own scheme for lowering city taxes was adopted by the reformers. Late in his first term he announced a 24 percent slash in
the tax rate for the coming year. Even the genteel *Boston
Transcript* was moved to applause when he vetoed an aldermanic order to rip up a sidewalk along Boston Common. By the
time he came up for re-election, at the end of one year in office,
Mugwump municipal reformers such as Henry Putnam, William
Minot, and John T. Wheelwright were chanting O'Brien's praises.
Another Mugwump returned from a trip to Washington to report
that President Cleveland hoped every good citizen of Boston
would support O'Brien's struggle for better government. The
Mugwump *Boston Herald* warbled, "It would take but a slight
change to make Mayor O'Brien a model in the chief office of the
city, and, if elected for another year, we shall expect him to use
the ample powers given that office under the new charter with
even less regard to party trammels than he has shown in the
year now drawing to a close." Just before the election O'Brien
was ushered into the presence of the august Massachusetts
Reform Club, assembled at the Parker House for dinner and
speeches. This was the acid test. Measuring his audience, O'Brien
solemnly announced that he believed in civil service reform. He
sat down to enthusiastic applause. A few days later he was easily
re-elected to a second term, and Cleveland Democrats basked
in his achievement. As Collector Saltonstall wrote hopefully to
Secretary Endicott, O'Brien's "tremendous majority of 8,500

shows the true status of the President, of yourself and the rest of us, as regards the party . . . We need not be worried." [18]

Mugwump votes swelled O'Brien's totals, but his majority was built on the work of Pat Maguire's organization. O'Brien was Maguire's man throughout his mayoralty. Significantly the only Democratic opposition to O'Brien came from among the North End followers of Ben Butler. One swallow did not make an Irish summer. Nevertheless Hugh O'Brien was an important token of the determination among some Irish leaders that their growing power in the city was not to be reviled and feared by proper Bostonians. City government under O'Brien was not in all respects a monument to municipal enlightenment as Mugwumps defined it, and their feelings toward him cooled as time went on. Still, he was an honest, efficient mayor, and kept jobbery mostly below the point of scandal. Many a Mugwump found himself forced by O'Brien's conduct of his office to a more charitable view of the Irish Democracy of Boston.

In Washington meanwhile, Grover Cleveland's patronage decisions began to reflect greater sensitivity to the demands of organization Democrats across the country. He had risked party revolt to meet his Mugwump obligations during his first year in office. Now he gently urged Massachusetts Mugwumps to fall in with the Democrats and form a single administration party in the state. His new appointments enforced the request. The Boston postmastership went to a neutral party, a minor Civil War hero who had settled recently in Boston. Another veteran, a popular Irishman from East Cambridge, became Surveyor of the Port of Boston, and the attractive Irish lawyer John E. Fitzgerald—a special favorite with the Mugwumps—replaced Eben Pillsbury at the office of internal revenue. A distinguished western Massachusetts lawyer, vintage Democrat George M. Stearns of Chicopee Falls, became federal district attorney for Boston. For the moment all these choices fostered harmony.[19]

In the spring of 1886, as a result, plans for a separate Mugwump organization in Boston were laid quietly to one side and many of the younger Mugwumps moved delicately toward merger with the Democratic party. "The great difficulty," explained George Fred Williams, "lies in obviating the suspicion which many good Democrats have, that we Mugwumps wish to take possession of their party; it must be so managed that they will understand that we wish the Democratic party to take possession of us." It began to look very much as if the Mugwump maiden had lost her coyness. For their part, Massachusetts Democrats were in a courting mood. Dollars were a leading reason. Elections were not to be won without money—money for rallies and strategic dinners, money for paying the poll taxes of the party faithful, money for naturalization fees to speed the annual corral of immigrant voters. Cleveland's rejection of Peter Butler for the collectorship had closed the purses of many habitual patrons, and the wealth of Mugwumps John Murray Forbes, Henry L. Pierce, and Henry Lee Higginson seemed a tempting alternative. Absorption of the Mugwumps, if it were politically possible, was the obvious path toward a state-wide Democratic majority. Democratic leaders set to work. *"The Cleveland party is under weigh in this state,"* Williams announced joyfully in April.[20]

The upshot of these genial sentiments was the selection of Mugwump John F. Andrew as the Democratic candidate for governor in 1886. To hold the labor vote, party strategists named Frank K. Foster, a local leader in the Knights of Labor and former supporter of Ben Butler, for lieutenant governor. The Mugwumps came into the fray with a rush, glad for a recess from righteous inactivity. Even Foster's presence on the ticket did not deter them. "I wish they had given you a better Lieutenant," Winslow Warren wrote to Andrew, "but yet if Foster is a decent fellow I don't regret giving a chance to an honest labor reformer." Andrew's Republican foe was the shovel magnate Oliver Ames, and that added zest to the fight. It was, as Williams put it, "a splendid canvass." Moorfield Storey contributed a vibrant address, and Richard Henry Dana left the Republican party in a bracing open letter. Winslow Warren summed up the Mugwump view for Carl Schurz:

We are embarking on another vigorous fight here for Andrew upon the same lines as 1884. The Democrats have been forced up to a good platform and an excellent candidate and have vindicated by this surrender our position the past two years. They are united and full of fight and so are we . . . We put the fight on the Cleveland basis, ignore personalities as much as possible, and go in to overthrow the Lodge, Long and Ames machine which is as despotic and unprincipled as any old spoils machine. We want all the help we can get as this is a skirmish fight for 1888 and the defeat of Ames would practically knock out Blaine in Massachusetts . . . Codman, Pierce, Clarke, Forbes and all the brethren are solid . . .[21]

The elation lasted until election day. Ames beat Andrew soundly at the polls, and in succeeding months the Mugwump-Democratic honeymoon went to pieces as suddenly as it had been consummated. Both parties discovered that they could not live together on the terms laid down in 1886. Andrew had disappointed the Democrats. Not only had he set the Mugwump stance on a sensitive point by refusing to contribute money for his own campaign, but he had been reluctant to take to the stump. Moreover he ran almost five thousand votes behind his running mate Frank Foster. Evidently the labor vote of the Ben Butler era had not lost all its cohesion. Enlivened by the Knights of Labor surge of 1886, the old Butler faction had split its votes between Foster and Ames (who was a popular employer) and punished the Democrats for running a Mugwump gentleman for governor. The lesson was one which Democratic strategists could not afford to forget for the future. Forced to a choice between the prosperous Mugwump and the numerous laborer, they faced a hard dilemma. If they spurned the support of either, the chance for a state majority went glimmering.[22]

Moreover the experiment of 1886 did not indicate, as Mugwumps had imagined, a Democratic surrender to Mugwump principle. Civil service remained a hard lump in the Democratic belly. The quarrel over patronage was not confined to federal offices. Ever since the Mugwumps had succeeded in pushing a state civil service law through the legislature in 1884, professional politicians had waged a bipartisan guerrilla warfare to enfeeble it. The 1884 law, as fashioned by Richard Henry Dana and Josiah Quincy, had created a state commission with powers of enforcement over Massachusetts cities as well as the state government and placed municipal laborers on the classified list. Its provisions were designed to slash the bond that tied public employment to local politicians' influence. Specifically it sought to halt the systematic distribution by city aldermen of employment tickets (which brought a good price in money and votes from men eager for work) and the massive hiring of surplus laborers just before elections. By ending this traditional system of municipal employment the Mugwumps hoped to bring the urban laborer closer to their own ideal of the "sturdy independent working man." In practice the law aimed squarely at Boston Democrats. Its municipal application was left optional for every city in the state except Boston, whose fire and labor force made up the bulk of the 4,200 jobs on the commission's classified list.[23]

When the law went into effect, Pat Maguire called it a piece of "sentimental snobbery," and in jigging verse the *Republic* derided the imposition of merit examinations on manual labor:

> We shall see some queer mutations
>   And improvements not a few;
> Firemen now must know equations
>   And be up in Euclid too.
> Practical we are, not narrow—
>   Here the proof of that appears;
> Men who wheel the nimble barrow
>   Must be civil engineers![24]

Boston Democrats quickly went to work to find ways of evading the law. One loophole exploited in and about City Hall was the exemption of messengers from the classified list. This provision, in the absence of any prohibition against transfers between white-collar jobs, resulted in an astonishing number of former messengers filtering quietly upward through the city's bureaucracy. Meanwhile efforts to amend the law excited annual crises at the State House. The favorite proposal was a veterans exemption amendment, which would go far to empty the law of meaning. As one Mugwump noted, "With four thousand offices to distribute among ninety-seven thousand ex-soldiers it will readily be seen that our civil service commission will have very little to

do. The political bosses will have things their own way." The
veterans exemption was beaten down in 1885 and 1886. Finally
in June 1887 the amendment passed and Governor Ames signed
it. Civil service reform had sustained a serious setback in
Massachusetts.[25]

The same year Pat Maguire, as zealous a patronage hunter as
Patrick Collins had been in earlier years, lost patience with the
hiring policies of Collector Saltonstall and the Boston Post-
master and touched off a new feud over federal jobs. Maguire
launched an investigation of "offensive partisanship" among
local federal officeholders, and his "smelling committee" reported that after two years of Democratic rule, 83 percent of the
federal jobs in Massachusetts remained in Republican hands.
(Others were certain this statistic was far off the mark. Saltonstall, of course, appointed many deserving and qualified Democrats. One of them was the grandfather of a future President, a
bright young Irishman from the North End named John F.
Fitzgerald,—not yet known to Boston as Honey Fitz.) Maguire's
report protested scornfully against the Mugwump belief that the
retention of Republicans in office "is in some way involved in
the reform of the civil service, and that this civil service reform,
as they interpret it, is of more consequence than the success of
the Democratic party." The issue was out in the open, and the
gloves were off.[26]

Stunned by Maguire's sudden belligerence, by the garroting
of the state civil service law, and by mounting evidence from
other states of Cleveland's Republican removals, the Mugwumps
fled hastily from contact with the Democratic party. "I still
expect to support Cleveland next year," Moorfield Storey wrote
to John F. Andrew, "but I think it better that he should not
count on our support so that he may feel it important to do something more for reform. It will probably strengthen us if Massa-
chusets does not go Democratic this year." Then Storey sounded
the Mugwump articles of faith: "The Republican party has
nothing to offer, and all the indications are that the time for a
new party is fast approaching. We want to keep ourselves meanwhile free from entangling alliances."[27]

Democrats seemed undismayed. At the party's state convention of 1887 the keynote speaker summed up the party's anti-Mugwump, anti-civil service mood:

We hear much said of an ideal government—a golden age of politics, that theorists and so-called reformers, who seldom touch the earth, find in the clouds and in their dreams, in which is drawn the fine lines of civil service, where party organization is unimportant, party work unknown, and where absolute political virtue is incarnate, and universal. Common mortals may seek for this elysium, but they cannot reach it. The Independents think they have found it . . .

Democrats had nothing to fear from Mugwumpery, the speaker continued. Third parties would come and go, but party government would endure. The party system was no menace; its practitioners did good and patriotic duty. The great threat to national well-being was "an aristocracy of office-holders" fattening on the notion they were "beyond reach, from any cause, by political discipline or party restraint." Proponents of cooperation with the Mugwumps listened with chagrin. One wrote philosophically, "Our roosters have to crow and fight once in a while and misbehave and demean themselves and then they settle down . . . It is useless to hold up a broom before them. They are filled with the fury of the fight and the frenzy of attack." [28]

For governor the convention nominated Henry Lovering, a Lynn shoemaker who had lost his seat in Congress to Henry Cabot Lodge the year before. Lovering epitomized much of what the Mugwumps disliked in American politics. A military hero—he had ridden with Sheridan in the Shenandoah and lost a leg at Winchester—Lovering was active after the war in the Knights of St. Crispin, a cell of labor radicalism, had helped nurse the Massachusetts ten-hour law through the legislature, and as a Congressman had been strong for pensions and greenbacks. Among Mugwumps his popularity with veterans and working men stamped him as an erratic, unreliable party hack. The Reform Club recommended that, rather than support Lovering, members should vote Republican, Prohibitionist, or not at all. On election day in 1887, Lovering lost by almost twice the margin Andrew had the year before.[29]

As the end of Cleveland's first term approached, his supporters in Massachusetts were further apart than when it began, and their prospects dimmer. The queer alliance between Democrats and Mugwumps had proved seriously unstable. As long as civil service reform transfixed the Mugwump mind, and as long as Democratic leaders had to spend their energies in opposition to the merit system, permanent cooperation was impossible. The spoils issue was too symptomatic of their differences. It aggravated the peculiar minoritarian bent of both groups. The Democrats, especially the Irish Democrats of Boston, had been a minority for too long to accept the ethic of self-denial. Lacking the incentive, vision, and money for broad advances in statewide politics, they showed a chronic weakness for the local and the expedient. They found it hard to shake off the inertia of long political isolation in New England. A compact minority with a vested interest in survival, caught in the spell of psychological conservatism, they sought limited, practical gains, grasping hard-won fragments for their small store of political power. The spoils of party patronage were a crucial counter in their strategy.

On the other hand the Mugwumps showed how volatile a militant new minority could be. Large in view, diffuse and intangible in numerical strength, they tended to treat local politics as a counter in national affairs. With little stake in the set political patterns of the recent past, they championed disruptive changes, hoping through civil service reform to assert the ethical leadership of their class despite their lack of numbers. Meanwhile they gloried in party flux and instability. And they had a fatal fondness for the technique of righteous defeat. Balancing the advantages of compromise against the joys of revolt, they often seemed to prefer a well-staged failure to an ambiguous victory. Finally, neither minority seemed able to forget for long the cleavage of ethnic rancor that divided them. In this situation, future cooperation awaited a new issue for their diverse interests to cluster around, and the energies of new, unembittered leadership.

CHAPTER FOUR · THE TARIFF AND
THE YOUNG DEMOCRATS

IN A popular travelogue published in 1887 a New England writer described his visit to Yellowstone Park, where he was much taken by the steamy natural wonders. Curiously one of the geysers was called "Mugwump." Upon asking his guide for an explanation, the visiter was advised to wait and watch it perform.

We waited. It was a spring some six feet in diameter. Clouds of steam began to rise; then came a thunderous, groaning roar, as if all the warring elements of the earth were about to burst forth. The waters began to rise as if to threaten our safety. Then came the supreme effort, and amid groans and sobs a tiny stream of water rose six feet into the air. It trembled there for a brief moment, then fell, and all was still.[1]

Massachusetts Mugwumps might not have enjoyed the joke. Three years after their magnificent victory of 1884, they had little further to show for their effort. From among them now and then came confessions of disillusion over their small success. To George Fred Williams, who had whipped himself to a froth over the patronage battles of Cleveland's first years as President, the future at times looked quite blank. He confided to a friend in January 1887,

An hour ago, I had concluded that my pet reform of the civil service was a failure. Evidence has accumulated that we may not expect from the President any definite action respecting the civil service by which we may realize the non-partisan theory . . . I said to myself, "My work is done;" I have done *my share* in the last two or three years, given my time, injured my business, incurred enmities and jealousies; now that there is no way to secure from the President the knot which will keep the work done from unravelling, what is there left for me to do? Some good has been done the country, but now that I am only plied by office-holders in whom I have no personal interest, I may as well regain my freedom by announcing myself *out of politics.* It would really have taken little, an hour ago, to get from me a public declaration that I should definitely abandon politics.[2]

Williams had often betrayed dissatisfaction with civil service reform as a vehicle for his ambitions. His letters now crackled with references to "civil service cranks," "growlers," and "theorists," as each succeeding crisis over patronage jeopardized the Mugwump future in the Democratic party. Williams was not the only disenchanted Mugwump. Winslow Warren, commenting on Cleveland's blurred attitude toward the merit system, saw no more cause for indignation:

His party does not believe in it nor does the Republican, and our men are a queer mixture of idealists and croakers with a sprinkling of men too practical to expect the millennium in a day. We make much noise for our number but really have got more out of the fears and hopes of both parties than we had a right to expect.[3]

The year 1887 marked a watershed for the Mugwumps. Civil service by then had lost much of its clutch on their emotions. Now that the reform had been institutionalized by the Pendleton Act and by Dana's Massachusetts law, efforts to advance the cause had thrown the Mugwumps on the defensive and branded them as politically suspect. Further agitation more often than not served only to darken their personal chances for political advancement. The civil service crusade had been blunted by partial fulfillment under Grover Cleveland.

By 1887 intimations of political stagnation began to cross the minds of Democrats, Republicans, and Mugwumps alike. Grover Cleveland in his stolid and unimaginative way had liquidated many of the public concerns of earlier years. The good gray rectitude of his administration silenced doubts about the capacity of the Democratic party to govern the country. The issue of corruption in high places, which had gripped the country for twenty years, seemed momentarily old-fashioned. Cleveland could point to few other important achievements. The party

battles that marked his first years in office were muffled, inde-
cisive, and mostly devoid of ideology. Public policy seemed
somehow detached and irrelevant to private preoccupations.
With no perceptible aid or interference from Washington, the
country was shaking off the sluggish economic trance of recent
years, and good times seemed to be returning. Less seemed to
separate the two parties than ever before, and the voting public
looked forward to Cleveland's re-election, if not with enthusiasm, at least with equanimity. "If we don't meander forth and
stir up something for ourselves in the next House," Republican
congressional leader Tom Reed wrote to Henry Cabot Lodge in
September 1887, "death on the palest of horses will be riding
hard after us." [4]

Political stalemate bred no commensurate sense of security for
men of orthodoxy. Along with the Mugwumps, the leaders of
both parties rested their particular structures of political belief
on a common assumption of social stability which began to give
way in the late 1880's. The "Great Uprising" of the Knights of
Labor, detonated in the national consciousness by the Hay-
market riot in Chicago in May 1886, was the main warning. The
surge of the Knights reached its crisis quickly and began to fall
away before the year was out. But the following winter witnessed a rash of strikes across the country, flaring without warning and dying as fast. The rising of 1886 had left a charged air,
instantly detectable to keen observers. "How much changed
America seems to me within the last three years!" Lord Bryce
exclaimed to Thomas Wentworth Higginson on his return to the
United States in 1887. The newspapers, he added, were full of
labor troubles scarcely heard of in 1883.[5]

For Higginson and the other residents of Cambridge, labor
violence exploded close at home in February 1887. Early that
month the car men of the Cambridge Horse Railroad Company
struck for easier hours. The city's Democratic mayor, William E.
Russell, told the strikers he was duty bound to guarantee continued service to Boston and offered police protection to the
company to keep the horse cars running. When enough scabs
had been hired, the cars began to roll again. On the night of

16 February, a large crowd of strike sympathizers, tough men from "Dublin," East Cambridge, and Boston, milled about Harvard Square, heaving rocks at the cars as they came through and working over the scabs. The entire Cambridge police force was at the scene, helpless and ignored. Frantically seeking an end to violence, Mayor Russell now pleaded with the company to suspend service. (Years later Russell's admiring neighbors along Brattle Street remembered this as the single act of weakness in his career.) After three days of relative calm, another mob of two thousand men sought to halt the cars, till they were scattered by mounted police firing pistols overhead. Taking no chances, Russell called for two companies of state militia. These, together with police reinforcements from nearby towns, kept the peace until the strike was broken.[6]

It was against this background of social turbulence, flashing into open discord in Boston and suburban cities, in Fall River and the other mill towns, and in isolated rail junctions across the state, that tariff reform suddenly became the driving issue of Grover Cleveland's followers in Massachusetts. A peculiar conjunction of frustrated ambition and social anxiety made tariff agitation a fitting tactic for orthodoxy defending itself. If civil service reform was the means by which gentlemen accustomed to social respect tried to disrupt political convention, tariff reform became the means by which they tried to secure power in a society that was getting out of hand. Their most persuasive leader, as it developed, would be the young mayor of Cambridge, William E. Russell.

The origins of New England tariff reform sentiment go far back behind the 1880's. They are woven like a darkening fleck in the pattern of commercial decay that marked the history of nineteenth-century New England. Protection had first come to New England in the 1820's when cotton textile entrepreneurs secured a tariff for their thriving young industry. The commitment to protection was strengthened in 1861 when New England allied with mid-Atlantic manufacturing interests to pass the Morrill Tariff. Cotton textile makers were increasingly devoted to protection in the postwar decades, and their prosperity was

a main prop of Republican supremacy in New England. The
boot and shoe industry, which, like the textile makers, had
access to domestic raw materials, also enjoyed good times. As
the Republican tariff coalition extended its commitments to
embrace the burgeoning West, however, a growing number of
New England economic interests began to feel pinched. As the
protective tariff was the shield of young industry, opposition to it
sprang from among men less interested in production than in
trade. Boston's railroaders and shippers formed a core of low-
tariff sentiment which carried over from before the war. The
rising national tariff level had cut into the shippers' trade, and,
as they believed, was clearing the seas of the American flag.
Decay crept across the port of Boston as the Berkshire Hills
isolated New England from the main trunk of the country's rail
system. Boston money poured west to build the Michigan Central, the Chicago, Burlington, & Quincy, the Atchison, Topeka,
& Santa Fe, the Mexican Central, and the stockyards of Chicago
and Kansas City. Dividends came back to Boston pockets, but
the commerce of the West went to New York. The hard facts of
geography, despite compensating rate differentials, condemned
Boston to provincial inferiority. Although the Boston & Albany
had consolidated lines across the state by 1867 and prospered
from its linkage with the New York Central, Boston merchants
resisted dependence on New York. In desperation the state
spent fifteen million dollars boring the Hoosac Tunnel through
the Berkshire range to create a separate route to the golden
West. But by no stratagem could Boston control its own lines
beyond the Berkshires. Measured by the hope which dug it, the
Hoosac Tunnel was a resounding failure. As one New Englander remarked, it was "like buying a bung-hole and failing
to buy the barrel round it." [7]

To compensate for the isolation of New England from the rest
of the American continent, Boston's shippers and importers had
long favored a reduction of the tariff level to loosen and expand
foreign trade. By the 1880's, as the first substantial wave of
trust-building swept through the domestic economy, a growing
number of established New England manufacturers began to

agree with them. The competition with new industrial combines in Pennsylvania and the West had started to hurt. The enormous growth of the Pennsylvania iron and steel industry, fed by large, convenient coal fields, forced New England iron works—which had depended on charcoal from depleted forests—to look for their own sources of coal. The best fields near by were in Nova Scotia. But reliance on imported coal carried the penalty of tariff duties. Similarly, New England canners believed their business was being artificially constricted by the import duty on tin. New England shipbuilders believed their industry had declined because of the high copper tariff protecting western mining monopolies. Most importantly, perhaps, New England woolen makers felt they suffered from the protection extended to western wool growers. Each resentment made converts to tariff reform. Together they fed a growing faith that free raw materials were the proper panacea for New England's economic pains.[8]

Neither economic blight nor the cure suggested could by itself incite public agitation. Education, political appeal, and popular emotion were needed to mature the issue. Through the postwar years New England produced an impressive body of tariff reform theoreticians and advocates. Led by Harvard, her colleges perpetuated the calm, rational consensus of classical economics in which reform thinking could flourish. Original speculations came mostly from nonacademic publicists, however. Foremost among these was David A. Wells, whose experience as a Washington tax expert during the Civil War had convinced him of the fallacies of high protection and won him warm enemies among Republican tariff sponsors. For years thereafter, Wells campaigned earnestly for lower tariffs by pamphlet and letter from his home in Norwich, Connecticut. In Boston, Gamaliel Bradford and Edward Atkinson often swung their wide-ranging attention to the tariff question. But New England reform sentiment lacked cohesion and visceral appeal before the late eighties. Neither party had done much to fix the tariff issue with a partisan flavor. Commitments when ventured were often cool and perfunctory. Thus when William

Endicott accepted the Democratic nomination for governor in 1884, he had called the tariff a business matter beyond politics and urged "readjustment . . . in a wise and liberal spirit." Gamaliel Bradford agreed that permanent business well-being required more than anything else a settled tariff policy; wholesale reduction would only usher in disaster. Bradford foresaw a solemn future for the cause. "What is needed," he wrote, "is public discussion, scientific treatment, and gradual reform," officially guided by the Treasury Department in Washington. Wary of the taint of radicalism enveloping the phrase "free trade," Boston's tariff reformers proceeded with caution. Edward Atkinson's insurance contracts with cotton textile mill owners muted what would otherwise have been a strident voice against high protection. Atkinson's reluctance to flaunt the cause in the face of skeptical businessmen was symptomatic. Early in 1884, reformers hopefully organized the Massachusetts Tariff Reform League with Charles Francis Adams, Jr., as president and Josiah Quincy as executive secretary. When they attempted to inject the tariff issue into the contest between Blaine and Cleveland, however, League members won only token support. And a year later when Quincy sought to raise money for a series of lectures, he discovered general apathy among expected patrons.[9]

The issue fared better in 1886. The *Boston Transcript* called that year's congressional campaign the first tariff reform contest in Massachusetts history. Several avowed tariff reformers got into the running, and four were elected. The leading Democrat among them was John E. Russell of Leicester. Russell was a genial, old-fashioned Jeffersonian who wore the label "free trader" with pride when most politicians took it as a smear. Well into middle age by 1886, he had traveled widely in his youth through Europe, South America, and the West and then settled down fifty miles from Boston amid the soft hills of Worcester County to breed racing horses and blooded sheep. The panic of 1873 left him a changed man, anxious for the future of the rural life he loved. Beginning in 1880 Russell spent several years as secretary of the Massachusetts Board of Agriculture. His close knowledge of scientific breeding and cultivation, together with his concern for the sad economy of rural New England, made him widely popular among New England farmers. By winning election to Congress in 1886 as a free trader from a rock-ribbed Republican district, he demonstrated that tariff reform had possibilities beyond the circle of commercial Boston. Shrewd, witty, and cosmopolitan, beyond the years of his ambition, Russell won the affection of Grover Cleveland and William C. Whitney while in Washington and helped link Massachusetts Democrats to the power structure of the national party. Before Cleveland's famous tariff message of 1887 regenerated his party, John E. Russell was the foremost tariff reform Democrat in Massachusetts.[10]

By 1886 many Massachusetts Mugwumps, tiring of the fight for civil service, gazed longingly at the tariff issue as a lifeline from political isolation. Thus Charles Codman, who confessed to Cleveland a year before, "I have no standing in a political party but am an outcast and a wanderer," now wrote to William Everett:

> I should be glad (and in this I rather expect you to agree with me) to act with the Democratic party whenever the issue is clearly made on the tariff question between it and the high Republican protectionists. We are drifting to that position every day, I believe, and it is inevitable that sooner or later the line will be drawn. When it is, I think that we shall know on which side to take our stand.

And shortly before Cleveland sent his tariff message to Congress in December 1887, President Eliot of Harvard was toying with his favorite notion of a third party, this one to fortify the civil service cause with the fresh energies of tariff reform.[11]

There is evidence that when Mugwump leaders in New York learned of Cleveland's intention to devote his entire annual message of 1887 to a demand for tariff reform, they caught their breath, conferred together, and urged the President to reconsider. There was no such hesitation in Massachusetts. There Cleveland's message met with an electric response. The clamor it raised dominated political dialogue for years thereafter. The anxieties of Mugwumps, Democrats, and men of commerce had finally converged and found their voice. The Tariff Reform

League went happily to work and scheduled a massive dinner to ratify Cleveland's message. George Fred Williams, his flagging spirits revived, hurried off to Washington to hunt guests. He landed a senator and three congressmen, all from the South. (Secretary of the Treasury Fairchild wanted to come, but Cleveland vetoed his appearance, according to Williams. The President had apparently been numbed by the cold reception to his message in the Republican press and felt there should be no further prodding from the executive branch.) Massachusetts Republicans accepted the challenge to tariff debate confident that Cleveland had delivered them a winning issue for the coming presidential election. With a few exceptions, New England cotton textile interests squarely opposed tinkering with protection. The Arkwright Club, the cotton manufacturers' chief political organization, was happy to foot the bill for a campaign against revision. Cleveland seemed to have swallowed the free traders' bait, and protectionists were sure that the mass of voters, in Boston and elsewhere, would decide against him.[12]

Despite their own hard suspicion that the tariff message dimmed Democratic chances at the polls in 1888, Mugwumps and Democrats rejoiced in their new issue. Tariff reform had many uses for Cleveland's followers. Most obviously it provided terms for reconciliation where civil service had kept them divided. This consideration more than compensated for the doubtful appeal of tariff reform at the ballot box. A crusade to lower duties on imported raw materials was admittedly not calculated to strike fire among the Democratic rank-and-file. Most urban workers accepted the tariff as protection for them as well as their employers. "Free raw materials" did smack of "free trade." And to Irish ears, free trade was "English" and therefore damned. Clearly there was need for education on these points. But Irish leaders in Boston were willing to play along. Unlike "snivel service," tariff reform agitation did not affront their self-interest. They could pay lip service as easily to the theory of the loyal-voter-as-abused-consumer as they could to the theory of the loyal-voter-as-protected-laborer. The loyalty of the Boston Irish to the Democratic party was a condition, not a theory. Tariff reform touched a more lively nerve of self-interest among the party's potential patrons. Railroad men, shippers, and importers who called themselves Democrats had as much at stake in lower tariffs as railroad men, shippers, and importers who called themselves Mugwumps. Whatever the intellectual and social disparity between Democrats like Henry M. Whitney and Leopold Morse and Mugwumps like John Murray Forbes and Henry L. Pierce, the hope of looser, freer trade gave them a common denominator. Unity of purpose among such men was an obvious boon.

At two vital points in the party structure, then, the tariff issue eased tensions and dissolved the barrier between Mugwump and Democrat. As a notion in the minds of thoughtful young Yankee lawyers, tariff reform also answered a profound need. It was something to believe in. Whether couched in terms of relief for consumers paying swollen prices for protected goods, or in terms of ending unequal subsidies to special interests, or in terms of killing the proliferation of industrial monopolies, the issue gave the Democratic party a fresh and ennobling image. It revived memories of a Jeffersonian equalitarian tradition long dulled by the heritage of the Civil War. It brought the value of federal economy into play against the treasury surplus created by twenty years of high protection. It made the facts of federal patronage to corporate industry a foil for dreams of a golden, atomistic past. It focused the ideal of the autonomous American individual standing free of his government, asking no favors, a single citizen among equal millions. Above all, the tariff reform issue fitted a stubborn faith in the tenets of classical economics just at a time when they were being called into question with abrupt and startling insistence. The tariff issue rightly used could be a powerful weapon for combating economic heresy among trade-unionists and labor agitators. Here was a chance for educated men to assert themselves. If the harmonious, classical, free and fluid market place of goods and services celebrated in the textbooks could be shown to remain a valid model for economic reality, the current bent of the working man toward militant organization, disruptive strikes, and class-oriented poli-

tics could be ascribed to ignorance or misinstruction. The
tariff reformers diagnosed the pains of industrial society as resulting not from any internal malady but from an artificial,
external encumbrance fixed in place by thoughtless, self-serving
politicians. Their prescription vindicated the classical model.
Remove the encumbrance and the free market would flourish
for the benefit of all. Remove the encumbrance and the nightmare of labor violence would dissolve with the dawn. Remove
the encumbrance and monopoly would disappear. If the sum
of individual interests in American society did not add up to the
public good, proper tariff revision would make it so.

Tariff reform was an issue for economic and social conservatives. Its advocates hoped to avert attention from intrinsic social
conflict in their community and so maintain their claim to community leadership. But this is not to say that tariff reform was
a sham issue, a herring drawn across the picket line. Clustering
about it were all the ideals associated with a minimal exercise of
governmental power in the economy. The sufficiency of the individual, the harmony of labor and capital, the excellence of free
intercourse among men and nations—these precepts gave the
reform moral and emotional force. Among politicians and
thoughtful men it inspired passions and loyalties more compelling than civil service ever had.

Tariff reform shook Boston's educated community at its roots.
In 1889 Harvard College momentarily became the storm center
of the dispute. For years past there had been talk that Harvard
was a spawning bed for low-tariff ideas. Most of the gossip concerned the teaching of a brisk young political economist named
Frank Taussig. For all his expertise with tariffs, Taussig was
anxious to dispel any impression that his lectures were aimed
against protection. He had no taste for political debate. He
preferred, he said, "to do my teaching quietly and soberly, and
avoid anything that would lay me open to the charge of being
partisan." But powerful Republican alumni were in no mood to
give Taussig a free hand in subverting Harvard undergraduates.
Finally a committee headed by the Republican John T. Morse
investigated Taussig's department and reported an intolerable

situation to the Harvard Board of Overseers. In the opinion of a committee majority, economic instruction had become so distorted by free-trade doctrine that Harvard was lined up on one side of a political issue involving the welfare of whole generations. The report continued:

These members of your committee regard the present organization of the department at Harvard as illiberal, one-sided, and therefore unjust to the student. It seems to them a somewhat singular thing that an institution which owes so much of the support and of the wealth which have made it prosperous to a community of protectionists and to the gifts of money earned in protected industries, should now so obstinately refuse to recognize protection except as a heresy, and should so pointedly contemn the opinions of so large a body of its neighbors and natural friends. They think that Harvard College ought at least to afford protection a respectful hearing.

A minority dissent, appended to the report by Mugwump Henry Putnam, took up Taussig's cause and asserted the principle of academic freedom in spirited language. Championing the "free and disinterested pursuit of truth," Putnam labeled the suggestion of Harvard's supposed obligation to its wealthy benefactors "extraordinary and unworthy":

If any wealthy donors and patrons of the College have expressly or impliedly made it a condition of their generous gifts that specific economic doctrines should be taught, and that the opinions of the College should be immutably fixed and mortgaged in perpetuity in the midst of a free community and in a world of change and progress, the College could better afford to return every dollar of their donations than to submit to such conditions. Its professors could better be starved than either pledged or subsidized in matters of scientific opinion.

Frank Taussig ran no risk of starving. Defenders swarmed to his side. President Eliot supported hm, and the whole community of Mugwumps and Cleveland Democrats rallied round him. Morse's majority report came in for stern criticism from the *Boston Herald* and the *Transcript* and from Godkin's *Nation*. Before the storm died, Morse accurately described himself in a letter to Henry Cabot Lodge as having been "searchingly har-rowed." [13]

Meanwhile, despite Grover Cleveland's narrow defeat by Benjamin Harrison in the presidential election of 1888, the Massachusetts Democratic party was passing through exciting changes. One striking index of the transition was the changing attitude toward the party within the Massachusetts Reform Club. Fewer than a dozen members of that Mugwump body had been prepared to call themselves Democrats when Cleveland first took office back in 1885. Over the next four years sentiment fluctuated wildly in ratio with Cleveland's changing reputation as a civil service reformer, but his removal from office in 1889 cleared the air. Now that the nagging complication of supporting an incumbent Democratic president was eliminated, and the tariff issue enhanced the Democratic party's role as the national party of opposition, a majority of Mugwumps were willing to abandon independent status and call themselves Cleveland Democrats. By 1889 most influential members of the Reform Club had gone over to the Democratic party. In November 1891 a spokesman stated that the club was almost wholly Democratic. The forty-odd members who continued to insist upon being called Mugwumps were regarded as obstructionists. Generally speaking the fusion between Mugwumps and Cleveland Demo-crats would remain intact until Cleveland's return to the presi-dency and the onset of economic crisis in 1893.[14]

But the Reform Club was not the instrument of the change reflected in its members' politics. It remained a polite Yankee forum, where gentlemen made speeches and waited for ap-plause or rebuttal. Its purpose was protest, not action. Fresh, authentic leadership for the Democratic party emerged among men who had come of age politically since 1884, inspired by Cleveland's presidency, men whose choice of party was original, natural, and voluntary. They differed from the Mugwumps mainly in this accident of age; they too were mostly Harvard-educated Yankee lawyers. But the livery of party did not chafe them. Because they experienced no crisis of conscience in flock-ing to Cleveland's colors, they had fewer qualms about the doubtful respectability of their chosen party. Their willingness to work with the leaders of the Boston Irish had been built into their decision to enter politics. They brought vigor, flexibility, and respect for compromise to the Yankee wing of the party.

Sherman Hoar, Charles S. Hamlin, and Nathan Matthews were representative of these young Democrats. Hoar was a nephew of the Republican Senator and the son of President Grant's Attorney General. A native of Concord, he passed through Harvard with the class of 1882. His handsome, robust features happened to catch the eye of a fellow townsman, the sculptor Daniel Chester French, and so today in Harvard Yard Hoar is enshrined in anonymity as the bronze face of John Harvard. His modeling and schooling completed, Hoar joined Moorfield Storey's Boston law firm. In contrast with Storey, he was untroubled by the Mugwump sense of conflict between private career and public office, or by worry that dabbling in politics might entail financial sacrifice. "On the question of money," he wrote a friend in 1886, "I can assure you from observation in my own family that public position attracts clients and that with long vacations to work in, a lawyer even in public life need not fear of losing his clientage." Hoar started running for office in 1886. A hard-talking, self-confident, blunt, and somewhat overbearing young man, he had the sense to cultivate a personal following among the Irish. His right-hand man was Charles Scannell, a Boston Democrat whose aggressive partisanship was no small factor in Hoar's election to Congress in 1890.[15]

Charles S. Hamlin, Harvard class of '83, entered Boston law practice in 1886 and was running for the state senate a year later. In his prim, polished way he was a competent debater and promptly earned a reputation for prowess in untangling complex tariff arguments. Hamlin sought public office as the moth seeks the flame, trying hard and often. He lived in Ward Twenty-one of Boston, the home territory of Democratic boss Pat Maguire. In later years he fondly recalled Maguire's friendship and support. But he never won an election. Maguire could hand him nominations but not majorities. Ever hopeful, Hamlin applied himself to organization routine, worked into the private councils of the party, and wound up as Assistant Secretary of the Treasury in Cleveland's second administration.[16]

Nathan Matthews, born in Boston's West End, graduated from Harvard in 1875 and then spent two years at Leipzig studying jurisprudence and political economy. Returning to Boston, he took up law practice and became expert in tax and realty. A large, rather formidable person behind his pince-nez and floppy mustache, Matthews valued honesty, efficiency, thrift, and power. When he entered politics in 1886, Democratic leaders instantly responded to his strong nature, and he was one of them within a year. Matthews had particular success in working out practical terms of party cooperation with Pat Maguire. This liaison would result in Maguire's selection of Matthews for the Boston mayoralty a few years later.[17]

Scores of young men like Hoar, Hamlin, and Matthews joined the Massachusetts Democracy during Cleveland's first administration: Joseph Lee, Mugwump banker Henry Lee's son who later gained local fame as a champion of municipal playgrounds; Thomas Jefferson Coolidge, Jr., whose more famous father was a leading Republican businessman; Sigourney Butler, son of Peter Butler and law partner to Richard Olney; Robert Treat Paine III, the son of the prominent philanthropist—these and others more obscure toyed momentarily with the notion of careers in politics. It was the tariff issue, more than any other factor, which charged them with a sense of ideological purpose. Out of their excited discussions about the future emerged the Young Men's Democratic Club of Massachusetts, the organization which would soon become the main agency of Cleveland Democracy in Massachusetts. Launched late in January 1888, the club was over a hundred strong by the following spring and growing fast. Within a year it had five hundred members, most of them living in the four counties surrounding Boston—Suffolk, Middlesex, Norfolk, and Essex. It attracted ambitious Mugwumps like Josiah Quincy, John F. Andrew, and George Fred Williams who had decided to pin their fortunes to the Democratic party. Several aspiring Irish politicians joined in the first months. Wealthy party patrons like the clothier Leopold Morse, the traction magnate Henry M. Whitney, the newspaper publisher Charles H. Taylor, and Henry Reed of Boston's sugar interests were charter members.[18] The varied membership raised certain problems in defining goals and compromising differences. The club's announced concern was to agitate the tariff issue and prove the Jeffersonian case in state and national politics. But some members, particularly those nurtured in Mugwumpery, hoped to use it as a stick for beating local Irish bosses. "You must join the Young Men's Democratic Club and help it to rescue the party from Maguire's hands and those of his ilk," the irrepressible George Fred Williams wrote a friend. Others recognized that cooperation between Irish and Yankee was an essential condition of Democratic success in Massachusetts. Under the guidance of Maguire's friend Nathan Matthews, who tended to dominate policy discussions from the outset, the Y.M.D.C. became a force for ethnic cohesion within the party. Matthews was determined that the energies keyed up by the tariff issue should not be vented in local squabbles between "bosses" and "reformers." Without the forty thousand Democratic votes from the wards of Boston, the party would go nowhere. The way to harmony was nicely specified in the aims of the club listed in its constitution:

To foster and disseminate Democratic principles; to secure the active participation in politics of those who have hitherto been indifferent to political duties, or who have been prevented from performing them; to bring about the election of honest and capable men to all public offices; and to secure the purity of elections; *but the Club shall take no part in municipal politics.*[19] [Italics added.]

In other words, politics were to be purified by democratic ideals and Democratic activism, but no one was to interfere with local satrapies. Unlike the Mugwump Reform Club, the Y.M.D.C. did not become a sounding board for Maguire's detractors. Instead, its leaders concentrated on winning control of the Democratic State Committee and creating a state majority. The membership of the Y.M.D.C. steadily broadened in character and geographical distribution. Increasing numbers of clerks, tradesmen, and teachers joined the lawyers, politicians, and

Boston capitalists who had signed up at the outset. A growing percentage came from cities outside the sphere of Boston. New members in the early nineties included such eminent people as Brooks Adams, Charles Francis Adams, Edward Atkinson, and Louis Brandeis. Donovans, Sullivans, and O'Briens swarmed in alongside. This diversity was no mere show. The club ultimately touched party workers throughout the state and suffused them with the enthusiasm of its founders. In 1891 the Young Men's Democratic Club was plausibly described by William E. Russell as "the strongest political organization in New England." [20]

William E. Russell had reason to praise the club. He was its main political product and beneficiary. Behind the ambitions of this young Cambridge Democrat gathered all the momentum of the revival that had begun in 1888. His personal qualities and political ideals so aptly registered the character of Cleveland Democracy that the man and the movement he led in Massachusetts became almost indistinguishable. From its bright beginning to its abrupt end, Russell's career provided a sensitive gauge for measuring the potential of conservative reform. His fortunes and the fortunes of his party rose and fell in unison.

The first William Russell settled in Cambridge in 1645. Eight generations of Massachusetts farmers, tradesmen, and lawyers linked him to the boy born on January 6, 1857, and christened William Eustis. Billy Russell, as he was known in Cambridge all his life, was the youngest son in a family of eleven. His father, Charles Theodore Russell, Harvard class of '37, was a Boston lawyer and Cambridge politician who had known Daniel Webster and was a Whig because of it. Along with others of his kind, C. T. Russell drifted into the Democratic party in the 1850's when Webster's following fell apart. He served several terms in the state legislature and was mayor of Cambridge during the Civil War. In the postwar decades, as his sons began to run the family law firm, Russell took up the teaching of law at Boston University. Meanwhile he acquired the stature of a Democratic patriarch in Cambridge. He lived until 1895, in his home on Sparks Street, celebrated for his flourishing white beard and his stories of Daniel Webster.[21]

His son Billy grew up while Cambridge turned into a city around him. A boy could still fish and swim in Fresh Pond, or he could fight with Irish gangs down by the Charles. Billy Russell was adept at either pastime. Betweentimes he camped at Walden Pond, collected mongrel dogs, and tried to climb the tower of Harvard's new Memorial Hall. At sixteen he entered Harvard with the class of 1877. Neither he nor his class set marks for scholarly diligence. Seventy-seven's most famous club, according to a contemporary, was the Picnic Club. The leading by-law of this splendid organization provided that if anyone, at any time, decided to go on a picnic, all members had to go with him. Russell's classmate Barrett Wendell recalled theirs as the "most discordant class which ever vexed the authorities and traditions of Harvard." As Wendell remembered it, his classmates fell into two feuding groups: the ordinary fellows and the society men. Russell was a society man but no partisan; he managed to keep a foot in either camp. Membership in Hasty Pudding and even Dickie failed to stamp him irretrievably as a clubbie. He was at his most ordinary in the classroom. He fared well enough in history and political economy and starred in ethics, but language, math, and chemistry kept him floundering. Friends recalled him as a guileless, healthy youth, "as fond of green fields as Greek roots." He evidently divided his best energies between sports and politics. A short, wiry boy, standing five feet eight inches, he was a good man in a boat, a skillful boxer, and—by one estimate—the best rifle shot in the college. Football was taking shape at Harvard in the seventies, and Russell threw himself into the new game with abandon. He kicked two years on the varsity rush line until he broke his nose and then settled for the job of manager. Politics came next. In the fall of his senior year Yard life was enlivened by the presidential campaign between Hayes and Tilden. Harvard boys favored Hayes five to one. A militant debater with his father's party to uphold, Russell spoke repeatedly for Tilden in campus rallies and won an easy reputation as the most ardent Democrat in his class.[22]

Russell's preparation for a career had about it the cast of inevitability. After graduation he entered Boston University Law

School, where his father taught, and carried all before him. He was class orator, wrote a prize-winning legal essay, and graduated with the first *summa cum laude* ever conferred by the school. In 1880 he was admitted to the Suffolk bar and promptly joined his brothers in the family law firm. A year later, when he was twenty-four, some Cambridge friends decided to boost him into the city's common council. On election day when Russell arrived at the polls he saw his friends distributing stickers bearing his name to paste on the regular ballot. Pleasantly surprised, he set about making up more stickers and was elected. During the next three years, first as councilman and then as alderman, Russell spiced the city's politics with his impudence and widened his following. Cambridge city government had long been loose, offhand, and mediocre, and his cocky enterprise refreshed the town. He was elected mayor on a nonpartisan reform ticket in 1884 and re-elected annually for three years following, twice running unopposed. The Cambridge mayoralty was traditionally an office of modest power, involving little more than spare-time effort. Aldermen and departmental committees made most decisions, and the mayor either resisted or acquiesced. When Russell took office the city's treasury was empty and its citizens saddled with what was then regarded as a high tax rate. By the end of one year much had changed. The reform administration implemented the state's new civil service law among municipal employees, paid city bills, funded the debt, balanced the budget, and cut the tax rate to the lowest level in a decade. "Pay as you go" became a Cambridge motto. Yet Russell was able to claim that as much or more money had been spent for schools, streets, lamps, sewers, health, fire, and police protection, and public charity as in years past. By the testimony of one of its most distinguished residents, Charles Eliot Norton, Cambridge became the best-governed city in Massachusetts while Russell was mayor. When Russell embarked on his last term in 1887, President Eliot of Harvard wrote to him, "Your re-election by so handsome a majority is wholesome for the city, very satisfactory to the friends of pure politics and good order, and just to you." [23]

By any standard and certainly by those of Massachusetts Democrats in the 1880's, Russell's mayoralty was a remarkable tour de force. Not yet thirty when he returned to the full-time practice of law in 1888, he was already the focus of anticipation among party workers and Democratic club men all over the state. His youth and early success seemed emblematic of their hopes. A trim man with high forehead, ruddy color, and a pleasant, clean-shaven, slightly homely face, Russell—like any good politician—cultivated his party's image of himself. His cool gray eyes now reflected a candid and collected manner, the honed intelligence of a first-rate lawyer, and a gift for quick perception of popular moods. His rivals among the younger Democrats tagged Russell as a man on the make. They were right.[24]

Russell was acquiring the special magnetism of rising politicians. Men crowded near him not only for his personal friendship but out of ambition, self-gratification, and for protection. Already in Cambridge he had shown a flair for befriending prosperous and influential townsmen. One source of his strength as mayor was his close acquaintance with Charles Raymond, a local street railroad entrepreneur, and J. Q. Bennett, president of the city's largest electrical plant. When the swashbuckling Henry M. Whitney of Boston decided to buy up the street rail lines into Cambridge, Raymond sold out to him and Bennett agreed to supply him with electrical power. It was through Raymond and Bennett that Russell came to know Whitney. Both in politics and law, intimacy with powerful men in the booming urban utilities business was a valuable asset. Russell also profited from friendship with Frederick H. Rindge, a fellow Cantabrigian and Harvard classmate possessed of great wealth and generous instincts. Through Russell's mediation Cambridge received huge sums of money from Rindge earmarked for a new city hall, a public library, and a manual training school. Nor did Russell neglect his ties among the established gentility. When he considered running for Congress in 1886 promises of financial support came from Henry L. Pierce, William C. Endicott, Henry Lee, and John Murray Forbes. Professor Shaler even offered to raise two hundred dollars among the Harvard faculty. Two years later when Russell ran for governor, Harvard graduates were stationed at the polls in all the larger Massachusetts cities to pass out ballot stickers bearing his name to Republican voters. ("Untidy chaps with stickers would only deter people from using them," a Harvard man explained.)[25]

This confidence in Russell displayed by wealthy, gentle, and educated contemporaries was less remarkable than his popularity among voters variously referred to as the Irish, the masses, or the slums. He interpreted himself with equal ease to both ends of the social spectrum. This was perhaps his supreme political achievement. Cambridge in the 1880's, like so many other Massachusetts cities, had become preoccupied with the social disparities in its midst. The Irish were coming over from Boston in large numbers, filling East Cambridge, and aspiring to political power. Solicitous for their city's future, Cambridge residents watched the Celtic migration across the Charles with some foreboding. Russell managed to mollify both Irish aspirations and Yankee fears through his own success. Using the Democratic party as his bond of sympathy with the Irish, he conducted himself as mayor in such a way as to please Yankee citizens. This was no easy strategy. His position became tenuous after 1886, when class consciousness among Irish laborers reached new heights. In the summer of 1886 he won approval among local Knights of Labor in settling a strike in a Cambridge meat-packing plant. The following winter he lost their affection when he acted to protect property rights against violence in the Cambridge street railway strike. But he never entirely forfeited the respect of Irish workers and unionists. And his own respect for them was as genuine and untroubled as his station allowed. Russell was an ostentatious democrat, a fact which always inspired a certain wonder among his friends. The Mugwump Robert Grant, who whiled away many a long night with Russell over cards, wrote years afterward that Russell "combined more admirably than any man I ever knew the personable sophistication of a man of affairs with an absolutely spontaneous faith in democracy. If I was democratic, it was solely through patriotic conviction tempered by innate reserves, but he seemed not only tolerant of the whole kettle of fish, but enamoured of it." (Judge Grant never forgot the time at a Cape Cod resort when Russell dressed him down for neglecting to greet their waitress when they met her strolling on the beach after dinner.) "We have placed the people on the throne," Russell told a Harvard commencement audience in the early nineties. "By inherent right and universal assent, they are the sovereign power beyond all question . . . We gratefully recognize this truth, and rejoice in established democracy." Russell challenged Harvard to drop its lingering distrust of democracy. "Let it not waste its energy in vain misgivings and idle complaints of popular sovereignty, or in mistaken efforts to thwart or hamper it," he urged. The true work of the university community was to qualify the people for wise rule, not to hector them for their mistakes.[26]

As an educated man and conservative reformer, Russell gained renown in Massachusetts for his generous democratic instincts. As a Democratic politician, he naturally offered his party as the people's surrogate. The Democratic party, he declared, was "the bulwark of the silent people" against selfish private interests who were warping the powers of government in their own behalf. In the eyes of the Democratic party, he said, government should be "a power to protect and encourage men to make the most of themselves, and not something for men to make the most out of." Russell was satisfied that his party's Jeffersonian tradition of local self-reliance could meet the reform needs of the 1880's. Accepting the Jeffersonian distrust of centralized political power, Russell had no trouble squaring his reformist goals with his party's historic sympathy for states rights, stringent economy in public administration, and the constraint of federal authority. For him there was no conflict between tradition and reform. He loved to quote Macaulay on the point: "It is now time for us to pay a decent, a rational, a manly reverence to our ancestors, not by superstitiously adhering to what they in other circumstances did, but by doing what they in our circumstances would have done." It was Russell's fortune to believe that Macaulay's formula could work. He admitted no doubt whether he and his fellow Yankee Democrats could discern what policies dead party heroes might have recommended for coping with a modern industrial community, or whether all their wisdom was still relevant. This confidence was more than stump rhetoric. Russell enjoyed a serene communion with the past around him, the past of his party, his native city, his family. The reforms he envisioned for his community involved no uprooting assault on what already existed. He suffered no sense of discontinuity from any cause. Change for him was simply the moving edge of familiar history. Able, attractive, self-confident, Russell moved rapidly to the head of his party in the late 1880's. He benefited from the complex tensions of anxiety and ambition playing on the minds of both Mugwumps and Democrats after 1886. When the fear stimulated by labor radicalism, in team with the vigor imbued by the tariff issue, pulled his party toward an uncertain future, this brisk, uncomplicated lawyer from Brattle Street became an oddly gallant guide.[27]

Russell's friends began to talk of running him for higher office while he was still mayor of Cambridge. In 1887 they entered his name in protest against the party spoilsmen's nomination of Henry Lovering for governor. A year later, with Grover Cleveland seeking re-election on the tariff issue, Russell became a logical choice to head the Democratic state ticket. Cleveland lost Massachusetts badly in 1888 and carried the state ticket down with him. But Russell ran for governor again in 1889 and 1890. Success in a state-wide election depended on patching Yankee differences with Democratic leaders in Boston. Russell had to guarantee the loyalty of the Irish. Only then could he turn to the task of changing the ponderous Republican voting habits of nonmetropolitan Yankee Massachusetts. His personal liaison with Irish leaders was slow in building. Contacts among Cambridge Irishmen were not overly useful in approaching powerful leaders like Pat Maguire. Nor was Russell's reputation as a Cambridge reformer any help. His dispatch in inaugurating the merit system among Cambridge employees, for instance, needed reckoning with. Moreover, his mayoralty had precipitated a great outpouring of proud civic virtue known as the

"Cambridge Idea," which resulted—among other things—in the closing of Cambridge saloons by popular referendum in 1886. Russell opposed the antisaloon ordinance, but as mayor he enforced it to the letter. In Irish eyes he therefore shared the stigma of prohibition. The liquor issue hampered his search for support among Boston Democrats. Over the years it had become habitual for Boston Democratic leaders to strike bargains with Republican majority managers in the state legislature in order to protect Boston's right to local option. The liquor issue produced an impossibly tangled skein of crises and secret deals in the lobbies of the state house and accentuated the bent of Boston Democratic leaders toward moods of expedient, insular self-interest. Russell's friends angrily agreed that he lost at least one race for governor because Boston "Saloon Democrats" had thrown their votes to the Republican candidate in return for Republican promises to squelch state-wide prohibition.[28]

Squabbles within the Irish organization added to Russell's troubles. Among Boston leaders, Pat Maguire's lieutenant Mike Cunniff had shown unusual interest in promoting the young Cambridge Democrat. But in 1888 Cunniff rocked the party organization by trying to unseat Maguire as the city's Democratic boss. Cunniff failed, fell from grace, and left Russell with the task of currying favor with the proud and foxy Maguire. Russell spared no effort. He cultivated the friendship of Irish lawyers like Thomas Gargan and Patrick Collins who had substantial influence on Maguire's behavior. Irish Home Rule suddenly became a fetish with Russell, and when he went abroad in the summer of 1890 he carried a letter of introduction to Parnell written by Boyle O'Reilly. Finally Russell satisfied Maguire that his ascendancy to party leadership was no threat to Maguire's interests in matters of patronage and prohibition. By 1890 Russell and Maguire had made their peace and were working together.[29]

Meanwhile with the help of the Young Men's Democratic Club, Russell embarked on the most intensive effort in a generation to fit together the little pieces of the Democratic party scattered across Massachusetts in lesser towns and cities. Club members provided him with a comprehensive series of reports describing in close detail the condition of local industries and the temper of local party factotums all over the state. In his three-year campaign to reach the State House, he marshaled every resource and spoke in the assembly halls and rail depots of towns where people could not remember ever seeing a Democratic candidate for governor before. And each year the self-imagery of the young Democrats surrounding Russell became more plausible to the voters of Massachusetts.[30]

The Democratic surge reached its crest in 1890. The chance of timing gave Yankee Democrats a crucial advantage. With Benjamin Harrison in the White House and Czar Reed cracking the whip in Congress, new high-tariff legislation was brewing in Washington. Following the advice of Grover Cleveland, Democratic leaders on Capitol Hill decided to give Republican protectionists a free hand with the new schedules and make political capital of the result. In Massachusetts the trick was to relate the tariff issue to state politics. Under the shrewd management of Josiah Quincy and a Boston Irishman named John McDonough, the Democratic minority in the state legislature produced a clear party division on the tariff question by introducing a series of resolutions favoring free raw materials. As each resolution came up for a vote, the Republican majority had to override a unanimous Democratic voting bloc to defeat it. The lines were now drawn. In the summer of 1890 Congress passed the McKinley Tariff and dropped into Democratic laps a bulging packet of evidence with which to drive home their case. The new rates went into effect just a month before the fall elections. Voters were persuaded that the immediate consequence would be to jack up consumer prices all along the line. The McKinley schedules on iron, tin, wool, and foodstuffs made a superb foil for the Yankee crusade for free raw materials.[31]

Massachusetts Democrats pressed their advantage. With Nathan Matthews and Josiah Quincy now running the state committee, the party organization was screwed up to its best performance in years. All across the state and especially near Boston, young Mugwumps and Yankee Democrats scrambled for nominations. In the Lowell-Lawrence district embracing the mill cities north of Boston, Moses T. Stevens, the wealthiest woolens manufacturer in America, decided to run for Congress as a low-tariff Democrat. John F. Andrew, Sherman Hoar, George Fred Williams, William Everett, and Charles Codman also won Democratic nominations for Congress and hit the stump immediately. Winslow Warren's son Charles, fresh out of Harvard, his career as constitutional historian not yet begun, threw himself into the campaign as a tariff agitator and wrote triumphantly to a friend of his success with a labor audience in Charlestown, "the hardest looking crowd imaginable, part of whom curiously enough did not seem to be Democrats." Edward Atkinson, a master of tariff statistics, fed Democratic campaigners a steady supply of facts and arguments and spoke for the cause himself in Brookline. The Bay State echoed with long, intricate speeches, fervently delivered, intently listened to, dissecting tariff rates on everything from chinaware to sulphuric acid. At the center of it all was little Billy Russell, the Democrat's best tariff speaker, looking like some precocious law student thrown into the breach, hands on his hips, pivoting on his toes from side to side, leveling his argument in a clear, resonant voice. Thomas Wentworth Higginson regarded Russell as the finest platform advocate he ever knew. He had, Higginson later recalled,

among all political speakers whom I have ever heard, the greatest simplicity and directness of statement, the most entire absence of trick, of claptrap, or of anything which would have lowered him. Striking directly at the main line of his argument, always well fortified, making his points uniformly clear, dealing sparingly in joke or anecdote, yet never failing to hold his audience, he was very near the ideal of a political speaker.

Russell on the stump, added Charles Eliot Norton, left a sting in the mind.[32]

Russell's tariff speeches were aimed mainly at answering the potent argument that high tariffs formed a protective wall around American workingmen, shielding them from the competition of foreign pauper labor. Reiterated for decades past, this argument had acquired the emotive force of acknowledged truth, and the mill worker of Massachusetts could accept it without intellectual effort. Russell found it a formidable barrier separating him from his labor audiences. To break it down he tried flattery: American wages, he argued, were higher than foreign wages not because of the tariff but because of the greater efficiency of the American laborer. The American earned more because he worked skillfully and produced more. Russell promised even more money in the workmen's pockets through tariff reduction: cheaper raw materials made for a cheaper product; its cheaper price increased demand at home and abroad; greater demand meant more work and higher wages. "What, then, does determine wages?" Russell asked a crowd of workers in Fall River. "Demand and supply and the efficiency of labor," came his crisp answer.[33]

The audiences listened quietly, politely. His economic analysis made some sense for the skilled labor force of New England's mature industries, but one doubts how many votes it changed. Russell was more successful when he used the tariff issue to probe the resentments growing out of New England's isolation from the postwar boom beyond the Hudson. In the best tradition of American political rhetoric he wove together a regional myth to move his listeners, a myth in which the tariff became the baneful agent destroying the simple republican prosperity of antebellum New England. One can link together images from his speeches to form the sequence of a wail. Before the Civil War, it would begin, New England was a happy place. ("In those days her agriculture thrived, her industries progressed by leaps and bounds, her commerce carried our flag into every part of the civilized world, and the New England coast rang with the music of anvil and of mallet . . .") Then during the war and after, greedy interests beyond New England wrested special favors from the federal government. ("It was the political shepherds of Ohio who had wool to sell . . . , the iron kings of Pennsylvania who had iron and steel to sell . . . , the Lime Trust with lime to sell, and the Glass Trust with glass to sell, and the owners of the coal mines of Pennsylvania with coal to sell,—these are the men who made the demand and who always stand behind high tariff duties.") The federal government under Republican control handed out favors at New England's expense and to her ruin. ("Languishing industries of Massachusetts cry out in distress that they be no longer throttled to satisfy the demand of Ohio and Pennsylvania. Our suffering woollen industry, our foreign commerce swept from the seas, and the unlighted fires of our glass and iron furnaces utter their emphatic and indignant protest . . .") But if the tariff blighted New England's economy, it had corrupted the moral temper of a whole nation. The people's government was now looked to as a treasure house of bounties. ("All classes of society have become demoralized by shouting around the gates of the palace, 'Give me a share of the spoils.'") Upon tariff reform depended not only New England's future, higher wages, and labor contentment, an end to trusts and government extravagance, but in the end the future of plain democracy. ("Because this reform means something more than any question of revenue or taxation, because it involves the fundamental principles of sound democratic government, and seeks to limit its power to public and to proper purposes, it is the most important question of the day,—the hopeful cure of the most threatening evil that has followed in the wake of the war. It is the people's cause. Its triumph is death to the control by organized wealth of elections and legislation, a restoration of political power to the people, and a guarantee that the people's law shall be used only for the people's interests.") Repeated year after year, in city after city, these were compelling words—tonic for a thwarted region. The man who spoke them became the most popular public figure in Massachusetts.[34]

Perhaps the best indication of the unifying chemistry of the tariff issue was the effort of Irish Democratic spokesmen to echo Russell's themes. Pat Maguire, who in the past had habitually accepted the protective tariff as an obscure but necessary fact of life, now dutifully recited low-tariff arguments to the readers of his newspaper. Noting the numbers of influential Bostonians who were joining the tariff crusade, Maguire's *Republic* lectured rather plaintively, "The masses of the Democratic party must keep step with this great procession, and to do this they must read and study and master the simple principles which lie at the very base of the agitation. The *Republic* will aid them as best it can . . ." True to his word, Maguire emphasized the benefits of lower tariffs to the working man, chided the Boston *Pilot* for opposing tariff reform as pro-British, and ripped into the voting record of New England congressmen on the McKinley Tariff bill. Finally reducing the question to workable shape, he announced in September 1890, "The leading issue in the coming campaign in Massachusetts will be the Republican neglect of Massachusetts in the distribution of tariff plums." Joseph O'Neil, the incumbent Irish Congressman from Boston, parroted Maguire's bemused support of tariff reform in his own campaign speeches. The issue was filling its most important political purpose, enabling Yankees and Irishmen to work in concert toward a stunning state-wide Democratic victory in 1890.

Of course the McKinley Tariff was not the only issue contributing to the electoral result. Massachusetts Republicans entered the campaign of 1890 seriously hobbled by factional quarrels over the make-up of their state ticket, and, more importantly, by a commitment on the part of their incumbent governor to strict enforcement of the state's liquor licensing laws. No doubt many urban voters were moved to vote Democratic as much by the spectre of prohibition as by the prospect of a rise in the cost of living through high tariffs. Nevertheless the Democratic use of the tariff issue in 1890 was shrewdly calculated to unify their party in the aura of a lofty reform movement transcending local party squabbles or mundane social habits and associations. This was what a Worcester Republican meant when he commented the day after the election that "Harvard College and the slums" had together scored a triumph for "free trade." [35]

It was a Democratic year. Throughout the entire nation Republican congressmen were tumbled out of office in November 1890, and a huge Democratic majority swept into the House of Representatives. New England Democrats secured their first sizable representation in Congress in thirty years. Of the twenty-six New England congressmen elected two years before, twenty-three had been Republicans. Now the Republican number fell to twelve, and fourteen jubilant Democrats joined them. Seven Democrats—including George Fred Williams, John F. Andrew, Sherman Hoar, Joseph O'Neil, and Moses T. Stevens—were elected in Massachusetts. And their leader, Billy Russell, was elected Governor. The Democratic boss of Westboro, a drowsy town nestled in the hills between Worcester and Boston, spoke for his party when he wrote to the state committee: "I think we can with a good deal of *Modesty* ask for some of your *Congratulations,* as our town went Democratic for the first time in the History of the *World.*" [36]

HAVING pushed their way to victory behind the tariff issue, Massachusetts Democrats talked long and loud for tariff reform through the early nineties. Yet of those who won election in 1890, only the small band that went to Congress had a chance to translate their issue into concrete results. The others remained in Massachusetts with their leader, William E. Russell, to determine what Cleveland Democracy could do for the state. This was no easy task. Success with the tariff issue was at best a murky mandate for reform at home. Moreover, the victory of 1890 had hardly been a landslide. Beside the state auditor, Russell was the only Democrat to win state-wide office, and in the legislature his party controlled neither branch.

Democratic prospects were limited in another sense. The political atmosphere of 1890 conspired with the institutions of Massachusetts state government to prevent decisive legislative results from following a change of governors. All over the state, but particularly in Boston, reform talk could be heard, from the press, the pulpit, even from some of the polite clubs and shabby boarding houses. Little knots of labor leaders, feminists, Nationalists, and dedicated visionaries of any cause gathered repeatedly in response to urgent posters on the doors of the Music Hall and Tremont Temple. But these agitations lacked consistency among themselves, and no single set of voices sounded above the noise with sustained force. Announced reformers remained radicals in spite of themselves, isolated from the mass of citizens and detached from the sources of political power in the state. "Reform" itself had little weight as a political value, and most professional politicians felt no particular incentive to reflect its aura. Moreover, Massachusetts Democrats discovered the tools of state government to be woefully defective even for the mild purposes of Cleveland Democracy. Neither the governor nor the legislature possessed the sanctions or prestige which made for swift, decisive action in the public interest. Together with the uncertain reputation of reform, the flawed character of state government militated against great achievements by the conservative young reformers of the Democratic party. Nor, finally, were Democratic leaders eager to stake their party to sweeping commitments toward social change. None of them intended to be headlong. Yet despite external hindrances and internal restraints, Cleveland Democrats would mark the state indelibly in their effort to define their goals.

William E. Russell was Governor of Massachusetts for three years. His re-elections were a feat unparalleled by any Democrat since the Civil War. He won them in the teeth of strenuous Republican efforts to put him out of sight. Russell's popular success as a Democrat gave contemporaries like Henry Cabot Lodge and Theodore Roosevelt many anxious moments in the early nineties. Lodge had gambled his career back in 1884 on continued Republican dominion in the Bay State. A revived Democratic party, tapping Mugwump prestige and the growing strength of Irish numbers, could badly upset his calculations. Although he turned aside all suggestions that he pit himself against Russell at the polls, Lodge directed the annual campaigns in 1891 and 1892 to return the young Cambridge Democrat to private life. Hoping to exploit the incongruity of Russell's Mugwump-Irish coalition, Lodge gathered figures to discredit the rising Democratic majority of Boston. Comparing the crime rate with the Democratic vote in the wards of Boston, he found a remarkable correlation. "These are the localities that give Democratic majorities," Lodge remarked in a prepared interview. "Go where they are and look, and then say whether you think a party that gets its votes in such quarters . . . is likely to give Massachusetts good government."[1]

As long as Billy Russell led it, the Democratic coalition hung together. In each annual election he tried to strengthen its base outside Boston. Just before election day in 1892 the governor executed a tactic that nicely illustrated his flair for hunting new supporters. Along with Patrick Collins, Congressman O'Neil, and Mayor Matthews of Boston, he whistle-stopped the length of Cape Cod (where Democrats were as scarce as the original Pequots), drawing curious crowds to the stations, shaking hands from the end of the car, accepting bouquets from schoolgirls, delivering little lectures on good government from dawn to dusk. Russell's "canvass of Cape Cod" was remembered long after its people had forgotten what he did as governor. His success on the stump outshone his accomplishments at the State House.[2]

His governorship promised to be one long ceremony. The prize he had won was a half-empty honor, annually competed for, imposing few responsibilities and fewer powers, and a wearing burden of social obligations. His official day began with a steady stream of morning visitors and lasted through banquets and speeches long into the night. After seven months in office Russell was near exhaustion. "I am overwhelmed by work and engagements of all kinds," he wrote a friend in July 1891, "so that I am almost broken down in health by overwork, and have not yet been able to get a vacation." Despite the pace demanded by the office, it had little meaning in the political processes of the state. The governorship of Massachusetts was a casualty of the American Revolution. The state constitution of 1780, while creating a stronger executive than most postrevolutionary constitutions, still reflected colonial distrust for royal governors. In peacetime the Massachusetts governor enjoyed only the vaguest of executive powers. His legislative initiative had come by usage to be confined to the recommendations of his annual inaugural address, which the legislature habitually disregarded, and occasional special messages. His only decisive power over legislation was the veto. Once a bill became law the governor found himself curiously detached from its operation. "The governor has almost nothing to do with the administration of the laws, in the broad and vital sense," a veteran State House observer wrote in the early nineties. "Ample machinery is provided for the enforcement of the laws without any action by the governor at all."[3]

The debility of the office resulted from encroachments on three sides. First, the governor's executive aides—his secretary of state, treasurer, attorney general, and auditor—had become in the course of the nineteenth century his elected associates, independent administrators who derived their power from the same source as the governor and who were not responsible to him. Secondly, the great bulk of state business was conducted by independent boards and commissions, over whom the governor had little control beyond his periodic appointments to fill carefully staggered vacancies. The marked increase in the policing functions of the state since the Civil War had sprouted a swarm of new commissions. By 1890 there were twenty-six such bodies, twenty-two of which had been created since 1865. Supervision over schools, charities, savings banks, insurance, labor and arbitration, railroads, corporations, prisons, civil service, gas and electricity, metropolitan police and sewage, taxes, and a host of other duties had been parceled out to these semiautonomous commissions. Some worked with efficiency and purpose. Others, lacking sustained oversight, had become quiet, musty nests of mediocrity, complaisance, and corruption. Finally, the Massachusetts governor was saddled with an elected executive council, one of three remaining among the states of the union. The council wielded veto power not only over the governor's appointments, but, more vitally, over his attempts at removal. The council was another creation of the constitution of 1780, a proud, archaic body whose prestige seemed to grow as its usefulness declined. The Mugwump Gamaliel Bradford, an amateur expert in administrative reform, found it thoroughly characteristic that outside the executive offices at the State House hung a sign in large letters, "Council Chamber," without so much as an allusion to the existence of a governor within.[4]

This dark maze of vested, independent power trapped the governor in virtual administrative impotence. His writ ran hardly anywhere. Of the three hundred commission officers in the state, Russell estimated he had the power to remove just eight. One hundred and twenty were beyond the reach of any executive control during their tenure. The rest could be removed only with the consent of the council or by impeachment. With the power of removal went the key to effective executive responsibility. "It may be said," Gamaliel Bradford commented, "that there is not a single official in the state, except his private secretary and his ornamental staff, to whom the governor can give an order with any means of enforcing it." Russell's isolation in the governor's chair was compounded by his loneliness as a Democrat. With the council and the legislature in Republican control, administrative reform inevitably became a partisan issue. Having reaped such benefits as they could from the administrative morass created under their long tenure, Republican leaders cheerfully defended the system's most patent abuses. Russell was not the first Democrat to register a protest. When Ben Butler had been governor in 1883 he tried to push his own bill through the legislature to magnify his powers. When the bill died in committee Butler had to content himself with empty forms. The blustering old campaigner became the first governor in decades to insist on the title of "Supreme Executive Magistrate." [5]

Russell promptly pressed the fight for more executive power. He took many of his ideas about possible reforms from Seth Low's pioneering work as mayor of Brooklyn in the early 1880's. Low championed the simple proposition that an executive ought to be given the power he needed to become responsible to the people for the government he headed. "Power always brings with it responsibility, and great responsibility exercised in the face of the community is a very sobering influence," Low had remarked; ". . . a system of concentrated responsibility accompanied by corresponding power and opportunity appeals to all that is best in a man." Russell's experience with an antiquated mayoralty in Cambridge, his deepening knowledge of the office he had now won, and his impatient ambition made him a fervent apostle of Seth Low's principles. Each of his annual messages to the legislature hammered at the theme. His recommendations boiled down to an insistence that he be connected with the processes of government around him. The existing static routine of tangled and untended government seemed to deny any chance for a purposeful surge of popular will. Russell's anger focused on the executive council. Abolish the council or render it harmless, give sole power of removal to the governor, establish clear currents of impulse and response between the governor and all the departments, bureaus, and commissions of the state, and so enable the governor to transmit some of the popular purpose registered at the polls—these were Russell's demands on the legislature. Testy old Gamaliel Bradford cheered him on. "I doubt if you realize fully the extent of what you are doing," Bradford wrote to Russell. "That is, I believe, appearing as the first of Governors or Presidents who has fairly fired the first gun in what is to be the fiercest political battle ever fought in this country, that between executive and legislature. You do not believe this but when you come to look back on it forty years hence you will." [6]

Nothing ever came of Russell's fight. In the contest between the restless Governor and the Republican legislative majority, the legislature held all the high cards. A special joint committee was appointed to consider Russell's demands. Bradford, Thomas Wentworth Higginson, Professor Shaler of Harvard, and President Francis A. Walker of M.I.T. trooped in to testify in Russell's behalf. A year passed before the committee rendered its judgment: expansion of the governor's powers might lead to personal aggrandizement, tyranny, and corruption. And there the matter rested. In retrospect Gamaliel Bradford was partly right. Russell fired an early gun in the battle for administrative reform and reorganization which would preoccupy many Progressives in later years. But in the atmosphere of the early nineties his proposals met swift oblivion. And since forgotten battles over dead issues can seem dull and trite, it is worth noting that most of his suggested changes continue to be agitated for in Massachusetts today. [7]

Such power as existed in the state government concentrated in the legislature, lurking about the cracked leather chairs, varnished portraits, and brass spittoons of the State House cloakrooms. The Englishman Lord Bryce counted the General Court of Massachusetts among the finest legislatures in America. This

was a tolerant and relative judgment. The General Court shared
many of the flaws which Bryce found common among American
legislatures. A body of 240 representatives and 40 senators,
annually elected and poorly paid, low on experience and technical skill, parochial and timid in view, it deserved the strictures of
its harsher critics. Its stubborn resistance to Governor Russell's
demand for administrative reform contrasted sharply with its
generally plastic behavior. In the eyes of Yankee reformers, the
legislature's chief characteristic was its rubbery compliance with
the force of money. There existed in the 1890's an enormous disparity between the power, prestige, and strength of purpose of
private corporate wealth and that of public legislative assemblies. Cash could shape the law of the Bay State, even if venality
was not as often the order of the day as in the legislatures of
New York and Pennsylvania. Imperious, highly paid corporation
lobbyists sauntered about the State House cloakrooms, lounged
in the Senate reading room, received their mail at the legislative
post office. Railroads doing business in the state supplied members with free passes. (Richard Henry Dana protested this practice at a stockholder's meeting of the Old Colony Railway in
1883. Officials of the line replied serenely that when they wanted
something from the legislature it was convenient to have the
members under obligation; the custom was too profitable to be
given up.) Railroads, importers, out-of-state corporations anxious
for kind tax treatment, manufacturers worried about labor laws,
and the new entrepreneurs in electricity, gas, and rapid transit
all had men working for them at the State House. Competition
for utility franchises was particularly vigorous. Lobbying was
nonpartisan. Henry Reed, agent for Henry O. Havemeyer's sugar
trust and the Boston sugar refineries, was a powerful Democrat,
but most others played both parties. R. A. Southworth, a
shadowy but potent State House lobbyist, was, for instance, on
good terms with the Republican Henry Cabot Lodge despite
his job as legislative agent for the Democrat Henry M. Whitney.
Since Republicans controlled the legislature throughout the
period, they received the brunt of attention from organized
wealth. Havemeyer, asked by a United States senate investigat-

ing committee why the sugar trust should support Democrats in New York and Republicans in Massachusetts, explained candidly, "wherever there is a dominant party, wherever the majority is very large, that is the party that gets the contribution, because that is the party which controls the local matters." [8]

Moralistic men observing the General Court from the outside noted the activity of "the lobby" (as it was called), examined resulting legislation, and concluded that the legislature was shot through with corruption. Moorfield Storey charged that the influence of the lobby could be traced across the entire legislative process from the nomination of representatives in their home districts to the final roll call on the floor of the legislature. The real power in the legislature, Storey decided, was a close-knit, self-interested group of experienced lobbyists who secured in each electoral district in the state the nomination and election of pliable candidates for the legislature. The lobby used this docile voting bloc to wrest promises from the Speaker and Senate President on the composition of crucial committees. Thereafter any private corporation seeking a law or franchise was forced to employ the lobby to guide its measure through a rigged legislature. Refusal to play the game incurred the lobby's active opposition. Storey quoted a professional Boston lobbyist:

When a private interest comes up and tries to obtain legislation for its own particular ends, and does not employ any regular lobby . . . , the lobby might feel free to discuss its merits in a somewhat critical spirit, and oppose it actively if an opposition interest employed them. It is, I believe, an axiom in law that a man who pleads his own cause has a fool for a client.

According to Storey a pattern of systematic secret shakedowns had wholly perverted the lawmaking processes of Massachusetts.[9]

There was some substance in Storey's analysis. In 1893 when the Boston and Maine Railway wanted to gain legislative approval for a merger action, the Boston corporation lawyer Richard Olney advised caution, "The lobby will antagonize the legislation unless paid," Olney noted, "—and the price is likely to be large." When another Boston lawyer, Louis Brandeis, asked

a liquor lobbyist in the confidence of his office to list the state
legislators who could be bribed, the lobbyist did so calmly and
efficiently, to Brandeis' dismay. The lobby was a potent agency
for swinging votes. But it existed on the sufferance of single-
minded businessmen with things to do, who preferred the con-
venience of the pay-off to explosive and messy exposés. And the
whole sorry system assumed an apathetic public whose attitude
toward its legislature was a nice mix of ignorance and cynicism.
What strikes one is not the corruption but the silence.[10]

Men experienced in the ways of the General Court believed
that only a small percentage of its 280 members were conscious
corruptionists. Jobbery centered mainly in the Senate where
membership was small and individual votes counted for more.
According to one observer, the House of Representatives contained two small groups of venal members known as "chain
gangs," that played the lobby's game with franchise bills and
often held a balance of power on issues which divided the whole
membership. Apprenticeship in the chain gang prepared one
for quick graduation to the lobby, which consisted largely of
former representatives and senators. But most legislators had
no permanent obligation to the lobby. What they lacked was not
honesty but will. The legislature as a lawmaking institution was
passive and inert, and individual members had little to fall back
on when outside pressure was applied. Both city and rural
members felt exposed, small, and vulnerable. Those from Boston
had less prestige than others. The Boston seats were generally
either rewards for hack service rendered in city politics or way
stations for ambitious men with their eye on Congress or a possible mayoralty. Moreover, a Boston member lived close to his
constituents, who kept him hopping with demands for patronage. And since the best source of new jobs in the city was the
burgeoning utilities companies, patronage responsibilities created obligations to gas and traction magnates, obligations which
came due on roll calls. But if city members scrambled for the
main chance, their small-town colleagues brought even less cohesion to the State House. Most of them passed through on rota-
tion, their seat a prize that moved annually by prearrangement

from town to town within their district. The result for both city
and town was ephemeral, disorganized, and expedient representation.[11]

The whole cluster of problems surrounding the legislature—
the lobby, the use of money by corporate wealth, the intimate
relations between job hunters and franchise seekers—came to a
head in the summer of 1890, just before William E. Russell was
elected governor. It confronted the young Democratic reformers
in an embarrassing shape and revealed the limits of conservative
reform. On the afternoon of June 10, 1890, during final action on
a franchise bill granting special privileges to the West End
Railway Company, a freshman member of the legislature rose to
demand an investigation of possible corruption involved in the
bill's passage. The audacious legislator was the Mugwump
lawyer George Fred Williams, who had been elected to the
legislature as a Democrat the previous fall. The president of the
West End Railway Company, the largest street railway company
in the world, was Henry M. Whitney, the powerful Democratic
traction entrepreneur. Whitney had been trying for several years
to electrify and consolidate all the trolley lines leading into
Boston from its suburbs. He had gotten his original charter for
this purpose from the General Court in 1887 and had moved
steadily toward his goal. Now he proposed to build an elevated
railroad through the densest part of downtown Boston to connect
the lines coming into the city in a single strand. He had run up
against stiff competition from rival syndicates, but in 1890 they
strangely left the field and Whitney's West End petition became
the chief business of the legislative session. His publicity campaign for a comprehensive metropolitan Boston transit system hit
a crescendo the same year, and the newspapers were filled with
long articles about his broad-gauged plans for the city. Whitney's
drive transcended party lines. The genteel *Boston Transcript*,
the Mugwump *Herald,* and the Democratic *Globe* all ran his
articles and backed his ventures editorially. So did Pat Maguire's
Republic. And so at the other extreme did the *Boston Journal,*
New England's leading Republican newspaper, whose editor
had a financial stake in Whitney's syndicate. The success of

Whitney's schemes promised dollars for Boston investors, jobs for Boston politicians, and a solution of sorts to Boston's pressing transportation problems. When Whitney spent money, many people were involved.[12]

No sooner had George Fred Williams finished his call for an investigation of Whitney's methods in securing his new franchise than several of Williams' colleagues were on their feet demanding that he be censured for calling the legislature's integrity into question. But the Democratic house leader, Josiah Quincy, knew from years of close association with the Dedham firebrand that there was no silencing him. The legislature had nothing to gain by squelching Williams, Quincy advised, and everything to lose. The investigation got under way the next day. It produced an immediate sensation. According to testimony, Whitney and his associates had laid plans to push their elevated franchise through the legislature months before the session began. Agents of the West End Company had combed the state seeking support among candidates for the 1890 session. Whitney paid a rival syndicate a large sum of money to guarantee a clear field. Over two dozen State House lobbyists were in the employ of the West End as the bill progressed through committee. Eight eminent attorneys had been retained by the company. Two of these were former Massachusetts governors. More unsettling to the Democratic party, two others were Patrick Collins, the state's most popular Irish Democrat, and William E. Russell, then on the brink of his third try for the governorship. All sides agreed that Collins and Russell had been retained for legitimate legal services, but the public revelation of their tie with Whitney sent a tremor through the party. Inquiry further revealed that Whitney had entertained scores of legislators at the Algonquin Club, providing them with carriages, plying them with food and liquor, and then—in the bluff words of Whitney's counsel—explaining to them with "rustic eloquence . . . that he wanted an elevated road and wanted a charter." The West End Company admitted to spending 33,000 dollars to secure the charter. There was widespread conviction that the actual sum was near 250,000 dollars.[13]

The response of Williams' contemporaries to the furor he

ignited was instructive. For an act that would have fixed the
stamp of progressive hero on him a decade later, he was pilloried
by his political enemies and shunned by reformist friends.
Democrats were understandably reluctant to side with him
against Whitney. While Pat Maguire's *Republic* fretted editorially over the "loose criticism of corporations which is now
the fashion," William E. Russell visited Williams and asked him
quietly to call off the fight. Boston daily newspapers, among
which Whitney had distributed several thousand dollars to print
his promotional articles, responded to the scandal with a tone
of anxious regret. The pristine lawyer Moorfield Storey responded to Williams' appeal for legal assistance during the
investigation with elaborate apologies, one piled on the other.
And Josiah Quincy disappointed his erstwhile Mugwump friend
by fashioning an official report of the investigation which virtually absolved Whitney of blame. Years later Williams remarked that it was his battle with the West End Company in
1890 that set him apart from his fellow reformers for the rest of
his career.[14]

Democratic leaders had tacitly agreed to swing the spotlight
of notoriety away from Henry M. Whitney and focus it upon the
lobby. Quincy's report set the tone. It mildly reproved the West
End Company for stating its case too zealously; the lobby should
be used "in as sparing a manner as possible." Whitney's systematic wining and dining of legislators, the report further cautioned, was "an error in judgment." Whitney actually came off
better than Williams, whom the report criticized for bringing his
fellow legislators into disrepute. The ink was hardly dry on
Quincy's report before a relieved legislature completed its approval of Whitney's elevated franchise. As the *Nation* commented from New York, the Massachusetts lobby investigation
had come to "a lame and impotent conclusion." But the lobby
issue did not die. Josiah Quincy promptly submitted a bill to
regulate the operations of "the third house." He regarded the
principle behind the bill as "novel in American legislation." It
accepted the lobby as an established political institution, impossible to eliminate. Quincy reasoned that the evil of the lobby

flowed from the secrecy of its operations. He proposed to legalize the lobby and dry up its pernicious influence by publicity. His bill provided that all lobbyists were to register at the beginning of each legislative session, indicating their employers and their purposes. At the end of the session they were to file a report of their expenditures, salaries, and fees. "It is not a measure," Quincy conceded, "which aims at changing human nature, or working any very radical reform. It recognizes that lobbying has been, is, and will be, a settled fact in connection with legislation." Quincy's bill passed into law with no opposition.[15]

By shifting the burden of blame from Whitney to the lobby, Democrats could shrug off some of the embarrassment that Williams' revelations had caused. Governor Russell managed to establish himself as a fervent opponent of the lobby, despite his association with Whitney. Following Quincy's lead after he became governor, Russell urged more stringent guarantees of publicity about the lobby and a curb on the lavish entertainment of legislators by private interests. And he called on the General Court to create adequate general incorporation laws in order to end the constant scramble for charters, franchises, and special privileges. Uniform laws of incorporation would not only help to rationalize the law, Russell argued, they would also cut the nexus that bound the legislature, the lobby, and privilege-seeking corporations together under the State House dome. "The efforts of the Massachusetts Governor and his friends to break down the lobby evil will be watched with great interest by reformers in all other states," the *Nation* now commented. "There can be no doubt that he has made the first formal move in a reform in which all defenders of honest government must take a hand."[16]

The lobby reforms of Quincy and Russell did not probe very far. Few new general laws were passed during Russell's governorship. And lobbyists continued to get things done for their clients. Unless publicity excited people, it could not hinder the operations of special influence. The foes of the lobby suffered in the early nineties from a timid press and a timid legislature in their effort to arouse public concern. But they were also hobbled by their own reluctance to call into question the power behind the lobby—the arrogant, buccaneering power of organized wealth. So long as Massachusetts Democrats depended on men like Henry M. Whitney to hold the party together with money and jobs, their reputation as a party of reform remained dubious. Whitney remained a powerful, enigmatic figure in the private councils of the party. He cast a long shadow as the "Harry" of other people's correspondence, the man looked to for help in meeting campaign deficits or swinging voting blocs, the name invoked in crucial patronage discussions, the one who gave the splendid parties when election victories were to be celebrated. In 1890, a year of rising party fortunes, it was possible for both George Fred Williams and Henry M. Whitney to advance their clashing aims within the Democratic party. Williams was elected to Congress four months after the West End crisis from which Whitney gained his franchise. The party would not always be so fortunate. Seventeen years later Whitney decided to try for the governorship. By then enough had changed that when Williams again attacked him, the result was a party fiasco.[17]

The West End episode clarified the nature of the General Court. Clinging to the precedents which made it the center of governing power in the state, it nevertheless submitted passively to any forceful interest that put the lawmaking machinery to its own use. But no single interest had a monopoly on the services available at the State House. Any body of petitioners could get a hearing for its views. Any shrewd legislator could bring his project to a vote. Facilities were open to any group with the money or wit to use them. Thus, paradoxically, during the same years that men like Henry M. Whitney wrested franchises, merger options, and tax privileges from the General Court, men like Richard Henry Dana and Josiah Quincy were fashioning and passing laws that put Massachusetts in the van of reform among American states.

Quincy and Dana had gone down separate political paths since they worked together in 1884 to push the state civil service law through the General Court. Quincy, just four years out of

Harvard when he bolted the Republican party in 1884 and itching for a career in politics, had promptly abandoned Mugwumpery to become a loyal Cleveland Democrat. By 1887 he had won election to the legislature and established himself overnight as a leader of the Democratic minority on Beacon Hill. Over the next five years he gained a reputation as the most industrious and talented lawmaker in the General Court. Meanwhile Richard Henry Dana followed the practice of private law and avoided party ties, but he remained charged with an enthusiasm for good government. He loved to tinker with legislation. Unlike most Mugwumps he had no wish to shun the grimy details of the political process. If politics were rotten, there were to his mind specific reasons and specific cures. Of course a general moral uplift would help, but what was not so clear, Dana insisted, was "the powerful effect that mere mechanism exercises on morality." If the laws on the books encouraged fraud, violence, and bribery, he felt there was little sense in launching a flood of moral invective against the party system. Precisely how were laws passed? How could they be changed? Which party was to get the credit or the blame? In the government of Massachusetts, Dana wrote to a fellow Mugwump, "there is no leader, or even party, that is under our system responsible for bad or good legislation as a rule. Sometimes party lines are drawn, but generally not, and who are you to hold for failure to pass a good law, or the passage of a bad one?" Dana believed that the responsibility lay with individual, interested men to take their petitions for reform into the committee rooms of the legislature and nurse them along day by day until they became effective law. Following his convictions, this big, earnest, cheerful lawyer became a familiar figure on Beacon Hill.[18]

His proudest achievement was the secret ballot. While working as an official at the Cambridge polling places on election day, Dana had been struck by the chronic disorder of traditional voting methods. In Massachusetts as elsewhere each party printed its own distinctively colored ballots and hired party workers to pass them out at the voting places and see that they were safely cast. Different ballots were printed for each district to fit the local slate. Independent candidates distributed stickers for their supporters to paste on party ballots. Others, more enterprising, might print their own ballots with their name deftly inserted in the slate of the strongest party. The result was a frenetic, expensive, and often violent election day. A careful citizen might succeed in voting as he wished, but so long as he had to make a public selection of his ballot from among the many thrust at him, his choice was rarely a secret. Moreover, the system encouraged enormous campaign expenditures, Dana observed, and widespread bribery in urban precincts. Convinced that reform was both necessary and possible, he enlisted the support of civil service friends, several labor organizations, and a few disgruntled politicians. In 1888, after careful planning and revision, they worked a bill through an apathetic legislature to inaugurate a secret ballot in Massachusetts. It went into effect a year later. "I went about the polls," Dana recalled, "especially in the districts that used to be rough and noisy, where I had seen a man's coat torn off his back, crowds pushing voters away and ballots taken out of men's hands and others substituted . . . All was going on very quietly and in a perfectly dignified manner and that alone was almost worth the whole of our efforts to obtain the law." [19]

The secret ballot, which was quickly adopted in other states after 1889, did produce more orderly elections. Dana was satisfied that it had greatly diminished bribery and intimidation at the polls as well. The state now assumed the expense of printing and distributing official ballots on which the names of all candidates appeared in alphabetical order, and the voter now marked his ballot in the privacy of the voting booth. By ending the complex system of party printing and distribution the new law cut ballot costs by over half and reduced to some degree the influence of campaign contributions on electoral results. Professional politicians of both parties judged the secret ballot from the standpoint of self-interest. Since the most publicized election violence had occurred in heavily Democratic city districts where local Republicans often voted at their own risk, Republican leaders tended to smile more broadly on the reform than

Democrats. The issue split Massachusetts Democrats. Yankee Democrats favored the new law for the same reasons that Mugwumps did: it dignified the democratic process and encouraged independent voting. Irish Democrats believed with some justice that the secret ballot, like civil service, was aimed at loosening the bonds of mutual obligation holding Irish leader and Irish voter together in party loyalty. In Irish districts the old party ballot had served many purposes other than determining the outcome of elections. Ward bosses had issued it as a token of political fealty, and voters had cast it either to curry party favor or to pay off a political debt or to earn a spare dollar. Irish leaders complained that the new secret ballot was a cumbrous and irritating burden on the voter, its long list of choices a purposeful discouragement to the unlettered city man who came to the polls to support his party. Boston Irish leaders had worked in vain to kill the bill in the legislature. Thereafter they tried repeatedly to amend the law to restore straight-ticket voting. "A man who goes to the polls has his mind made up on the question of how he is to vote," Pat Maguire's *Republic* grumbled. "He ought not to be compelled by the state to hunt for his candidates. Their names and their political affiliations should be before him in an orderly, plain and systematic manner. If this antipodean novelty is to stay with us it should be made as unobjectionable as possible." But the secret ballot did not generate the friction civil service had. Partisan precinct workers soon applied their special ingenuity to the new ballots, and if the act of voting was now less turbulent, it was hardly less disciplined.[20]

Legislative reformers next turned to the task of reducing the influence of private campaign contributions on the election process. Josiah Quincy hoped to regulate party contributions in the same way he hoped to regulate the State House lobby—by the glare of publicity. With Dana's help he fashioned the Massachusetts Corrupt Practices Act which became law in 1892. This act simply required both major parties to account for the sources of their campaign money and indicate how they spent it. The new law placed no limit on either contributions or expenditures. No bar was placed on contributions by candidates; nothing was done to stop the ancient practice of dunning political aspirants for the price of a nomination. While setting a mild precedent for democratic virtue, the law probably cured less than anyone cared to admit. Still the *Nation* called it "by far the best of the few that have been adopted in this country." Josiah Quincy admitted that the sanction of publicity did not appreciably reduce party spending, but he noted with satisfaction that many sensitive patrons began cutting the size of their contributions when the law took effect. The chairman of the Republican state finance committee, George Lyman, took a dim view of Quincy's motives. "The Corrupt Practices Act," he wrote, "is the finest bulwark for the squeaker as well as the empty-pursed. If all accounts are to be trusted, one Josiah is vastly interested in Republican observance of that enactment." [21]

A final measure designed to separate money from voting was the removal of the long-standing poll tax qualification for voting from the Massachusetts constitution. Both parties had customarily paid this dollar tax for poorer citizens to attract their votes, and the practice widened in the 1880's as Democrats whittled away at the Republican state majority. Poll tax payments were a particular burden on the Democrats since they drew most of their votes from the poorer urban populace. Along with the large sums annually spent to accelerate the naturalization of immigrant voters, the poll tax had become a serious drain on party finances. By the early nineties Massachusetts Democrats were spending up to fifty thousand dollars a year on poll taxes alone, necessitating pleas for funds from party leaders in other states. In 1891 Grover Cleveland helped organize a collection in New York City for money to pay the tax of Democratic voters in the Bay State. And with the advent of the secret ballot it was hard to know how well the money was being spent. Democrats of every stripe disliked the poll tax and united in attacking it. Governor Russell gave the issue a smooth polish by inverting the archaic Federalist doctrine of the social stake: "This tax deprives a man of his vote because of his poverty only. It forgets that his very poverty makes him the more dependent upon the efficient administration of laws that are wise, just, and honest, and that our democratic idea of government requires that he be given a voice in the making of these laws." Russell added ominously that if the poor were denied the chance to vent their grievances at the ballot box they might try less peaceful ways of making their power felt. Largely because of sustained Democratic agitation, the poll tax was abolished as a qualification for voting by popular referendum in 1891.[22]

These successive bursts of political reform—the secret ballot act of 1888, the lobby regulation act of 1890, the poll tax aboli-tion of 1891, and the corrupt practices act of 1892—varied widely in their impact on the political life of the state. They were significant not only for the changes they impelled but for the anxieties they codified. All four measures reflected a desire to ban coercion from the democratic process, whether it occurred in the polling places of the South End or the cloakrooms of the State House. All betrayed a profound mistrust for the swelling power of wealth, the political imbalance caused by the force and prestige that money gave to its possessors. All reflected a fear of political decisions reached out of court and under the table, decisions ignoring what a reasonable man might have called the merits of the case. They were, essentially, the solution of Yankee lawyers for the abuse of Yankee law. They stood as token of the lawyer's highest ethic, his respect for the law as guarantor of reasonable and equal justice. They denoted as did the drive for tariff reform a hope that statute books might mirror deliberation, reason, and equality before the law as democratic virtues, rather than mocking them by distortion. These reforms, while bipartisan in the support they attracted, opened up the pure strain of Cleveland Democracy. When they became law their sponsors hurried eagerly to announce their achievement to the country at large. They were the fine show pieces of conserva-tive reform.

Yankee Democrats tackled the proliferating social problems of urban living with less gusto. Their conceptions of reform pro-vided no ready answers for the rude, intruding task of coping with a sprawling industrial community. The vital, grimy world of metropolitan Boston filled them with regret for the past and nagging doubts about the future, but not with the zealous indignation of men with certain formulas for action. A sense of rural virtue, reinforced by the august traditions of the New England town, transfixed them as they gazed on the life of the city. The grip of the past on their thinking loosened slowly and painfully. "The most serious problem which the statesman of our day has to face," Professor Shaler wrote to Governor Russell, "concerns the maintenance of this precious heritage of the motives of local government which have been transmitted to us by our forefathers. To effect this end at a time when our people are gathering in ever increasing numbers into our great cities is a very grave task. The question is how to maintain the ancient training in these vast aggregations.[23]

Professor Shaler's words touched a hard dilemma in the minds of urban Yankee Democrats. Their heritage taught them that the vitality of American democracy had been generated from small, self-sufficient, political cells planted across the New England land by Puritan fathers 250 years before. This assumption was poor mental baggage for city life. When ingrained habits of thought associated democracy with slow cellular growth over centuries, men found it easy and natural to identify the sudden sprawl of urban industrial society as a malignancy. The irony of this conviction deepened with increasing evidence that rural New England's democratic wellsprings were going dry. The empty farmhouses of the hill country made bleak monuments to a way of life whose promise had disappeared. Impatient sons and daughters of old-stock families were abandoning their rocky farms for the lure of the city or the West, leaving sluggish relatives to intermarry and scratch a living among the pine thickets and second growth. Town after town, isolated from the railroads, watched its population age and dwindle, its churches weaken, its social and political life decay. Town offices went begging; indolent selectmen and constables held their places by default. Stagnation and sameness made for aimless brooding after imagined wrongs and the occasional relief of violence. Murder, rape, and robbery punctuated the rural town routine as commonly as in the city. In the 1880's the per capita murder rate of western Massachusetts was consistently higher than that of Boston. But small-town virtue lost little of its clutch on urban minds for being a cracked myth.[24]

A compelling configuration of facts forced Yankee Democrats to accept the city as a place of promise as well as menace. For one thing, the steady urbanization of Massachusetts had made her cities the obvious dynamo of her economy. By 1890, 62 percent of the state's population, 67 percent of its invested industrial capital, and 72 percent of its taxable property were found in cities. Secondly, immigrants composed a rising percentage of Massachusetts residents until by the mid-eighties one out of three in the state were foreign-born. In Boston in 1885, 34 percent of the population was foreign-born, and in mill cities like Fall River and Holyoke immigrants approached a majority. If these newcomers were to adjust their lives to the ways of American democracy, it must be without reference to traditions peculiar to the New England past. Finally, realistic and tough-minded Yankee politicians sensed by 1890 that the future of the Democratic party lay with the newcomers. Men like Governor Russell, Josiah Quincy, and Nathan Matthews knew that continued acquiescence in their own leadership depended on their skill in bending their inherited convictions to meet the interest of the urban immigrant.[25]

Home Rule for Boston was one issue around which Yankee Democrats and Irish Democrats could align themselves in the legislature as champions of urban democracy. The issue had a lengthy history. Decades earlier, as the migrant Irish proletariat filled out Boston's slums and began its long assault on New England sensibilities, native politicians had sought to rescue Boston's instruments of social control by putting them under state jurisdiction. Nativistic anxiety over Irish mores was the tainted germ of state-supervised metropolitan planning in Massachusetts. In 1863 a committee of the legislature reported:

It is necessary to adopt the metropolitan principle in order to prevent the elements which are destructive of property and laws from keeping practical control of the city, and so, from the size and wealth of Boston and the intimacy of its relations with the whole state, undermining the prosperity and peace of the commonwealth . . . Moreover, large classes having the right of citizens but not the welfare of government at heart, always run into large cities as the common sewers of the state, and are ready to make use of just such machinery as the present system affords to them to make the material, moral and legal interests of society and the state subservient to their passion and their will.[26]

Finally in 1885 the Republican state legislature transferred control of the Boston police force from the city government to a metropolitan police commission. The new commission, appointed by the governor, not only controlled Boston's police but supervised liquor licensing in the city as well. Commission proponents claimed that gambling, prostitution, and traffic in saloon licenses would all decline now that Boston's finest were responsible to the state rather than to municipal politicians. Critics of the new arrangement countered that majority rule had been purposely hobbled in Boston and charged that gamblers, liquor dealers, and Boston policemen were flocking into the Republican party for protection against the discipline of the commission. Boston Democrats, of course, unanimously opposed state control of city police. Pat Maguire, to whom the police commission was a personal affront, never tired of mocking the motives behind it. When, a few years after the change had been effected, a Protestant clergyman complained about continued vice in the city, Maguire's *Republic* sputtered sarcastically, "The venerable hayseed legislators from Podunk and other rural sections, aided by Boston hypocrites and frauds, lay and clerical, deprived Boston of the control of her police for the purpose of making her a moral city." For his part, Governor Russell adroitly turned tables on the Republican legislature by charging that its creation of the metropolitan commission reflected a loss of faith in the New England democratic tradition of local responsibility it professed to be protecting. Invoking Jefferson, John Adams, Tocqueville, John Fiske, Lord Bryce, and Judge Thomas M. Cooley in testimony to the special genius of New England local democracy, Russell remarked of the commission that "such a wide departure from the spirit of our institutions and the teaching of the fathers has brought only evil results. A law founded on a mistrust of the people, removing government beyond their reach, and officials beyond their control, is certain to lead to grave abuses." Addressing a native-American audience at Ashfield in the Berkshires, Russell added another note of Jeffersonian localism. "I believe it far better to leave to the public spirit of a community to work out its salvation, if need be, after a period of suffering, rather than to interfere with its self-government by forcing upon it the power of the state." [27]

But all of Russell's rhetoric could not blink the fact that the mystique of New England town government assumed a racial homogeneity and a shared fund of social traditions. The concept of metropolitan organization to cure Boston's growing pains had originated as a disciplinary remedy for controlling alien behavior. And so long as the metropolitan concept remained a distinctly political issue in Massachusetts, raising questions about the limits of authority in city government, it was likely to bruise ethnic feelings and foster reactionary localism. But gradually metropolitan thinking outgrew its repressive political connotations and became an inspiration to urban planning. By 1890 it was exciting the minds of Boston's public leaders with a bright vision of the city's economic future. A dawning awareness of the potential excellence of city life contributed to urban awakening. As a Mugwump civic leader grudgingly acknowledged in 1893, the finest intelligence, education, philanthropic spirit, and executive capacity were to be found in cities as plentifully as ignorance, folly, and vice. "If the powers of evil are concentrated and organized in cities as nowhere else," he added, "so also are the powers of good, and nowhere can the battle between the two be fought out to so great advantage." [28]

To save the city by building a metropolis: this became the new urban strategy of Yankee Democrats. In their plans for a greater Boston, Henry M. Whitney's clanking trolley cars figured appropriately large. Whitney's prestige in Boston was not the simple sum of his economic and political power. His broadgauged, well-publicized plans for knitting Boston suburbs to the

city by metropolitan transit had captured civic imagination. For
a few fleeting years around 1890 Whitney's scheme seemed to
provide a wondering city with a solution for the conflict between small-town values and urban needs. Whitney's original
interest in trolleys had been incidental to his real-estate speculations in Brookline and Brighton, suburbs to the south of Boston.
To enhance the value of his tracts he built a horsecar line from
Boston to Brookline in 1886, thus grafting his own fragment
into the city's disjointed local transit facilities. Then Whitney
saw the opportunities in rapid transit. Within three more years
he had bought out his chief rivals, consolidated in a single
system the lines running into Boston from all directions, and introduced electric cars to replace the horse. (This last innovation
rubbed two ways. Governor Russell was knocked off his horse
by an electric trolley while riding into Boston one day in 1891,
and Cambridge dames objected to the new era on the grounds
that electricity reduced neighborliness at Harvard Square.)
Whitney envisioned two great fanlike trolley networks, one
spreading south of Boston through Dorchester, Roxbury, and
Brookline, the other north through Cambridge, Charlestown,
Somerville, and Malden. The two fans would converge and
connect in an elevated track over downtown Boston. Whitney
propagandized an enchanting picture of the benefits which
would accrue to the city from rapid transit. His system would
ensure Boston's future as the commercial hub for her sprawling
suburbs. And it would provide a sure safety valve for the social
pressures of the congested city. Cheap rapid transit would put
suburban living within the reach of all social classes. By drawing
Boston's labor force from dirty urban slums and boarding houses
out into the sunshine of the surrounding countryside, electric
trolleys could transform the area around the city into a smiling
garden metropolis, all at a nickel a ride. The miracle of electricity would bring white cottages, green land, and fresh air as
therapy for the crowded city.[29]

Whitney and his claque created an exciting image, the more
appealing for its smooth merger of philanthropy and private
profit. Wealthy men with consciences, worried about the city

as a spawning ground for social hatred and uneasy at the public paternalism that industrial society seemed to demand, reached eagerly at the vision. "Is there a blessing physical or moral beyond a good home—for us all?" asked Henry Lee Higginson. "Can anyone raise as good children in a city for the whole year as in the country? Think what a blessing to a hardworking man as a small house and yard in Everett or Dedham or any country town is." Edward Atkinson hit on a slogan, "Every Man His Own Landlord," drew up plans for a model suburb on the edge of Brookline, and urged Whitney to link the area into his trolley network. Rapid transit, said Governor Russell, "would surely and effectively tend to dissipate the crowded centres of sickness, misery, and vice which so readily gather in the hearts of our great cities. Make transit to the suburbs easy, swift, and cheap, and the squalid tenement-houses of the city cannot compete, as experience shows, with the attractions of a country home." The suddenly larger physical dimensions that the advent of electric traction made possible for the modern city momentarily looked like a panacea for urban ills. If the free-wheeling capitalist adventures of men like Whitney could empty the city's slums, scatter their gladdened occupants out over the breast of the New England landscape, and make money for farsighted investors to boot, then the jungle of industrial society lost some of its terror.[30]

Whitney succeeded too well. Reality quickly intruded on the dream. His plans for an elevated road over the city were suddenly seen to jeopardize a wide swath of historic Boston and were voted down by public referendum in 1893. Meanwhile, fast electric transit from the suburbs created an appalling traffic jam in the center of the city. Raking in the profits of his cars backed up along Tremont and Washington Streets, Whitney stubbornly opposed the subway construction which the city finally inaugurated in 1894. Then, just as the traction snarl was at its worst, he abandoned his transportation schemes for brighter prospects in Canadian coal gas. A callous, heavy-handed entrepreneur, Whitney had laid the groundwork in the early nineties for the sordid, complex traction battles that preoccupied Boston for a decade and more thereafter. But he also, almost incidentally, had helped to bring the concept of metropolitan planning to a glow among Boston's civic leaders.[31]

One immediate result—the development of a metropolitan park system accessible to city dwellers—again suggested the mixture of motives that gave the metropolitan concept its appeal. The street railways had provided a direct example to recreational park development by fashioning their own small parks and amusement centers at the country end of their lines in order to build up outgoing traffic from the city. The happy week-end crowds in these parks testified to the role of rapid transit in the urban culture of the 1890's. But sustained leadership in the park movement came from nonbusiness groups, apprehensive at the sprawl of the city symbolized by the raucous trolley. In the late 1880's small bands of civic-minded men and women among the Boston suburbs had launched an agitation to preserve historic landmarks and natural scenery from piecemeal encroachment by real-estate speculators, traction companies, and near-sighted town governments. From this agitation emerged two young men who were to make the metropolitan Boston park system the preoccupation of their lives: Charles Eliot and Sylvester Baxter. Eliot, the son of Harvard's president and a disciple of Frederick Law Olmsted, had embarked on a promising career in landscape architecture. Baxter, a Mugwump journalist from Malden and disciple of the Utopian novelist Edward Bellamy, has been mainly renowned as an organizer of Bellamy's Nationalist movement in Boston. To both of these men, park development seemed an essential antidote for the ravages of city life. Both were informed by a compelling sense of social urgency. "The herding of the very poor in city slums breeds a degraded race," Eliot wrote in 1890. "The lack of opportunity for innocent recreation drives hundreds to amuse themselves in ways that are not innocent. The tremendous competition for the opportunity to work breeds that discontent, and anger, and despair, which leads to anarchy, and feeds the fires of that volcano under the city which the alarmists tell us is so soon to break forth." When Eliot's boyhood friend Billy Russell became governor, Eliot saw a chance for action. He urged on Russell the establishment of a metropolitan park commission to develop some of the remaining vacant land around Boston and thus preserve what he called "the healing influence of Nature's scenery" for the city's populace. The notion won Russell's sympathy, and after two years of sustained civic pressure on the legislature the commission came into being.[32]

Governor Russell promptly appointed the Bellamyite Sylvester Baxter to be secretary of the Metropolitan Park Commission and hired young Charles Eliot as the commission's technical consultant. For ballast he persuaded Charles Francis Adams to assume the chairmanship. During the next few years the park commission took great strides toward providing greater Boston with an imaginative system of parks, forest preserves, picnic grounds, and sparkling watercourses. While a bit taken aback by the driving energy of his young associates, Charles Francis Adams later wrote in his autobiography of his labors with the park commission, "I greatly doubt whether at any period of my life, or in any way, I have done work more useful or so permanent in character, as that I did in this connection." The finest single product of the commission sprang from the imagination of Charles Eliot. This was Revere Beach, a long and gently curving arc of white sand along the ocean north of Boston, just twenty minutes from the city by rapid transit. Cleared of a ramshackle array of shanties, saloons, and gambling dens and equipped with public bath houses, pavilions, and bicycle paths, Revere Beach overnight became the favorite summer resort of Boston's urban masses. So it remains to this day, although Charles Eliot would hardly recognize his creation.[33]

Metropolitan planning had growing appeal for Cleveland Democrats approaching urban problems with the assumptions of suburban gentlemen. By accentuating the shared interests of a broadly diverse and mobile population working and playing cheerfully for the betterment of the whole community, the mystique of the metropolis oddly reinforced the models of classical economy. The attitude of Yankee Democrats toward park development derived in part from the same ultimate values as their enthusiasm for tariff reform. As long as metropolitan

planning bore results so obviously benign as woodland parks
and bathing beaches or eased solutions to hard problems of
water supply and sewage disposal, there were few to cavil. But
the planning enthusiasts had been overly optimistic. Neither
rapid transit nor suburban parks could lance the sore of city
slum life. And too often the workers' new suburban districts—as
in Everett, Malden, and Somerville—fell sadly short of the dream
of arcadian paradise. Instead of bringing the country into the
metropolis, rapid transit had merely exported the slums to the
suburbs.[34] And metropolitan thinking drew up short when
political and ethnic differences came into play. Boston's satellite
cities never accepted any scheme for merging their local governmental functions with those of the parent city. Boston's inability
to soften the hostile edge dividing her Yankee and Irish peoples
continued to plague the city's history. The metropolitan principle was a palliative, not a panacea. Moreover, it was clearly
irrelevant to basic problems of economic conflict in Massachusetts' urban population. Industrial strife between workers and
employers, aggravated by absentee ownership of corporations
and competition from other sections of the country on the one
hand, and the tightened organization of labor on the other, resisted treatment within the terms of community cooperation.

Yankee Democratic politicians wrestled with the labor problem with no more enthusiasm than had Mugwump amateurs.
It was characteristic of them to work around the question,
probing for indirect solutions to labor conflict in tariff reform,
civic philanthropy, and even in moral crusades against electoral
corruption. To intervene directly in the dispute between labor
and capital and cast the lot of government for one against the
other ran counter to all their social instincts. Such action would
seem to ratify economic class distinctions, acknowledge flaws
in the classical model of merging economic interests, and, worst
of all, imbue government with a positive economic function
smacking of paternalism. Nevertheless, the Cleveland Democrats
of Massachusetts pressed quietly and steadily for factory reform.
In so doing, they did not act wholly in defiance of their instincts. Their training did not dictate the neutral impotence of

government at every level. The federal structure of American government had in practice broken up the monolithic sanction of laissez faire across the nineteenth century. Scruples about federal paternalism, recently reinforced by judicial precedent, instilled in many Yankee Democrats a corresponding sense of larger responsibilities in the state sphere. The police power of the state to protect the health and safety of its citizens remained a lively and flexible notion in Massachusetts. Yet in the last analysis Cleveland Democrats approached the labor problem not as theoreticians but as alert and humane politicians. The impressive burst of labor reform that coincided with Democratic revival in Massachusetts was a function of practical necessities, not political philosophy.

Massachusetts had longer experience with industrial strife than any other state in the union, having pioneered the factory system well before the Civil War. Bay State politicians had been bothered by the factory since the Lowell mill girls walked out on their first strike back in the 1830's and began petitioning for shorter hours. The General Court took its time responding, but Massachusetts staked a claim as the country's leader in labor legislation in the decade after the Civil War. The great landmark was the ten-hour law of 1874, fixing a sixty-hour week for women and children employed in factories. Although years were needed to plug holes in its language and guarantee its enforcement, the ten-hour law contributed decisively to the practice of a sixty-hour work week in Massachusetts mills by the 1880's. The combined efforts of militant working class agitators led by Ira Steward and reformist intellectuals like Wendell Phillips had secured the ten-hour law after more than a decade of debate. For a decade thereafter few important fresh advances for labor came out of the General Court. First Wendell Phillips and then Ben Butler passed from the public scene, leaving the worker with no politically potent advocate in the state. The depression of the mid-eighties cut labor's bargaining power further. Moreover, the bent of the increasingly influential Knights of Labor toward fuzzy dreams of class-free society, co-operative ownership of factories, and universal reform tended to distract labor's attention away from the piecemeal gains possible through orthodox legislative politics.[35]

Then, as the Knights reached the height of their power and militance, the lull ended. In 1886 over seven hundred strikes occurred in Massachusetts, more than twice as many as in the five previous years put together. Simultaneously, new labor reform bills began to issue from the labor committees of the General Court in startling numbers, and many of them became law. They were sponsored in almost every case by Democrats and won the overwhelming support of the Democratic minority in the legislature. Often their passage was delayed for years until a sufficient number of Republicans could be broken away to vote against the inclination of their party. Labor legislation always required bipartisan support to pass. At no time during these years was the legislature more than 45 percent Democratic. The figure was often much lower. But on labor issues the Democrats were a disciplined band, led by skillful and energetic men who exploited the sluggish institutions of the legislature as easily as did Henry M. Whitney. From 1886 to 1893 the Democratic party rightly claimed a reputation as the "labor party" in Massachusetts. Opposition to labor legislation came mainly from manufacturers and particularly from powerful textile makers who charged that the cumulative effect of the new laws was to cut profits and drive capital out of the state. Whatever validity the charge had, manufacturers lacked the sure support of Republican legislators which labor enjoyed among the Democrats.[36]

The Democratic legislative leaders were a diverse group. Michael McEttrick, a dashing, rawboned native of Roxbury celebrated for his youthful feats in long-distance walking, looked after the bread-and-butter interests of the Boston Irish, the largest single working-class bloc in the party. Robert Howard and James Mellen represented smaller pools of Democratic support from the mill towns. Howard was an English-born cotton operative from Fall River and secretary of the Fall River mule spinners' union. Mellen was the radical editor of a working-class newspaper in Worcester. Both men were returned to the legislature year after year, building up seniority and strategic friend-

ships. Edward Moseley of Newburyport, a maverick businessman who had joined the Knights of Labor along with his
workers, was also an influential legislator until Grover Cleveland
made him secretary of the Interstate Commerce Commission in
1887. But in the framing of labor laws (as in the framing and
passing of so many other reforms) the acknowledged leader of
the Democrats was the remarkable former Mugwump Josiah
Quincy. Quincy had been elected to the General Court in 1886
with the help of Knights of Labor votes. During the next five
years this taciturn, calculating young patrician worked with cold
intensity to create a solid foundation of labor support for Cleveland Democrats in Massachusetts. Where many of his kind
regarded the mounting self-consciousness of urban laborers as
a threat to social safety, Quincy saw it as a party opportunity.[37]

Jolted by the labor uprising of 1886, the General Court hopefully created a state board of arbitration and conciliation to look
into labor disputes and seek agreeable settlements. Of the
board's three members, one was to represent labor, another capital, and the third the neutral interest of the state. Well-inten-
tioned but toothless and loosely drawn, this legislation reflected
little more than official faith in ultimate industrial harmony. But
it served notice of aroused legislative concern. The same year
more tangible evidence of sympathy for labor came in a law
providing for weekly wage payment of factory workers. This
measure had been blocked for years by manufacturers who
claimed the extra bookkeeping costs would force a cut in wages.
Labor spokesmen favored it, charging that the prevailing time
gap between payments caused too many workers to fall into debt
to their employers. The passage of the weekly payments law in
1886 marked a significant shift in the relative political power of
laborer and employer.[38]

The pace of reform picked up in 1887 with Quincy's arrival in
the legislature. The session had hardly gotten under way before
he moved that the house committee on labor be ordered to
consider the expediency of new legislation comparable to the
Consolidated Factory and Workshop Act passed by the British
Parliament in 1878. Quincy's colleagues, their curiosity aroused

by a twenty-eight-year-old Harvard dude interesting himself in such matters, approved his motion. Over the next two years Quincy translated it into a dozen separate labor laws, most of which he drafted himself. They dealt mainly with factory working conditions and the rights and privileges of factory workers: new requirements for factory construction and fire escapes, proper toilet facilities, proper ventilation to remove fumes and dirt, a prohibition against the use of children to clean moving machinery, uniform meal hours for women and children. Lest these laws meet the common fate of exhortatory humanitarian legislation, Quincy added to his barrage a law empowering factory inspectors to enter factories and making enforcement of state regulations a matter of legal compulsion. Meanwhile the arbitration law of 1886 was redrawn to enable the arbitration board to call witnesses and examine wage account books. In 1888, after years of urging by a Boston lawyer named Charles Gershom Fall, the legislature inaugurated the country's first experiment in employers' liability. The same year Quincy pushed through a comprehensive revision of the state's child labor law, raising the prohibitory age from ten to thirteen and strengthening provisions for enforcement. He also successfully sponsored a general law for the incorporation of trade-unions which did away with the cumbrous former method of granting special charters to individual unions on application. This was the first of several laws to fortify the rights and prestige of organized labor. In 1890 a union label bill passed. Two laws of 1892 dealt with labor intimidation, one barring employers from exacting worker agreements not to join a union and the other prohibiting the use of out-of-state private police to put down strikes.[39]

By the early nineties Massachusetts was the paragon of states among the friends of American labor. A close student in the field wrote for an English journal in 1891: "To Massachusetts belongs the honor of first place in the character and comprehensiveness of her labor laws, and in the wisdom and thoroughness with which she enforces them. She has led the way and served as the model for other states." To the Bay State trade-unionists this was all very well. But in their minds ameliorative factory reform was tangential to the root question of hours. The average skilled worker was less concerned about his working conditions than he was with the length of time he had to spend at his job. Union leaders, who had to do their organizing work at night after long hours in the shop, shared this view. Moreover, the record showed that a shortening of hours was generally followed by a hike in hourly wages. By 1890 organized labor in Massachusetts felt the time had come to improve on the sixty-hour week established in the 1870's. Governor Russell agreed, and threw Democratic party approval behind a new reduction in hours. Believing as he did that the Federal Constitution forbade national hours legislation and recognizing the dependence of Massachusetts industries on skilled labor, Russell argued the state must maintain a liberal labor policy as a matter of expediency as well as justice. "While a general reduction in the hours of labor must be brought about mainly by the organized action of employees," Russell told the legislature, ". . . the State should lend its cooperation and the weight of its example in this direction." The courts of Massachusetts had made public regulation of hours possible by acquiescing in a legal maneuver through the maze of nineteenth-century jurisprudence. In theory, hours regulation flew in the face of the hallowed doctrine of free contract which denied to no man the right to work as long as he wanted. But in accordance with long English practice, the fiction of free contract was circumvented by another—that hours laws applied only to women and children who as wards of the state came under the protection of the state's police power. In practice, of course, the routine of the factory imposed uniform hours on all workers, and if the state limited the working day for part of the labor force, the rest benefited from the same limitation. Yet another means by which the state could indirectly support shorter hours for factory workers was the passage of maximum hours laws for publicly employed labor.[40]

Advances on both these flanks were made in the early nineties. State and municipal workers won a nine-hour day, and in 1892 the legislature passed the fifty-eight-hour week for women and children. In both houses the fifty-eight-hour bill passed with virtually unanimous Democratic support and was opposed by a majority of Republicans. The law gave Massachusetts the shortest and best-enforced work week in the United States. And it paid clear dividends to Billy Russell. During the subsequent campaign of 1892, state senator Robert Howard, the Fall River mule spinner, noticed that mill superintendents in Fall River were vigorously proselytizing for the Republican party among their workers. Howard went to work putting up notices all over the city: "Workingmen! I appeal to you to vote for William E. Russell, who recommended and signed the 58 hour law, for governor. Robert Howard, Senator." Russell carried Fall River and the state and returned to the governorship for his third term. His good standing with labor was doubtless one reason why he ran ahead of Grover Cleveland in Massachusetts.[41]

Where labor reforms did not collide head on with the dogma of free contract, and where they attracted support from union leaders and laborers who could vote, Cleveland Democrats were easily persuaded to take labor's side. But when their humanitarian instincts were pitted alone against the sanctity of contract on an issue involving workers with no political power, Cleveland Democrats struggled with a hard choice. In the early 1890's a problem of unfamiliar and frightening proportions forced a choice upon them. This was the sweating system, a nasty kind of slum-based manufacture spreading suddenly through the clothing industry of eastern cities. Despite widespread, nonpartisan anxiety over the sweatshop, no solution had been found when William E. Russell became governor. The search for a remedy to sweatshop labor clarified the limits of the reformism he represented.

The rudiments of the sweating system had flourished in the United States for decades. In Massachusetts they could be traced to the flood of Irish immigration in the late 1840's. A sudden demand for military clothing during the Civil War had further stimulated the leasing of piecework out of factories to small workshops and slum homes. The Boston fire of 1872, desolating the clothing district along Summer Street, gave fresh impetus to home manufacture. But the virulent spread of the sweatshop in the late eighties was part of a larger contagion which centered in New York City. There the widening flow of immigrants through Castle Island into the vast tenement districts of the city had fixed the sweating system beyond eradication in the postwar decades. The first effort at public regulation came in 1883 when young state assemblyman Theodore Roosevelt, appalled by what he saw of cigar manufacturing among sweated tenement workers, pushed a reform measure through the New York legislature. When the state supreme court found the law unconstitutional, society's power to act against the evil seemed paralyzed.[42]

In the mid-eighties Boston's skilled tailors and cutters, who normally completed the unfinished goods of local clothing manufacturers, began to suffer a slack in available work. A union investigation verified their suspicion that Boston clothing makers were sending their goods to New York to be finished by sweated labor. Anxious to stop this threat to their own livelihood, the tailors began agitating for a Massachusetts ban on sweated goods imported from New York. What they neglected to emphasize, and therefore what the public was slow to understand, was that the sweating system was not merely an external menace but was rapidly entrenching itself in the slums of Boston. In October, 1890, a reporter for the *Boston Herald* spent several days wandering through the crowded back alleys of the North End gathering data on the sweatshop. The *Herald* ran his findings as a lead story. The piece was no muckraking exposé. But recorded among the many scenes of "smiling, contented poverty" was graphic evidence that what had happened in New York was happening in Boston a decade later. As in New York the sweatshop fed on a new wave of immigration. In the late eighties the character of immigrants arriving in Boston seemed reminiscent of the Irish deluge forty years before. The people stumbling by the shipload on to East Boston piers were now chiefly Russian Jews, victims of Czarist persecution, rootless, unwanted, looking for some way to begin life over again. In the early nineties Italian and Portuguese immigration increased rapidly, adding to the sudden glut. The newcomers swarmed into the oldest parts of the city, the battered North and West Ends, looking for rooms and work. They were the bewildered labor force that made the sweating system possible.[43]

Boston clothing manufacturers readily adapted to their new circumstance. They had always operated on a contract basis, employing skilled cutters to cut the cloth to pattern, tailors to finish the custom clothing, and workshops of unskilled laborers to finish the cheaper grades. In theory at least, all these phases of the industry came under the surveillance of state factory inspectors. Now, however, the pressure of competition from New York inspired the manufacturers to broaden the contracting system beyond the range of established workshops into the homes of the new immigrants. Most manufacturers welcomed this chance to lower overhead while expanding production. In the bargain they escaped responsibility for their workers' well-being. Indeed, it was a rare manufacturer who knew who his employees were, where they worked, or what they were getting paid. The grinding harshness of tenement industry, tempered as it was only by the limits of human endurance, produced scores of men who leaped at the chance to become middlemen between clothing merchants and their scattered labor force. A year or two in the slums of the new world proved an effective spur to upward mobility for anyone who could pick up the local language and a little ready cash. These sweaters competed ravenously for bids on the manufacturers' unfinished goods. Then, to eke out a profit for themselves, they subcontracted batches of material among the rooms and attics of their racial kin. Here in dark squalor beyond the eyes of state inspectors, Jewish, Portuguese, and Italian families worked day and night stitching pants and coats together at a few pennies a garment. Conditions in Boston never plumbed the depths of filth and degradation reached in New York, but they were appalling nevertheless. An atmosphere of soiled bedding, smoky black walls, bones and rotten food littering the floors, and the strong stench of human excrement pervaded the rooms where these people worked. The long hours, foul environment, and niggardly wages that sweating transmitted like a blight made it too vicious a mode of exploitation to be ignored for long. But urban gentlemen needed no special sympathy for the victimized tenement worker to react indignantly to the exposure of the sweatshop. The threat to the health of the whole community from vermin-infested, slum-made clothing was cause enough for alarm. It was as a public health menace that sweating first concerned the Boston conscience.[44]

William E. Russell became aroused over the sweatshop problem through his friendship with Reverend Emory J. Haynes, social-gospel minister of the People's Church in Boston's South End and president of the Anti-Tenement House League. Pressed by Haynes, other League spokesmen, and union leaders, Russell defined the sweatshop as a matter of government concern as soon as he became governor. Shortly after his inauguration in 1891 he ordered the state factory inspection team (the only administrative force over which he had clear control) to investigate the prevalence of sweating in Boston. He received a hurried and sketchy report that focused mainly on the importation of sweated goods from New York and emphasized the hygienic dangers of this commerce for the consuming public. The inspectors found Boston clothing manufacturers close-mouthed about their involvement with the sweating system. Seeking further information, Russell turned to Horace Wadlin, the efficient and dedicated chief of the Massachusetts Bureau of Labor Statistics. Wadlin reported that almost 50 percent of Boston's clothing output was being contracted out to piecework laborers in Boston itself, and that piecework contracting made a dead letter of state laws regulating the working day. The spread of the sweatshop was driving wages down inexorably and disrupting steady employment. Wadlin stressed the danger to the worker rather than the danger to the consumer. The blight of sweating, he predicted, would "lower the standard of living of all workers engaged in the industry, and any industrial system that does this is the source of social evils far greater than any infection that may possibly be found in the product turned out under it." Russell forwarded Wadlin's report and that of the factory inspectors to the legislature. In a special message he asked that legislation be immediately passed to bring the sweating evil under control.[45]

The legislature responded with unaccustomed speed. The resulting law, entitled "An Act To Prevent the Manufacture and Sale of Clothing Made in Unhealthy Places," defined any dwelling where clothing was made as a workshop subject to state inspection. All operators of such places were required to register with the state inspectors and keep their clothing free from vermin and disease. Hygienic violations would result in closing the workshops for public safety. As a deterrent against the sale of New York City tenement-made clothing in Massachusetts, all retailers of such goods were required to indicate by label in what city they were made. The sweatshop law of 1891 was the first successful attempt to cope with the sweating problem. It started a chain reaction among other industrial states. New York passed a similar law in 1892 and Pennsylvania, New Jersey, and Illinois soon followed suit. As a Philadelphia social worker observed, "the decision Massachusetts has come to throws the burden on the other states either of sustaining further than heretofore the sweated industries or of maintaining a higher social standard in the enforcement of the law." Billy Russell counted his role in the chain reaction against the sweatshop among his proudest achievements as governor. But critics of the Massachusetts law, including labor leaders trying to organize the sweated workers, charged that it failed to come to grips with the basic source of the trouble, the system of contract and subcontract by which clothing manufacturers escaped responsibility for the wages and welfare of their employees. By leaving the web of contract intact while placing responsibility for clean working conditions on the workers themselves, the law penalized the victims of the evil it sought to regulate. In the event the critics were proved right. Sweatshop conditions in Boston improved markedly after 1891, but the wages of the unskilled immigrant clothing workers remained miserably low.[46]

The response of Massachusetts Democrats to the sweating problem typified their effort to combat social evil while jeopardizing as little as possible the economic interests which produced the evil. Joseph Lee, a Cleveland Democrat from suburban Brookline, mused over the delicate problem, posed by the sweatshop, of protecting workers' health without raising con-

sumer prices. Laws which sought to remedy a single flaw, he
wrote, inevitably spilled over into other areas with unintended
effects. Perhaps there was wisdom in "our inherited unwillingness to interfere with any man's liberty as to his choice of a
way of making a living, and especially our unwillingness to
interfere with him in his own home, whether he chooses to work
in it or not . . ." Yet on the other hand, he acknowledged, "One
may doubt whether liberty to work under unhealthy conditions
is an essentially valuable possession . . ." [47] This last admission
was puzzled, tentative, groping. Bound still by nineteenth-century legal abstractions, Yankee Democrats could not always
bring themselves to press the issue further. The sweatshop law,
with its provisions for registration, inspection, and labeling, reflected once again a tendency to fall back on the power of
publicity to eradicate an evil believed to be beyond the power
of government to outlaw. By carefully skirting the whole issue
of labor contract, the law paid obeisance to the sanctity of individual economic rights which governments could not touch. The
one qualification on the inviolability of contract—that public
health and safety be preserved—was in this case a slender reed
on which to hang any notion of the public interest.

As they searched for adequate responses to the problems of
urban society, Yankee Democrats were hindered both by political circumstance and internal scruples. Despite the successful
wooing of the Mugwumps, the Democratic party remained a
minority coalition of vested interests, bound by obligations to
the Boston financial and commercial community, to local Irish
organizations, to organized labor. These obligations always competed with one another. Frequently they clashed. Rarely did
they all pull in a common direction. To have brought this contentious coalition together at all and made it a going concern in
Republican New England seemed a remarkable feat to contemporary observers. "I do not believe that the full significance of
the change in sentiment in Massachusetts has yet been realized,"
a New York friend of Grover Cleveland wrote to Governor
Russell in 1892.

To my mind it is one of the most significant contributions to free
government that we have yet seen. That you and your friends should

have been able to take a party composed of heterogeneous elements, largely made up of a population which to the ordinary mind has not yet thoroughly assimilated itself to American institutions and to bring about such great results is not only significant but wonderful. All over the country our friends are asking, "well, can we rise to the Massachusetts standard; can we adapt our varied population to the political necessities of the situation as well as our friends in Massachusetts have done?" [48]

As responses to political necessities the reforms achieved in Massachusetts by Cleveland Democrats probed the limits of the possible. If in retrospect they seemed halting, timid, and mild, it was not only because their advocates were leaders of a minority coalition. The Yankee leaders of the party were politicians by choice, but they were lawyers by profession. And few callings bound their members more tightly to the precepts of the pre-industrial past. Orthodox American legal thought was still largely enmeshed in a system of natural rights dating from the eighteenth century. "The condition of legal education in this country," the liberal economist Richard T. Ely wrote in 1891, "becomes apparent when it is stated that the political and economic science implied and expressed in Blackstone's Commentaries on the laws of England is still regarded as sound doctrine by at least nine American lawyers out of ten." The legal profession thickly insulated its practitioners from thoughts of more drastic reform exciting college professors, journalists, artists, feminists, and working-class intellectuals around them. Few lawyers could muster much enthusiasm for the broad vistas of environmentalist thinking evoked by Professor Ely and others, or for the positive uses of public law which the environmentalists proposed. Governor Russell's own words suggest how his generous reform instincts were circumscribed by his legalistic inheritance. The law, he declared, "deals everywhere with man, and as an individual moral agent, with freedom of will, and corresponding right and responsibility." This conception of the law sharply limited its potential as a tool of reform. "It is the infringement of some right," Russell insisted, "and not merely detriment to some interest, which justifies the interference of government. For its duty is the protection, not the support of the people." Using

Edward Bellamy's Nationalist movement as a case in point, Russell said, "It runs counter to a law of nature which, establishing individual right, imposes individual responsibility." [49]

Yet their veneration for the law as the final bastion of natural rights did not trap Yankee Democrats in completely passive obedience to static legal fictions. They looked to the law for an ideal body of governing rules weighing with precise equality on all men, universally valid, blind to wealth, status, or secret influence. The law, Governor Russell repeated endlessly, was the people's law. What pulled these Yankee Democrats from the conservative moorings of their profession was their recognition that the law was in increasing instances no such thing. Everywhere around them they saw the law enforcing and augmenting the new inequalities of urban industrial society. Both as practicing lawyers and as practical politicians they knew that the law had been distorted from its ideal and put to use in behalf of private purposes and goals—serving "interests" instead of "rights." Their muted militance as reformers stemmed from this sense of the law's abuse. Their most characteristic proposals for change sought to restore to public law its equalizing function, and so restore to politics some of the public respect they valued for themselves as lawyers. Beyond this, they supported reforms of social amelioration only where such reforms could be justified in terms of the legal rights of those affected. Bewitched by the ethos of natural rights, they could press no further along the path of reform than their party obligations took them. Neither their legal conscience nor their party's commitments allowed them to formulate a notion of the general *public* interest above the clash of individual rights and private interests which obsessed them. So long as they believed that simply equalizing the impact of the law could save democracy in the savage urban world of the 1890's, they could conceive no justification for sustained public control or social planning. They would try to ride the tiger but had no notion how to tame it.

CHAPTER SIX · THE CITY:
EFFORTS AT COOPERATION

IN THE last years of the nineteenth century the city of Boston came under Irish political domination. This passage of control from established Yankee to aggressive Celt has been remarked upon by numerous historians and celebrated or lamented in scores of memoirs and biographies. The impression gained from these retrospective glances is that the transfer of power was angry and cataclysmic, a jagged spark leaping from one pole to its opposite. But closer examination suggests a more gradual succession of changes, at a pace determined as much by Irish caution as by Yankee tenacity. The first Irish mayor, Hugh O'Brien, who served from 1885 to 1888, had astonished apprehensive Yankees by his moderation and attracted sizable Mugwump support in his early years in office. Essentially the same coalition that elected O'Brien, heavily weighted as it was with Irish numbers, won the mayoralty in the nineties for two Yankee Democratic reformers: Nathan Matthews who served from 1891 to 1894, and Josiah Quincy who served from 1896 to the end of the century. O'Brien, Matthews, and Quincy all tapped the resources of an Irish city organization whose leaders were remarkably sympathetic to the motives of Cleveland Democracy. How could this odd alliance hang together? How could Irish and Yankee politicians work together in the teeth of the tragic cleavage of cultural distrust between Paddy and Brahmin? How long could their efforts at cooperation prevail before the pull of ethnic loyalty defeated them? How can one account for the renewed pattern of Irish subservience to Yankee leadership after Hugh O'Brien's mayoralty?

Much of the answer lay in the character of Pat Maguire, the last city-wide Irish Democratic boss in Boston's history and the political embodiment of the prospering immigrant's quest for respectable security. The organization Maguire led was a weak shadow of the implacable, despotic machine his critics thought he controlled. The Democratic party in Boston sprawled awkwardly across the city's twenty-five wards, a loose federation of ward dynasties fashioned from fears, favors, and the clan rivalries of the Old Sod. The Irish enjoyed their kaleidoscopic political game almost as much as they said they did. Ward politics was a violent, everlasting contest, with gusty pretenders always eager to knock sluggish leaders from control and strike up new alliances across the city. Shifting loyalties among the fractious petty titans of East and South Boston and the West, North, and South Ends aborted the Irish monolith from which proper Bostonians thought they were retreating. But after 1884 Pat Maguire managed to pull Irish leaders together and impose on them a rough unity of purpose in state- and city-wide elections. He rarely emerged from the cloud of suspicion obscuring his "machine" from clear public view. Aside from brief service on the governor's council in the early eighties, Maguire never sought the prestige of elective office. The caucus and the conclave were his habitat. Democratic state and national conventions found him in regular attendance, and he was a veteran of thirty years on the Democratic City Committee. The city committee—a rough assembly of delegates from the ward organizations meeting periodically to ratify the current balance of power in the city—was Maguire's governing mechanism. Most of the decisions on policies and candidates endorsed by the committee originated in the back rooms of Maguire's real-estate office on Washington Street in downtown Boston. Maguire seemed to fit the classic mold of the urban boss in the gilded age. A short, erect, stocky man with a thick red face and black mustache, he had the long memory and the mercurial temper demanded by his calling. Like an Indian, men quipped, he never forgave an enemy or forgot a friend. His explosive rages when he thought he had been crossed changed many a young career. Men either did his bidding or avoided him.[1]

All this fitted the type. But Pat Maguire was a different breed from the Boston bosses who came after him, and the difference tells much about the changing character of Boston politics in the last years of the nineteenth century. He had been born in County Monaghan in 1838. Seven years later he emigrated to Prince Edward Island in the Maritime Provinces. There in the village of Charlottetown he learned the printer's trade, and by 1850 he had come south to Boston in search of better openings. Maguire learned his American politics in the newspaper composing rooms, along the city's crowded streets, and in the hot discussions that spiced life at his Milk Street boarding house. He watched from the curb as Anthony Burns was marched down State Street to the wharf and back to slavery in the spring of 1854. From what he could make of the quarrel between abolitionists and slaveowners, squatter sovereignty seemed a sensible solution, and Stephen Douglas was his first American hero. When the Civil War broke out, Maguire was working for the Democratic *Boston Post,* and he already had his seat on the party's city committee. There he hitched his fortunes to Michael Doherty, the leading potentate in the city's Irish Democracy in the early postwar years. Doherty was a prosperous liquor dealer, president of the Boston Beer Company, director of several Irish Catholic savings and charitable societies, and treasurer of the Democratic City Committee for almost two decades before his death in 1883. Maguire's friendship with Doherty opened new horizons in both business and politics. When he was twenty-eight, he left the printer's case and set himself up in real estate. Speculation in the rapidly filling land south of Boston paid off handsomely, and by the 1870's he was a person of some substance.[2]

Having attached himself politically to the respectable Yankee Democrat F. O. Prince, and through Prince to Grover Cleveland, Maguire was instrumental along with Patrick Collins in holding Irish voters in the Cleveland camp in 1884. Then, one month after Cleveland's victory, Maguire engineered the election of Hugh O'Brien to the Boston mayoralty. "We can fancy our friend Maguire," the New York *Irish-American* chortled, "leaning up against the 'Old South' and bidding the Hub and the rest of mankind to bring on some more political worlds for him to conquer." Through the eighties Maguire entrenched himself in the life of his city. In 1888 he beat down the only serious challenge to his political supremacy when his erstwhile lieutenant, Mike Cunniff, contested his leadership unsuccessfully. By the early nineties Maguire had moved out from downtown Boston to a choice suburban residential district in Roxbury and began building new houses all around his own home. Meanwhile his personal weekly, the *Republic,* catered increasingly to the tastes of Boston's growing Irish Catholic middle class. Maguire had a stake in his society.[3]

By 1890 he was ready to swing his city organization behind the rising Yankee Democratic leaders in Massachusetts. This was more than a gamble for new power. Maguire respected Grover Cleveland, valued his acquaintance, and longed for tokens of reciprocal esteem from the men around him. Mugwump barbs bit deep, and Maguire never forgave Godkin's *Nation* for its comment in 1887 that he was "probably the silliest and most impudent demagogue who has ever figured in American politics." If Yankees would only defer to his authority in the city, he was willing to dress his ranks under the Cleveland banner. His own mature political tastes, in fact, matched the Yankee penchant for good order and propriety. (Democratic politics were on a much higher plane when he was a boy, he once primly informed a reporter.) Maguire worried that the turbulence of Boston ward politics would make the Irish unreliable and disreputable recruits for Cleveland Democracy. "When young men reared in a Republican atmosphere come over to our ranks; when men of mature years, disgusted with the policy of their party, seek a political asylum with us, is not the time for Democrats to imperil party success by internecine strife," Maguire's *Republic* lectured its readers. The Irish must be worthy of cooperation.[4]

Maguire's efforts at discipline were supported by Boston's most respected Irish public figures. Chief among these were Patrick Collins and Thomas Gargan, the city's leading Irish lawyers. Like Collins, Gargan had withdrawn from active politics in the 1880's to attend to a booming law practice. The son of a prosperous contractor who had emigrated to Boston before the famine, he had been privately schooled, served briefly as a union officer in the war, trained for the law at Boston University, and spent some time in the state legislature. Through the law he had lifted himself to a place of influence in the community. Like Collins he was a winning Democratic stump speaker. In 1885 he was picked as the first Irish Catholic to deliver Boston's hallowed annual Fourth of July Address and used the occasion to affirm an Irish sense of participation in the American past. (Gargan having cracked the Yankee monopoly on official Fourth of July oratory, Irishman and Yankee alternated yearly in the post of Independence Day speaker for the rest of the century.) Pat Maguire's management of the Boston Democrats went far to enforce the rapport between immigrant and native stock which Gargan, like Collins, found so valuable.[5]

Younger Irish leaders like Congressman Joseph O'Neil had also discovered the wisdom of cooperation. O'Neil's career makes a striking success story. Born into an immigrant family in Fall River in 1853 and brought to Boston as a boy, he had wandered from job to job, first in printing, then shoe-selling, carpentry, news-vending, and crockery. While still in his twenties he won election to the Boston school committee and later to the legislature, where he became a fervent disciple of Ben Butler. Then O'Neil got interested in rapid transit and became president of an experimental elevated trolley line running between Cambridge and Boston. The taste of business responsibility was chastening. By 1888 he had shed his Butler enthusiasms, worked back into the grace of the local Democratic party, and won Patrick Collins' vacated seat in Congress. In Washington he proved an effective, diligent errand boy for Boston businessmen and a shrewd bargainer at the pork barrel. He disliked civil service agitators and had no fondness for Grover Cleveland, but he seized on the issue of tariff reform to clinch his new respectability in Boston. "This is a business age," O'Neil announced in 1890, "and we are essentially a business community . . . The passage of the McKinley bill was a direct blow to the business interests of this section of the country." A shrewd, jovial, "professional Irishman," O'Neil attached himself to a succession of rising Yankee Democrats; first John F. Andrew, then William E. Russell, and later Richard Olney received his flattering attentions. He was Pat Maguire's kind of man.[6]

In their effort to swing their people behind the leadership of Cleveland Democrats in Massachusetts, Maguire, Collins, Gargan, and O'Neil gained leverage from the local world of Irish journalism. Along with Maguire's *Republic, Donahoe's Magazine* and the Boston *Pilot* were the most influential spokesmen for Catholic social opinion in the city. Patrick Donahoe, founder of both the *Pilot* and *Donahoe's,* rivaled Collins and John Boyle O'Reilly as Boston's best loved Irishman. *Donahoe's* was a monthly family magazine filled with pleasant stories, gentle object lessons, and homely Catholic wisdom. It tried to avoid partisan politics. Every issue in the early nineties carried a banner line from Archbishop Ireland's pen: "The future of the Irish people in this country will depend largely upon their capability of assuming an independent attitude in American politics." Yet in its passing comments on men and issues *Donahoe's* invariably stated the Democratic case. The *Pilot* under O'Reilly's editorship was militantly Democratic and bolder in its social commentary than *Donahoe's* or Maguire's *Republic.* O'Reilly's poetic and passionate soul transcended the confines of Irish Boston, and his editorial range spilled over the edge of Catholic social belief in many places as he tried to bring his readers some inkling of the possibilities for social change in the American environment. But in politics he was a loyal party man with many friends among the Mugwumps. Having swallowed Grover Cleveland in 1884, he supported him warmly four years later. After O'Reilly's death in 1890 Patrick Donahoe regained control of the *Pilot,* and under its new editor, James J. Roche, the paper hewed more closely to Catholic orthodoxy.[7]

The reigning social assumptions of the Catholic community helped Irish leaders justify their quest for allies among Yankee Democrats. The historic reluctance of the Church to sanction drastic changes in the terms of temporal life gave Irish politicians as sturdy a rationale for social conservatism as the legal tradition of natural rights gave Yankee contemporaries. Prosperous and self-made men, the Irish leaders had little sympathy for the radicalism many an Irish laborer absorbed from the Knights of Labor in the eighties. The logic of politics ensured their support of Josiah Quincy's labor laws and they warmly backed the aspirations of the trade union movement. But caution tempered their advice to Irish workers. They hated the red flag both as Catholics and as lawyers, realtors, and politicians. "Combined labor can enforce its just claims to a fair and equitable dividend upon the product of its energies, by agitation and by harmonious action," the *Republic* warned after the May Day demonstrations in 1890. "But if it allows itself to be directed or managed by the crowd of reckless socialists and atheists who are trying to use the grievances of the wage-workers as a lever to undermine the foundations of civil government it will forfeit public confidence and come to grief." The harmony of labor and capital, rooted in acceptance of the distinction between the two, was a key value in Irish-American orthodoxy. Arbitration and generous private charity, as means of softening the distinction, won quiet favor. But Irish leaders' distrust of public welfare programs was often as fierce as any Yankee Jeffersonian's. "Our political faith teaches the lesson that the people should support the government," Governor Russell's Irish Catholic running mate said in 1892; "but not that the government should provide for the limp, the lame, or the lazy . . ." [8]

Irish leaders had a serene confidence that the competitive business ethic, the profit system of an expanding business economy, could solve the social riddles which the Catholic church and the Democratic party shied from. Joseph O'Neil, the poor boy from Fall River who came to Boston and made good, was invited to deliver the annual Fourth of July Address in the depression year 1894. His speech was a jumbled, rushing paean of faith in the headlong progress of the American people. The current depression merely underscored for him the abnormality of the country's pace. The American urge to compete, he felt, would bring a fast cure to economic misery by recharging the commercial energies of the nation. The grim alternative of socialist paternalism could only sap ambition and blight individual hopes. Deprive a boy of the need to make his own way in the world and you open the door to national decadence:

> The hope of advancement, the desire for a higher station, a broader field of usefulness, are the hope of this Republic in the future, just as they are the mainspring of the individual, and the cause of the wonderful prosperity and remarkable progress we have made . . . Take them away, remove all ambition from the mind of the young, endeavor to make this a paternal government, progress and energy will cease, socialism and paternalism step in, and dissolution and disruption must inevitably follow. The man struggling for a livelihood becomes a better citizen when he owns a little home, takes a greater interest in the affairs of the government, and helps lift up the average of his immediate neighborhood.

O'Neil's faith was not unusual. Confidence in the benign powers of private enterprise was deeply embedded in Boston Irish orthodoxy. A passage in *Donahoe's Magazine*, about a businessman who discovered that life was conducted on business principles, wrapped his perception with the ultimate sanction: he meant "not only that the universe stands for the dollar, but that the universe is governed by unvarying laws, that promptness, exactness, thoroughness, and honesty are wrought into its very fibre. On these business principles all life is conducted—if not by men, at least by that Power which is behind man." [9]

With these precepts as their guides to right behavior, Irish leaders were anxious to shake off the image of the shiftless, brawling, alcoholic paddy fixed in the native American mind. "For tin-pan and broom-handle bruises," ran one characteristic observation of Irish behavior, "for nocturnal disturbances of drunken men and women, for the unremitting bellow of brazen voices, there is no place like an Irish street. When one sees a man rolled down stairs by his wife and mother-in-law, armed with a tin dish and a rolling pin, the air thick with dust and expletives, we know that his name is Pat." Whatever their domestic mores, most Irishmen remained isolated from the respectable Yankee world of trained professions and higher commerce. By the mid-nineties the Irish made up over 60 percent of the city's population, but they constituted a vastly larger percentage of its labor force. Most Irish workers remained unskilled, though in certain trades, notably those connected with building—contracting, masonry, and carpentry—they had made good advances. Most of the postal workers and policemen were of Irish extraction, and the Irish enjoyed a virtual monopoly on the city's manual labor force. But according to the findings of an Irish lawyer in 1896, his people could boast of not a single large bank manager, and only one representative on the floor of the Boston stock exchange. The Irish controlled one savings bank and one small local trust company, were without representation in the new field of life insurance, and contributed less than one percent of the city's lawyers, doctors, dentists, architects, and civil engineers. This disparity between Irish numbers and occupational diversity did not breed automatic resentment among Irish spokesmen toward Yankee domination of business and the professions. It remained as much an incentive to greater efforts toward mobility as it did a cause of class hostility. Men like Patrick Collins and Thomas Gargan gained much of their prestige in Irish Catholic Boston from their intimacy with the mighty men of State Street, from their success in crossing the barriers separating most Irishmen from the Yankee world. For those who had secured their own success on Yankee terms, emulation of the dominant minority still seemed a valid strategy.[10]

Religious and ethnic controversies plaguing Boston's immigrant population gave point to those Irish leaders who counseled cooperation with Yankee Democrats. A main cause of community disruption was the arrival of new ethnic groups which cramped the Irish at points where the Yankees left them unchallenged. Canadians from the Maritime Provinces had been coming to Boston in search of work ever since the Civil War. By the 1880's they composed the largest ethnic group in the city after the Irish and Yankees. They were a floating throng, often staying only for a season to earn quick wages, filling the downtown boarding houses, their roots in Boston shallow and easily broken. Friction with the Irish centered in the highly seasonal building trades where Irish union labor concentrated. Canadian construction workers shunned the unions and accepted wage scales that undercut the gains made by the Irish. Relations between the two groups were further embittered by religious and political strife. The spirited Protestantism of the Canadians, intensified by close city life under a hostile Catholic majority, found release in direct attacks against the local Catholic hierarchy and the Democratic party. The British-American Society, formed in 1887, began to naturalize and organize voters against Irish power in local politics and seized the banner of public education to discredit the parochial school program launched by the Church in Boston in the early eighties. The Society attracted eager allies among Boston's Protestant clergy and won scattered sympathy among established Yankees worried over growing Catholic power in New England. The ensuing Boston school controversy seemed to Irish politicians to mark a revival of the Know-Nothingism of the 1850's, imperiling their narrow majority control of the city. City elections bore them out. Anti-Catholic agitation, tacitly abetted by local Republicans, contributed decisively to Irish Mayor Hugh O'Brien's ouster in 1888. The following year another Irish Catholic Democrat, Owen Galvin, lost the mayoralty by an even wider margin.[11]

Meanwhile the coalition of Canadians and native Protestant evangelists, bolstered by Boston feminists, shifted its concern from the parochial school toward an effort to purge the Boston public school committee of Irish Catholics. How else, the Protestants reasoned, could the schools be freed from the dead hand of political control by the Democratic machine? One Protestant minister addressing a church rally in 1894 conjured a Catholic conspiracy behind the plight of Boston's public schools:

> I am afraid that at City Hall, whoever is Mayor, Patrick Maguire is boss, and if there is not hostility there is indifference to the public schools. If the public schools are not adequate enough and if there is no place for the child but in the street, then there is an excuse for the parochial school, and I am afraid that the children are turned into the street for a purpose.

Religious bitterness deepened after 1893 with the spread of
the American Protective Association to Massachusetts. As in
earlier years Republicans sought to exploit anti-Catholic sentiment for political gain. They connived secretly with the A.P.A.
in what one Republican leader privately called an "entente
cordiale," and for a time actually submitted to A.P.A. demands
in the construction of campaign platforms while shaping the
party's state ticket to attract A.P.A. votes. In Boston, A.P.A.
activity sharpened religious and ethnic feelings already aggravated by the school controversy. Lashed by the editorial violence
of a local A.P.A. sheet, the *Daily Standard,* Boston anti-Catholicism reached an ugly climax on July 4, 1895, when an A.P.A.
parade through East Boston degenerated into sporadic rioting,
bloodshed, and one death by gunfire.[12]

Irish leaders thought they saw yet another hostile menace in
the fast-growing Italian colony in the North End. Relations between the Irish and the Italians had been bad from the outset.
The Italians began arriving in Boston in large numbers in the
late 1880's. Mostly tenant farmers from the barren hillsides of
southern Italy, unskilled, illiterate and penniless, they fell in
easily with arrangements for gang hiring developed among
steamship agents, petty Italian bankers and padrones, and urban
contractors. Irish politicians complained that the growing pool
of cheap, mobile, Italian labor in the city was ruining wage
standards and spoiling chances for employment among unskilled
Irishmen. The Italian menace also had religious overtones:
many of the newcomers brought with them a lingering hatred
for the Church instilled by a lengthy history of Papal opposition
to Italian national unification. But there was no staying the new
immigration. As the North End filled with the unwelcome inter-
lopers, Irish families began their exodus to Charlestown, Dorchester, and Roxbury, retreating in emulation of the Yankees
before them. For Pat Maguire the fresh sea of new immigrants
was an obvious threat to community stability. Noting the sudden
increase of new arrivals in 1890, Maguire's *Republic* declared,
"These people are the very scourings of the slums of Italy. They
are imbued with socialistic ideas, taught under the Crispi

method of civilization to despise religion and to be indifferent as
to their political and social mores. They are a dangerous as
well as an undesirable element." [13]

The changing North End beckoned those who sought to put
Irish animosity toward the newcomers to some advantage. Republican politicians tried desperately to organize North End
political clubs to prepare Italians for Republican citizenship;
social workers sought to wean them from the clutch of street-
corner politicians; A.P.A. agitators fanned the flames of Italian
anticlericalism. The agitators had the easiest chore. Italians ap-
preciated sympathy from any quarter for their peculiar attitude
toward Rome. In September, 1895, during a North End cele-
bration commemorating the completed Risorgimento, an Italian
priest presented a floral bouquet to an agent of the A.P.A. *Daily
Standard,* as "homage of a people who, having had for long
centuries the practical experience of clerical oppression, salute
the Boston *Daily Standard,* a representative of liberty which,
righteously jealous of its rights, would prevent the well known
papal ambitions in this free land." In time antipapism would
abate among Italian immigrants, and the A.P.A. would disappear, but resentment against the Church would find new
confirmation in the slow rise of Italian priests in the New England Catholic hierarchy.[14]

Irish leaders found themselves in an awkward and vulnerable
position in the early nineties. Baffled by these fresh outbreaks
of religious and ethnic bitterness so reminiscent of their boyhood, anxious for the gains they thought they had consolidated
for their people, men like Maguire, Collins, and Gargan sought
out the best protection they could find. Instinctively they looked
to their party as the surest link in their attachment to the
community where they had made good. Through the Democratic
party they hoped to affirm a sense of responsible fellowship
transcending religious or class divisions. In this connection,
Maguire missed few opportunities to drive home to his readers
the lesson of Republican complicity in the anti-Catholic revival
and Republican conniving with the A.P.A. If every Republican
was not a nativist, the reasoning went, every nativist was prob-

ably a Republican. But striking such blows in print was a partisan luxury. Throughout the school controversies Maguire's *Republic* had appealed for mutual tolerance to avoid a sectarian war which would "not only blacken the reputation of the community, but injure its business, interrupt its commercial progress, and stay, for a time, the healthy development of its institutions." The noisy anti-Catholic ravings of migrant Canadians and imported evangelists did not, the *Republic* insisted, "represent the conservative sense of the average Boston Protestant." [15]

Irish confidence in the protective sanity of the older Yankee community was not misplaced. When anti-Catholics tried to drive a bill through the legislature in the late eighties for state inspection of parochial schools, Irish Democrats had enlisted impressive Yankee support in their fight against it. President Eliot of Harvard and the redoubtable Thomas Wentworth Higginson, among others, spoke eloquently against the proscriptive aspects of the measure, while Nathan Matthews joined Thomas Gargan in attacking it as a socialistic exercise of state authority. (Josiah Quincy was caught favoring the bill, whose political implications he was slow to grasp, and escaped embarrassment only by beating a hasty retreat.) Throughout the years of A.P.A. virulence in Massachusetts, Yankee Democrats led by Matthews, Governor Russell, and George Fred Williams stoutly defended Irish Catholics against their detractors. (Williams, however, remarked in his diary in 1895, "I wish the Irish politicians had not given the A.P.A. so much ground to stand on.") Yankee and Irish Democrats alike realized that self-interest required them to maintain their party as a bridge across community differences. Despite Yankee distaste for Irish mores and Irish scorn for gentlemen who had never worked a precinct, each group brought to the task of cooperation a respect for the other's sensitivities. For a time in the nineties they produced striking results.[16]

In no area was collaboration more apparent than in negotiations over jobs and nominations. Pat Maguire, for instance, had helped the Mugwump Robert Grant get his job on the Boston water commission, had nursed the political ambitions of young

Charles S. Hamlin, and was acknowledged to have been instrumental in swinging John F. Andrew's election to Congress in 1888. In 1890 the *Republic* endorsed Yankee congressional candidates despite their Mugwump past. A Democratic governor after 1890 and a Democratic President after 1892 opened up new sources of patronage for Irish and Yankees to divide. As in the 1880's, the patronage issue ruffled ethnic pride, but now negotiations were direct and frank. When Congressman O'Neil felt Irishmen were getting short shrift in state patronage he wrote bluntly to Governor Russell, "I hope you will not make the mistake of F. O. Prince who believed that there were half a dozen men with Irish blood who had brains but that the balance was fit only to fill places with less than a thousand a year. You can well afford to divide even." And Russell shot back, "I am the last man in the state against whom any criticism can be justly brought that I have distinguished between men on account of race, religion or anything of that nature." Russell recounted his pride in the opposition he had aroused among Canadian immigrants because of his sympathy for Irish aspirations and challenged O'Neil to re-examine his record of recent state appointments. He admitted he could not mollify every faction in the party: "You know as well as I do, Joe, that it is impossible to give satisfaction in appointments to office, or to avoid a great deal of disappointment." Russell gave the Irish as much satisfaction as he could squeeze past the Republican legislature. He managed to place prominent Irishmen on the state railroad commission, the Boston police commission, and the metropolitan sewer commission, and he found his unsuccessful Irish running mate a judgeship on the superior bench. In 1892 he used all his influence with Grover Cleveland to land for Patrick Collins the richest piece of patronage the President had to give—the forty thousand dollar-a-year post of Consul General in London. During Cleveland's second administration federal jobs in Massachusetts were dealt out among Yankees and Irishmen with almost mathematical precision. "I think with five Yankees now in office here and two Irishmen," Sherman Hoar advised Attorney General Olney in 1894, "another Irishman would be good politics." Patronage had become the politicians' balance wheel for ethnic equilibrium.[17]

Underlying these hard-headed calculations among Democratic leaders was a shared fund of social agreement around which both camps naturally clustered despite their ethnic differences. The merger of Catholic and Jeffersonian conservatism created among them a proximate but fundamental consensus. When Pope Leo XIII published his famous encyclical on the condition of labor in 1891, it served as a summary confirmation of accepted social thought in Democratic Boston. The Delphic judgments of *Rerum Novarum* won applause from both the conservative and liberal quarters of American Catholicism. Yet its salient doctrines defined with rare precision the range of theory tolerated by Boston Irish political leaders: the priority of the individual and his family over the state; the natural right to possess private property; the necessity of labor organization to secure just wages by free contract; the need for public regulation of working conditions for women and children; the ultimate harmony of labor and capital; the dignity of poverty; the alleviation of social conflict between rich and poor by "beautiful charity" from the one and "tranquil resignation" from the other. But for the source, these doctrines might have served as well as a manifesto for the Yankee followers of Grover Cleveland.[18]

An interesting if less crucial concurrence of views was the common Democratic opposition to woman suffrage. If Boston Democrats had their way, neither Bridget's calloused palm nor the soft glove of the Yankee lady would ever shadow the ballot box. Irish antipathy toward woman suffrage stemmed from Catholic focus on the family as a prime source of social virtue. "You are not called upon to occupy a prominent position before the world," lectured *Donahoe's* in "A Word to Girls," "but you are called upon to exercise that home influence which shall make the world better. Remain where God places you: some of the noblest conquests have been achieved in a humble home." Clerical apprehension over the increase of religious tension which might follow the political activation of Catholic women reinforced Irish opposition to female voting. For their part

Yankee Democrats and Mugwumps were by no means unanimous in opposition to woman suffrage. Josiah Quincy and Thomas Wentworth Higginson favored it, for instance. But most held a position close to the Catholic view, for a variety of reasons. Some doubtless nursed a quiet fear that extension of the voting privilege to immigrant women would compound the danger of democracy running amuck. Many doubted the wisdom of granting the vote to their own wives. Often the wives agreed. The first chairman of the Massachusetts Association Opposed to the Extension of Suffrage to Women, established in 1895, was Mrs. Henry M. Whitney, wife of the Democratic traction magnate. Neither the character of Boston politics nor the character of Boston society in the late nineteenth century nurtured acceptance of female political activism. A kind of social monasticism governed the polite adult life of the city. Gentlemen hurried from the ladies after dinner to get to their cigars and sober talk, and so carefully drawn were the reigning forms that only a cad would refer to an unmarried girl by her first name. In Victorian Boston the veiled peculiarities of the female seemed an insuperable bar to her political equality. Obliging women to vote, William E. Russell declared, would pull them from their firesides "into the busy turmoil of a politician's life,—a life unsuited to their tastes and at variance with their modesty and sensitive natures . . ." Russell cited Milton on the point:

> For contemplation he and valor formed
> For softness she and sweet attractive grace.

For Charles R. Codman, female incapacity in the art of war and violence clinched the matter. Codman deemed it "unphilosophical that the non-combatant element of the community should be in a possible position to outvote the combatant element." (John Boyle O'Reilly agreed exactly: "Roughly stated," he concluded, "the voting population ought to represent the fighting population.") For the Mugwump Frederic J. Stimson, woman suffrage struck at the heart of the marriage contract, and, he grandly announced, marriage, private property, and personal liberty from state control "are so inseparably bound

together that neither one may fall without the other two." Irish
Catholics observing the annual march of suffrage petitioners to
the General Court detected an equally ominous threat. "The
leaders in the movement to secure the ballot for women in
municipal elections," Pat Maguire's *Republic* finally decided in
1895, "are simply and solely female A.P.A.'s." At times the
woman suffrage hearings at the State House degenerated into
raw verbal cat fights as epithets about "amazons" and "priests in
politics" flew back and forth between petitioners and Irish
legislators. "If we should bring our women to the polls," Boston's
Jerry Donovan shouted at the end of one such session, "we could
bury you people that have been talking as you have today."
When with evident misgivings Republican leaders embraced the
cause of woman suffrage in the early nineties, the union of
Democrats against it was confirmed.[19]

Prohibition was another issue which found Yankee Democrats
defending Irish mores. Whatever their private thoughts about
the use of liquor and the problem of temperance, they willingly
aligned themselves against the coercive proposals of Massachusetts Prohibitionists. The liquor question, like the school
issue, the A.P.A., and woman suffrage, was laden with nativistic
anti-Catholic overtones. It was also tangled with the issue of
urban home rule, as had been made clear when the Republican legislature took from Boston her control over her police and
saloon licenses simultaneously. The central role of the saloon in
the social life of the urban Irishman, as well as the generous
support of the Democratic party by brewers like Boston's Jacob
Pfaff, made insistence on local option an obvious Democratic
answer to the Prohibitionists. The question of immigration restriction provided Yankee Democrats with another chance to
practice tactful self-restraint. Few active Democrats joined the
genteel Immigration Restriction League born in Yankee Boston
in 1894. In any event, anxiety over alien hordes was directed
not at the Irish but at the new immigrants from southeastern
Europe, people whom the Boston Irish regarded with almost as
much distaste as did native-born Yankees. Seeking an appro-
priate stance on the immigration issue, Democrats were usually

reduced to an awkward silence, broken occasionally by calculated reference to the "English-speaking peoples" as bound together in common interest. Meanwhile, however, they mustered
militant resistance to all proposals for tightening restrictions on
the naturalization of immigrants already arrived, recognizing
that the votes of the newcomers were an important source of
Democratic strength.[20]

Of all these formulas for cooperation no one in itself was a
satisfactory solvent for the differences outstanding between
Yankee and Irish Democrats. Each provided individual Yankees
with grounds for private distrust of Irish power in Boston. Taken
together, they constituted a profound Yankee concession to the
legitimacy of that power. It was a concession dictated by political necessity rather than personal preference, but it clothed Irish
aspirations with a dignity which their leaders deeply valued.
Yankee Democrats in effect ceded control of the city to the Irish
in return for a chance to forge a Democratic majority in the
state. The remarkable sequel is that Irish leaders accepted their
trust with great caution, some reluctance, and a convincing show
of obsequious restraint. A decade would pass before they sought
to seize what was theirs.

The fate of Hugh O'Brien was one initial reason. When
O'Brien went down to defeat in the mayoral election of 1888
after a campaign laced with sectarian strife, and another Irishman was more badly beaten the next year, Pat Maguire decided
to pull in his horns. Weighing Irish political aggrandizement
against the cost in community embitterment, he chose harmony.
Beginning in 1890 he compelled his fellow Irishmen to forego
competing for Boston's choicest political prize and accept the
safer strategy of running established, respectable Protestant
Democrats for mayor. The fruits of City Hall, he decided, must
after all continue to drop from Yankee hands. Searching for a
suitable candidate for the mayoralty, Maguire first seized on a
suggestion in the columns of the Boston *Pilot* that the Democrats
run Charles H. Taylor, editor of the city's leading Democratic
daily, the *Boston Globe*. Taylor would have suited nicely. A
powerful and loyal Democrat, privy to the party's highest coun-

cils and yet associated in the public mind not with grimy machine politics but genial, folksy, community journalism, he seemed an apt choice to lead his party back into control of City Hall. But Taylor preferred to protect his profitable public image and declined the bid. Maguire then turned to his austere friend Nathan Matthews, the leading organizer of the Young Men's Democratic Clubs. Matthews' strong partisanship had not dimmed his legal reputation in Boston, and he wore a plausible aura of Yankee reform. He promptly accepted Maguire's proffer, and after a purposeful campaign carried twenty of the city's twenty-five wards—including Back Bay's silk-stocking Republican district. In January 1891 Matthews settled down to four years of vigorous management of the city's public affairs, and Maguire's strategy was put to the test.[21]

The mayoralty was no figurehead position. The new city charter of 1885 had reinforced the authority of the post by stripping the common council and board of aldermen of their executive functions and by giving the mayor broad powers of appointment and removal in the city departments and an item veto over aldermanic appropriations. Matthews was the first mayor to fulfill the vision of the charter framers by demonstrating the merit of concentrated executive authority. His administration was hardheaded, businesslike, and financially stringent. To the applause of Yankee Boston he resisted repeated efforts by the legislature and board of aldermen to play the pork barrel with city appropriations and pad municipal operating expenses. Humorless and autocratic, Matthews was not a lovable mayor. Yet he used his office to force workable solutions to chronic urban problems. Mainly through his persistence Boston began digging its downtown subway to cut into the tangled trolley traffic near Boston Common. He launched an investigation of the city's inadequate water supply with the result that in 1895 a comprehensive metropolitan water works was inaugurated. Under Matthews, municipal park development accelerated, and the city assumed the task of watering dusty streets at public expense. Over the startled objections of interested aldermen, Matthews embarked on a celebrated war against the price manipulations of Boston gas companies, and his exposures helped slash city gas rates by roughly 25 percent. In sum, he used his office to demonstrate the feasibility in Democratic Boston of majority rule under stern executive direction. Amateur municipal reformers applauded Matthews as a "reform mayor." Toward the end of his mayoralty the Republican president of the Boston Municipal League, Samuel Capen, declared that city offices were filled with men as honest and capable as any in the past. Capen felt municipal conduct in Boston to be a just cause for civic pride and participation. "When a man is called upon by his fellow-citizens to serve in the city government," he said, summoning his absolutes, "it is just as honorable as to be a director in a bank or a professor in Harvard University." Adding to the chorus of praise, Mugwumps like Edward Atkinson and Moorfield Storey concluded that Matthews had gone far to crystallize their favorite image of city government as a business corporation.[22]

Matthews for his part rejected, however, the reformers' analogy between municipal government and corporate enterprise as impractical and fallacious. He felt this notion, so popular a canon of good government in the earnest reform thought of the 1890's, ignored the hard fact that city governments were organized not to make money for private profit but to spend money for public benefit—to provide for the health, safety, comfort, and education of the city's people. While he regarded extravagant spending as the besetting difficulty of city government, he rejected any solution by which businessmen might run the city as they would a railroad. Any such corporate analogy, he argued, with its implicit definition of the good citizen as shareholder, drove its adherents to favor limitations on the political power of the unpropertied immigrant. (Moorfield Storey, for instance, favored tripling the residence requirement for naturalized voters.) "If the American people cannot in time solve the problem of city government on the basis of universal suffrage," Matthews declared, "then democracy itself is a failure." Moreover, he rejected the reformers' plea for nonpartisan municipal elections as detrimental to Boston's peculiar religious and social mixture. Municipal affairs were unavoidably political, he argued,

and people would divide over them in partisan fashion. Far
better to borrow the irrelevant loyalties of the national parties
than to inflame local religious and ethnic feeling by dividing
into polar social camps. Much the same arguments, he believed,
applied to proposals for introducing proportional representation into the city government—it would turn the city council into
a squabbling swarm of ethnic factions. Behind Matthews' polite
quarrels with his reformist admirers loomed, of course, the city's
irrepressible conflict between Brahmin and Celt and the hope
he shared with Pat Maguire that the Democratic party might be
used to head it off. Matthews and Maguire remained on good
terms. While resisting the special aggrandizing projects of aldermanic cliques, Matthews recognized his obligations to the Irish
organization. Irish infiltration through the lower realms of city
offices, which had begun in earnest under Hugh O'Brien, continued in the 1890's. In return Maguire mustered sizable majorities for Matthews every time he ran for re-election. The strange
alliance seemed to be working.[23]

During Matthews' fourth year in office, however, the massive
onset of depression exhausted his definition of reform and un-
strung the coalition he and Maguire had put together. The
rocking Wall Street panic of May 1893 began to make its impact
on industrial New England by early fall. The initial effect of
depression varied among occupational groups. As the Boston
correspondent of the *Hartford Courant* noted early in December, "the pinch of the hard times is not severely felt by the class
who generally buy Christmas presents." At the same time, however, a survey of three dozen Boston craft unions indicated that
37 percent of their members were unemployed during the two
preceding months. Depression struck hardest at New England's
clothing, leather, and woolen industries, fusing factors that had
begun to disrupt manufacturing patterns well before the panic.
The causes seemed to include the fresh influx of cheap immigrant labor, the pressure of technological change toward overhaul of factory and business organization, and a noticeable
decline in consumer demand for boots and clothing from the
agrarian South and West. These combined to produce heavy

unemployment in Massachusetts in the winter and spring of 1894. In Boston conditions were worst at the outset in the congested clothing industry. As the depression spread out the building, printing, and machinists' trades were seriously hit. Mass hardship confronted Boston with a sudden social and political emergency.[24]

Individual proposals for coping with the depression ranged across a wide spectrum. Edward Bellamy recommended on the one hand that the state establish economically self-sufficient communities of the unemployed to serve as pilot plants for his Nationalist dreams. On the other, one J. G. Thorpe of Cambridge suggested that habitual tramps be given six-month jail sentences. A respected Harvard political economist expressed a prevailing view among the more thoughtful men of Cambridge when he explained to Richard Henry Dana over lunch at Young's "how nine out of ten unemployed were 'tramps' but the other one was a genuine sufferer, how the actual existence of the real sufferer gave birth to the socialist movement, how the latter was growing more than the people generally had any idea of, how a labor test, hard but varied work with wages . . . freely given would help weed out the tramps and help the worthy, and how that would be an answer to the socialists." The crisis tended to congeal orthodox attitudes toward support of the unfortunate: to be efficacious, aid should be personal, voluntary, and discriminating. Depression must not drag the country blindly toward public paternalism. Politicians of neither party doubted the proper response of government to the unemployment problem. No attempt was made in Massachusetts to distribute state-financed relief, and no appeal for aid was made to Washington. Governor Russell's Republican successor declared at his inauguration in January 1894, "If the people are compelled to get along from hand to mouth, to pinch, to economize, to practice self-denial, it is reasonable and just that their condition should be reflected in the conduct and affairs of the Commonwealth . . . If the individual citizen must retrench and economize, why should not the state retrench and economize as well?" No Democratic leader cared to challenge this powerful logic.[25]

The assumed incapacity of the state threw the whole burden of relief on the local community. In Boston Mayor Matthews reacted with initial vigor. As early as September 1893, anticipating a grim winter, he had issued extra numbers of municipal bonds to finance over thirty new building projects. He ordered city departments to keep on as large a labor force as possible without increasing normal costs and to expedite projected plans for street, sewer, and park development. In December he called a public meeting to air the unemployment problem. From this meeting emerged the Citizen's Relief Committee, the organization which carried the main load of relief work in the city during the first winter of depression. The committee managed to tap Boston's philanthropic resources for just over 100,000 dollars. Most of this money was distributed as wages among 5,761 unemployed men and women carefully screened by committee aides. (For lack of proper qualifications 1,699 applicants were denied relief.) Women were put to work making rag rugs, a pastime chosen because it competed with no established commercial enterprise, while men labored at city sewer projects, alley-cleaning, and earth-moving details. As an experiment in swift, large-scale administration of the work test, the activity of the Citizen's Relief Committee was cause for pardonable self-congratulation among its members. As alleviation for unemployment it was sadly inadequate. Most of the men accepted for work relief were put on rotating shifts, working every second or third week. Among skilled laborers relief assistance often amounted to a week's wages over long months of idleness. The money the committee paid out in wages could hardly compensate for the estimated 1,500,000 dollars lost through unemployment in Boston. The working class had no representative on the Citizen's Relief Committee. Control remained in the hands of Yankee philanthropists and charity workers—public spirited upper-class men and women who could not abandon the moral preconceptions which had brought them to charity work in the first place. Pervading all their reports was the determination that relief should be selective, reinforcing virtue where it could be found among the unemployed. Otherwise the emergency would establish bad precedents. "Relief-work suggests to many the possibility of depending on others to invent work for them instead of hunting it themselves," cautioned one committee member, "and thus instead of truly helping the community it tends to create artificially a new dependent class." [26]

While the Citizen's Relief Committee fretted over its responsibilities, and Mayor Matthews struggled to meet his, Boston's working class grew restless. Mounting unemployment made Faneuil Hall the scene of repeated radical agitations. In mid-February 1894, a band of six hundred jobless workers stormed the State House and demanded work of the governor, only to be ejected by hastily summoned police. A few weeks later socialists, Nationalists, and labor leaders assembled on the floor of the state house of representatives to debate the unemployment question. (One upshot was a political union of radical splinter groups which lasted through the fall elections.) On a cold, bleak Sunday afternoon in March, fifteen hundred workers gathered on Boston Common to hear the touring Kansas Populist Mary E. Lease raise her peculiar brand of hell. Meanwhile resentment ran high against wage cutting by employers and the city's increasing use of cheap Italian contract labor. Among Irish Democrats demands rose for more generous treatment from the city government. In the teeth of falling wages and intense competition for scarce jobs, the municipal labor force with its two-dollar-a-day pay rate became an ideal haven. City patronage at its lowest level was looked on as a potential buffer between the party faithful and urban distress.[27]

But under Nathan Matthews the hope of the faithful was not realized. Matthews argued that the city was legally unable to spend or borrow extra funds for the relief of the unemployed because of restrictions placed on city spending by the state legislature. Moreover, he refused to try to loosen these restrictions. They represented to his mind a basic American principle of divided government which was "the chief defense of the American people and their free institutions against the insidious encroachment of socialism . . ." The stress of hard times had revealed Matthews as a stout ideologue of social orthodoxy.

"The main reliance of every community in emergencies like the present," he had concluded, "must be the generosity and public spirit of its individual citizens." His root convictions steadily crippled his executive drive as the depression ground on. He retired from City Hall at the end of 1894 congratulating himself that no money had been spent by the city for the sole purpose of furnishing relief for the unemployed. The dangerous strategy of relieving distress by creating unnecessary work had proved a failure wherever it had been tried, he claimed. Yet he saw a dark future. The belief was gaining ground, he noted,

that the community in its corporate capacity owes a liberal living to its individual members. A gradual change has come over the spirit of the people; and a large part of a population once the most independent and self-reliant in the world is now clamoring for support, as individuals or in classes, from the government of this country— federal, state, and city. These symptoms . . . constitute the chief danger of popular government, and a danger that will be greater before it is less: the demand for a systematic distribution of wealth by taxes.

To meet this threatening mood, he would marshal the best virtues of the nineteenth century: "Let us aim to remain a body of self-respecting, self-supporting American citizens, and not permit ourselves to be transformed into a pauperized community of Nationalists and socialists." Nathan Matthews had entered public life a sturdy Democratic reformer. He returned to private life a narrow, fearful conservative, his robust reform energies stunted by economic collapse.[28]

Economic crisis cast a pall over Pat Maguire's Democratic organization. As Matthews completed his stewardship, Maguire glumly looked around the city for another mayoral candidate who met his specifications for perpetuating the Yankee-Irish alliance in city politics. Finally he tapped an elegant Back Bay lawyer named Francis Peabody, a close friend of Matthews and Governor Russell. Peabody was a ludicrous choice, and his candidacy a painful parody of Maguire's peculiar coalition strategy. He sprang from the Essex County Peabodys and was the brother of Endicott Peabody, the founder of Groton. Edu-

cated at Trinity College, Cambridge, and prepared for the law
at Lincoln's Inn, he had been quietly practicing law in Boston
since 1880, living on Commonwealth Avenue in the winter and
summering at Nahant. Aside from directing a small crusade in
1891 to drive peddlers from the streets of Boston and serving
as a "general" on Governor Russell's tinseled military staff, he
had never taken an active part in public life. The news of his
nomination sent a wave of fresh discontent rumbling through
the party's lower echelons. One incredulous Irish Democrat
declared: "Mr. Peabody is not a representative Democrat. His
only qualifications for office seem to be his connection with
society clubs, his possession of money, which it is expected he
will spend freely, his close and intimate relationship to Mayor
Matthews, and his holding of the office of president and director
of a score or more of corporations." Trying to appease the Irish,
night after night Peabody left his Back Bay drawing room to
visit party rallies, "for the purpose of getting acquainted with
the rank and file of the Democracy." It was no use. Some Irish
Democrats bolted, others sat on their hands, Peabody was soundly beaten, and an equally respectable Republican became Mayor
of Boston.[29]

The Peabody disaster underscored the bankruptcy of Pat
Maguire's formula for political success in the grim era ushered
in by the panic of 1893. In the mid-nineties Maguire's control of
the city organization began to give way. A month after Peabody's
defeat Maguire indicated he was about ready to yield the reins
on the Democratic city committee. No sharp break occurred;
Maguire's grip loosened slowly. But an era was perceptibly
passing. Under the stress of hard times the older suburban Irish
leadership of Maguire, Collins, Gargan, and O'Neil, who for
years had directed the fortunes of their people from their soft
perch on the ladder of success, lost its logic and appeal. Power
sifted down and settled with an altogether different breed, the
men who ran the wards. Among these, three young Irishmen—
James Donovan, Martin Lomasney, and John F. Fitzgerald—rose
to contest what Pat Maguire's passing might augur for the city's
future. All three were born in Boston and had grown up in the

city since the Civil War. Now they bossed the desolate tenement districts clustering around the commercial center of downtown Boston. Each of them, surrounded by a loyal cadre of heelers and hangers-on, hoarded political power against the Italians and Jews who pushed into their districts to find new homes. The ward bosses were steady fixtures in the rootless limbo of the slums, exploiting the political vacuum created by Irish retreat before the new immigration. In effect they ruled an abandoned city rarely entered by outsiders. Older and more prominent Irish leaders had judiciously broken their ties with the grimy downtown back streets of their boyhood, while Back Bay Brahmins seldom passed through except in summer carriages en route to the North Shore or the Cunard Piers. The power the slum politicians wielded was theirs by default.[30]

Smiling Jim Donovan of the South End came closest to being Pat Maguire's protégé. Born in 1859, Donovan had quit school at age eleven for the greater enticements of politics, won election to the city council at age twenty-two, entered the state legislature at age twenty-four, and sat on the governor's council at age thirty-three. His influence in the Democratic city committee grew apace, and, after 1892, under Maguire's tutelage, he was committee chairman. There his ambition ended. Living alone on dingy Emerald Street, he became a fast friend of first-generation Irishmen who clung to the South End. A big, open-faced, nattily dressed street-corner politician with a ready grin, Donovan was an early craftsman in the art of the Irish funeral. His district was a dismal, nondescript area to which a Boston social worker applied the harrowing label "city wilderness." The South End had fallen apart as a residential area after 1880 when prosperous Yankees deserted it for Back Bay, and their former dwellings were partitioned into tenements and boarding houses. By the 1890's the South End population was heterogeneous, but the Irish still predominated in numbers and political power. Donovan's aim was to maintain Irish domination in both the South End and in the city. Blunt, breezy, and affable, he sought by scattered alliances across the city to hold Maguire's coalition together among ward leaders.[31]

On the other side of Boston Common behind the State House, where Beacon Hill sloped down from Yankee gentility to the brackish Charles, lay Ward Eight, the famous West End empire of Martin Lomasney. Lomasney became a myth in his own lifetime, the essence of the Irish ward boss. He came up the hard way. Born in the West End in 1859 of poor Irish parents who shortly died, he spent his boyhood as a lonely urchin of the city streets and grew up with a cold, suspicious eye on the world around him. After scraping together a living as a boot-black, errand boy, and metal spinner, he got into politics by chasing down voters in the city election in 1876, was rewarded with a job on a city construction gang, and later became a lamp-lighter. While still in his twenties he began fighting his own ward leaders and finally ousted them in 1886. By 1890 Lomas-ney's Ward Eight organization was the tightest in the city, and his power to deliver its vote absolutely according to promise became a byword among his rivals. He called himself a "six o'clock Democrat"; he had idolized Ben Butler in his youth, thought little of Grover Cleveland, and admired Cleveland's arch rival in New York politics, the crafty David B. Hill. In Boston politics Lomasney was unpredictable. The only man who had his confidence was his brother Joe. His relations with Pat Maguire were cool; he had a weakness for sudden factional alliance with Republicans; yet as an alderman he was Mayor Matthews' most loyal supporter. By 1895 he was restless for greater power in the city. Meanwhile the West End was chang-ing swiftly around him. The Irish had won control of the area in the 1880's but were now themselves retreating before Jewish immigrants from the North End. Lomasney ignored the Jews at first, but soon was working hard to fit them into his organization. His tough compassion for the people whose lives he dominated would in time become as legendary as his mammoth jaw. He ruled the West End with a clenched fist, feared equally by social workers and parish priests.[32]

Casting about for allies in the city, Lomasney hit on his neighbor in the North End, John F. Fitzgerald. Fitzgerald made an odd accomplice. Unlike Donovan and Lomasney, he had been born into a prosperous family. His parents were lace-curtain Irish who kept a brisk business in groceries and liquor in the heart of the North End. Young Fitzgerald received a good education in Boston's public schools and studied for a time at Harvard before his father died, after which he landed a job at the Boston Customs House under Leverett Saltonstall. He won his politician's spurs in the state legislature in 1893 pushing for free trolley transfers, an eight-hour day for city workers, and protection for Irish laborers against Italian contract gangs. In Ward Six of the North End, where a small remnant of Irish families with firm business and political stakes clung to power against the tide of voteless Italians and Jews, Fitzgerald and his friends ran an Irish rotten borough. Fitzgerald's warm ties with the Catholic Church, and especially St. Stephen's in the North End, were useful in his political progress. So was the cooperation of aspiring Irishmen who had moved across the harbor to Charlestown and East Boston but flocked back to the North End for Mass and politics. An attractive, articulate, cocky bantam of a man on whom the nicknames "Little Napoleon" and "Honey Fitz" stuck like burrs, Fitzgerald gathered around him a large coterie of bright-eyed, well-dressed, hustling young Irishmen. In the depression year 1894 he decided the time was right for a strike against the established order in Boston politics. Announcing that Boston needed a fresh face in Washington, he challenged Joseph O'Neil for his congressional seat. This was a bold move. O'Neil had City Hall, Pat Maguire, the *Boston Globe,* and the good will of many businessmen on his side. But Fitzgerald gambled shrewdly for the support of Martin Lomasney. Having won it, he sent his followers scavenging through the city for discontented voters. Meanwhile he swept back and forth across the district with his fife and drum corps, his carriage lit with torches, pumping hands and singing songs. He beat O'Neil for the nomination hands down and won the fall election.[33]

The new power of Fitzgerald, Lomasney, and Donovan registered a natural evolution of youth rising against age. But depression accelerated the tempo of change. Over 30 percent of the applicants for relief in 1894 came from the wards controlled by these three men. The misery of unemployment in the city's tenement districts deepened the disparity between orthodox notions of what society owed to its poor and what the poor wanted. In the gap stood the ward boss. Over the long pull he proved to be a far surer source of security than private charity. Martin Lomasney alone, it was estimated, controlled city jobs worth eighty thousand dollars in salaries, a sum almost equal to what Boston's Citizen's Relief Committee dispensed in wages during the one winter it operated. Moreover when private employers—building contractors, gas companies, railways, freight companies—needed hands, they went to Lomasney, Donovan, and Fitzgerald, not to Pat Maguire or Joseph O'Neil. The ward leader remained close to his power, accessible, serviceable, fitting snugly at the apex of his subtle society of street-corner gangs, saloons, clubs, and caucuses. (When Honey Fitz married and moved out to Concord in the late nineties he lost his status as ward boss and was promptly taunted as a carpetbagger.) Irish leaders remained in power in the South, West, and North Ends despite the influx of new ethnic groups. Even before the Italians and Jews began to vote they began to bow to Irish leadership. Lomasney found the West End Jews a constant headache but he had his agents waiting at the pier when each new shipload of aliens debarked. Fitzgerald, who as a state senator had complained vehemently about Italian contract labor, by 1896 was singing praises to Italian virtues and denouncing advocates of immigration restriction. By the end of the nineties over half the Italian voters in the North End were Democrats by habit, and their padrones were trusted party lieutenants. Irish ward leaders who had nailed down the ethnic vote could afford some skepticism in judging Maguire's policy of collaboration with suburban Yankee Democrats. The working terms of compromise Maguire had accepted smacked too much of subservience. The good opinion of Yankee Boston was no longer a condition of either survival or success in city politics. Each of the rising young Irishmen calculated a separate strategy for self-advancement. Where Smiling Jim Donovan toiled amiably in the line of succession behind Pat Maguire, Lomasney and Fitzgerald counted on insurgency for success. Both were head-strong, free-lance politicians prepared to throw their autonomous power wherever it hit hardest at any given time. If the Democratic party were to regain control of the city government under the stern new conditions created by depression, men like Fitzgerald and Lomasney would have to be reckoned with, and their proud new power recognized in party arrangements.[34]

Whether under these circumstances intraparty cooperation between the leaders of the Yankee and Irish segments of the city's population would still be possible remained in doubt. Efforts to paper over the widening ethnic split only served to illuminate the anxieties of men on either side. One touching example occurred at an otherwise unremarkable meeting of the Democratic city committee in June 1896. When the time came to elect officers for the coming year, an obscure South Boston Yankee was nominated for committee vice-president. The Irishman who nominated him argued that the committee ought to have at least one Yankee on it, "lest we be charged with being a party of inverted Know-Nothingism." The suggestion was greeted with hearty applause and the lonely Yankee was elected by acclamation. No one knew whether this little tribute to ethnic harmony was a promise or an epitaph.[35]

WHILE Massachusetts Democrats worked to fix the stamp of Cleveland Democracy on the state and city, they waged a desperate fight to keep their ideals alive in the national party. Rallied by Grover Cleveland's tariff message of 1887 to push to victory in Massachusetts, they vowed to make the tariff issue the militant war cry of national reform in the decade ahead. These ambitious young Democrats believed they were the cutting edge of Cleveland's brand of Democracy, and they anticipated long service in the front rank of party leadership. In 1890 they had good reason for their dream. Yet before another three years were out they found themselves entering dark thickets of party strife, struggling to save their careers.

With the tariff issue they had hoped to swing New England behind New York and the New South and forge a seaboard alliance which would serve the Democratic party as well in the future as the protectionist entente between New England, Pennsylvania, and the Middle West had served the Republican party in the recent past. Cooperation between Cleveland Democrats in New England and New York rose naturally from a likeness of men and motives. A bedrock consensus about what was important in politics joined Bostonians with New Yorkers like George F. Parker, Charles S. Fairchild, William C. Whitney, the Straus brothers, and Henry Villard in a fushion of purpose. Both groups represented what they were fond of calling "the better element" in the Democratic party. Both were anxious to lift the party beyond the reach of its own spoilsmen and to protect Grover Cleveland from the machinations of David B. Hill, the bête noir of New York politics. Both groups, moreover, responded sympathetically to the biases of Wall and State

Streets, sharing as they did a sense that the national welfare was a natural residue of autonomous business interests. The alliance between New England and the New South was more complex and more tenuous—a working bargain whereby Yankee Democrats leaned on the power of southern politicians while Yankee dollars built the New South. Both sides sought to exploit economic developments already underway. Capital from New York and Boston had been moving south in growing proportion since 1877, building the railroads and industries which philosophers of the New South hoped would erase the memory of civil war and southern defeat. Henry W. Grady, editor of the *Atlanta Constitution* and the New South's most compelling publicist, put it concisely: "We have sowed towns and cities in the place of theories and put business above politics." [1]

Southern awakening in the 1880's was a broad-gauged, indigenous undertaking. But part of the original impulse came from outside. Among the pioneers of the New South was Edward Atkinson, Boston's ubiquitous Mugwump economist. Spurred by New England textile manufacturers' dissatisfaction with the quality of raw cotton arriving from the South, Atkinson had started in 1880 to promote the education of Southerners to their obligations and opportunities. Not only ought the South to gin better cotton, Atkinson felt; the region ought to recognize the economic diversity latent in its resources. Many powerful Southerners agreed. In the eyes of Yankee cotton manufacturers the revival soon threatened to get out of hand. The attention Atkinson had focused on the problems of raw cotton production ironically contributed to the rise of southern cotton mills. By trying to improve the source of supply for the New England textile industry he had inadvertently helped to foster a lively manufacturing rival. Atkinson and other Bostonians were naturally anxious to develop those kinds of southern industry which might supplement rather than compete with New England's economy. Harvard's Kentucky-born Professor Nathaniel Shaler argued, for instance, that southern iron and mineral industries might seek out markets in Africa and South America and thus widen the flow of international trade by which

so many New Englanders set store. Together with potent New
York capitalists like Abram S. Hewitt and enthusiastic Southerners such as John C. Calhoun's sons John and Patrick, Boston
began investing strongly in southern mines, timber, and railroads.[2]

Meanwhile the South and the border states began to produce
a new generation of political leaders sympathetic to the business
aspirations of the New South—Roger Mills of Texas, Hoke Smith
of Georgia, William L. Wilson of West Virginia, John G. Carlisle of Kentucky. Such men were a powerful arm of Cleveland
Democracy in the South, and ambitious young Yankee politicians like William E. Russell prudently cultivated their friendship and esteem. In the budding alliance between New England
and the New South the resurrection of Thomas Jefferson as
patron saint of the Democratic party played an important part.
Yankee Democrats happily embraced as their own the vision
deduced from Jefferson of a simple, decentralized, individual-
istic society geared to free-moving and expanding commerce.
One nagging incongruity needed reckoning with: New England's abolitionist heritage. Yankee advocates of the southern
entente were compelled out of self-respect to announce, in effect,
that the southern Negro no longer posed a serious national
problem. Where racial conflict remained in the South, economic
resurgence promised a certain cure. In an industrial South
the Negro could slash all remaining ties with his plantation
past. Edward Atkinson, himself an old abolitionist, lectured
Southerners on the right of the Negro to political equality, but
acknowledged to a Virginian, "The progress of the Negro in
property, education, and influence righteously obtained, is the
marvel of the present century." Southern spokesmen like Henry
W. Grady assured New Englanders that Negro emancipation
was virtually complete in the South, and that Negroes and whites
lived together in cordial harmony. Release from the institution
of slavery was the "jewel," Grady explained, which Southerners
had found in the "toad's head of defeat." Yankee Democrats,
anxious to wish away obstacles to sectional alliance, echoed
these jolly views. Early in 1890 William E. Russell traveled to

Atlanta to address a dinner in memory of Grady, who had died suddenly after a Boston speaking engagement. Russell's Atlanta speech eulogized the New South for the rancor it had liquidated and the new sectional compact it made possible. After touring New Orleans in the company of southern railroad magnate John H. Inman, Russell returned to Boston and reported to Atkinson:

My visit was very delightful, and I believe useful to me in an educational way. I certainly got much new light on the South, its prosperity and progress, and on the relation between the races. The one strong impression that I received from all in reference to the races was, that there was not a hostile, but a very friendly feeling (often affectionate) between the races . . .

His conscience cleaned on that point, Russell was eager to get on with the politics of business brotherhood between North and South.[3]

Boston's warm solicitude for the New South contrasted sharply with her untrusting and slightly resentful attitude toward the West. The robust continent beyond the Ohio reminded thoughtful Bostonians of New England's relative economic stagnation and prompted talk of ignorant, crass, western heedlessness. The West was felt to be lacking in good sense, irresponsible in politics, and unreliable in business. The Mugwump banker Henry P. Kidder, for instance, laid much of James G. Blaine's popularity to "the blind enthusiasm" of Westerners who were "remote from great cities [and] not familiar with the business of the country," while George Fred Williams told Carl Schurz the South must be cultivated "to counteract the materialism of the West in politics." Commercial Boston was, of course, deeply committed to western development, and particularly to western railroads. Bostonians owned large blocks of stock in the Chicago, Burlington, & Quincy, and the Atchison, Topeka, & Santa Fe, as well as seats on their boards of directors. Young Boston railroad lawyers knew the region from trips out on the line. ("And we were told," F. J. Stimson recalled with a flourish, "—travelling in private cars over our railroads in those wide-open spaces where men are men—to pull down the shades of our dining-car over the oysters and champagne lest the native take a shot at them.") If Boston tapped the West, Boston sensed that the West was beyond control. Her interest involved little of the patronizing camaraderie which adorned investment in the South. When the year 1887 brought an abrupt end to the western land boom, Boston's investments in railroads and land mortgages further poisoned her relations with the West. The broken bubble of expansion sent land values plummeting and exposed the wild overbuilding of towns and railroads. In the new gray light of western hard times bitterness spread among both debtors and creditors. More than one Bostonian, nursing his losses, regretted his ventures in the western boom. Mistrust had been confirmed.[4]

The political implications of the reversal dawned slowly. Most eastern Democrats paid scant attention to the first stirrings of agrarian radicalism in the South and West in the late eighties. The realization that agricultural depression might rend the bonds between New England and the New South and foment a radical alliance between southern and western farmers came as a delayed shock. It jolted Democrats at the precise moment of their greatest victory—their election triumph of 1890. Having fought through to success against the McKinley Tariff, Yankee Democrats felt an uneasy chill as they examined the nationwide congressional returns. New England had gone Democratic, but barely. Elsewhere the Democractic sweep had reached huge proportions. Cleveland Democrats registered their most impressive gains in the upper Midwest, but there the tariff had vied with prohibition and local school disputes as a rallying issue. Moreover, Democratic victory margins had been widened in many districts by agrarian third-party tickets that bit into normal Republican strength. Many Democrats found themselves shifting to absorb agrarian demands in order to clinch victory. Events elsewhere were even more unsettling. Populists surged to a majority in Kansas and Nebraska. Through the South the Farmers Alliance, an organization built on the distress of agriculture, wrested control of local Democratic organizations from conservative hands, elected three governors, majorities in eight state legislatures, and several dozen congressmen.[5]

To New Englanders the chief threat posed by agrarian radicalism was the fresh impetus it gave to the ancient debtor's demand for cheap money. What if heedless currency agitation should now drown out the maturing debate between protectionists and tariff revisionists? The resounding Democratic victory of 1890 provided at best an unwieldy and intemperate majority for tariff reform. At worst it turned the Democratic party into a Trojan horse for free silver. "The great danger to be guarded against," Edward Atkinson warned the day after the election, "is, I think, a sudden outbreak of the slow-moving and unintelligent farmers and farm laborers, who with those associated with them, constitute a majority of the people. They may become so enraged with the McKinley bill as to make a destructive rush in the opposite direction without regard to conditions." Atkinson's mood typified the fears of the tariff reformers. Swallowing their verve, they were immobilized overnight by caution. "Now moderation and calm judgment is needed to restrain injudicious action," Winslow Warren wrote to his old friend William Everett. "The magnitude of the victory alarms me and the brakes must be applied to prevent disaster." [6]

In the months following the election, anxiety over silver inflation replaced zest for tariff reform in the priority of concerns among influential Bostonians. Before the fall of 1890 a tolerant if ambiguous attitude toward silver had prevailed in the city. Earlier that year a Republican Congress had passed the Sherman Silver Purchase Act providing for an increase in federal currency proportionate with government purchase of 4.5 million ounces of silver per month. Boston's initial reaction to the Silver Purchase Act was mild to the point of serenity. Republican financier T. Jefferson Coolidge was surprised to find so little objection to it among Boston bankers and businessmen; the bill was almost popular on State Street. "In my own private judgment," Coolidge wrote to Congressman Henry Cabot Lodge, "I do not think that the additional purchase of twenty-five millions of silver a month will drive out enough gold for some years to come, to cause any financial difficulty." The banker Henry Lee Higginson showed a like flexibility. "To tell you the truth," Higginson admitted to Lodge, "I have had rather a fancy for a reasonable amount of silver for a good many years, and I often doubt whether we cannot use silver and gold both; often doubt whether there is gold enough to do the business of the world. At least, I do not feel at all sure that the man who would throw silver out of the window understands the case in the least . . ." The commercial community had long been torn between the investor's natural preference for the steady deflation of the post-war decades and the financier's hunch that the nation lacked adequate currency for economic expansion. Meanwhile the cause of international bimetallism—by which gold and silver might be recognized as valid coin at a ratio agreed on among all nations—was winning many respectable advocates in Boston under the leadership of President Francis A. Walker of M.I.T.[7]

However, when the failure of Baring Brothers in London in the fall of 1890 touched off a wave of selling in American securities held abroad, State Street was quick to attribute it to European distrust of congressional silver legislation. "Do not scare the business community . . . ," Higginson wrote to Lodge in November, 1890. "It is not a matter of opinion, it is a matter of fact that Europe has been greatly scared by our silver law of last summer." From 1890 on, State Street's litmuslike sensitivity to wavering European confidence in the American economy was a crucial factor in the response of Cleveland Democrats to silver legislation.[8]

While business optimism faltered, the newly elected Yankee tariff reformers fretted anxiously through the year-long waiting period before they could take their seats in Congress. In January 1891 their grim premonitions were confirmed when a free-silver bill passed the lameduck Senate with almost unanimous Democratic support. Even before they had a chance to urge their convictions on Congress, their party bid fair to lose its credit among influential Mugwump supporters at home. Once again Edward Atkinson spoke for the latter. If the Democrats were going to cave in on silver, he warned Grover Cleveland, "I know what action will be taken by those who have carried Massachusetts on the tariff issue for the Democratic party. They look upon the tariff as *second* in importance to the maintenance of a sound currency, and they will not support a party which commits itself at the present time to the free coinage of silver." Privately Atkinson expressed himself with more heat. If the Democrats went wrong on the money question he and his kind would help "crush them into powder," he told a friend, "as they ought to be crushed if they behave like fools." [9]

Anxious to avert this fate, Boston Mayor Nathan Matthews called a Faneuil Hall open meeting to protest against the Senate free-silver bill. The gathering was bipartisan but Democrats Josiah Quincy and Henry M. Whitney and Mugwumps Henry Lee Higginson, H. L. Pierce, and Edward Atkinson were conspicuous in the crowd. Banker Higginson set the tone in his brief speech. Styling himself and his audience as plain workingmen seeking a fair chance to work at a fair day's pay, he stressed that their fortunes rested on the confidence of Europe. "Rich and full of capital as this country is," he argued, "it needs all the possible capital it can get from Europe to develop its farms, mines, and railroads. But the present course of legislation tends directly to the restriction of capital." Congress must be made to reconsider its course, "chiefly on account of workingmen who are suffering most from the cheap dollar." Boston mustered its resources. A committee of nine was dispatched to Washington to head off the silver bill. Banks began contributing to an "education fund." The secretary of the Reform Club hurried to New York and points west to rally Mugwumps and businessmen to the fight. Atkinson fired off blunt letters to the South: 'It would be useless to offer any further opportunities for investment in the South until the bill for the free coinage of silver is killed so that it cannot be resurrected. Everything in that line has stopped hereabout. I think it would be judicious for you to notify your Southern friends to that effect. If the solid South is for free silver coinage, the solid South thereby declines any further Northern capital." Less truculently, Governor Russell reminded West Virginia's William L. Wilson of the political implications of free silver. With Mugwump support Democrats could strengthen their hold on New England, Russell said. Without it they would return to obscurity. The national party would make a huge mistake to ignore Democratic growth in New England. The alliance of business and politics between Democrats North and South would carry the country in the presidential election of 1892 if not broken up. Far better, Russell concluded, to unite the seaboard around tariff reform than yield to the "impulsive movement" of the plains toward free silver.[10]

Yankee Democrats breathed easier when Grover Cleveland affirmed his opposition to free coinage in his famous "silver letter" of February 10, 1891. After that the menace seemed to fade. The silver bill failed in the House of Representatives and Bostonians lauded the ex-President. Cleveland Democracy had asserted its purpose and prevailed. "When capital is allied with right, capital and right together will be sure to win," Edward Atkinson had written in January, at the outset of the crisis. Now men began to speak of the silver movement in the past tense. Surrendering happily to his ego, Atkinson wrote to Charles Nordhoff, "I think the Free Coinage Bill would have passed by default except for the Boston meeting. We turned it. The movement is nearly if not quite dead. It will be of no importance in '92." [11]

But the silver issue would not die. When the Congress elected in 1890 finally convened in December 1891, the Massachusetts tariff reformers, led by George Fred Williams, John F. Andrew, and Sherman Hoar, instantly discovered how time had tarnished their cause. In the winter of 1891–92 Washington was a maelstrom of contending forces. Tariff reformers clashed with currency reformers; doctrinaires on either side confronted unyielding vested interests on the other. New England's erstwhile southern allies were found to be evasive about free iron and coal, and one after the other southern congressmen toppled to free silver, terrified by the power of the Farmers Alliance at home. "If we bow to the storm temporarily," William L. Wilson wrote to Carl Schurz, "we retain our seats and lose our self-respect. If we face the storm even in this unnecessary phase of it, we lose our places and our opportunity to fight for tariff reform." [12] Senator Gorman of Maryland led a powerful Democratic bloc prepared to compromise with the West on currency reform in order to avert passage of a Republican Force Bill authorizing federal control of elections in the South. (The Force Bill's leading proponent, Massachusetts Republican Henry Cabot Lodge, knew what he was about.) Senator Hill of New York, casting over troubled waters, led another Democratic faction eager to embarrass Grover Cleveland with the silver issue. With the presidential nominating convention only a few months off the Democratic party was profoundly divided as to whether its salvation lay in embracing silver or abjuring it.

For Yankee Democrats the session was a dreary sequence of disappointment. The contest between silver and the tariff began with a battle for the House speakership between southern Democrats Roger Mills of Texas and Charles Crisp of Georgia. The choice between them was a choice of issues. While wobbly on silver, Mills was perhaps the most ardent tariff reformer in the party and a warm proponent of the alliance between New England and the New South. Crisp, in contrast, was a shuffler on the tariff and friendly to silver. George Fred Williams defined the stakes involved in their rivalry in a trenchant memo to his colleagues:

It must not be forgotten that when New England Democrats fight against free-silver coinage, it must be a fight to the death. We could not carry one Congressional district with free silver . . . The business community and the prominent contributors to our campaign funds would not justify a vote against Mills. Mr. Mills' success is second only to Russell's success in importance to us . . . What security should we have that his defeat would not be taken as the triumph of free silver, and be followed by a new craze in Congress. The Democrats of New England would then go down like a school of porgies to the bottom of the sea.[13]

Yet even the Massachusetts delegation was divided between Mills and Crisp. Its ranking member, Boston's Joseph O'Neil, had committed himself to Crisp and to the Gorman-Hill strategy of temporizing with silver. O'Neil's defection accentuated the plight of the tariff reformers. A querulous letter from Mills warned them: "If I shall be defeated you will see the end of

New England's hope for free coal ore and raw materials." In the end all but four New England Democrats voted for Mills. But Crisp defeated him, then refused him the chairmanship of the vital Ways and Means Committee, and buried his New England supporters with hopeless committee assignments.[14]

With Crisp, Gorman, and Hill dominating party strategy in Washington, and the Republicans clinging to control in the Senate, Democrats were doomed to write an empty finish to their great victory of 1890. Gorman, an organization politician to the fingertips, hoped to hold his party together by tossing a sop to both tariff reformers and silverites in the form of ringing resolutions, adjourn Congress early, and prepare for the fall election. Boston's Joseph O'Neil was privy to Gorman's plans, and he was confident the silverites could be put off with meaningless promises from the East. Now he wrote home to Governor Russell and urged that to strengthen Gorman's hand State Street ought to publish a few stories about the brightening prospects for international bimetallism.[15]

To William E. Russell, watching the congressional turmoil from a distance, this was a bitter potion. He could not have opposed the Gorman strategy more emphatically: party principle must not be sacrificed in a crafty search for party unity. Russell was not blind to the plight of western and southern farmers. In fact he happily quoted Farmers Alliance fulminations against the protective tariff in his own speeches. As long as he could associate agrarian unrest with dissatisfaction over national tariff policy he remained the farmers' friend. What the farmer needed, Russell would argue, was a chance to buy his goods in the same free market of supply and demand as he sold his crops; this, together with broadened overseas markets to relieve domestic overproduction, would solve the agricultural problem. Meanwhile, for politicians to tinker with the money supply against the will of high finance could only spell disaster. Russell like Grover Cleveland turned a hard face on currency reform. As Cleveland's personal friend and disciple, he was anxious for Cleveland's renomination in 1892. Beyond that, he was already grooming himself as the New Yorker's future successor in the

Democratic party. If the party in any way identified itself with
free silver, his strength in New England would wash away and
his political future topple. In the winter of 1892, replying to
O'Neil's apologies for Gorman's temporizing strategy, Governor
Russell vented his exasperation in an anguished wail:

The Democratic party should not by word or act become committed
to silver. It defeats us absolutely in New England, undoes all the
progress we have made in Massachusetts, and sets us back where we
are in a hopeless fight for years to come. Whether right or wrong,
you and I know the sentiment is so universal and overwhelming
against silver here that we should lose entirely the support from business and conservative interests . . . For God's sake where is the gain
to come by committing the party to it with the certainty of defeat
here in the East? . . . Time is against silver, and good crops are against
silver. To commit our party to it is not merely to lose the election of
'92 with absolute certainty, to tie the hands of all of us who have
fought for years here through defeat to victory, but in my judgment
is to commit the party to a policy and an issue which they will repent
of in years to come most bitterly . . . [We are] merely pleading for
the life of our party here, and asking the national party on the eve
of a presidential election not to split in two on a controverted issue
where we are all united on tariff reform . . . We are heart and soul
with them on the tariff. We are heart and soul with them against
Force Bills, for economy and every Democratic principle, and we are
loyal to the last drop of blood to our party and its faith. We do not
agree on silver. Silver is death to Democracy in the East.[16]

Three weeks later, in early February 1892, "Silver Dick" Bland
of Missouri reported a free-silver bill out of the House Committee on Coinage, and the beleaguered Massachusetts Democrats prepared for what they thought might well be their last
stand. Once again Bostonians took pen in hand, rallied old
friends, entrained for distant cities. Governor Russell made a
personal appearance in Washington to plead with party leaders.
George Fred Williams protested for the minority on Bland's
coinage committee. Borrowing a page from banker Henry Lee
Higginson, Williams affected to speak for the working masses
against free silver. Cheapening the currency, he argued, would
hurt the poor and help the rich. It was the rich who had suffi-

cient credit to borrow, the rich who were the debtors of the country. The rich would benefit from inflation, not the hapless farmer. On the House floor Williams attempted to answer the silverites' argument that free silver would loosen the grip of eastern mortgage holders on bankrupt western farmers. Eastern money invested in western mortgages, he claimed, came not from powerful trust estates but out of the pockets of "comparatively poor people" whose income would be jeopardized by cheapened dollars. In the privacy of party caucus Williams repeated the New England political argument: the party must choose between the Democratic alliance of North and South or the Farmers Alliance of South and West. To this a Missouri Democrat replied that he would gladly swap Williams for "Sockless Jerry" Simpson, the Kansas Populist.[17]

While silverites remained unimpressed by Yankee pleas, finally the requirements of party unity prevailed and a commitment to silver was once more averted. With large numbers of southern and midwestern Democrats fearful but undecided, scurrying in and out of the silver camp for temporary advantage, the silver issue remained fluid and subject to manipulation by party leaders. Strategy prevailed over ideology and Bland's silver bill died on a motion to table. Tariff reformers drew a long breath. Through the balance of the session they tried to create some record on the tariff to take home to the voters and party patrons in the fall. John F. Andrew introduced a series of "pop-gun" reductions on specific raw materials including coal and iron ore; Governor Russell sent off letters to key leaders on Capitol Hill urging action on them; Sherman Hoar and Charles Hamlin tried to break down William L. Wilson's opposition to the "pop-gun" method. It was no use. Andrew's bills never reached a vote. For the moment resistance to silver was all that the New Englanders could gain from their party. In calculating party needs neither the Crisp-Hill-Gorman coalition nor the politicians of the New South would set aside any special favors for the frail Democracy of New England. Andrew, Williams, Hoar, and the other Massachusetts Democrats returned to their districts in the summer of 1892 with nothing to show but their scars.[18]

In a single session of Congress most of the reform zeal of Yankee Democrats was played out. They had been elected as a coherent, ambitious band; they came home tired, abused, defeated individuals. The first session of the Fifty-second Congress at the beginning of the nineties telescoped a decade for Massachusetts Democrats, anticipating the whole bitter history of their party's downfall after 1893. The fratricidal strife between free silver and the tariff would continue to plague the national party and finally tear it apart, but for Yankee Democrats much of the damage was done by the summer of 1892. Thereafter Cleveland Democracy in Massachusetts ceased to be a movement and became a holding action. The atmosphere within the party grew petty, sour, and waspish as lonely politicians competed to salvage their careers from the general misfortune. The years from 1892 to 1896 were a time when individual achievements counted heavily for individuals but meant less and less for the party. For Democratic politicians as for the general populace they were years of deepening gloom.

Such was the air in Massachusetts, and across the nation, when Grover Cleveland served as President a second time. His easy election in 1892 concealed only briefly the crisis that would soon undo him. His nomination by the Democrats had ended months of intricate connniving among his enemies in Congress, Tammany Hall, and in the South and West to destroy him with the silver issue. Cleveland by now was a frank and massive bulwark of the conservative virtues, a rock for sound money and fiscal confidence against the "lunacy of poverty." The radical revolt of agrarian America he regarded with impassive scorn, convinced of the foolishness of questioning Democratic orthodoxy, especially the sovereign remedy of tariff reform. His invincible disdain for the agrarian rebels in his party made Cleveland a refuge for eastern Democrats, including those in Massachusetts. Yankee politicians, tariff reformers, Mugwumps, State Street financiers gathered behind him in relief, drawing on his strength where they doubted their own.[19]

Most important Massachusetts Democrats had known no other leader but Cleveland and hurried to line up behind his nomination. ("Every time these callow Mugwumps get together they adopt resolutions without end in praise of Grover Cleveland," remarked Joe Lomasney of Boston's West End.) Cleveland's managers were anxious for an early counterthrust from Massachusetts against Senator Hill, who nailed down the New York delegation in a snap convention. But in the Boston atmosphere of 1892 merely mustering a show of popular support for Cleveland seemed hard. A mass meeting had to be canceled for fear the crisis over silver would drain it of enthusiasm. The best to be hoped for was a loyal delegation to the national convention. A favorite-son boom in the Democratic press for Governor Russell made even this seem doubtful. And Boss Pat Maguire, fighting sturdily for Cleveland, had all he could do to suppress lingering Irish fondness for Senator Hill. Finally William C. Whitney, Cleveland's most potent manager, pulled the Massachusetts Democracy to its feet as he started his masterful nationwide search for delegates. Whitney sent money to Boston to guarantee a friendly delegation, called Bay State party organizers to his secret preconvention conference in New York to plot final strategy, and at the Chicago convention in June Cleveland carried twenty-four of Massachusetts' thirty votes in his first ballot sweep. "It wasn't a fight at all . . . ," Whitney gloated afterwards to Carl Schurz. "It was a grand and enthusiastic rush over the whole field—you never saw anything like it before." The nomination looked like a romp, but it had taken long months, tough talk, and a generous purse. A few days after the convention Whitney received from his old Yankee friend John E. Russell a check for 470 dollars, "your final dividend on investment in Mass[achusetts]." [20]

The campaign of 1892 was quiet, desultory, and dull. The outbreak of labor warfare in Homestead, Pennsylvania, and—nearer home—the lurid axe murder of Lizzie Borden's parents in Fall River, outstripped orthodox politicking in popular interest. Boston politicians made the most of their solemn trips to Buzzards Bay, at the base of Cape Cod where Cleveland spent the summer, to fish and talk politics with their candidate. Governor Russell, seeking his third election, campaigned mostly on his

own, exploiting his unique appeal in the state. Democratic
congressmen worked unhappily to mend fences and obscure their
barren records. ("I dread the campaign, do not you?" George
Fred Williams wrote to Russell. Morosely he added, "I hope to
be defeated this fall; I have no more desire to remain in office
than I had to enter it.") As ever, tariff talk seasoned most oratory,
but little new could be added to the issue. Cleveland's supporters
worked hard to minimize his party's infection by free silver. "In
the Democratic party the friends of free silver have been defeated," declared a Mugwump pamphlet, "and its candidate is a
man who has never swerved from his outspoken opposition to
all legislation which tends to debase the standard of value."
Other Cleveland literature made much of a plank in the Democratic platform favoring revival of state bank currency as a
solution to scarce money in the South and West. This proposal,
part of the price paid at Chicago for a sound-money plank, won
praise from Boston entrepreneurs familiar with credit difficulties
in the South. But on the whole the Democratic cause excited
little public enthusiasm. Josiah Quincy, searching for a catalyst,
suggested that a meeting between Cleveland and old Ben Butler
might enliven the party faithful, but Cleveland regarded Butler
as a dishonorable man and refused to invite him to Buzzards
Bay. Next, a party rally was scheduled in Woburn with an
appearance by Cleveland as the promised attraction. But party
leaders decided to cancel when they learned that a rival crowd
would gather in Woburn the same day to honor prizefighter Jim
Corbett. Corbett, they feared, might outdraw Cleveland.[21]

Cleveland lost Massachusetts to Benjamin Harrison. On the
record of past elections Whitney and the national committee
had not counted on the state. In the magnitude of Cleveland's
national victory (achieved in large part by Populist inroads in the
Republican Midwest), his failure to carry Massachusetts in 1892
surprised no one. What was disheartening was the defeat of the
young Yankee tariff reformers on whom brisk hopes had ridden
two years before. The Massachusetts Democratic delegation to
Congress fell from seven to three; George Fred Williams, Sherman Hoar, and John F. Andrew all went down. No single cause

accounted for their failure. Some laid it to state redistricting the year before, and this had doubtless added to Democratic troubles. Yet the redistricting plan had passed the legislature with bipartisan support and Democratic leaders had professed satisfaction with it. Another factor was neglect of constituents: none of the Yankee congressmen had been avid patronage hunters. But as important a cause as any was the failure of the Yankees to make good on the Democratic promise of 1890. Tariff reform had attracted money and votes in 1890. Resistance to silver and inaction on the tariff attracted neither in 1892. Governor Russell alone escaped the Democratic rout. While Cleveland was losing the state to President Harrison by 26,000 votes, Russell squeaked by to re-election as governor by 2,500 votes. His victory was a singular feat, and it enhanced his reputation as one of the party's brightest young men. Godkin's *Nation* called it "one of the greatest personal triumphs ever achieved by a public man in this country," and added that "no man of his generation has a brighter political future before him, and the best of it is that he deserves all that he has had or may yet receive." Some of Russell's colleagues thought otherwise. Resentment ran high against his ability to avoid the stigma of defeat. With the tide running out on Cleveland Democracy in Massachusetts, Russell's glittering national reputation and popular appeal cost him in political friendships at home. The Cleveland Democrat John E. Russell summed up the local feeling succinctly in the wake of the election: "I am greatly disappointed in Massachusetts in this hour of victory . . . The election of Wm. E. R. with an adverse council and legislature and strong vote for Harrison is no triumph. It is only a continuance of the protest against the local machine. At a critical moment we have lost our influence in Congress." [22]

Yankee Democrats watched Cleveland's second administration with a less heady sense of involvement than they had the first. Meanwhile, Democratic strength in Massachusetts ebbed steadily, receding to its base in Boston. By the time Russell left the governor's chair in December 1893 the hope of turning the Bay State into an anchor of New England Democracy had about collapsed. The grand strategy of seaboard axis between Yankee Democrats and the Democrats of the New South now seemed a fond, youthful illusion. With the Southern Populist revolt steadily gaining momentum, Cleveland's administration from the cabinet down became a haven for southern casualties of the agrarian uprising.[23] In Massachusetts one saw a comparable trend. With the notable exception of Boston's Richard Olney, Democratic participation in the new administration was mainly confined to men who had tired of competing for elective office. In fact the decision whether to accept the solace of patronage from President Cleveland was weighed by virtually every important Democratic politician in the state after 1892. Governor Russell, John F. Andrew, and George Fred Williams shunned the quest for plums and returned to private law practice. On the other hand, Patrick Collins landed the London consul-generalship, Charles S. Hamlin became Assistant Secretary of the Treasury, Sherman Hoar became a United States District Attorney and Joseph O'Neil a United States Subtreasurer in Boston, and Josiah Quincy became Assistant Secretary of State. All but Quincy had eagerly sought their jobs.

Cleveland's selection of Richard Olney to be his Attorney General resulted from a determination to ground the new administration in commercial Boston through the traditional New England cabinet member. Cleveland first considered Olney for Secretary of State and later Secretary of Navy, but Olney indicated his preference for the Justice Department. Cleveland's attraction to him was irrelevant to state politics. Olney's habits had made him an inconspicuous Democrat, although he was an effective fund raiser for important campaigns. An occasional game of tennis with Governor Russell had kept him on happy terms with the local party hierarchy. Since 1884 he had applied himself to corporation law and become Boston's leading railroad lawyer. A self-confident, hard-headed man of bulldog virtues, he enjoyed enormous respect among clients and colleagues. If his cabinet appointment startled politicians it alarmed some of his clients. "What will become of the Boston & Maine?" wailed one of its directors. The president of the Chicago, Burlington, &

Quincy took a more statesmanlike view. "In a certain sense of course the C. B. & Q. loses by your appointment," he wrote to Olney, "but in a larger sense it in common with every property interest gains. I consider every share of my stock worth more today than yesterday. The danger to property lies in the tendency of politicians to pander to ignorant public opinion, and a strong cabinet while it cannot make the laws can influence the opinion which does make them." The railroaders knew their man. Cleveland's second cabinet, with Olney its strongest member, placed protection to property at the summit of its aims.[24]

Panic and depression, set in motion by events long preceding Cleveland's inaugural in March 1893, gave the new administration early opportunity to show its hand. Financial distress shunted aside hopes for tariff reform at the outset and gave priority to the nation's fiscal problem. From Boston as from New York, advice during the first months of Cleveland's new term aimed at a single goal: the repeal of the Sherman Silver Purchase Act. As European investment in the United States contracted after 1890 and gold left the country, eastern businessmen and bankers attributed the squeeze to silver inflation. Meanwhile the heavy spending of the Harrison administration had combined with the machinery of the Silver Purchase Act to lower drastically the resources of the federal treasury. As the government's gold reserve dwindled steadily toward the sacred one hundred million-dollar minimum a sick chill clutched the financial community. Talk of bimetallism quieted in the East, and preservation of the gold standard became the mania of Cleveland Democrats. In the session of Congress beginning in December 1892, lameduck Congressmen George Fred Williams and John F. Andrew pressed gamely for a Purchase Act repealer. But their efforts were no more successful than their fight for tariff reform the year before. Congress refused to budge.[25]

By the time Cleveland took office, State Street quivered with anxiety over the condition of business. Henry Lee Higginson's letters to Washington in the spring of 1893 chart his fear as the crisis broke. On April 19: "People are in a state to be thrown into a panic at any minute, and, if it comes, and gold is withdrawn, it will be a panic that will wake the dead . . ." On May 5: "We have had the worst day in my experience on the stock exchange, followed by a much quieter feeling and a rally. Pray remember that it is very good people that have been suffering these last few days and not the stock gamblers . . ." On June 2: "I have never seen such a state of affairs as exists at present, and it grows worse daily. Since . . . April things have gone very badly indeed. Everybody is paralyzed . . . everyone expects considerable financial failures." [26]

Despite the panic, Cleveland resisted intense pressure from New York and Boston to call an immediate special session of Congress and attempt repeal of the Silver Purchase Act. He preferred to use the panic as a lesson in fiscal reality to the silver inflationists. The constricting effect of the panic as it spread across the country would teach the South and West, he hoped, the folly of pursuing cheap money as a national policy. State Street took a dim view of the President's pedagogical approach to economic crisis. Government inaction ran against "the business sense of the better part of the country," Higginson lectured Richard Olney. "It seems to me," C. C. Jackson added, "that the Westerners and Southerners must be fully impressed already with the fact that for *some* reason a great deal of gold is hoarded and a great many capitalists and bankers are unwilling to loan them money in their usual easy way—and I can't see what more they will know about the situation next September." The bankers feared that Cleveland's astringent policy would simply increase the clamor from the interior for free silver.[27]

Finally Cleveland agreed to a special session in August. Bankers and Democrats girded for battle. Speaking for both groups in Boston, Sigourney Butler suggested that newspapers in the interior be bought up by willing eastern banks to swing editorial opinion. "Lee, Higginson & Co. are very anxious to do something," he wrote to Olney. "They feel patriotic and want to show it." Edward Atkinson bombarded Washington with "clinching arguments" for repeal until Roger Mills of Texas told him bluntly, "I do not think that anything you have said . . . could induce the men who are fighting the President's position to agree to a speedy repeal of the Sherman Act. The silver mine owning interest will exhaust every power they can to delay to the last moment the passage of the repeal bill and, if possible, to defeat it." Assistant Secretary of State Josiah Quincy found himself consulting constantly with the President on the use of state department patronage to garner doubtful votes. As the fight continued on Capitol Hill, some Cleveland Democrats played quietly with the idea of compromise with the silverites. But Quincy tested sentiment along State Street and found it adamant for repeal. "The thing has gone too far," he reported to presidential adviser Daniel Lamont, "and if we give up beaten now and accept a compromise we shall never hear the last of it, I am afraid. I think a good many business men will try the Democratic party by the test whether it will insist on a vote on this measure, and will act with it or against it in the future as this question is determined." A few days later Cleveland closed the door on compromise, and on October 30, the repealer finally passed.[28]

This victory for gold was little help to Massachusetts Democrats. With hard times fastening down on Boston and the nation, Governor Russell prudently retired from state politics while his record still gleamed, and the Democratic vote in the state fell off sharply in 1893. The party managed to pick up one congressional seat before depression set in when William Everett, the doughty old Mugwump schoolmaster, won Henry Cabot Lodge's vacated seat in a special election. But Everett won by the slimmest of margins and his success was a weak ray among enveloping shadows. By 1894, when the administration finally moved to reform the tariff and make good on Democratic promises of the past six years, the President's friends in Massachusetts watched from the sidelines, hoping for little, expecting the worst. Forgotten were the ringing epithets and gallant charges of the past. Now the chief wish was to get the thing over with. Politicians agreed with businessmen that delay and uncertainty over tariff reform were postponing chances for recovery. Cautious investors and employers were waiting for Congress to define the terms of new risks, the argument ran. Mugwump banker Henry Lee expressed the prevailing impatience in a public letter to the New England Tariff Reform League:

> Is there a man in business of any sort whose progress is not arrested, whose prosperity is not diminished, by doubt as to tariff legislation?
>
> Protectionists look with dread, you and I with hope, upon tariff reform; but both reformers and protectionists long for a determination of the question, a period to the present stagnation.
>
> We have been already tortured and nauseated by the silver demagogues in the Senate! May we escape tariff egotists and cranks!
>
> If the Democrats cannot use the power they possess, they will be dispossessed by the exasperated and earnest people.[29]

Irritation turned to disgust as the low tariff schedules of Congressman William L. Wilson were systematically pulled apart and revised upward in the Senate under Senator A. P. Gorman's cool direction. "That wretched Senate is giving us all away," Winslow Warren wrote to William Everett. ". . . while I hope to see the party succeed—if it has no principles to stand by and for, of what good is it?" Everett, who was discovering that life as a freshman Congressman was no match for his carefully nursed dream of public eminence, watched the desecration helplessly. When the final Wilson-Gorman Tariff came to a vote, he refused to support it. But most tariff reformers in Boston accepted its meager gains, noting the law's improvement on the McKinley Tariff of 1890, and were heartily relieved to be done with the issue. It was a measure of the sapped vitality of the tariff reform movement by 1894 that the income tax clause inserted in the Wilson bill by western Democratic congressmen aroused more concern among Massachusetts Democrats than did Senator Gorman's tariff amendments. While the *Labor Leader*, Boston's trade-union weekly, and Pat Maguire's *Republic* favored the income tax, most Democratic leaders, Irish and Yankee, found the provision highly distasteful.[30]

Ironically, Pat Maguire, a late convert to tariff reform, had become its most strident advocate in Boston. The *Republic*'s assaults on protection compared favorably with the most fervent Mugwump forays of the past. When Maguire warmed to an issue his editorial imagination knew no bounds. In the *Republic's* view, the depression resulted directly from Republican protectionist policy which generated domestic monopoly, price-fixing, stagnation, and ultimate paralysis. To supplement this hypothesis the *Republic* suggested further that protectionist manufacturers had shut down their factories in order to prevent tariff reform. Along similar lines, the paper found sinister implications behind Coxey's Army—that ragtail band of unemployed which momentarily diverted attention from the congressional tariff fight by marching on Washington in the spring of 1894. Noting Coxey's origins in protectionist Ohio and the route of his army through protectionist Pennsylvania (whose industrial towns fed and sheltered his men), the *Republic* concluded that Coxey was secretly sponsored by protectionists seeking to embarrass Grover Cleveland and enlist labor in the cause of high protection. No doubt some Democratic readers found solace in these explanations of their party's plight.[31]

Eighteen-ninety-four, a frightening year for most Americans, accelerated the downward spiral of Democratic fortunes. When the elections that year were over, New England had one lonely Democrat in Congress—Boston's John F. Fitzgerald—as compared with the thirteen elected in 1890. Defeat was more than statistical. The threat to social stability implied in Coxey's Army was fulfilled in July in the violence of Chicago's Pullman strike. Depression, industrial strife, contention over silver and disappointment over the tariff combined to drain Yankee reformers of desire for further innovation in national affairs. By 1895 their glad adventure in tariff reform was ended. Josiah Quincy, a founder of the Tariff Reform League eleven years before, delivered the keynote address at the Democratic state convention in 1895. His comments on the tariff betrayed his party's exhaustion:

> The Democratic party now occupies the position of conservator of the industrial peace. It defends the maintenance of the present status. It occupies the conservative position. It has had its day in court, and its work is on trial before the jury of public opinion. It is willing to leave it there. All it asks is time for the formation of an intelligent opinion.

Privately the tariff reformers admitted nostalgia for the lost mood of the 1880's. In contrast the future seemed empty of hope. "How confused the future of our politics looks to me now," William L. Wilson wrote to a friend in Massachusetts. "The magnificent army which we rallied by ten years hard but inspiring work, to carry out the reform of the Tariff, has been so long involved in internecine war that it seems a collection of hostile camps." [32]

In Massachusetts, Wilson's words were borne out in the splintering of the entente between regular Democrats and those Mugwumps who had delicately entered the party on the strength of the tariff issue in the eighties. Concern over the abuses of high protection had kept Democrats and Mugwumps together since 1887. Now the possibility of silver replacing the tariff as the cohesive issue of the national party had gone far to loosen Mugwumps from Democratic ties. Admiration for Grover Cleveland was once more clouded by doubts about his party. Dissatisfaction was vented in characteristic style. Mugwumps began to talk about a new party. Tariff reformers unworried over silver could remain Democrats, the talk ran. Men who believed in protection and sound money were natural Republicans. But where could the low-tariff, sound-money man go? As early as 1891 Mugwump advocates of a new party had coined a name—the Columbian Party. Let the Columbians organize at once, they suggested, seize Grover Cleveland as their own, and free him of the burden of being a Democrat. Edward Atkinson, a passing proponent of the notion, saw a parallel in the Free-Soil party of his youth, and urged it on Cleveland's supporters. The Columbian Party died unsung when Cleveland accepted his own party's nomination in 1892. But Mugwump discontent steadily gathered force.[33]

Mugwump expectations for Cleveland's second administration were modest and subdued, bearing no trace of the exhilaration of 1884. The views of Charles Francis Adams, published in *Forum,* were perhaps too fatalistic to be typical but indicated the worn-out anticipation of his kind. Adams now regarded tariff reform as a vain illusion. Protectionism was a disease fixed in the blood of the people, he noted, spreading among laborers and capitalists alike, corrupting the truths of Jefferson and Adam

Smith. To expect Cleveland to check this general malaise was preposterous. "Like other sweeping natural movements," Adams wrote, "this one must work itself out in a natural way and in its own time." Prospects for progress in civil service reform were somewhat brighter; the President might hasten the cure for the office-seeking epidemic by promptly expanding the classified list. But for the rest, Adams concluded that "there is no reasonable ground to suppose that this country, in entering upon the second administration of President Cleveland, enters upon any new era in its existence at all." [34]

Many of Adams' fellow Mugwumps found the new issues of the nineties, particularly the silver question, unpleasant and worrisome but essentially uninteresting. They waited out the crisis over repeal of the Silver Purchase Act with growing restlessness, anxious to reimpose the simple moral terms of political judgment which the civil service issue had provided a decade before. Discussing the new administration's patronage performance over the first seven months, Moorfield Storey wrote to Carl Schurz, "In judging Cleveland we must, I suppose, make allowances for a man engaged in a desperate contest with his own party on the silver question, but I confess myself much disappointed . . . I have not felt like saying much till the silver fight is over, but after that I think we should open fire all along the line." Storey could hardly wait. The bitterest patronage controversy of the 1890's was already under way. At the October 1893 meeting of the Reform Club in Boston Storey launched an attack on Josiah Quincy's record as Cleveland's Assistant Secretary of State which brought long-standing private misgivings about Quincy's behavior boiling into the open air. When the controversy subsided Mugwumps and Democrats stood farther apart than at any time since 1887. [35]

Mugwump distrust for Quincy had waxed with his rising power in the Democratic party. By 1893 the silent Brahmin seemed on the threshold of a career as promising as Governor Russell's. He was the recognized manager of party affairs in Massachusetts. Called by William C. Whitney to New York to help manage the Cleveland campaign of 1892, he had moved

within the center circle of the national party structure. He mixed
political acumen with a capacity for hard work which astonished
all who knew him. Through the campaign he had directed both
the propaganda bureau of the national committee in New York
and Governor Russell's state campaign in Boston, traveling between the two cities by night train. All this served only to
blacken his fame among the Mugwumps. One wrote to Carl
Schurz in December 1892:

> Hereabouts my Independent friends fear the influence of Josiah
> Quincy in our Massachusetts matters. Quincy is a man of small nature
> who is engaged in putting his opponents "in a hole" and although of
> one of our "first families" is the remnant of a glorious past as far as
> political virtue is concerned. Nevertheless he is most active and
> skilful in campaigning, untiring, fertile in expedients, but alas! ready
> for very low measures and men to gain party advantage. He is as you
> know always before the public, is a National Committee man, and
> has no other color than Regular Democratic in dark shade.[36]

When Grover Cleveland asked the Republican Judge Walter
Q. Gresham to be his Secretary of State, Gresham accepted on
the condition that he be relieved of all patronage responsibilities.
Cleveland's adviser Daniel Lamont then asked Josiah Quincy
to serve as Gresham's Assistant Secretary and distribute the
consular patronage for the new administration. Quincy took the
job reluctantly, knowing it would shatter the remains of his
reputation as a civil service reformer. His stay in the Capitol
was dismal from beginning to end. The post he served was traditionally regarded as among the pleasantest in Washington. Yet
it was surrounded by ambiguities which became explicit in 1893.
The American consular service was in sorry shape by the end of
the nineteenth century. Regarded with derision in the press and
with easy contempt by politicians, it was a lush source of party
patronage. During the four years of the Harrison administration
75 percent of the consular offices changed hands, and the quality
of the service remained poor. Yet its long association across the
century with American men of letters, established by Irving,
Motley, Hawthorne, Howells, Bret Harte, and others, had vested
it with a glow of virtue in the New England mind. In 1886 a

speaker at the Reform Club had described it as the last area left in American public service for the educated amateur. Rising levels of American trade and tourism had increased the consuls' burdens. ("If I were to do all they seem to expect," one complained from Glasgow in 1885, "I should have to be as learned as Edward Atkinson.") Consular posts nevertheless continued to be regarded by many as sinecures for gentlemen of merit and worthy avocation, and when Josiah Quincy assumed his duties requests for places promptly began to arrive from genteel Boston. They competed on his desk with letters from Democratic politicians the nation over.[37]

Quincy's task was complicated further by the crisis over repeal of the Sherman Silver Purchase Act. With votes hanging on every administration move, he worked under President Cleveland's close guidance in choosing his men. First things came first. Consular posts must be used as bait to win reluctant congressmen to the administration side in the fight for repeal. While Cleveland and Quincy tried to reward competence wherever they had a chance, the President did not feel he could jeopardize chances for repeal by raising congressional hackles over patronage. In the scramble for votes no holds were barred, and Quincy's work violated many niceties. The sight of this erstwhile Brahmin civil service reformer dealing in offices over the counter in coarse, time-honored Washington tradition was a spectacle Mugwumps could not abide. Quincy's old Harvard classmate, Theodore Roosevelt, a member of the civil service commission at the time, reported to the Mugwumps regularly on Quincy's behavior, relishing the irony of the situation. Quincy was turning out consuls at five times the rate of his predecessor, Roosevelt reported to Carl Schurz: "he hunts through the departments for patronage places as a pig hunts truffles." New England Mugwumps watched with pursed lips. "A fine employment for a Josiah Quincy," one commented. "But Quincys have not been born as *large* as they were in older times. Adamses are ahead." Sensitive to mounting criticism, Quincy mustered tortured arguments to defend his course. While acknowledging the politics behind his appointments he insisted they had not lowered the quality of the service. What special virtue lay in retaining men who had gotten places themselves through political influence, he asked Schurz, if in removing them he could achieve greater efficiency? He concluded plausibly: "We may fairly be asked to be judged by the character of our appointees." [38]

But Quincy had violated the high canon of civil service reform by admitting partisan motives. By October Mugwumps could contain themselves no longer. Moorfield Storey engaged Quincy in blunt debate at the Reform Club. Godkin's *Nation*—which earlier had approved Quincy's arguments for quick removals—now lashed him for publicly defending himself ("Mr. Quincy's shame is great enough without such glorying in it."). *Good Government,* the organ of the Civil Service Reform League, joined the chorus of rebuke ("To try to keep one's toes in the Reform stirrups while seated astride the spoils saddle is neither honest or patriotic."). The League itself considered whether to invoke its ultimate sanction and expel Quincy from its membership.[39]

After seven months in Washington, Quincy finished his thankless task and came home. Democrats were glad to have him back. "While I think your presence there is a great help to the administration," Governor Russell had written to him earlier in the year, "I believe it can get along without you far easier than the Democratic party here in Massachusetts . . . I know I only speak the voice of the whole party when I say we are all most earnest that you should be back here if you can without too much sacrifice to manage things as you have in the past." But Quincy came home under a cloud. Early in 1894 a Boston Republican reported to Senator Lodge that Quincy had "lost caste here in every way so much that I doubt if he [will be] able to recover the lost ground. I hear him spoken of by most every one, regardless of politics, as being either a fool or a knave . . ." Quincy's rupture with Moorfield Storey enforced the stigma he carried as the price of his political power. By mixing too candidly with political necessities he had violated a cardinal rule of public behavior among Cleveland Democrats. He lacked the gift, so common among that breed, for protesting his own virtue.

So he paid the politician's penalty for lack of pretense. Success in the repeal fight brought accolades to Grover Cleveland. Success in winning Massachusetts elections had brought accolades to William E. Russell. Quincy's contribution to these events had won only public opprobrium. Now suddenly he discovered he had traveled beyond the pale, and ranked in the Mugwump mind with the Hills and Gormans of the Democratic party.[40]

Quincy continued as party chairman for the next two years, trying to work the old formulas for Democratic success in Massachusetts. But the failure of tariff reform and resurgent Mugwump concern for civil service reform proved formidable obstacles. Contributions from wealthy Mugwump patrons like John Murray Forbes, Henry L. Pierce, and Charles R. Codman were no longer forthcoming. In 1894, for the first time in years, the Mugwumps refused to publish their annual "Address to the Independent Voters of Massachusetts" whose glittering list of supporting names had fortified Democrats in the past. Moorfield Storey, now thoroughly disgusted with Democratic civil service performance, had always written the Address in earlier years. "I haven't cared to touch it this year," he told a reporter. So far had Democrats and Mugwumps fallen out that not even Cleveland's appointment of the conscientious old Mugwump Winslow Warren as Collector of the Port of Boston could mollify his friends. When Warren intimated that he planned to hire some Democrats where the rules permitted, the Reform Club solemnly dispatched a committee of three to reprimand him. When Warren suggested at the Reform Club that under present economic conditions other problems pressed more heavily on the government than civil service reform, Richard Henry Dana interrupted him, shouting: "No! No! I don't believe it!" In the teeth of depression, violence, and political disaster, the Mugwumps kept up their chant for civil service reform with remarkable persistence. It made a hollow echo now down deserted corridors, a cry of wistful and tired nostalgia.[41]

The searing blasts of depression did not, of course, leave the Mugwumps untouched. Many of them depended on their investments, and some had been hit hard by the panic. If their material losses averaged out to insignificance next to the mass poverty of unemployment, the experience could be withering nevertheless. "They were for me years of simple Hell," Charles Francis Adams recalled, "years during which I had to throw everything aside, and devote myself to rehabilitating a wreck . . . The dislocation this event caused—coming just when it did— shattered my whole scheme of life. Breaking in upon it, it broke it up. I was sixty-three years old, and a tired man, when at last the effects of the 1893 convulsion wore themselves out, and my mind was once more at ease . . ." [42] Depression did greater violence to the Mugwump conception of reform. For years men like Adams had argued against corruption and party dictation in American public life. The apathy of "the people" before the base spectacle of American politics had appalled them. They had repeatedly demanded that the public arouse itself. Now, under economic duress, the public was very much aroused. "The people," from the followers of Tom Watson and Mary E. Lease to those of Jacob Coxey, Gene Debs, and Daniel DeLeon, were trumpeting their angry demands. Meanwhile both major political parties were fending off challenges by agrarians and silverites in a harsh contest for party control. The new mood of the nineties, embittered by hard times and accumulated social grievance, mocked the Mugwumps' old demand. It was an ugly jest.

The Mugwump clung doggedly to his moral precepts. Moorfield Storey, addressing the American Bar Association in 1894, confessed shock at the bloody rioting of the Pullman Strike in Chicago, where a year before the White City of the World Exposition had crowned four hundred years of American progress. But the disparity between the current crisis and the tranquillity of earlier years forced no change in Storey's diagnosis of the national malady. Refusing to take the resentments of farmers, laborers, and the unemployed at face value, he traced society's sickness as in the past to the corruption of politicians. The disease had merely worsened to the point where now "bribery is made the excuse for anarchy." If only the lower classes could trust their elected officials, Storey felt, they would suffer depres-

sion miseries with little protest. Storey did not question the
excellence of prevailing sound-money policies, taxation policies,
urban franchise policies, or railroad policies. But when wise laws
were bought, he insisted, the damage was beyond calculation.
Once the people were convinced that

> their misery at any minute is the result of laws purchased by their
> employers or creditors, if they have lost their faith in peaceful agita-
> tion and relief within the law, they will begin to consider how they
> can help themselves, law or no law. Populist movements, Coxey
> armies, Chicago, Homestead, and Pittsburgh strikes are symptoms,
> and symptoms to which we cannot close our eyes . . . Honesty is
> justice and it is the cornerstone of self-government. Foreign war,
> pestilence, and disaster unite and strengthen a people, but no govern-
> ment can long resist the insidious influence of general corruption.[43]

Honesty is justice. In this small equation Storey distilled the
Mugwump response to the social tumult of the 1890's.

The politics of economic crisis had reduced the Mugwump-
Democratic alliance to a cipher. By 1895 the remaining friends
of Grover Cleveland stood at bay, without allies and without
issues. Late in August Democratic party leaders in Massachusetts
gathered at the Algonquin Club in Boston for a birthday party
in honor of Charles S. Hamlin, the able, colorless lawyer whom
Cleveland had made Assistant Secretary of the Treasury. With
the table cleared and pleasantries completed, William E. Russell,
Josiah Quincy, Colonel Taylor of the *Globe*, and the rest grimly
turned on Hamlin and asked him to run for governor. Of course
there was no chance of winning—since Russell's narrow victory
in 1892 the Democratic state-wide vote had dwindled seriously—
but Hamlin's candidacy would at least guarantee the Cleveland
administration an honorable hearing. Moreover, party tradition
dictated that a man could make three runs for the governorship,
and prospects could not fail to brighten in the next two years.
Meanwhile the party leadership would be in reliable hands. It
was feared that if Hamlin refused, the nomination would go by
default to the only man who wanted it—former Congressman
George Fred Williams. Despite urgent pleading, Hamlin rejected
the bid, and Williams was nominated at the state convention.[44]

Democrats had harbored a vague distrust for George Fred Williams ever since his sudden attack on the West End Railroad Company back in 1890. In his strident righteousness Williams had accumulated many enemies in both parties. As Pat Maguire's *Republic* carefully put it in 1895, "his chief element of weakness as a politician has been his frankness in discussing issues and policies." Williams was an erratic and unrestrained campaigner. He rarely pulled his punches, and his colleagues were never quite sure they would not be grazed. And although his social relationships and public pronouncements had stamped him as a normal Cleveland Democrat, his volatile, questing mind made him prey to reform proposals his more conservative associates could not accept. When he tried to insert planks in his 1895 campaign platform demanding public regulation of telephone rates and free trolley transfers, they were struck out by timid party leaders. Undaunted, Williams waged a bold campaign attuned to class tension and industrial unrest. His election eve speeches in Boston were honed to a radical edge. Colleagues listened uneasily while Williams announced: "The history of civilization has been the record of a struggle against privileged classes who through the possession of the government, through violence, or through extortion in taxation, have aimed to support themselves in luxury and power at the expense of the toilers of the earth." Democrats had not talked like this in years. In an atmosphere of economic depression and widespread unemployment Williams' language seemed to smack of desperate, irresponsible demagoguery. Orthodox party leaders must have felt a glum relief when on election day Williams polled the lowest Democratic vote of the decade thus far.[45]

Cleveland Democrats approached the presidential year 1896 with little enthusiasm. Whatever faction controlled the national party machinery in the crucial months before the nominating convention, there seemed scant prospect that Cleveland's successor in the White House could be a Democrat. The Republican tide, mounting since the crash of 1893, seemed sure of cresting in 1896. Democratic party leaders thought less of the slim possibility of victory than they did of maintaining the integrity of their party as they knew it. Opposition to silver—opposition to agrarian control of the party—became a grim, uniting faith. "National decency," "honor," and "civilization" were now at stake. Any Yankee politician with the effrontery to challenge orthodoxy courted swift oblivion. As they prepared with other bastions of eastern Democracy to help as they could in the coming struggle with the West, Massachusetts Democrats had little inkling that the silver issue would shatter their ranks at home.

CHAPTER EIGHT · 1896

EIGHTEEN-NINETY-SIX was a year of trauma for the Democratic party. In July, at the party's national convention in Chicago, the contest between Cleveland Democrats and free-silver insurgents reached its last crisis. In one mighty effort southern and western agrarian Democrats snapped the leading strings that had bound them to the eastern seaboard for a generation. Suddenly Grover Cleveland's followers were dispossessed, as their party became the vehicle of angry Populistic protest. Their own political loyalties were strained beyond the breaking point. The campaign of 1896 left the Democratic party a broken heap. In few states were Democrats able to preserve intact that subtle machinery of precedent and accommodation which had allowed them to live together under a common label. Americans were witness to a rare event—the splintering of a national party organization by the implacable demands of sectional interest and radical ideas. Across the country, in places where it mattered little in the final count, the campaign precipitated rending discord among local Democrats. One of these places was Boston.

When the year began Cleveland Democrats were strangely unprepared for the shock awaiting them. Dismayed as they were with the sorry fortunes of the administration, they seemed reluctant to face up to the possibility that the year might bring party disruption as well as party defeat. An agrarian leader later wrote,

One of the curious features of the movement . . . looking to the organization of the [silver] Democrats in the party for the purpose of capturing the Chicago Convention was the fact that the Eastern Democrats seemed to be utterly incapable of comprehending what we were doing. While we openly stated our purpose, the knowledge that we had succeeded came upon them like a thunder-clap, and this, notwithstanding the fact that we had given information to the papers, all along, showing just the progress we were making.[1]

From January to June eastern Democrats made no concerted effort to renovate the instruments of convention control they had used so efficiently in the past. Activity was hindered by the stubborn passivity of the administration. Grover Cleveland sulked ponderously in the White House, awaiting party defeat with a certainty that it would somehow vindicate him. For months his calculated silence about a third term and his refusal to encourage other candidates kept his followers musing anxiously over strategy. Lacking presidential leadership, Cleveland Democrats found their restlessness souring into jealousy and mutual suspicion. Communication among party managers in Washington, New York, Boston, and the outposts of the West was random and unsatisfactory. The party Warwick of the past, William C. Whitney, had cooled over the administration's gold policy and was no longer in close touch with the President. Having made a realistic assessment of the political climate, Whitney was mostly occupied in squelching talk of his own candidacy. Up until the eve of the convention eastern party leaders could agree on little except the hope that the party would not topple to free silver. It became axiomatic among them that the fight over a platform would be decisive. If honest money were sustained, then surely a suitable candidate could be found. Even with Cleveland and Whitney out of the running, there were plenty of eastern aspirants. In administration circles Secretary of the Treasury John G. Carlisle was regarded as a likely candidate. Outside Washington, Cleveland Democrats preferred someone untainted by the President's recent record. Speculation centered about Cleveland's old rival David B. Hill, Governor Pattison of Pennsylvania, and, above all, William E. Russell of Massachusetts.[2]

Billy Russell was as well equipped as any man to carry forward the principles of Cleveland Democracy. Happily out of politics during the past three grim years, he had just turned thirty-nine. From the years of his governorship he retained a

brilliant national reputation as speaker, vote getter, and executive. Journalists and editors from Adolph Ochs and Henry
Watterson to Walter Hines Page and Richard Watson Gilder
sought his friendship, influence, and opinion. The liberal economist Richard T. Ely had once sent for a copy of a speech;
Wisconsin Democrats requested details about his labor legislation; the Indiana boss Tom Taggart had urged him to stump
the Hoosier country in 1892. Flowers, cigars, and babies had
been named after him. The crowning accolade came when
Orison Swett Marden, the well-known chronicler of pluck, principle, and push, in preparation for a new book, sought Russell's
advice to aspiring youth, along with that of William Gladstone,
Otto von Bismarck, and John Wanamaker. The years from 1893
to 1896, so disastrous for Russell's party, were a pleasant inter-
lude in his own career. Relaxing in the comfort of his Brattle
Street home amid the oil sketches, painted tiles, and bric-a-brac
commemorating his success, summering at fashionable Coolidge
Point, Manchester-By-The-Sea, on the North Shore, he savored
the private fruits of public eminence and found them good. The
family law office on State Street bustled with activity, and the
light duties of referee for several major life insurance companies
paid a generous extra salary. Russell, however, remained ambitious.[3]

He had been often spoken of as presidential timber in 1892
during the months when it had seemed that Cleveland could not
be nominated. Russell's potential backing had extended beyond
New England into the South and Midwest. Ohio Governor James
E. Campbell, among others, had been ready to support him. But
Russell had bided his time. His acquaintance with Cleveland
had by then ripened into warm friendship, and along with
Richard Watson Gilder and the actor Joseph Jefferson, he became a welcome member of Cleveland's fishing circle at Buzzards Bay. The night Cleveland was nominated in 1892, Russell
was with him at Gray Gables, keeping tabs on the convention
by telegraphic wire from Chicago. Cleveland was in his own
words "exceedingly fond of Russell," and despite twenty years'
difference in age the two men got on famously.[4]

After 1892 they saw and heard less of each other. Observers laid this to Russell's singular gubernatorial victory that year while Cleveland was losing Massachusetts, or, alternatively, to Russell's pique at being ignored in the formation of Cleveland's second cabinet. Nevertheless Russell remained a stout defender of administration policy. In articles for *Forum, North American Review,* and *Century Magazine,* he attributed the depression to the cynical indulgence of the Republicans under Harrison and tried to allay fears about Democratic weakness for free silver. Meanwhile he resolutely kept his eye glued on the tariff issue as his party's best hope for future success. As the next presidential election approached, Russell began to draw away from close identification with the administration. In November 1895, writing in *Century,* he ended a defense of his party with the careful suggestion that it needed new leadership. Democrats, he said, had no right "to demand or expect that he who has so gallantly led them in three campaigns, and twice to victory, will again be their standard-bearer. His own wish, no doubt, will be to retire on the laurels he has well won to a rest he has well earned." When the Venezuela boundary crisis broke in December 1895, Russell, following the predominant sentiment of State Street and most Mugwumps, criticized the President's bellicose message to Great Britain and went so far as to suggest that the Monroe Doctrine be submitted to arbitration to discover what it meant. By early 1896 Russell had established himself as a friendly critic of the administration and yet was widely regarded in the East as Cleveland's logical successor in the party.[5]

In February 1896 a group of Cleveland Democrats in New York sounded Russell on the possibility of his running for the nomination. Russell was receptive. It was no year for a Democrat, but a creditable showing by a man of his youth would count heavily toward future preference. Friends immediately laid plans to secure his endorsement as a favorite son. This was no easy hurdle. Russell's abstention from state politics after 1893, his refusal to stump for a lost cause, had sat poorly with local party leaders. They were in no mood now to flock to his colors. In fact they launched a tentative flank attack, seeking to embarrass Russell over the Venezuela crisis by endorsing Secretary of State Richard Olney. But Olney was angered at being placed in competition with Russell and insisted that his name be dropped from discussion. When Russell formally announced in April that he was a candidate for President, Massachusetts party leaders followed Josiah Quincy's lead and swung behind the former governor. Russell now calculated on solid New England support, probable backing from New York and New Jersey, and whatever help could be salvaged from the wreck of southern business conservatism. A superb opportunity to attract national attention to his cause came when the National Association of Democratic Clubs selected Russell to deliver the annual Jefferson Day address at Monticello. On April 13, before an impressive gathering of cabinet members, senators and congressmen, reporters and reverent pilgrims at Jefferson's home, Russell spoke fervently for party unity and hard money. Even the silver men in the crowd acknowledged his appeal. But if Russell's friends had hoped for a laying on of hands, they were disappointed. President Cleveland failed to attend, and Senator Daniel of Virginia shattered the ceremonial harmony by attacking Russell's views in a vigorous rebuttal.[6]

Russell's chances seemed to brighten momentarily in May. New Jersey came into his camp. *Leslie's Weekly* ran a flattering promotional article about him. The probability that the Republicans would nominate the Ohio protectionist William McKinley strengthened the logic of Russell's candidacy for those who hoped to restore the tariff as the central issue of American politics. McKinley's doubtful record on silver would be helpful. But Republicans remained serenely confident. "All this talk here that if Billy Russell is put up as against McKinley the latter will be defeated," a prominent Boston Republican snorted, "is stuff." From Ohio a partner in Mark Hanna's coal and iron business wrote solicitously to Russell, "I hope you will win, though judging from what little overflows 'the political rooms of this shop,' I hope your campaign will not come this year, for I fear it will have too heavy a load to carry." By June, as state after state in the South and West named free-silver delegates to the

Democratic convention, Russell's chances blackened. His supporters outside Massachusetts, a flimsy coalition of Mugwumps, former congressmen, and terrified southern conservatives like Virginia's Governor O'Ferrall, had received no encouragement from the administration or national party leaders. Michigan's Don Dickinson had Cleveland's ear in these weeks and (according to Washington gossip) was actively opposing Russell. Meanwhile rumors flew about Boston that George Fred Williams was threatening to challenge Russell at the convention. The gamble with destiny had apparently come to nothing.[7]

Then the picture suddenly changed. In St. Louis on June 18 the Republicans nominated McKinley. In New York the same day the old Democratic kingmaker William C. Whitney sent off a hurried note to Russell in Boston. Whitney had canceled his departure for Europe and launched a last-minute effort to save his party from the boiling anarchy of the West. Perhaps it could be done after all, by opposing McKinley with a militant tariff reformer. "Now is your time," Whitney wrote to Russell. "Come with me to Chicago and we will do one of two things—either beat down this craze or save the *esprit de corps* of the eastern democracy by most emphatic action. The last is probably all we can do, but there is more duty in that at the present time than in anything else." Whitney knew that the only hope of averting a western sweep of the convention lay in shrewd use of the party rule requiring two-thirds support for the nomination. His note implied that a third-party nomination was probably all that Russell could realistically hope for. Russell wanted none of this. In a long, careful reply to Whitney he agreed to go to Chicago, but not as an avowed candidate. "I could not and would not be a candidate of any bolting convention if one were held," he added. "Of course it is too early yet to say what action sound money Democrats should take in case the convention goes for free silver. I am very much in doubt if a bolt would be desirable or of any use, but whether there is one or not, if I go to Chicago I must go with my whole heart in the fight for sound money and without any personal interest in the result." Russell had not closed the door. If by some miracle eastern Democrats could control the convention he would be available. This was good enough for Whitney. He scrawled a quick reply:

Thanks for your letter. Do not take any action about candidacy at present. There will be no bolt and no third ticket, . . .

But the fight we make will help any man around whom it centres. Unless you wish it we will not make it on you but do not take any action without we have had a chance to talk.

Show this to any friend you choose. I haven't time to argue or discuss at this moment.[8]

For all his sudden thrashing energy, Whitney could do little to cut through the defeatist lethargy of Cleveland Democrats. Dickinson and others remained suspicious of his motives. Cleveland sat in the White House grumbling over Whitney's failure to keep him informed. Trusting lieutenants in the South and West, accustomed to the peremptory commands of the past, fretted in doubt and confusion. ("There are thousands of plain Democrats like myself," Col. William C. P. Breckinridge wrote from Kentucky, "who are ignorant of the plans of the Eastern leaders, who are patiently and loyally waiting . . .") Whitney had no plans but to cling to the slim advantage of the two-thirds rule and plead for forbearance from the silverites. In a memorandum distributed for use in Chicago by Russell and others he dwelt on the familiar dangers of free silver at length, and then concluded in a pathetic plea:

The Democrats of the East and North know that they always have been, and are today, the truest friends of the people in other sections of the country. They have been tried over and over again, often at times when devotion to principle meant personal or business ostracism, and have never been found wanting. Now they are informed by the new leaders of the South and West, some of whose names have not long been familiar to the people of the country, that they are no longer wanted in the Democratic party.

Can it be possible that those who assume this attitude truly represent the millions of men throughout the South and West who certainly hitherto have seemed to entertain a fraternal feeling towards their fellow-Democrats in the North and East?[9]

Each day brought news which made the rebellion seem more

profound and pervasive than ever. As Billy Russell prepared to leave for Chicago he sustained another jolt. On the morning of July 2 George Fred Williams announced his conversion to free silver. "The time has come for a great popular uprising," Williams declared, "and I propose to be in it." This stunning bolt instantly split the Massachusetts delegation and hamstrung Russell in his own city. At one stroke George Fred Williams paid off a debt of resentment accumulating since 1890 and shattered the Democratic party in Massachusetts. That afternoon Russell left Boston to join Whitney's private trainload of politicians, editors, and financiers bound for Chicago. With these travelers, agents of the once-awesome power of the eastern Democracy, rode Russell's final hopes for the presidency. "You have beyond any man in this country the ability to utilize this great occasion . . . ," Whitney had told him a few days before. "Do not neglect this great opportunity." With his party on the edge of ruin and his own career in jeopardy at home, Russell could find little solace even in Whitney's support. He arrived in Chicago a tormented man.[10]

For four days Whitney's sound-money forces worked frantically to organize their resistance before the convention opened. But it was obvious from their first hours in Chicago that eastern money and eastern oratory carried no weight. The hotels swarmed with a new breed of Democrat, many of whom had never attended a national convention before, rough, confident, lacking deference, men of baggy pants and hard eye whose voices snapped in hot defiance as they prepared to seize a party. For Democrats of every vintage and persuasion the crisis of a decade neared resolution on July 9 as the convention opened debate on its platform. The majority report declared for free silver and opposed any further agitation of the tariff issue until the money question was settled. It criticized the Supreme Court for finding the income tax unconstitutional. It criticized civil service reform for tending to establish life tenure for public officials. It boldly criticized Grover Cleveland's intervention in the Pullman strike and his trafficking with the House of Morgan to cushion the gold reserve. It praised the tradition against third terms. One after another the planks added up to a calculated indictment by an insurgent majority of the management of public affairs under Cleveland Democrats.[11]

The Easterners mustered a final defense. Hill of New York, Vilas of Wisconsin, and Billy Russell of Massachusetts were chosen to protest against the majority will. Russell waited his turn in taut anxiety. Several witnesses later recalled his intense nervousness, his bitter mumblings, his pale face, and harried eye, all in stark contrast to his usual easy calm. Finally his time came. Standing frail, small, and tired before the great hostile crowd, he made his last appeal to the new democracy of the West. Acknowledging that he spoke for a state and region that lacked the power to enforce its views in the convention, he asked only for pause and reconsideration. All that was left now was the ability to protest, not bitterly, not with hostility, but with sadness:

We did not think that we should . . . be invited under new and radical leadership to a new and radical policy; that we should be asked to give up vital principles for which we have labored and suffered, repudiate Democratic platforms and administrations, and at the demands of a section urging expediency be asked to adopt a policy which many of us believe invites perils to our country and disaster to our party . . .

Oh, that from this great majority, with its power, there might come the one word of concession and conciliation . . .

It was the last speech of Russell's life. He was hardly heard. When he finished, a chesty, black-haired man hurried down the aisle from the Nebraska delegation and mounted the platform two steps at a time. It was in response to the pleas of Russell, Hill, and Vilas that William Jennings Bryan delivered his famous declaration of defiance. "If protection has slain its thousands," Bryan cried, while Russell listened in wilted exhaustion, "the gold standard has slain its tens of thousands!" The convention hall fell silent before this powerful voice. The new Democratic party had found its issue and its leader. A day later George Fred Williams, in open enmity to Russell now, seconded Bryan's nomination for the presidency.[12]

Russell left Chicago a broken man. After spending a day at his summer place on Coolidge Point and another at his office in Boston, he departed with old companions for a rest in the quiet of the Canadian forest. On July 16, in a log cabin in Quebec on a river off the Bay of Chaleur, he died in his sleep. A heart ailment was given as the probable cause. His native city responded with open sorrow. At Cambridge City Hall, while high winds flapped the black-draped bunting, thirty thousand passed his casket. President Cleveland attended the funeral, gray-faced and visibly aged. Boston's Irish Catholic poet, Louise Imogen Guiney, composing her grief in solemn lines, saluted

> One sunny strength illimitably needed,
> Felled by the Hewer in the Northern wild.

In a long letter to the *Transcript*, Russell's Harvard classmate Barrett Wendell searched for the meaning of the event. Russell, "by temperament perhaps the most ardent man of the people whom our time has known," had possessed a remarkable ability to unite a whole community behind him, regardless of race or class. Wendell wondered how long the very notion of community could survive in New England as unequal wealth bred growing differences of temper, education, and belief between rich and poor. It was a rare politician whom both classes could still comprehend. "Such a figure," Wendell concluded, "we have lost in Russell. The profound sense of public bereavement, so spontaneously evinced, then is no trivial fact . . . It expresses how classes and masses alike realize the transcendent value of an interpreter." The symbolism of Russell's death was not lost on the rest of the country. In the formal expressions of regret carried in the press one noted a sense that the conservative wing of the Democratic party had lost more than an able lieutenant; it had lost much of its resilience for the future.[13]

Meanwhile the rest of the Massachusetts delegation had returned from Chicago. On July 14, George Fred Williams arrived home in Boston, traveling on a separate train. Williams' decision to bolt for free silver was the definitive choice of his career. "In taking this step of supporting a silver Democrat," he had told a *Boston Globe* reporter before the convention, "I realize that I am doomed politically in Massachusetts, and that I shall never be forgiven by men who claim to be Democrats. I realize also that these men can punish me socially and financially, but I invite the persecution with a conscientious feeling that I am doing right by voicing the sentiments of an outraged public." The shock of Williams' heresy spread far and fast. John Hay wrote banteringly to Henry Adams of a fellow passenger on the *Teutonic* homeward bound from England, one of Williams' most devoted followers: "He goes up and down the deck, repeating to himself passages out of G. F.'s anti-silver speeches, and sighing, how are the mighty fallen . . ." In New York, Williams' old mentor Carl Schurz read the news in amazement. "Can this be true?" he asked. "It seems incredible. What is the trouble with Williams?"[14]

One obvious motive was Williams' profound jealousy for Billy Russell. His diary, kept briefly the year before, reeks of the bad blood between the two men:

I stand in his way from now on. He aspires to the *Presidency!* Poor little puffed up play actor, who is so sincere that he thinks he is really Julius Caesar when he is playing the part . . . He must make a fight against me now, as I shall ruin his chances even of honorable mention as a Presidential candidate. But if he dares to oppose me openly, and gives me justification, I can and will crush him beyond recognition.[15]

When the chance came to join in Russell's destruction, Williams seized it eagerly. But his sudden conversion to free silver was more than a cynical act of retribution for past resentments.

Poised always on the edge of any social or political group he belonged to, Williams retained throughout his long life a flair for the romantic, the melodramatic, the unexpected. His latest act was only one evidence among many of his maverick instinct. Tall, red-haired, aristocratic in bearing, he had unsettled his Democratic colleagues repeatedly in recent years. He was a loyal, busy Cleveland man over most of the decade after 1884, but he ached to be tapped for greater things. Barriers in his path to eminence only confirmed his headstrong ways. "Ingrati-

tude, opposition, indifference and cruelty are in waiting for
him, who attacks the wrong," he had written back in 1887; "it is
pardonable to falter, but cowardly to retreat." Predictably his
intense behavior provoked strong comment. William Everett
once told the Reform Club, "I thank God that Mr. Williams has
been foreordained for the glorious purpose of getting people
mad." Others reacted with less enthusiasm. Moorfield Storey,
who yielded to few men in his outspoken ways, once called
Williams "the most indiscreet man on the stump that I know,"
and found much to distrust in his scrambling conduct through
the eighties. In 1890 Williams had gained his first important
chance for fame. His election to Congress, following on the heels
of his turbulent investigation of the West End trolley franchise,
made him a man to be reckoned with in the Massachusetts
Democratic party. In Washington his buoyant, aggressive ways
had marked him with a special reputation among freshman congressmen. His defeat for re-election in 1892 was an abrupt come-
uppance.[16]

Returning to private practice in Boston, Williams experienced
considerable success as an advocate. But the missionary flame did
not die. He hungered for the public causes. "Our salvation must
be worked out through the politician, after all," he wrote to
Charles Francis Adams, "and the lazy and indifferent count but
little here as elsewhere. The evils to be surmounted seem to me
so numerous that I value the frequent opportunity to reach the
people." Meanwhile Williams brooded over his own failure as a
politician. Among his constituents, and among the Boston Irish,
he was regarded as a "dude"—an overeducated, loud-voiced,
arrogant young man who refused to knuckle under to bosses or
to public whims. His congressional fight against silver left him
dissatisfied despite the plaudits it won him on State Street. "The
success of the silver fight gave me standing among business men
and generally as a fighter," he wrote in his diary in 1895, "but
that side of the question is not quite the 'popular' side in the
people's hearts." Williams now began a groping reassessment
of his political faith. He worried whether the controversy over
silver might not lose Democratic tariff reformers stout allies

among western Populists. Moreover, he sensed that behind the tariff issue lay a vastly more profound national problem—the power of the trusts, feeding on protection, extorting public franchises, fixing prices by combination. Williams' dislike of corporate wealth, always lively since his exposé of Henry M. Whitney's West End Company, made him hope that some path could be found through the tariff issue to a new alignment of forces within the Democratic party. If the party could identify itself as the relentless enemy of the trusts, and the champion of the little man everywhere against organized wealth, the ruinous cleavage over silver between eastern and western Democrats might yet be sealed off.[17]

Because of his attempts to probe beyond the accepted limits of party orthodoxy, Williams was one of the few politicians of his day to win praise from Edward Bellamy's Nationalists. In fact, the writer Hamlin Garland, a charter member of the First Nationalist Club of Boston, based his reformist novel, *A Member of the Third House,* on Williams' West End investigation. An important source of Williams' deepening radicalism was his intimacy with Boston's working newspapermen. In particular he had struck up a close friendship with Sylvester Baxter, the Boston journalist who played a key role in the formation of the First Nationalist Club. Baxter became Williams' window on the left. Through the early nineties he kept up a drumfire of advice and criticism, chiding "Dear Fred" for his myopic notions about currency, lecturing him on the fallacies of Jeffersonian laissez faire, sending him Populist tracts, recommending to him the works of Boston's radical economist Frank Parsons, and forever urging him to come the whole way toward national ownership of railroads, telephone, and telegraph. As much as any man, Baxter figured behind Williams' bolt to Bryan. By the spring of 1896 Williams was convinced that the currency issue had produced a false division in national politics. Unhappy over his party's conservative retreat in the face of depression and free silver, he decided that his own public career was not going to end on the altar of the gold standard. "My views upon free coinage have very considerably changed . . . ," he wrote an

acquaintance early in July, "and certainly in view of the fact that
the Democratic party is the one party upon which we can rely
to check the dangerous monopolistic tendency of the day, I am
not willing to sacrifice my share of the popular movement in
favor of a monetary system that is radically bad . . ." [18]

Shortly after announcing his conversion, Williams declared
that he would fight to be renominated as the Democratic candidate for Governor of Massachusetts. [19] By embarking on this
course he thrust the issue of Bryanism to the very center of
Boston politics and exploded the liveliest political battle of the
decade. His tactic instantly split the Democratic party into three
contending factions: the supporters of Bryan and Williams; the
Gold Democrats; and the Boston Irish organization.

Bryan's nomination had breathed life into Boston radicalism.
When Williams returned to Boston from the Chicago convention
as Bryan's new ally, he was paraded from the depot to Faneuil
Hall for an uproarious reception. The throng there was an odd
array: men who had wandered without a party since the days of
bold Ben Butler; Nationalists and Populists who had been
watching the mounting revolt of the South and West with a
paternal enthusiasm; minor city politicians discomfited by the
discipline of Pat Maguire's organization; a sizable sprinkling of
trade unionists. What they shared in common was the fact that
for all of them the party of President Cleveland had proved an
ultimate disappointment. Crowding into Faneuil Hall to honor
their new leader, they felt their meeting marked the birth of a
new party from the cracked casing of Cleveland Democracy. [20]

When it became apparent that the regular party organization
was in no mood to make way for the insurgent Bryanites, they
quickly organized themselves to do battle with the old guard.
The Bryan-Sewall-Williams Club, thrown together late in July,
reflected in its leadership the incongruous following Bryan had
lured in Boston. At one extreme were gentlemen of wealth and
breeding like Henry Jaquith and Robert Treat Paine III. Jaquith,
a prosperous young corporation lawyer, had been president of
Boston's Hancock Bank until April 1896. But his free-silver convictions had aroused his directors' ire and they forced his resig-

nation. Delighted to have a man of these credentials in their midst, the Bryanites promptly appointed Jaquith treasurer of the B-S-W Club. Robert Treat Paine III was a more delicate flower. Descended from a signer of the Declaration of Independence, he was the son of Boston's leading philanthropist. Having bustled fruitlessly for years as a Democratic sport in Beacon Hill ward politics, he had more recently become an active member of Boston's Immigration Restriction League. A sensitive, vulnerable young man of generous instincts, Paine saw in the Bryan movement a mass protest of the native American working classes against deprivation, and he wanted to help direct it.[21]

Balanced off against these heartfelt sympathies for Bryan and free silver was an enthusiasm for local party rebellion among minor city politicians whose ambitions had been cramped by Boston's regular Democratic organization. George Fred Williams' heartiest allies in the city came from this quarter. Veteran losers in ward politics and the scramble for municipal patronage, they were ready to clutch at any straw—even Bryanism—to better their luck. Typical was one Timothy Coakley, a lean, fiery, political adventurer who for years had been waging a thoroughly unsuccessful vendetta against City Hall and Pat Maguire. *Harper's Weekly*, in an acid but accurate comment, described Coakley as "an ambitious, strenuous, glib young Irishman, who has been through bankruptcy once or twice, and who looks back on politics as a sort of prolonged wake." Another of Williams' political lieutenants was Thomas F. Keenan, a reporter and state legislator who had recently stirred his colleagues in the State House with a proposal for the legalization of prostitution in Massachusetts. Keenan was mainly renowned as a militant opponent of woman suffrage. Added to the likes of Coakley and Keenan, and reinforcing their petty resentments and awkward stratagems, were several free-lance Democrats from satellite communities surrounding Boston happy to have a crack at unseating the city influence. As allies and advisors to George Fred Williams these men made up a doubtful ballast.[22]

Support of yet another caliber came from the leadership of organized labor in Massachusetts. Frank Foster, Boston's foremost trade unionist, was on the platform waiting to speak for labor when George Fred Williams came home from Chicago to Faneuil Hall. A hard-headed, articulate Yankee typographer, Foster had followed Ben Butler in the early 1880's and worked for the Knights of Labor in the rising of 1886. While he accepted a Democratic nomination for lieutenant-governor that year, he remained aloof from the party organization and turned his talents instead to forging a state affiliate of the American Federation of Labor. Meanwhile he edited the Boston weekly, *Labor Leader.* His prime loyalty was to the trade union, and he labored incessantly for factory reform at the State House in the early nineties. He got results, and so came to accept the strategic necessities of orthodox two-party politics. He also accepted the wage economy and the class-structured society it produced. Distrusting the finespun formulas of Boston's intellectual radicals, he watched with jaundiced eye while local Nationalists, Populists, and Socialists involved the state AFL in a hapless third-party merger in 1894. Foster retained a deep distaste for committing his union movement to utopian ends or political splinter groups of any kind. But now, in 1896, he saw a chance to throw in again with a major party. He had read the Chicago platform enthusiastically. The plank condemning the use of federal injunctions in local labor disputes captured him for Bryan. The strike-breaking injunction seemed to menace the life of free unions, and for protection from it Foster would swallow free silver. What mattered was that at last he could fight the unions' fight from within the Democratic party. To the crowd in Faneuil Hall he declared:

> Those of us who for nearly a quarter of a century have been protesting against the crucifixion of the laboring man upon the cross of gold are only too glad that the time has come when a great party organization preaches the same doctrine . . . There are those of us . . . who do not bow down before gods of gold or silver either. The keynote was struck tonight by Mr. Williams . . . that there are no longer any political questions but the question of the welfare of the common people, the question of bread and butter . . .[23]

Convinced he had witnessed a reincarnation of the Democratic party, Foster turned the *Labor Leader* into a Bryan sheet and eagerly sought a place on the speakers list of the Democratic national committee. Other prominent Massachusetts labor leaders followed suit. Harry Lloyd, a Populist carpenter and official of Boston's Central Labor Union, spoke often at Democratic rallies across the state and toured New York and Ohio in Bryan's cause. George E. McNeill, the grand old man of the Massachusetts labor movement, and James Mellen, the radical Democratic legislator from Worcester, also supported Bryan. Whether they could persuade the rank and file of workingmen to do the same remained in doubt.[24]

Heterodox patricians and lawyers, castoff urban politicians, labor organizers, local Populists, and all the perennial camp followers of the radical fringe—all summer through Williams' noisy headquarters on Tremont Street crowded the strange allies who were the chief hope in New England of Bryan's new democracy.

Early in August the Massachusetts Bryanites gained yet another accomplice when Brooks Adams came in to Boston from Quincy and offered his services to George Fred Williams. On August 11 he and Williams addressed a Bryan rally together in Quincy. For Adams it was an exciting but trying experience. Stump speaking was not his métier, nor were the followers of Bryan altogether comforting companions. Since 1884, and his rush of activity in behalf of Grover Cleveland, Adams had relapsed to the role of passive observer of the political scene. He approved of the Democratic resurgence in his own state, judging from an effusive little note he sent to William E. Russell after the 1892 election. ("In all the Commonwealth of Massachusetts," he had written, "I do not believe there is a man who is more rejoiced at your great victory than I.") Reactivated in 1893, he became a member of the Democratic state committee, helped draft party platforms, and made an occasional speech. Thereafter the crisis over silver preoccupied him, and he tried to organize a nonpartisan group of politicians, financiers, and educators to convert New England to international bimetallism. In the process his contempt for the "gold bugs" mounted. They had destroyed Grover Cleveland, he commented to Henry Cabot

Lodge, and now they were after the Republicans. No disaster would stay them. Of one Boston banker stricken by the panic, Adams wrote in 1894, "I think . . . he would be cheerfully crucified for gold—the fool." Adams' maturing pessimism found expression in his *The Law of Civilization and Decay,* published in 1895. Meanwhile his wife and brother Charles, concerned by his "morbid, excited condition, and his inherited tendency to worry," considered whether he might be persuaded to accept the post of city librarian of Boston. Instead Brooks Adams left for a tour of India. He returned in the spring of 1896 expecting to play the pariah for his conviction of America's approaching doom. But rebellion was in the air and he was eager to watch. When George Fred Williams bolted to free silver, Adams invited him out to dinner, and had his vanity stroked by Williams' remark that Adams' views had played a part in the conversion. Aroused by now to see what else might happen, Adams went to Chicago to watch the Democrats nominate a presidential candidate, hoping the prize would fall to silver Republican Henry M. Teller. He was thunderstruck by what he witnessed. To his brother Henry he wrote:

> We have monkeyed, and now we have the explosion. I went to look at the Chicago Convention, and of all the sights I have ever seen it was one of the most impressive. I know now precisely what the convention looked like in 1789. If ever I saw revolution it was in that meeting . . . There was no arguing with those men. They meant business and they have nominated Bryan, thirty six years old, and a man, as far as I can understand, exactly of the type of the men of the Revolution. The waters are out and we are all washed away. There is no compromise. The Populists will unite on Bryan, and we shall have all the substratum against all of capital . . .[25]

On which side should an Adams stand? An aristocrat constricted by hatred for State Street, Brooks Adams was torn between an inclination to goad events toward chaos and a distaste for the men who had gotten control of the silver movement. Through the summer of 1896 he vacillated between involvement and disillusion, in that dilemma his generation of Adamses knew so well: the sardonic observer aching to be on the stage. Bryan kindled his hot sense of impending catastrophe; yet Bryan's election would push men of Adams' breed still further from the sources of power. Moreover, Adams doubted whether Bryan's kind had the capacity to run the country. They were society's rejected survivals, he wrote, without money or ability or cohesion. Yet, after all, he stood with them against gold and he "had to get up and testify or be marked as a coward." So Adams found himself speaking for silver with George Fred Williams at the Quincy rally. The corner on gold had to be broken, he argued, and prices made to rise or else America's agrarian class—already headed toward socialism—would rock the country with continued uprisings and imperil republican institutions. Forty million farmers could not be suppressed. They must be listened to, if only in self-defense. Adams had worked hard on this cunning argument and was proud of it. Williams had it printed as a silver tract, yet as Brooks wrote to Henry, "not a mouse has squeaked on the other side." But the effort had sapped him: "I do not want office, I do not want responsibility, I do not want to fight . . ." When Williams asked him for more help, he pleaded bad health. Prostrated by fever, he lay at Quincy and sought instruction in books on the French Revolution. When the Massachusetts Bryanites named him as a presidential elector, he was ready to wash his hands of involvement. On October 8 he asked that his name be removed from the ballot "as I probably shall be absent from the country at the time of the election." At the end of the month he took ship for England and the waters of Bath. He did not leave without a certain regret. There had been a point, just before Chicago, when he thought he could touch the events of history and feel them respond. It had passed quickly. A week before the election, in a remarkably sober letter to his brother, he wrote, "Had Teller and McLean been nominated I should have been as close to them as a man could be; but you can't be on all sides at once. I chose mine, Williams chose his; Bryan carried the convention and, as far as New England was concerned, Williams became the only man. Had Teller been nominated I should have stood equally alone." Once again an Adams' venture into politics ended in melancholy retreat.[26]

Aside from his sympathy for silver, Brooks Adams' reaction to the events of Chicago was similar to those of other New Englanders whose attraction to the Democratic party dated from the Cleveland campaign of 1884. The respected oracles of conservative reform in Boston agreed with Adams that some force more awful than free silver had been loosed by Bryan's nomination. The shock in the Chicago platform was not its currency plank. Boston had braced for that. "Free silver," President Eliot wrote to Thomas Wentworth Higginson, "is a question on which the community might divide without manifesting on any large scale an immoral quality in either party; but there are other matters in the Chicago Platform which seem to me fundamentally immoral . . ." For Charles Hamlin it was the attack on Grover Cleveland for sending troops to Chicago during the Pullman Strike. That was enough, Hamlin wrote in his diary, to condemn the platform even if it had declared for gold. For others it was the criticism of the Supreme Court, or of the civil service. For Moorfield Storey: "The financial issue is simply an excuse. The campaign will be fought against socialism . . ." For Winslow Warren: "They have overthrown the Constitution of the United States. They have done away with the Supreme Court. They have endorsed everything which tends to the overthrow of the Republic. I expected that they would come out for silver . . . but the remainder of the platform is worse than the silver plank." [27]

The Yankee followers of Grover Cleveland found themselves after Chicago without a party. Their problem that summer was not ideological but tactical. They knew exactly what they thought of William Jennings Bryan. But they wanted to oppose him without having to vote for William McKinley, the Ohio protectionist. They spent most of the summer looking for a man to head a Gold Democratic ticket. Through July they gathered every few days in the law offices of Nathan Matthews to sort alternatives. The former mayor of Boston, gruff and quarrelsome now, refused to make the run himself. But he insisted on repudiating the results at Chicago. He did not intend, Matthews said, to take his politics from "the Populists of the West and the white trash of the South." By the end of July most Cleveland Democrats were agreed on the need to bolt. A poll of the Young Men's Democratic Club revealed that of 838 members responding, 673—80 percent—wanted to condemn the Chicago platform. On July 31 the Gold Democrats issued a manifesto pointing to the special mission of the Democratic party they had known—preservation of sound money, limited government, the liberty of the individual—and decrying its abandonment to Populism, repudiation, and dishonor.[28]

Among the men who signed this document was Louis D. Brandeis. The same day Brandeis volunteered for duty on the stump, and frequently during the next months he spoke for the Gold Democrats. This was his first major effort at political campaigning. Yet oddly enough Brandeis' public career before 1896 paralleled George Fred Williams' in several ways. The two men were in fact friends, despite what Brandeis later called Williams' inordinate vanity. Both had bolted to Cleveland in 1884, and in the eighties they were fellow members of a rather exclusive Boston law club. During the West End investigation of 1890 Brandeis was one of the few Boston lawyers who responded to Williams' appeal for help. Williams afterwards wrote to Brandeis and urged him to throw in his lot with the young reformers of the Democratic party:

Knowing from your appreciation of my work in the last Legislature how heartily you sympathize with such work, I venture to ask, if you cannot get time to study some particular measure and identify yourself with it: this much for the State. Some of us have given ourselves up to this work, and I believe our participation in politics has done much to steer the people toward Democracy. You belong with us and your influence would help amazingly . . .

Brandeis had accepted the challenge and took up a fight against the state liquor lobby. Then he turned his interest to the care of Boston's paupers. In 1897 he would begin his famous work as "People's Attorney" against New England's traction magnates. But unlike Williams, Brandeis had an ingrained moderation about him, a distaste for drastic change that his awakening reform instincts did not alter. Moreover, he was a stunning success at corporate law and by 1896 approached the status of a millionaire. A man of liberal motives who had traveled brilliantly through life thus far, Brandeis insisted on working for reform within the urban business world where he had achieved success. The animus against that world fomented by the Bryanites in 1896 blocked them from Brandeis' support. In the flux of forces that broke up the Democratic party in 1896, Brandeis found himself in the ranks of the Gold Democrats as much from repulsion as attraction.[29]

By reading themselves out of the Democratic party the Gold Democrats lost all hold over the struggle for party control between Williams and the regular state organization. Striking out on their own under the leadership of former Mayor Matthews, Sigourney Butler, and the genteel Irish lawyer, Thomas J. Gargan, they opened liaison with the national third-party movement in New York and the Midwest, and sent a delegation to the Indianapolis convention that nominated Illinois Senator John M. Palmer for President. The search for someone to lead a state Gold Democratic ticket ended with odd fitness on seventy-eight-year-old Frederick O. Prince, the last survivor of that small band of old-line commercial Democrats who entered politics a half century before under the Whig wing of Daniel Webster. A ring of fearful reaction marked the Gold Democrats' last appeal:

> There is no danger that the advocates of free silver will elect their candidates in Massachusetts; but there is danger that the doctrines of the Chicago Platform may spread through the community, and that the Democratic party may permanently descend to become the party of social disorder . . . Today we find arrayed against each other, and supporting antagonistic principles, all the conservative, thoughtful men and formerly trusted leaders of both political parties on the one hand, and all the revolutionary and dishonest elements on the other . . . If this division is to be permanent, it forbodes evil for the future of the republic . . .

As one of their number put it, the Gold Democrats were not "dreamers, or romancers, or theorists; they were not professional reformers who cannot stay put. They were men who have fought with the Democratic party for years." They had not bolted for the joy of new adventure. They had not formed a third party merely to ensure the election of William McKinley. They had acted as they did because they wanted badly to restore the past, to perpetuate the party and principles of Grover Cleveland. They had no taste for complicity with Republicans. It was true that in asserting their independence from the perversions of Populism they served as a convenient stalking horse for Mark Hanna. But there was more irony than calculation in their circumstance.[30]

Irony deepened in the case of those other former Cleveland men, the Mugwumps. The prospect of a Democratic party gone to smash gave the Mugwumps small anxiety. Most of them, in fact, had contemplated this prospect with the enthusiasm of veteran bolters. One wrote to George Fred Williams shortly before Chicago (unaware of Williams' impending conversion to free silver):

As you know it has long been a truism with most educated men that the interests of the country would be promoted by the disruption of both of the old parties and a new political crystallization . . . Personally I am not without hope that the able minority may find some way to control the wayward and headstrong majority. Failing in that, such independent action as that in which we both took part . . . in 1884 would seem to me to promise far better results than any submission to a majority gone mad.[31]

Submission to a majority gone mad was what the Mugwumps were determined above all else to avoid. For a decade and more they had served as the self-constituted conscience of American politics, casting judgment on the quality of a majoritarian society, confident they were uniquely equipped to discern the good from the evil. Whether the goal was civil service reform or lower tariffs, for the Mugwumps the great issue had been the corruption of special privilege vested in men manifestly less worthy than themselves. In their innocence they had come to regard their own participation in politics as the vital reform of their era. They had watched unhappily as the moral structure of their politics gave way under the economic stress of the nineties. Since the fight for repeal of the Sherman Silver Purchase Act they had found it increasingly difficult to reach political judgments that other men would heed. The moral alternatives of the new decade gave small satisfaction. Now in 1896 morality was thoroughly blurred. The alternative to Altgeld's Bryan was Hanna's Mc-Kinley. And the issue, they sensed, had gotten to a deeper level. Special privilege to the Bryanite was not simply an abuse of political morality but a denial of economic justice.

In the contest of 1896 the Mugwumps abandoned their moral independence and rejoined their class. That they had no other choice was hard for them to understand. Conditioned since 1884 to respond to political crisis by departing rather than joining, they searched for something to leave and some place to go. "What our 'bolt' is to be I know not," one Mugwump wrote breathlessly on the eve of Bryan's nomination, "but bolt it should be and that quickly and with ardor no matter how small in numbers." Recalling the inspirational leadership from New York in 1884, Boston Mugwumps urged Carl Schurz to lead a new bolt. But Schurz replied that any new movement should be led by a union of Republican and Democratic businessmen, rather than the old "political" Mugwumps. Schurz admitted he had not been able to arouse much enthusiasm among Republican businessmen for his scheme.[32]

That was before Chicago. By mid-July businessmen of both parties were coming together to beat down Bryan. The New York Chamber of Commerce now appointed a committee to collect funds for the Republican campaign in the East and the Gold Democratic cause in the Midwest. James Loeb, a young Harvard-educated New York financier, took up this work with an enthusiasm reminiscent of 1884. "The crystallization of the third party movement," Loeb wrote to Schurz, "may prove to be the first harbinger of good things. The opportunity for building up a new, clean, intelligent Democracy resting on the *real* convictions of the laboring class—of course, after we have got through educating them—presents attractive possibilities to my mind." One project toward this end was a theatrical production entitled "Sixteen to One," to tour the Midwest starring Joseph Jefferson. The plot called for a silver victory followed by starvation and death in the last act. In this and other ways Loeb and his friends strove zestfully to educate the workingman.[33]

Boston Mugwumps regarded the Gold Democratic movement somewhat ruefully, and few of them took much active part in it. Anxious as any to defeat Bryan, the Mugwumps were dismayed at the tactics necessary to accomplish the end, and they were saddened by the political impotence imposed on them by their alignment with eastern businessmen. "Unlike yourself," Charles Francis Adams wrote to Schurz, "I am so placed that I can do nothing to affect results in this campaign. Every one I could possibly influence thinks as I do; while those who think otherwise regard me as belonging essentially to the 'classes,' and as, therefore, not even entitled to a hearing, much less to any degree of confidence, on the part of what they are pleased to call 'the masses.'" Adams lent his name to the Gold Democratic cause, but little else. William Everett was one of the few Yankee Mugwumps to take up the campaign with any enthusiasm. He stumped the Midwest for the Gold Democrats, his rhetorical abilities in top form. (At Indianapolis a seventeen-year-old budding historian named Claude Bowers heard Everett and was enormously, if temporarily, impressed.) Many other Mugwumps were undecided whom to support. Aversion to McKinley's tariff record—and to Mark Hanna—mingled with fear that failure to vote Republican might make possible Bryan's victory. Many quiet lower-class voters were doubtless attracted to free silver— "Just how many," Charles R. Codman mused, "no one can tell. Under the Australian ballot they can vote for Bryan and no one will be the wiser. Are we safe then even here in supporting Palmer?" For those with a tougher faith in the democratic process, the choice was difficult for other reasons. The buoyant old radical Thomas Wentworth Higginson, summering at his country place in New Hampshire, felt a certain nagging kinship with the Bryanites and sent veiled congratulations to George Fred Williams for his course. But Higginson could not accept free silver, and he disliked the memories of Ben Butler which the Bryan cause aroused in him. So he remained on the side line. Years later he would confess that his failure to vote for Bryan was the biggest political mistake of his life.[34]

The campaign of 1896, venting issues long submerged by the

Mugwumps' conception of reform, shoved them outside the narrow limits of their effectiveness, and suddenly they were irrelevant. No more could they purge the nation by purging themselves. Most of them slipped finally into the thin ranks of the Gold Democrats, aware that a vote for Palmer was after all a vote for McKinley, knowing their action would bring no flicker of the catharsis of 1884.

Meanwhile the dispute between Massachusetts Bryanites and Democratic regulars had turned into a naked struggle for power. George Fred Williams' determination to win control of local party machinery brought Pat Maguire out of semiretirement for his last battle. At Chicago Maguire had listened to Bryan with a strange exhilaration. But when Williams brought the West's rebellion home with him to Boston, Maguire set his face against it. He was willing to support Bryan from a safe distance, out of regularity. But he bitterly resented Williams' bolt to Bryan for the leverage it gave to dissidents within the Boston party organization. As he watched the city's Democratic freebooters and malcontents flocking into Williams' B-S-W Club, Maguire settled into surly reaction. His gloom deepened as Williams mounted his attack. From the pages of his *Republic*, Maguire spat epithets all summer at Williams and his "reckless band of guerrillas" and threw sand in every scheme for compromise.[35]

In contrast the younger Irish leaders—Martin Lomasney of the West End, John F. Fitzgerald of the North End, and James Donovan of the South End—maneuvered to accommodate the Bryanites. Bryan himself had not particularly impressed them. Lomasney remarked later on that it was John Peter Altgeld who caught his fancy at Chicago. But in the summer of 1896 Boston's Irish politicians were less concerned with Bryan than they were with George Fred Williams. They aimed to control the city on their own terms whatever the national outcome. Williams must be humored. If they rejected him out of hand and denied him the regular Democratic nomination for governor, they feared that he would use Bryan's blessing to run independently as a Silver Democrat and plant the strife of Chicago in the wards of Boston. And if Bryan should then win the presidency, Williams would control federal patronage in Massachusetts. Haunted by these calculations, Lomasney and Donovan had voted hopefully for Williams in the balloting for vice-president at Chicago. When this gambit failed the younger Irish leaders went out of their way to minimize differences. As one of them put it, "My trip to Chicago will not change my politics. I went a Democrat, have returned as such . . . The convention is over, its work is done, and no improvement can be made by getting excited about its results." He promised to work hard and get out a heavy vote for Bryan. Meanwhile, Williams would be allowed to run for governor again as the regular Democratic nominee. The hypocrisy of this arrangement was only superficial, even though it earned the Irish scorn from Gold Democrats and other men of principle. Control of the local machinery was what counted for the Irish. Their tactics were employed in cities all over the East in 1896.[36]

In Massachusetts Williams made a shambles of the Irish try for cooperation. The events of Chicago could not be played down. The Chicago platform split society at the seam, and virtually every Democrat found he had at last to leap for one side or the other. Williams' own speeches measured the widening gulf. Through July and August his arguments leaned heavily on free silver as a panacea for hard times. Not only would silver bring prosperity; it would unite the country and rid it of its enemies. Grover Cleveland's folly lay in gearing his financial policies to a limited gold supply and thereby delivering the country over to a powerful clique of international bankers who manipulated gold at will. J. P. Morgan was merely an errand boy for the bankers of Lombard Street. Williams delighted to call their roll—"Heidlebach, Eickleheimer and Company, L. Von Hauffman and Lazard Freres"—conjuring by incantation the republic's secret foes. To prick open the scars of Anglophobia among his listeners he styled the Chicago free-silver plank a declaration of economic independence from the British Empire. "England thought," he cried, "that she could pursue on this continent the policy which has been pursued in Africa and Asia of invading territory and planting there the English flag. But one determined word, which was an American word, has made this continent from now on an American continent that no foreign country dare invade." Meanwhile, in his early speeches, Williams tried to dissociate the free-silver issue from its radical origins. He accused the Boston press of trying to "convey the impression that we are advocating something startling, something heretical, something Populistic, something anarchistic, something that is utterly bad." Thus he sought to nail the charge that he was engaging in class politics.[37]

As the summer wore on Williams lost his caution. He began to swing around and talk less about unity against foreign danger than about the unhappy cleavages in American society. In his speeches silver fell away before the larger issue of political control in America: how long would the present alliance between government and corporate monopoly continue to deny the farmer and laborer access to the instruments of power by which they might redress their wrongs? The institutions of representative government, Williams insisted, had been perverted by the demands of business and needed radical overhaul. He would fuse the interest of the Boston workingman with those of western farmers and called on all who had felt the pinch of depression to join Bryan in revolt. "The failures in our country," he finally declared, "are now united in a popular uprising against the successes."[38]

This was class politics. Through September Williams carried it to a climax, stumping the wards of Boston. Standing tall and immaculate among his new allies, his pince-nez flashing in the torchlight, his angry voice ringing out into the night, the Dedham lawyer heaped scorn on the "successes"—the Sages, Vanderbilts, Astors, Morgans, and Rockefellers—and cried:

Need I apologize for asking the people of this country to give a little more influence to the unrepresented masses . . . , a little more power to the farmers and the workingman, and to take a little from that which has been exercised by these gentlemen and their associates in perverting the laws and doing injustice to thousands and inflicting misery throughout the length and breadth of our land?

If this was class politics, Williams declared, "it is time we had it." The next night he pressed home the indictment:

For years the people of this state and of every state in the Union have seen the popular interests ebbing away by reason of the control of legislatures, and even of the executives of states and of the bench itself, by a power that was apparently too great to feel the strong hand of the people. Now that this issue has been made it becomes a question whether we shall obey that power or at last it shall be brought down to obedience . . .

Let us go forward to the verdict with the consciousness of what there is as the true foundation of this fight. It is well enough to talk of free coinage of silver; it is well enough to discuss the other planks of the respective party platforms; but I firmly believe that this is a social and political question that has now got beyond the platforms of the parties, and must be read out of the purposes of the men who stand on the one side or the other.[39]

By September Williams had convinced himself that the Irish politicians of Boston were joined with State Street, Wall Street, and Lombard Street on the other side against him. For their part the Irish leaders locked arms with the regular state Democratic committee in stolid opposition to Williams' attempt to gain control of the party machinery. "It is not enough," Williams declared, "for the Democratic organization in Boston to be loyal to me . . . Mere lip service will not suffice . . . The purpose of this campaign is to wage war to the knife against our opponents, and only men who are willing to take the knife in hand and use it in the cause are fit to be leaders in this party . . ." To this end Williams tried to throw together rival organizations in the wards of Boston to seize local control from the Irish. The tactic failed miserably. At the crucial ward caucuses in September to choose delegates to the state nominating convention the insurgents, while scoring well elsewhere in the state, met complete defeat in Boston. In Ward Eight, for instance, Martin Lomasney beat Robert Treat Paine III by 525 to 21. The Bryanites charged the regulars and the Boston police force with fraud, collusion, and intimidation at the polls, but to no avail.[40]

Now Williams hatched a desperate scheme to guarantee control of the state convention by main force. Bryan had just begun a swing through the East, and he had promised Williams he would stop in Boston. Shuffling through the daily piles of requests for tickets to hear the young Nebraskan, Williams determined to score a coup. From Arthur Sewall, Bryan's phlegmatic running mate from Maine, he got a blank check for Bryan's schedule in New England. He then arranged to bring Bryan into the city on the eve of the state convention and merge Bryan's audience with his own outstate delegate strength. The presence of the golden-throated Westerner would tip the balance in his favor, Williams calculated, against the silent power of the Irish.[41]

On Friday night, September 25, seventy-five thousand people massed on Boston Common to hear Bryan. It was the largest crowd in most men's memories. What they heard across the evening air was a sober indictment of the gold standard and a sermon on free silver. Bryan's speech was moderate and ingratiating. It set in sharp relief the progress George Fred Williams had made toward a more comprehensive radicalism since Chicago. When Bryan finished he was pushed through the crowd to the Boston Music Hall, where the state convention was to open the next morning. There he spoke again to the packed house, cheering Williams in his fight. Then, with the presidential candidate's obvious approval, Williams called on the crowd to camp in the hall all night to bar its seizure by the city machine. Promptly a brass band struck up "Hold The Fort For I Am Coming." Wild excitement swept the hall. Williams and Bryan slipped off to spend the night at Williams' home in Dedham while reliable lieutenants stayed on to direct the operation at the Music Hall. The Bryanites barricaded all entrances with chairs and upturned tables. Impromptu speeches, songs, and card games consumed the hours, and about half the delegates lasted in the hall till dawn. Those who left and tried to re-enter were blocked by a cordon of Boston police. Events took on the aspect of a siege. Food and hot coffee were lowered into the hall from second-story windows. A luckless Bryanite from Somerville martyred himself on a live wire while carrying sandwiches up a fire escape.

Next morning about two hundred tired delegates milled in the street outside the hall while the rest hung on inside. When Williams arrived, braced by a good night's sleep, he declared the delegates in the street to be part of the convention in the hall and sent in orders to begin proceedings. Shortly thereafter he was nominated for governor. The nomination was approved by acclamation, indoors and out, and the whole throng retired to nearby Horticultural Hall to hear Williams accept the nomination and justify his actions. Thus, by the calculated manipulation of crowd psychology Williams got his nomination from his own people. The party regulars were outflanked but not outdone. With the blessing of the state committee Pat Maguire and his lieutenants assembled their charges near the State House and marched solemnly to Faneuil Hall to hold their own convention. There they swiftly nominated Williams for governor, accepted Martin Lomasney's resolution to adopt the Chicago platform, and named a committee to complete the ticket later. Two hours after it was called to order the Faneuil Hall convention adjourned, its leaders satisfied they still controlled the party organization.[42]

In the words of one delighted Republican observer, it was "a bully mess." Which convention was legal? The question provoked a dreary debate that lasted through October, defying resolution. Some of Williams' supporters questioned his wisdom in refusing to bargain with the regulars. Dismayed to see Bryan's cause degenerate in Boston to the level of a ward squabble, Harry Jaquith and Robert Treat Paine III, the wealthy patrons of the Boston Bryanites, felt conciliation was the wiser course. When Williams and his militant adviser Tim Coakley left Boston in October to stump the Midwest for Bryan, Paine and Jaquith used the chance to try for compromise. But Williams got wind of it and fired home a telegram from Chicago: "I absolutely refuse further negotiations with enemies on state commitee . . . Let them reckon with the people. They cannot have my hand to pull them from the ditch." In the end the state committee gave up trying. Its chairman finally resigned and told reporters, "You can announce it from the housetops that I will not vote for George Fred Williams."[43]

Boston Democrats thus came up to election day hopelessly divided. Even the Irish leaders ultimately broke ranks. While Maguire and his underlings concentrated on thwarting Williams, Martin Lomasney and Congressman Fitzgerald emphasized their independence of Maguire by working quietly for greater cooperation with the Bryanites. Tim Coakley, irreconcilable foe of the machine, tried to persuade Williams to extend the general ruin to Fitzgerald by denouncing his try for re-election to Congress. When Lomasney learned of this, he exploded in wrath. Fitzgerald declared tardily for free silver and Williams refused to support the man Coakley had gotten to run against him. But this was the last unparted strand. For the rest Williams by converting Bryan's crusade into a local party purge had painted proud Pat Maguire's machine as an instrument of power without principle, and he had crippled his own power in the bargain.[44]

By his slashing, headlong course Williams had moreover antagonized many voters who had been ready to vote for free silver. One potential supporter wrote to him: "You represent what we believe in; others who are being pushed to the front show no knowledge of the question at issue, and an ability only to divert attention from silver to internecine quarrels. You cannot run a successful campaign with egotists, boodlers, and bums in the front ranks." To add to their troubles, by October Bryan's followers had run out of money. Their campaign newspaper, the *Boston Evening Despatch,* folded two weeks before the election. Their campaign headquarters in Boston, a hive of activity in August, was quiet and all but deserted by October. The man in charge of the office struggled along on a single rented typewriter, had his telephone cut off for lack of funds, and was hounded by an unpaid washerwoman every time he used the elevator.[45]

But the surest omen of the Bryanites' defeat was the apathy for their cause among the working class. No single reason can be assigned for the Democrats' failure to arouse the labor vote in 1896. The tarheel editor Josephus Daniels recalled that as Bryan's campaign train traveled through the mill towns of New England he saw giant placards on the fronts of factories warning employees that work would stop if Bryan were elected. Mark Hanna had visited Boston, among other cities, to open the pocketbooks of terrified businessmen, and Republican money doubtless affected the vote in Massachusetts as elsewhere. The Boston cotton merchant Stephen Weld and the Republican state chairman together raised 428,000 dollars during the campaign. Bryanites were sure that the laboring man was being systematically bribed or threatened into supporting McKinley. The going price of votes was a common joke among Williams' followers. But the working man's reluctance to swing behind Bryan need not be laid entirely to corruption or fear. In Massachusetts the Bryan Democrats fell between two stools in their quest for labor support. To some, their appeal was too nebulous; to others, too heretical. For the minority of workers who had developed by the 1890's a distinctive, political class consciousness (these included old Butlerites, socialists, immigrant radicals, some trade unionists), the silver panacea simply was not convincing. It lacked clear relevance to long hours, oppressive foremen, dirty shops, or unemployment. In the shadow of a factory free silver was a dim abstraction. Bryan did little to identify his cause with labor's while he was in Massachusetts. In the shoe town of Lynn when he tried to expand on free silver to a crowd of restless workers, he was interrupted by the shout: "Talk about injunctions!" He responded weakly. Arbitration would replace injunctions "while we younger men are still alive," he hoped. Quickly he got back to gospel: "I recognize these things in our platform are material, and yet this contest is going to turn on the money question . . ." Neither Bryan the prairie evangelist nor Williams the Dedham patrician won many labor votes not already won by the Chicago platform. "I will favor the silver standard if I can be convinced to," a Cambridge immigrant told Williams, "but I neither favor gold or silver, for the times are too hard, and my own opinion is that the working people must get one of their own class for guiding the government . . ." [46]

But the majority of laborers did not regard themselves as a class apart from the rest of society, and perhaps they resented the Bryanites' effort to link their interests with the distant grievances of the West, to translate a sectional uprising into a class revolt. In Massachusetts George Fred Williams had tried frankly to turn Bryan's campaign into a struggle of poor men against wealth, of failures against success, of malcontents against the standing order. In a state where the Puritan ethic was not altogether forgotton, where rich and poor alike, Irishman or Yankee, were taught to regard success and respectability as unquestioned ideals, his appeal seemed like a challenge to the very moral fabric of life. Those who identified their aspirations with the values of their own society watched his effort with revulsion.

His campaign attracted mainly those who felt no such bond of identity or placed little value on it. Men dissatisfied with the constrictions of urban politics, who felt political progress to have been bottled up by the tacit agreement of men in power, seized a chance to join what seemed for a moment like a powerful movement for drastic reform and were catapulted into the Bryan camp. Bryan and Williams had attracted the militant leadership of organized labor, if not the rank and file. They had attracted several Bay State woman suffragists to the cause of free silver. They enjoyed the support, for what it was worth, of Massachusetts Populists and other restless orphans of the two-party system. They won attention in the pages of Boston's famous *Arena*, whose hardy editor, Benjamin O. Flower, turned his reformist journal into a sounding board for free silver and told Williams he was a worthy successor to Wendell Phillips. Several young Boston newspapermen worked hard for the local cause. And finally, after an evident struggle, the Democrat James Roche, editor of Boston's liberal Catholic *Pilot*, came over to Bryan.[47]

They were a lonely handful. In November Bryan lost Massachusetts along with every other state in the Northeast, and Williams plunged his party to a new low for the decade. Democrats won only seven of Boston's twenty-five wards where they had carried fourteen the year before.[48] But the frustration of the Bryanites went deeper than failure at the polls. They had expected that. The more telling defeat lay in their inability really to capture the Democratic party—to win converts to their cause from any of the groups that had clustered under the banner of Grover Cleveland and Billy Russell over the past decade. The Bryanites remained in November what they had been in July: a band of rootless, random individuals, without cash or cohesion, thrown together suddenly and without premeditation under brash and erratic leadership, and with no mature tradition of political radicalism to guide them. Whether they were disappointed men of destiny, wealthy patrons of the new and untried, trade-union leaders, journalists, suffragists, or rejected ward heelers, they proved to be political amateurs when they came up against an entrenched machine with an instinct for survival. They had failed utterly to effect a conquest of established organization by radical action. Militance fell before the citadel of power. But the wounding losses inflicted by the battle would endure. In their effort to bring Bryanism to Massachusetts, Williams and his followers had ruined their party in a flare of melodrama and discredited themselves in the eyes of the electorate. Their fate was not peculiar to Massachusetts. It suggests an important reason for Bryan's national defeat in 1896 and the impotence of the Democratic party in the years ahead.

CHAPTER NINE · MAYOR QUINCY'S BOSTON

BOSTON had massively and fearfully rejected Bryanism. But while the Irish organization of the city had been badly shaken, it remained intact. Boston returned John F. Fitzgerald to Congress, where he was once again the only Democrat from New England. Democratic candidates for the General Court carried thirteen of Boston's twenty-five wards, where Bryan and Williams won only seven.[1] The campaign left lasting scars among the Democrats of the city. In his vain effort to crack Irish control of their urban stronghold, George Fred Williams had driven a wedge of hostility between Boston's radical reformers and her reigning politicians. The uses to which he had put Bryanism had enlarged and multiplied the grounds of mistrust between "machine" and "antimachine" politicians.

Among Irish regulars the campaign of 1896 reinforced a tendency in the younger leaders to resort to individual expedients of self-interest at the expense of the common party cause. An important result of the national election for Massachusetts' future was its disintegrating effect on the disciplined Irish voting bloc which Pat Maguire had put together behind conservative Yankee reformers like William E. Russell and Nathan Matthews. In a sense Maguire himself was one of the casualties of the campaign. Three weeks after the election he died in Boston at age fifty-nine. Perhaps it is not entirely romantic to suppose that, as in the case of Billy Russell, the events of the preceding summer had shortened his career. During the campaign Maguire had taken refuge in the highest loyalty he knew—party regularity. To accommodate himself to Bryan he had sacrificed even his good opinion of Grover Cleveland. In October 1896 Maguire's *Republic* commented that Cleveland would leave the White House "discredited and hated by more than one-half the American people. This is certainly an inglorious ending of a career that gave promise of almost phenomenal brilliancy." The publication of this judgment may have been distasteful. It was also fruitless. Even party regularity proved unavailing for Maguire in the end, since Bryan supported Williams against the Irish organization in Boston. During the closing weeks of the campaign Maguire watched helplessly as his work of half a lifetime crumbled before Williams' assault. To the last week of his life he lashed out bitterly against his adversary for the wreck he had made of the Democratic party.[2]

Maguire's funeral was one of the largest and most elaborate Irish Boston had yet seen. The carriages behind his casket formed a line over half a mile long on the city streets, and hundreds were turned back at the church doors. Friend and foe alike recognized that with his passing a central prop of Irish-Yankee political cooperation fell away. Even the Brahmin *Boston Transcript*, for whom the Irish political boss was a wholly nasty breed, admitted a grudging respect for the dead Maguire:

> He was a man of strong, almost extraordinary personality . . . his life was almost a continuous warfare, rather more often with the mutinous in his own ranks than with his avowed opponents . . . The boss in politics is a boss in the wrong place. The policy which permits it is a pernicious one; but it is due to the man, who by hard fighting and no surrender so long held that position, to say that he showed less disposition to abuse his unnatural trust than most of those who have wielded power under similar conditions . . . He was a man of many admirable qualities, and the danger now is that his successor, whoever he may be, will not use the same questionable power with equal moderation, honesty, and regard for the public service.[3]

The *Transcript's* apprehensions were not unfounded. An episode in February 1897 gave proper Boston a small taste of what changes might come with the new order of Irish leaders. The previous fall local Republican strategists, banking on a McKinley landslide, had put up a Boston Negro, one Isaac Allen, to run against the only Irishman on the Governor's Council. Allen won. Lopsided pluralities in the silk-stocking districts of Back

Bay had tided him over losses in the Irish wards. Sitting politely
on the Governor's Council, Allen was a pretty feather in the
Yankee cap, and it stung the Irish like a face slap. Early in 1897
the state of Tennessee invited the Governor of Massachusetts
and his council to its centennial. To spare themselves the embarrassment of traveling with Allen to the South, his fellow Republicans arranged to exclude him from the trip. Martin Lomasney,
now a state senator from the West End, sprang callously to
Allen's defense. His words reveal the surly contempt growing
among Irish politicians for their Yankee rivals:

> Owing to the most intelligent constituency in the state, owing to
> the Back Bay district of Boston, an honorable colored gentleman has
> been elected to the executive council . . . Go forth, Governor of
> Massachusetts; go forth to the Tennessee exposition, but do not leave
> behind you the cultured gentleman who represents the Back Bay
> and the cream of Boston society . . . You sons of old Massachusetts,
> where Garrison and Phillips pleaded for equal rights, go forth, I say.
> You are going to face the music. Bring on the minstrels.[4]

This cynical outburst was significant less for its mockery of
Allen than for its scorn of Yankee pretense. Lomasney cared well
for the Negro minority (as well the Jewish and Italian minori-
ties) in the West End and feared no reprisals from this quarter.
In fact it was his entrenched position in the city which allowed
him to vent his penchant for disruptive ethnic appeals against
the older New England order. Increasingly as the century neared
its end and the Irish ward bosses grew in power, they turned in
on themselves and calculated their tactics with little regard for
Yankee gentlemen of either party and with slight reference to
party lines. Lomasney matched his mounting power with growing political agility. He worked out a close understanding with
Boston's Republican boss, Jesse Gove, and learned how to muster
Republican support at the State House when he needed it against
his fellow Boston Democrats. The fractious localism of the 1880's
was returning to flavor Irish thinking. Men like Lomasney would
take only a secondary interest in state affairs as long as control of
the state remained beyond their grasp. Meanwhile, in the city,
they meant to seize what was theirs whenever the opportunity
opened.

In this atmosphere, such cooperation as was possible between Irish and Yankee within the Democratic party survived the damaging events of 1896 largely through the efforts of Mayor Josiah Quincy. Quincy had been elected to the office in 1895 for a two-year term. Party leaders had turned to him that year in a final effort to work together on the terms laid down by Pat Maguire in the predepression era. Quincy's performance over the years since 1884 had erased his reputation as a Mugwump dilettante and had won the grudging admiration of city Democrats. Since his service in the state legislature he had become the pre-eminent party manager in the state. He had directed several gubernatorial campaigns, served as publicity director of the party's national committee during Cleveland's 1892 campaign, and earned the scars of a competent spoilsman during his rugged stint as Cleveland's assistant secretary of state in 1893. Irish confidence in his openhanded patronage policies won him the mayoral nomination in 1895. His good reputation among trade-unionists, social workers, and the unemployed bolstered the normal Democratic vote and won him the election by a larger margin than any in the past.[5] Now during the last years of the century, by cunning tactics and herculean labor, he managed to stretch the Yankee Democratic conception of political leadership far beyond the limits defined by his Democratic predecessor Nathan Matthews. And astonishingly, in the process he made Boston's city government for a brief time the cutting edge of urban reform in America.

Quincy's achievement as mayor was possible because, alone among Democratic leaders in Massachusetts, he escaped the stigma of involvement in the campaign of 1896. This had not been an easy trick. Both as mayor and as national committeeman, he had been in the thick of his party's politics right up to the Chicago convention. Having gone to Chicago and seen his party revolutionized, he quietly resigned from the national committee and went into political seclusion. While convinced of the dangerous consequences of a Bryan victory, he masterfully avoided any flat condemnation of the ticket and refused to bolt the party. As the campaign progressed his silence began to be noticed. One prominent Gold Democrat told him that Boston businessmen were grumbling over his evasions. Quincy had more to lose by reticence, he was warned, than by a bold stand for principle against the Bryanites. But Quincy would not speak out. His far-reaching plans for Boston were irrelevant to the issues raised in the Chicago platform. He refused to blight them by commitment in the national contest. In September he went out to Quincy to spend a night with his friend Brooks Adams and talk politics. In a letter to brother Henry a few days later, Brooks Adams quoted Quincy's quiet prognosis: " 'These fools talk as if this election will settle something, but it won't, it will only inflame. In my opinion a wise man will keep himself in reserve till he can see his way a little, for unless all signs fail the time is coming when there will be need for someone to take hold who is not used up.' " When Bryan's campaign train swung into Boston, Quincy offered the city's hospitality in a polite and proper letter. When in the wake of Williams' tumultuous Music Hall convention Pat Maguire marched his forces past City Hall to the Faneuil Hall convention, Quincy came out and saluted them with the gold-tipped wand of his office as they tramped by. He maintained his silent, measured neutrality through election day. He earned abuse for his course, but he accomplished his purpose.[6]

No one knew with certainty what his purposes were until they unfolded. Josiah Quincy was an enigmatic man. He was in his late thirties when he served as mayor—tall, lean, always carefully dressed, distant and distinguished in bearing. Dark, curling hair, deep-set brown eyes, and a full mustache set off his sober, hollow-cheeked face. He had moved into Boston from Quincy in 1891 and lived with his father in an old house on Charles Street well apart from Boston's fashionable quarter. As Mark DeWolfe Howe once noted, there was little of the conventional Bostonian in the Quincys. For years Josiah Quincy's friends had noted a chilly strangeness in him that often made them feel uncomfortable. A bachelor who was reputed to dislike women, he seemed to lack all interest in the polite small talk or easy compliments which won favor in Back Bay drawing rooms. Men constantly remarked on his calculated loneliness. "Generally I dine at the Club," Henry Adams commented in 1894, "and see queer, stray people, like myself. Two days ago, it was Joe Quincy." And Richard Henry Dana confided to his journal a year earlier, "Q is certainly sphinxlike. I never knew what to make of Q when working with him, but always assumed the best of him." [7]

New Englanders were accustomed to thinking well of Quincys. But this Josiah Quincy broke too many of the accepted rules. Even his own father had become concerned by his son's decision to enter the grimy arena of Boston city politics. A missionary urge was all very well, the elder Quincy advised, but the Boston mayoralty no longer took any skill except a willingness to please the bosses. Far better, the father concluded, to work for reform from a clean, safe, appointive post. Others had similar doubts about Quincy's political judgment. What alarmed his Yankee friends was the accumulating evidence that his obsession with practical politics had torn him from the principles of his class. The trouble was more than his willingness to strike bargains with the bosses over offices and votes. Quincy had clearly cast aside the pristine heritage of Jeffersonian conservatism common among Cleveland Democrats. One reason for this was doubtless his family's long-standing record of belief in social paternalism. During his boyhood, for instance, his grandfather had been an outspoken advocate of low-cost housing and transportation for working men. [8] In his own Harvard commencement oration back in 1880 Quincy had prophesied the motives which would guide his subsequent career in politics:

The world has entered upon a period of change. The miscarriages of our present form of civilization are exhibited with emphatic caricature. Upon the horizon may be seen indications of political and social convulsions that must be faced within the lives of many of us who are graduating today. The problem is to make the results of study and cultivated thought acceptable to the mass of the people; for it is into their hands that the government of all civilized states is now rapidly passing. [9]

For the next fifteen years Quincy grappled imaginatively with the task of meeting the demands of "the masses" by manipulating public institutions—in the legislature as labor reformer, in his native Quincy as the leader in a movement for municipal charter reform, in the councils of the Democratic party as party manager. Friends may have lamented his lack of principle, but like his great-grandfather and grandfather he found satisfaction in what he took to be the social responsibilities of his family.[10]

For Quincy the demands of the new urban, industrial environment of New England were serious but unfrightening. He had armed himself with two convictions which seemed heretical to many of his Harvard-trained Yankee contemporaries. First, his complete commitment to the Democratic party reflected a belief that the political party was not merely an unfortunate expedient but a crucial instrument of social progress. Secondly, he felt that specific extensions in the power of government should be judged by present need and not by established canons of historic principle or abstract logic. He lacked the eloquence or temperament to argue persuasively for these convictions, but he possessed in abundant measure the energy to act on them. In doing so, he ensured his isolation from his own class of people in the Boston community.[11]

Searching for new ideas and techniques with which to vindicate his views, Quincy turned from New England to Europe. He had traveled widely and intelligently in England and on the continent during the 1880's and remained an avid student of European governmental practice long after embarking on his own political career. It was the example of English factory legislation which had made him a champion of advanced labor reform in the Massachusetts legislature. Just as England had remained ahead of the continent in this vital area of social progress, Quincy believed, so Massachusetts must establish guidelines for the rest of the United States. Moving from state to city politics in the 1890's, he looked constantly for instruction to the great cities of the European continent. Berlin and Paris, he felt, despite their oligarchic governments had proved vastly more responsive than American cities to the needs of their massed inhabitants. Writing for the reformist magazine *Arena* in 1897, Quincy indicated that his studies had produced for him a fresh ideal for urban democratic government:

If we form our judgment not by the scope of the elective franchise, but by that of services rendered, we shall have to award the palm for variety and usefulness of municipal activity, for benefits conferred upon the masses of the people, to the foreign cities . . . In a score of different directions the interests of the average citizen are better and more fully cared for, his wants more fully met, in the great city of Europe than in that of America. Municipal government in the old world seems to be for the people, if not by the people.[12]

Quincy had clearly moved beyond the sense of municipal responsibility defined by Nathan Matthews in the early nineties, a definition bankrupted by depression and the decay of Irish political discipline. Quincy's task from 1896 to 1900 was to reduce his vision to specific proposals that would win him political support from the increasingly disparate social groups of greater Boston. Unlike Matthews he could not count on backing from Boston Mugwumps or from Republican Back Bay. Unlike Matthews he could not count on Pat Maguire. He hoped for the continued backing of the younger Irish leaders, but in any event support from the Irish would be insufficient by itself for mastery of the city.

Quincy's first bid for new recruits was widely hailed as a daring innovation. It seems in retrospect the tamest of his proposals. Soon after taking office at Boston's City Hall, he created a Merchants' Municipal Committee, a seven-man unpaid advisory board representing the powerful, highly centralized, commercial organizations of the city. This group of business leaders lacked any legal sanctions or initiative. Meeting twice a week with Quincy to discuss his programs, it served him in two valuable ways. Since a majority of its members were Republican, the committee opened for Quincy an avenue of communication with the leaders of the state legislature. Moreover, it served as a sounding board for thousands of businessmen who paid taxes in Boston but voted in the suburbs. Largely by means of his merchants' committee Quincy was able to embark on more radical schemes for the city without alienating the metropolitan business community or incurring the wrath of the General Court.[13]

Soon after Pat Maguire's death in November 1896, Quincy moved to preserve a semblance of the old unity among Irish leaders in the city. He created another extralegal body, composed of as many district leaders as could be cajoled in, to divide the patronage and plan the electioneering of the local party. This group, dubbed the Board of Strategy, met periodically in Quincy House behind City Hall and on occasion in the office of the Superintendent of Lamps. The Superintendent was Pat Maguire's old protégé, "Smiling Jim" Donovan of the South End, entrusted by Josiah Quincy with maintenance of the Board of Strategy as well as lamps. Other members included Donovan's disciple, John A. Keliher; the lawyer and ward boss, Joseph Corbett; the liquor dealer and boss of East Boston, Patrick J. Kennedy; and Congressman John F. Fitzgerald when he was in town. Quincy often joined their deliberations and was acknowledged to be the craftiest strategist of them all. He knew the price of their support, and during his mayoralty the Irish tightened their monopoly on city offices. Through the Board, and by calculated indulgence with jobs, Quincy won to his side for a while every important Democratic boss in the city, with one ominous exception. Martin Lomasney remained outside the Board of Strategy.[14]

Another group whose favor Quincy valued was organized labor. Many of Boston's trade-unionists had lost faith in the Democratic party during the recent depression years. But others remembered Quincy's splendid labor record in the state legislature and hoped for an end to certain hiring practices engaged in by the city in the past, now that he was mayor. Their resentment centered on municipal contracts by which city work was let out to private contractors who used the cheapest labor they could find. To woo the affection of organized labor, Quincy promoted the alternative system of direct hiring of union labor by the city. He expanded the city's public works department to include a division of electrical construction and a division of building repair, and by the end of his mayoralty hundreds of union men were gaining off-season employment from the city.

Quincy launched his boldest innovation in labor's behalf with an eye on the city's powerful typographical union, which had for years agitated for an end to a long-standing policy of contracting city printing out to private firms. First Quincy appointed a typographer to be Superintendent of Printing. He then arranged for the city to buy out an unused printing establishment and renovate its presses. In March 1897 Boston's municipal printing plant opened for business, staffed by Boston trade-unionists. Urban reformers across the country anxiously watched the fate of this experiment in what they called municipal socialism. To mollify the orthodox, Quincy could plausibly have argued that he was saving the city money. But he preferred to justify the venture in terms of its social value. He found it "highly desirable," he said in his mayoral address of 1897, "to make organized bodies of intelligent wage-earners feel that they are directly represented in the management of public business, particularly as such pertains to their several trades." The city printing operation quickly became a pilot plant for trade-union progress in Boston. Working conditions were the best in Boston; paid holidays became the rule; in 1899 an eight-hour day was inaugurated. Quincy looked ahead to the day when its workers in common with all city employees would receive retirement pensions. He was a warm advocate of municipal ownership and he rejected the arguments of those who felt that such advances must await wider application of the civil service rules. Municipal services must be extended in a growing city, he insisted, without waiting for an abstract elevation of its ethical standards. He refused to be immobilized by the narrow Yankee ethic of "good government" if it blocked realization of goals he felt to be more vital than efficiency.[15]

If he forfeited the support of Boston's leading Mugwumps by advertising these convictions, Quincy tapped a richer vein of civic virtue among the city's professional philanthropists—people such as the settlement worker Robert A. Woods, the social worker Alice N. Lincoln, and the playground enthusiast Joseph

Lee. Woods, director of Andover House in the South End, where he sought to interpret the social ethic of London's Toynbee Hall for the slums of Boston, most clearly indicated the temper of this group. Rubbing elbows with ward bosses in the South End, Woods had come to understand the impotence of reform aimed at rooting out the influence of such men in city government. He acknowledged that Boston's municipal reformers in the past had been skilled at opposing and preventing, but he regarded this as a negative contribution to urban politics, empty of permanent responsibility. Any reform drive which devoted itself solely to correcting the ethical behavior of politicians, he argued, would prove futile. For city dwellers judged these politicians not by their methods but by their usefulness. A boss like Woods's friend James Donovan of the South End thrived because he satisfied individual desires by doing private favors. The true task of the city reformer, Woods concluded, was to seek out these individual desires and translate them into public needs. If the city could dispense as a common blessing what was customarily awarded through the special influence of the ward boss, the boss might lose his secret sting and be reduced to a benign, responsible spokesman for his community.[16]

Woods found a sympathetic and responsive audience for his ideas when he met Josiah Quincy over lunch at St. Botolph's shortly before Quincy became mayor. The settlement worker's fertile, informed enthusiasm for social welfare schemes balanced well against the Brahmin politician's sophisticated expertise, and the two men embarked on a creative friendship. Between 1896 and 1900, Quincy launched the city on a festival of social innovations which aroused scorn in some, smiles in others, and wide-eyed admiration in many more. Woods became, in his own words, one of Quincy's "chief advisors . . . in all his social schemes" and remained fascinated by "this human sort of politics." Perhaps Woods's major contribution was to convert Quincy to a program of public baths for Boston. As Quincy's commissioner of baths, he supervised several projects which excited Quincy's deepest pride. "The city is now doing some

things for the people which were formerly thought to be outside
its scope," Quincy could soon write. "For instance, it has made
a good beginning at bathing them—or, at least, at helping and
encouraging them to bathe." During his tenure the city's outdoor
bath facilities expanded yearly, and charges for suits, soap, and
towels were lowered or dropped entirely. In 1898 Quincy opened
the Dover Street Bath House, its indoor marble showers another
monument to municipal socialism. Planted in the heart of the
South End slums, open year-round to men and women and free
to all, the Dover Street Bath House was soon cleaning Bostonians at the rate of thirty thousand a month. With this happy
precedent, indoor showers were soon installed in the Paul Revere
School in the North End, over the protests of alarmed conservatives on the Boston School Committee. Meanwhile, concrete
swimming pools were built in other tenement districts. The great
expansion of public bathing facilities, Joseph Lee later wrote,
was one of "Mayor Quincy's many contributions toward making
Boston a city in which it is an education to live." [17]

Baths were only the beginning. Inspired by Joseph Lee's
suggestions, Quincy effected a major change of emphasis in
Boston's recreational park program, a favorite preoccupation of
Cleveland Democrats in past years. Woodland retreats and
bubbling brooks were all very well, but they did not really touch
life in the slums. "When Josiah Quincy was Mayor," Lee commented, "he saw that the great omission in our playground
system was still the playground, and he set to work in a characteristically radical way to make up this deficiency." Quincy and
Lee aimed frankly at encouraging play in the middle of the city.
Strengthening the vigor and virtue of Boston's youth seemed to
them as worthy a goal as beautifying its landscape. Quincy told
the City Council: "I can hardly emphasize too strongly my
belief in the great benefit to the community, not only physi-
cally, but also socially, and even morally, of an extensive development of reasonable and properly directed athletics . . . there
is nothing visionary about the general proposition that the more
the community spends in bringing facilities for exercise . . .
within the reach of all, and in encouraging and properly direct-

ing their use, the less it will have to spend for the punishment of crime . . ." Armed with his environmentalist theories, Quincy marched up Beacon Hill and wrested half a million dollars from the state legislature to build playgrounds. Soon the city had cleared twenty-two spaces big enough for a game of baseball. For smaller children Quincy saw to it that some twenty school-yards were kept open in the summer and equipped with sand-boxes and matrons. He also began a summer camp for boys on one of the city-owned islands in Boston Harbor, and sponsored several municipal gymnasiums for winter sport. The public gymnasium which opened in East Boston in 1897 was the first of its kind in the United States.[18]

Quincy constantly sought new ways of strengthening the city government as an agency for surer protection of urban health and safety. For instance, he authorized a new bacteriological laboratory under the city Board of Health to study germ diseases, and this led to important hygienic reforms in the kitchens of municipal jails and orphanages. Meanwhile a tentative start was made toward an improvement of slum housing conditions. Under pressure generated by Robert A. Woods, Alice N. Lincoln, and Quincy himself, the state legislature granted new power to the Board of Health to purchase unsanitary tenement buildings at market price and tear them down. Continued pressure was needed to make the hesitant board members act on this fresh authority, but by 1901 over 140 dwellings and 80 stables had been torn down and space provided for new construction.[19]

Quincy matched his concern for the physical well-being of Boston's citizenry with a lively urge to refresh its cultural spirit. In this purpose he was aided by the Twentieth Century Club, a body which served Boston's urban progressives in much the same way the Reform Club had served her Mugwumps in earlier years. Founded in 1894 to awaken civic thought about the city's future, the Twentieth Century Club operated through a network of busy committees concerned with the quality of Boston's popular life and culture. In 1897 the club's educational com-mittee sponsored a series of free public lectures on timely topics for the working class. The lectures won a surprisingly warm

response. With his startling flair for innovation, Quincy there-
upon invited the education committee of the Twentieth Century
Club to become a municipal department and continue its work
at the city's expense. Quincy had a special interest in the musical
dimension of popular culture. He created a city music commission, encouraged it to organize a municipal brass band, and
revived public band concerts on the Common. Moving from the
oompah of the summer bandstand to the more classical, Quincy
gave public backing to a series of inexpensive symphonic concerts at the Music Hall. A special fifty-piece orchestra subsidized
by the Twentieth Century Club played to a packed hall through
the 1898–99 season, and music journals began to hum with discussion of the "Boston idea." Meanwhile a city string quartet
spread the gospel of municipal culture by traveling about to the
remoter districts of the city. In 1899 Quincy opened a public
hall in the South End for a municipal art exhibition and urged a
more direct public encouragement for this form of creative expression as for others.[20]

Following European precedent, Quincy made a policy of ap-
pointing unpaid advisory commissions of Boston do-gooders to
supervise his various experimental ventures. Similarly, he used
the device of the unpaid commission to direct disinterested but
sympathetic opinion to wide areas of the city's traditional business, including its jails, insane asylums, pauper homes, and
orphanages. At no time in the past had the humanitarian urges
of proper Boston been so systematically exploited by the city
government.

In his public speeches and private conversations, Quincy was
not always able to communicate the values which impelled his
efforts. But in one passage from his writings on American urban
problems, his dream for Boston was revealed:

The duty of a city is to promote the civilization, in the fullest
sense of the word, of all its citizens. No true civilization can exist
without the provision of some reasonable opportunities for exercising
the physical and mental faculties, of experiencing something of the
variety and of the healthful pleasures of life, or feeling at least the
degree of self-respect which personal cleanliness brings with it. The

people of a city constitute a community, in all which that significant term implies; their interests are inextricably bound up together, and everything which promotes the well-being of a large part of the population benefits all.[21]

Boston had not expected the compulsive vigor and unorthodox techniques with which Quincy sought to implement this vision. The coterie at City Hall watched him with puzzled anticipation. Social workers waited for his speeches and flocked to hear his annual addresses to the City Council. People learned to wonder what would happen next in Boston. The blank-faced, solemn young mayor rarely disappointed. Even as his projects took shape, his motives remained a mystery for most of his contemporaries. Despite the sense of noblesse oblige inherited from earlier Mayor Quincys and his obvious fascination with foreign municipal experiments, it was hard to judge how he had freed himself from the incubus of aristocratic impotence suffered by those other Quincy gentry, the Adamses, or from the milder inhibitions of the Mugwump Democrats with whom he had worked so closely for a decade. Many of his own kind found it easiest to lay his behavior to shallow opportunism. Brooks Adams acknowledged Quincy's shrewdness but claimed he lacked a shred of principle or conviction. The younger Charles Francis Adams dismissed Quincy with brief scorn: "When he is not a practical politician he is a visionary." Others professed distaste at Quincy's truckling to Irish Catholics, trade-unionists, and even Jews and Italians in awarding offices. Even some of those who served on his advisory commissions often wondered whether they were not being used as tools to placate public opinion. Quincy's fellow politicians rarely knew quite what to make of him. Many regarded his innovations as merely an ingenious new approach to patronage. "He is a pretty sly bird," one Republican leader observed to Henry Cabot Lodge. "The curious thing about it all is that I haven't yet found one single Democrat of first-class standing who has been willing to say to me personally that he believes in Josiah Quincy." [22]

Quincy had his believers. The former Boston Nationalist, Sylvester Baxter, surveying the mayor's achievements, thought he saw Edward Bellamy's "hand of the people" being put to work at last in the birthplace of the Nationalist movement. The organizer of the Twentieth Century Club, Edwin D. Mead, admitted reservations about Quincy's patronage politics, but lavished high praise on his administration of the city. "I believe immensely in his fundamental purpose," Mead wrote, "and in his ever purer and purer methods. No other municipal administrator in this country has equal knowledge of the great municipal movement in the modern world or is so impressed by its spirit. He has great imagination and looks at Boston in a great way. The making of the greatest mayor we have ever had is in him." In general Quincy's reputation improved as one got further from Boston, for many of his schemes were unprecedented in America. The secretary of the National Municipal League, addressing the annual Conference For Good City Government in Columbus, Ohio, in 1899, reported:

> The leadership of Mayor Quincy of Boston, in all matters relating to municipal progress and development, is too well known to need more than a passing reference. Mayor Quincy's administration has been characterized by a breadth of view and grasp of the municipal problem which place him at the head of American municipal administrators.

Similarly, the *Review of Reviews* in a survey of city government across the nation commented in 1899:

> For some years past it would seem that Boston has, among our larger cities, furnished the country with the best example of modern knowledge and ability applied to the conduct and development of the corporate life of a metropolitan city. Mayor Quincy has been singularly successful, and has earned the reputation of being the foremost practical expert in the science and art of municipal administration that we have in this country.[23]

Perhaps Quincy's most fervent admirers were the English Fabians Beatrice and Sidney Webb, who met him on their trip to the United States in 1898. Beatrice Webb found Quincy winning in appearance and intriguing in character—"quite the hero from the pages of a novel," she wrote of him in her diary. Over the course of several days in Boston, Quincy guided the Webbs through the grimy intricacies of Boston city government and quizzed them thoroughly on English politics, municipal theory, and trade-union activity. They came away deeply impressed by his candor, intellectual alertness, and practical skill. Beatrice Webb even speculated that but for his political isolation in Massachusetts he might some day be a candidate for the presidency.[24]

What most outside observers, and many in Boston, did not understand was that Josiah Quincy was losing a race against political oblivion. His explorations in municipal socialism were a hopeless effort to revive that sense of community—economic, social, and political—which had been the dearest ideal of Cleveland Democrats and which had been the basis of their claim to public leadership. Freed from the moral restraints of the Mugwumps by their condemnation of him in earlier spoils controversies, Quincy was now manipulating all the machinery of party and city government to preserve the only important value he still shared with his former associates. But by the turn of the century the stormy centrifugal forces of Boston democracy had ruined his effort.

Quincy faced down his first serious challenge when he sought re-election at the end of his first term in 1897. Within the Democratic party Boston Bryanites sought to regroup their forces by unseating him as mayor. Bent on revenge for Quincy's conduct in 1896, the Bryanites cited his reliance on the Board of Strategy as evidence of his subservience to the Irish machine and used his advocacy of a new unified rail terminal at South Station to paint him as a tool of New England rail magnates. Backed by George Fred Williams and Tim Coakley, an Irish lawyer named Tom Riley (a one-time follower of Ben Butler) entered the race against Quincy as the Bryanite candidate, thereby creating a three-cornered contest for the mayoralty. Massachusetts Republicans, sensing another Democratic donnybrook, happily encouraged Riley. Henry Cabot Lodge followed the campaign closely. If Curtis, the Republican candidate, could oust Quincy on the strength of the Bryanite defection, Republican

domination of Massachusetts would be complete, and Lodge's re-
election to the United States Senate a year hence would be in
the bag. "Riley will turn Quincy inside out," a Republican
strategist on the scene predicted to Lodge. "He has the venom,
he has the ability, he has the facts, and the result ought to be not
so much a large number of votes for Riley as an antagonism or
at least an indifference to Quincy . . ." Riley had venom to spare.
His attacks on Quincy honed the edge of bitterness left over
from 1896:

> Mayor Quincy is not a man of affairs. He is not versed in business.
> He does not understand finance. He has never been obliged to earn
> a living . . . He is sailing under the shadow of a mighty name, but it
> is only a shadow . . . I was not brought up with a silver spoon in my
> mouth. My infant limbs were not wrapped in purple and fine linen.
> The name I inherited, however dear to me, had no weight here. I am
> a child of toil . . .[25]

Against such invective Quincy's concessions to the Board of
Strategy and to organized labor paid off handsomely. Irish district leaders, even including Martin Lomasney, interpreted
Riley's campaign as another effort to wreck the party organization in the city, and they united against him. And Boston trade-
unionists knew their benefactor. Perhaps Quincy's most significant supporter in 1897 was the typographer Frank Foster.
Despite his conversion to Bryanism the year before, Foster
despised the strategies of factional politics and recognized in
Quincy a rare friend of the labor movement. Far from lending his
influence to Riley, Foster stumped the city in Quincy's behalf.
Quincy won by nearly the same margin as in 1895, despite Riley's
hatchet work. In the wake of his victory Henry Cabot Lodge's
chief Boston informant ruefully suggested that the only way to
beat Quincy was to run a strong man on the following promise:
"Independent of the tax payers, without regard to the expenses,
I propose to improve the city in the most advanced way, thereby
furthering the glory of our municipality and the employment of
the poor." [26]

But where Quincy survived the challenge of the Bryanites in
1897, he met his match when Martin Lomasney turned on him a

year later. In the months after his re-election tremendous pressure built up among regular Irish leaders to force Quincy to shape his program more directly to their benefit. Rather than bow to these fresh demands, Quincy intensified his own efforts to concentrate executive authority in the city government and rationalize its methods. Quincy's growing dissatisfaction with the Boston City Council and Board of Aldermen now verged on studied contempt. Council appropriations for wardrooms and "street improvements" ate into the city budget and forced Quincy to appeal repeatedly to the Republican state legislature for permission to borrow above the city debt limit in order to finance his own special projects. To remedy this situation Quincy attempted after his re-election to establish an independent Board of Apportionment with power to draw up a reasonable and "scientific" distribution of the city budget. (In line with this goal Quincy created a municipal bureau of statistics—the first in the country—and brought in a Johns Hopkins Ph.D. to direct it.) The state legislature's authorization of the Board of Apportionment precipitated a harsh contest between the mayor's ideal of rational city government under executive leadership and the jealous insistence of aldermen and council members for more consideration in the spread of largesse. With a sensitive issue now drawn between the Mayor and Irish organization Democrats, patchwork compromises in the meetings of the Board of Strategy were unavailing, and Quincy was suddenly exposed and vulnerable. The quarrel cast him in a role he had till now succeeded in avoiding: the haughty patrician intelligence trying to restrain a heedless majority.[27]

By 1898 no Yankee Democrat could thwart the Irish and survive. Martin Lomasney instantly seized his opportunity. Already worried about the impact of what he later called Quincy's "visionary ideas on government" upon his slum-based power, Lomasney quickly marshaled his resources in the General Court. By exploiting his influence among Republican leaders in the legislature, he engineered the repeal of Quincy's scheme for a municipal Board of Apportionment. After this crushing blow, the vendetta shifted back to City Hall, as Quincy began to comb the city payroll and Lomasney exploited letters stolen from Quincy's office. When the returns were in on the city council elections of 1898 Lomasney controlled a bloc of rebellious Democrats and willing Republicans large enough to elect one of his henchmen as president of the council. An investigation of Quincy's removals was promptly launched, and it ended in passage of what amounted to a vote of censure against the mayor. Meanwhile Quincy's program of city reform ground to a dead halt. He had to content himself with charges that the City Council had degenerated into a "municipal debating club" bent on obstruction and harassment, and offering foredoomed proposals for a unicameral city legislature further stripped of its powers. Quincy's last year in office was a political nightmare. His disgruntled advisers on the Board of Strategy had been put to rout by Lomasney's tactics and the Democrats of Boston divided into an angry swarm of wrangling factions.[28]

Quincy dropped all thought of running for a third term. Patrick Collins, the sage of the Irish Democracy, was brought out of political retirement in an effort to unite the party. But Martin Lomasney would not be appeased. He encouraged a rival Irish faction to oppose Collins and thereby ensured Democratic defeat in the mayoral election of 1899. Collins lost to a staid Republican businessman, who immediately set about liquidating Josiah Quincy's "insolvent utopia." Quincy left Boston in January 1900 for a tour of Europe, marriage, a lecture engagement at the London School of Economics, and a study of the latest English legislation. He would return to run unsuccessfully for governor in 1901 and to play a backstage role in Boston politics in later years. Despite well-publicized financial reversals he retained enough influence to help gather New England support for Woodrow Wilson in 1912. In the year before his death, at the Massachusetts Constitutional Convention of 1917–18, he would return briefly to the limelight to battle once again with Martin Lomasney over issues of executive authority and party discipline, and once again he would be defeated. For the rest, his political career ended at age forty when he left City Hall in 1900.[29]

Thirty years later Andrew J. Peters, another Harvard man who became Mayor of Boston, wrote Quincy's epitaph for the *Commonwealth History of Massachusetts:* "It was almost a fetish with him that the poor should have as ample facilities for recreation as the rich. Quincy was an ardent advocate of the management of city departments by unpaid boards. His expenditures of unusual sums to better the condition of less fortunate citizens proved the fallacy of a philanthropic administration." [30]

With these smug words Josiah Quincy has been assigned his place in Boston's history as an almost unremembered oddity. It is not surprising that he won no recognition in the pantheon of reform mayors who marked the onset of the Progressive Era in American politics. He differed from Cleveland's Tom Johnson, Toledo's "Golden Rule" Jones, Detroit's Hazen Pingree, and the others, in important ways. Unlike them, he attempted frankly to ground his program in cooperation with the local "machine." He was no colorful tribune leading a crusade against corruption. Beatrice Webb had concluded that under Quincy, Boston was "governed by its aristocracy working through a corrupt democracy." While her judgment was perhaps too crisply phrased to be wholly accurate, it was true that Quincy held power at the sufferance of a majority which never altogether trusted him. And when he ventured a concerted effort in favor of rational budgeting of city funds, comparable to the drives for business efficiency among Progressive mayors, it was quickly snuffed out by Boston's special breed of politicians. Moreover, circumstances in Massachusetts provided him with no opportunity to bring Boston's rail and traction magnates to heel in a vigorous assault upon monopoly. In any event, for all his desire to translate Fabian socialism into American urban politics, Quincy's theories of public ownership stopped at the edge of vested rail interests. In fact his campaign for a new union rail terminal in the South End, as well as his willingness to lease Boston's new subway to a private syndicate, provoked his critics to label him a friend of organized wealth. Boston's progressive, reform magazine *Arena,* which had hailed Quincy's socialist adventures as mayor, was listing him a few years later among the lackeys of New England's plutocrats.[31]

Quincy's mayoralty, for all its remarkable precedents and suggestions, stood not at the beginning of a political era but at the end. When he left office Cleveland Democracy ceased to be a vital force in Boston political life. Thereafter Irish Democrats increasingly controlled the city on their own terms. Whenever they could agree among themselves they elected their own mayors. Occasionally, as when Patrick Collins was elected in 1901 and later on under John F. Fitzgerald, a fleeting vestige of the old collaboration between Yankee and Irish revived in the Democratic party. And Collins' mayoralty proved remarkably faithful to the ideal of spartan economy which Nathan Matthews had followed in the early 1890's. Meanwhile, a few Irishmen managed to parlay their political contacts during the Cleveland era into business success. Thus Joseph O'Neil, the bluff Boston congressman who had befriended William E. Russell and Richard Olney, had turned to banking by the turn of the century. By the 1920's he was one of the city's wealthiest and most respected Irishmen. Joseph P. Kennedy, the son of the East Boston ward boss Patrick J. Kennedy, was perhaps only the most famous young Irishman to seek out Yankee acceptance in his drive for commercial fortune. But in Boston politics the future belonged not to those who staked their careers on social cohesion and party cooperation, but to those who thrived by fanning political dissidence and ethnic resentments. It belonged to Martin Lomasney, and ultimately to a young man who cast his first legal vote in 1896—James Michael Curley.

CHAPTER TEN · AFTERMATH

AFTER 1896 Cleveland Democrats had no coherent influence in American politics. Bryan's nomination marked a massive shift of power and purpose within the Democratic party. Its new agrarian leaders had written an end to the Yankee dream of a seaboard alliance between North and South by abandoning New York, New Jersey, and New England for the growing trans-Mississippi West. Eastern Democrats were left thrashing among themselves in the backwater of neglect. In many parts of the East at the turn of the century, as a result, one-party Republican control fixed itself with as great tenacity as Democratic rule in the South, and meaningful political competition all but disappeared. The political crisis of the mid-nineties had produced a radical imbalance in the two-party system throughout the industrial Northeast. This was reflected most emphatically in the overwhelmingly Republican composition of state legislatures and congressional delegations in the region. The comfortable margin of Republican power tended to blunt and diffuse the search of urban Americans for moderate reform through traditional partisan activity. This was one reason why the gathering forces of Progressivism made relatively slower headway in the East than beyond the Appalachians. Lacking the spur of competition from a well-organized party of opposition, many eastern Republican politicians were less responsive to the Progressive cry for reform than they otherwise might have been. For years Old Guard complacency remained untroubled by any serious need to secure Progressive votes through protective coloration. Not until the Democratic party emerged from its private wilderness in 1910 would the Progressive movement reach fulfillment in most Eastern state legislatures and in Congress.[1]

In Massachusetts the Democratic party took a full fourteen years to recover from the shock of 1896. By bringing Bryanism home to Massachusetts, George Fred Williams had forced his fellow Democrats to follow out their personal reactions to Bryan and the Chicago platform to unintended and often undesired public extremes. Men found themselves branded by the commitment they had had to make in 1896. For an entire generation of political leadership, the result was permanent fragmentation. The special character of Cleveland Democracy in Massachusetts—the cautious, conservative, ameliorating reformism best exemplified by William E. Russell—was invalidated by the events of 1896. Bryan's nomination, Williams' bolt, the deaths of Russell and Maguire, and the shock of the campaign itself combined to destroy the assumption of shared community values from which Cleveland Democracy drew its life. Thereafter conservative reform was an anachronism in the Democratic party. One was now an old-fashioned conservative or a radical reformer or a case-hardened Irishman. One's choice in 1896 made the difference.

Among the former followers of Grover Cleveland and Billy Russell, Massachusetts Mugwumps suffered as much as any after 1896. The futility of their long quest for independent political authority had been brought home to many of them by the role they played in the election of William McKinley. Few of them could stomach McKinley's subsequent behavior. Even Richard Henry Dana, more charitable than most of his breed toward Republicans, found the new administration in Washington hard to justify. Dana voted for McKinley in 1896 and again in 1900. But he admitted in his private journal, "President McKinley . . . has done nothing but has the same sweet, lovable, and ineffective disposition, hoping to please everybody and in the end, like a lump of dough, yielding to the greatest pressure." If the ascent of such a man to power was the end result of political upheaval, perhaps the Mugwump should re-examine his principles. For some the events of 1896 suggested the wisdom of closer and more sustained participation in partisan politics. One's cherished goals might stand a better chance of fulfillment if forced into the matrix of one party or the other by constant group pressure. Thus the young Mugwump Charles Warren sought to modify the hallowed doctrine of the bolt:

> While the independent who has no party designation at all, but who wanders from one party to another, may not have great weight, and may not be considered of great importance by party managers, the independent who is a party man until the principles he believes in are outraged, and who then *as* a party man votes against his party,—that is the independent whom party managers will now be forced to recognize, to consider, and to conciliate.[2]

Yet after 1896 the Mugwumps experienced more trouble than ever before in choosing between the parties, or even choosing principles to impose on one party or the other. Civil service no longer excited much debate, even at Reform Club meetings. And with the country bent on an orgy of high protection under McKinley, tariff reform seemed a fading vision. "I am a Free-Trader," Charles Francis Adams wrote to Henry Cabot Lodge in 1897, "yet I am quite willing to see the full experiment of protection tried to its logical end; I agree that the game is up for my life time." While the Mugwumps worried openly about trusts and plutocrats, their fear of expanding federal power made them constantly distrustful of techniques for closer public regulation of the economy. Through the nineties and early years of the new century, they regarded the Interstate Commerce Act and the Sherman Antitrust Act as ominous extensions of the government's capacity to intervene in a man's private affairs. They favored a milder, less coercive approach. Banking reform, profit sharing, the sanction of publicity for corporations as well as parties—all these remedies had their advocates among Mugwumps worried about economic conflict in America. But more often than not, hope struggled with despair. After threshing out the difficulties of profit sharing as a solution to factory friction, Charles R. Codman concluded in his journal, "Still it may come as free trade may come, or as universal peace may come, or as the Kingdom of God may come—and all these I believe will come—but when?"[3]

The aging Mugwumps' spirit had been beaten and tempered

by accumulating disappointments. As their dissatisfaction with McKinleyism mounted, they talked increasingly of the need for a party of responsible opposition in America. The stubborn vision of a new third party had not vanished entirely, but the Gold Democratic movement of 1896—and its contribution to McKinley's victory— had done much to cloud the dream. Perhaps, in retrospect, there was some merit after all in the old political equilibrium between the major parties. At least both parties had occasionally listened to gentlemen. But now, with the tattered Democratic minority in the hands of unreliable Westerners, and the ample Republican majority catering contentedly to the Hannas, Platts, and Quays, Mugwumpery made one a more irrelevant outsider than ever before. Acceptance of the two-party system was finally forced upon the Mugwumps at a time when both parties seemed impervious to their influence. In the years after 1896 Mugwumps agonized over the patent difficulties of fulfilling their new hope of responsible opposition through the Democratic party. The hysteria of 1896 receded quickly, and the next four years did much to establish the legitimacy of Bryanism in the Mugwump mind. But if they no longer identified Bryan with rabid anarchy, neither did they trust his leadership or accept the heresies of the Chicago platform. As long as domestic tensions shaped the concerns of national politics, neither the Republican nor the Democratic party promised safety for the Mugwumps' republic. The secretary of the Reform Club put the choice succinctly:

While there is little question that one of the chief causes of the distrust of Mr. Bryan is his attempt to array class against class, the rich against the poor, by his inflammatory speeches, a candid man must admit the danger that the constantly increasing influence of wealth in deciding and controlling the politics of the Republican party may of itself produce much the same effect as Mr. Bryan's speeches.[4]

Under these circumstances the advent of the Spanish-American War and the adventure in empire that followed it revived the flagging temper of the Mugwumps. Here at last was a bracing moral challenge to their cosmos to which they could respond unequivocally. Anti-imperialism provided a new ethical dimension to the economic and political conservatism of the Mugwumps. It also promised a way out of political isolation. By blurring domestic political divisions it seemed for a while to create grounds for opposition to McKinley within the two-party system.

Boston Mugwumps, especially those close to the financial community, had for years been skittish about American muscle-flexing overseas. The Venezuela crisis of 1895, breaking in on a depression at home, exasperated many State Streeters. The Mug-wump banker C. C. Jackson, in urging the Democratic party to resist overseas meddling, set the tone for years to come. He called for "a declaration in favor of promoting the industrial prosperity of the country by *minding our own business*,—by not interfering with foreign countries or foreign quarrels . . ." [5] In the wake of the campaign of 1896 Bostonians tended to judge mounting jingoism by its probable effect on the discontent of American farmers and laborers. Expansionists and anti-imperialists agreed that domestic dissatisfactions were boiling near the danger point. They disagreed whether imperialism would prove to be an outlet for these grievances, or an aggravation. Thus the Mug-wump Charles Francis Adams (who had regarded Cleveland's Venezuela message as "a disgraceful bit of drunken, diplomatic rhodomontade") wrote to Henry Cabot Lodge in 1897, "There is a time for everything—even for a brilliant, spirited, Roman-candle foreign policy; but, I submit, that time is not when the currency is hopelessly snarled up . . . , when trade and industry languish, when confidence is shaken, when popular discontent is widespread, when Bryanism and the Coxeyites are lying low . . ." A year later, during the early phase of the Spanish-American War, one of Lodge's imperialist friends, George H. Lyman of Boston, argued from Adams' premise to a diametrically opposed view. Empire, he wrote, "would give vent . . . to that restless spirit of our race which of late years has found its expression only in a desire for a change of government, institutions, and policies. From a political standpoint, always provided the thing is started right, it is bound to ensure the welfare of the Republi-can party for another generation." In the event, Lyman proved the more astute psychic analyst. [6]

The full implications of the war with Spain over Cuba became clear only after Admiral Dewey's victory in Manila Bay opened the prospect of an American overseas empire. Mugwumps were shocked at the unexpected lust for colonial possessions which seemed to clutch the American majority in the hour of victory over Spain. The probable costs of this appetite, economic, social, and moral, were frightening. One danger often cited was the expansion of the federal administrative and military arm which necessarily would follow the acquisition of overseas territory. Thus Charles Francis Adams argued at the Reform Club against taking the Philippines on the ground that it would require a standing army costing a hundred million dollars. (He concluded his remarks with a chilling glimpse into the future: "Gentlemen, an income tax looms up in the largest possible proportions.") But at bottom, most Mugwumps were anti-imperialists because they could not square the old, benign, republican ideals on which they had been bred with American imperial control of subject peoples beyond continental shores. To them the imperial distemper, in its acquisitive, domineering paternalism, augured the definitive rejection of a national record of honor, stability, and probity in the affairs of the world. The American democratic experiment, already threatened internally with the European diseases of class strife and social violence, was now apparently headed toward Old World expedients of aggression and conquest in its foregn policy. To a caustic critic of American mores like Charles Eliot Norton, the imperial phenomenon was almost vindication: "We have been living in a Fool's Paradise," Norton wrote to an English friend, "hoping that in the long run the better elements in our national life would get the upper hand, and that we should stumble along, with many a slip indeed, but on the whole in the right direction. But the war has suddenly roused us from this dream. America has rejected her old ideals, turned her back on her past, and chosen the path of barbarism . . ." As the rueful anti-imperialist crack had it, "Dewey took Manila with the loss of one man—and all our institutions."[7]

In the fall of 1898, as Washington wrestled with the large details of the peace with Spain, three Boston Mugwumps—Moorfield Storey, Gamaliel Bradford, and Edward Atkinson—formed the Anti-Imperialist League in Boston, and quickly the protest movement took on a broad and varied national dimension. Even in Massachusetts the League's membership list revealed those political incongruities which have often been cited as a weakness of the anti-imperialist movement. While most established Mugwumps were prominent in the cause, they had to work with, among others, that crusty old critic of Mugwumpery, Republican Senator George Frisbie Hoar; the aging labor radical, George E. McNeill; and the popular Boston Irishman, Patrick Collins. No doubt this diversity, as well as the advanced age of many of the League's leaders, hobbled their efforts at organizational unity and dynamism. But no local consensus, however intimate, could have saved them from confronting the fact that the most powerful anti-imperialist in the country was William Jennings Bryan. That was profoundly awkward.[8]

Bryan's assumption of the mantle of anti-imperialist leadership did not mean, as many Mugwumps hoped it would, that he was through with free silver. Thus he was accepted as a spokesman for the new cause with serious reluctance. But even those who disliked the man were tempted by the hope that his party might assume the role of responsible opposition by taking up the issue of anti-imperialism. As the election of 1900 approached a significant number of Mugwumps, most notably Moorfield Storey, Thomas Wentworth Higginson, and Charles R. Codman, decided to support Bryan for President. Moorfield Storey's behavior during that campaign illustrated vividly the problem Bryan posed. Storey's commitment to anti-imperialism propelled him further along the path of political expediency than he had ever traveled before. He acknowledged his dilemma with painful candor. "In a word," he wrote to George Frisbie Hoar in February 1900, "I want to vote against imperialism and I do not want to vote for Bryan." The following summer he toyed with the notion of accepting a national third-party nomination to appease those who shared his dilemma. Finally, reluctantly, he abandoned this project. A third party simply was not feasible, he told Carl Schurz. "I have long, as you know, desired a new party and have labored to bring it about for some sixteen years, and it is therefore a great disappointment to me that the way does not seem clear now." To John Jay Chapman he explained, "I wish to see the American people declare that the slaughter in the Philippine Islands shall stop and that they shall have their independence. This can only be done by the defeat of McKinley, and that means the election of Bryan . . . The end I wish I must work for openly and directly." Storey came out for Bryan in mid-September. A little later he decided to run for Congress as an anti-imperialist. He hoped for Democratic endorsement, but the Democrats of his district did not oblige, and so he ran independently. On election day his life-long distrust of successful politicians was confirmed by his resounding defeat. It was his first and last try for elective office. Thereafter Storey sought to convince himself that the cause of anti-imperialism had gained more in the long run by McKinley's re-election than it would have by Bryan's victory. "McKinley will work out his own damnation," he wrote, "and in so doing will teach the people of this country that imperialism is absolutely wrong, as it never could have been taught in any other way." His rationales had brought the most rigid of Mugwumps full circle. Only the durable Mugwump faith in the justification of principle through political defeat had clearly survived.[9]

The election of 1900 was the last in which the Mugwumps participated with any sense of group identity. Many could not bring themselves to vote for Bryan. Charles Francis Adams and Charles W. Eliot publicly announced their decision to support McKinley. Carl Schurz called his vote for Bryan in 1900 "the most distasteful thing I ever did." But whatever their personal solutions to the Bryan problem, Mugwump anti-imperialists agreed among themselves to support Democratic congressional candidates in order to create an effective opposition to McKinleyism in Washington. If their success at this tactic was modest, so by now were their hopes. As Adams put it in a letter to Schurz, "For educational purposes alone, aside from all others, we desire to bring about a condition of unstable political equilibrium during the next few years. Give the country time in which to reflect." [10]

Through the early years of the new century Adams' hope for equilibrium through opposition became the pervading desire of those Mugwumps who still retained an interest in political affairs. (It should be noted that the attrition rate among this number was high after 1896.) The feverish pace of national politics in the McKinley era had thoroughly alarmed them. Headlong and heedless, the country seemed bent on national self-glory. Meanwhile a certain cult of personality was evidently gathering around national leaders. McKinley's assassination, and the popular response to it, provided a sad lesson in the changing times. The secretary of the Reform Club expressed concern at the "importance attached by the world to the life of one American man as contra-distinguished from an act of our people or of our government. The political world felt the man was of importance. I venture to doubt whether it had ever felt so with reference to an American. The event is significant. It is a symptom of the Imperial disease from which we are suffering." McKinley's successor aggravated the Mugwumps' distaste for heroic leadership. Few of them were won over to Theodore Roosevelt's new kind of Republicanism, or to the Progressive movement in general. While sharing with the Progressives an urgent sense of political malaise, the Mugwump generation recoiled from Progressive solutions which swelled the power of organized society over the individual. Talk of "Theodore I" spiced conversations at the Reform Club, and Roosevelt's intervention in the 1902 coal strike was judged to be a "dangerous precedent" for the future. So out of sympathy with the Roosevelt Era was Moorfield Storey that he was delighted to find at the annual meeting of the American Bar Association in 1907 a widespread opposition to Roosevelt, an attitude which he associated with "a moral awakening all over the country." The panic of 1907 encouraged Storey to anticipate a slackening of national prosperity and "a chance of our knowing some adversity with its sweet uses." All that was needed, in his mind, was fresh blood to lead the coming reaction. But good men were hard to find. In 1908, as Roosevelt prepared to leave the White House, Storey once again decided that Bryan should become President. As he assured Charles Francis Adams, Bryan could accomplish nothing serious as long as the Republicans controlled Congress. The federal government would be deadlocked, and the country would have four more years to think where it was headed. The hope for pause was characteristic. Looking glumly out on the dawning years of the twentieth century, the Mugwump might well have remembered Howells' lines:

> We live, but a world has passed away
> with the years that perished to make us men.[11]

It would be an error to judge the Mugwumps solely on the behavior of their declining years, or to write them off as Yankee conservatives and leave this as explanation for their ineffectiveness as reformers. "Our best memories are that we have tried to fix ideals for other folks to live by," Barrett Wendell wrote of his generation as early as 1893. "We have done our best—not greatly, but honestly." [12] It is hard to imagine that any group of men caught up in American politics were ever guided by a more stringent code of ethics, or possessed by a more driving zeal to obey it, than were the Mugwumps. There is, of course, a line in our politics beyond which a man cannot insist on his own virtue without destroying his effectiveness. If the Mugwumps stepped across that line with self-righteous regularity, they did not do so with impunity. For all the excellence of their public virtue, their insistence on it as the highest good to which they could aspire was not only an intellectual conceit but a serious misdirection of talent. The reforms they recommended along the way were not irrelevant to the problems of their generation, however antedated they appear in retrospect. But the Mugwumps' moral arrogance precluded much achievement. If once in a while they had accepted the wisdom of the half loaf, they might have left the political arena with something more than the memory of their own integrity. They left little more than that in Massachusetts.

From 1896 until 1910, meanwhile, the Bay State Democratic party remained a split minority, consuming its energies in acrid internal strife. George Fred Williams never forgave former friends who resisted his behavior in 1896. Looking back on that campaign, Williams even professed a greater respect for the crass techniques of Mark Hanna than for the actions of the "cowards" in his own party. By maintaining control of the party nominating machinery Williams kept the Chicago platform, as well as his own enmities, bristling as live issues in Democratic state politics for half a decade after 1896. After one more try for the governorship in 1897, he secured loyal Bryanites to carry on the hopeless annual struggle. Opposed to him within the party were the power of Boston traction and rail interests, the potent but fickle leaders of the Boston Irish, and the remnants of Grover Cleveland's personal following. Meanwhile the state's Republican majority grew sleek and powerful. "All the Billy Russells that ever lived could not sway it for one moment . . . ," the state chairman proudly wrote to Henry Cabot Lodge in the summer of 1897.[13]

The blithe movement of the early nineties—whose most celebrated characteristic had been the hearty youth of its recruits—had come to a stunted end. By the end of the decade only Josiah Quincy among its leaders retained a hold in active politics, and the days of his influence were numbered. Dead with William E. Russell were the former Congressmen John F. Andrew (who died in 1895 at age forty-four), and Sherman Hoar (who contracted typhoid fever caring for the wounded of the war with Spain and died at age thirty-eight in 1898). Even a man so firmly established in the leadership of the Democratic youth movement as Nathan Matthews found himself a political cripple for having engineered the Gold Democratic bolt in Boston. Despite his earlier work as Mayor of Boston and organizer of the Young Men's Democratic Club, Matthews was denied as trivial an honor as the chairmanship of the Democratic state convention in 1904 because he had bolted the regular organization in 1896.[14]

Nor was Matthews the only young man to experience difficulties because of his Gold Democratic label. Louis Brandeis was challenged by Bryanites at a Democratic ward caucus in Boston shortly after the 1896 election on the grounds that he had no

business at a regular party meeting. The objection was over-
ruled and Brandeis continued to regard himself as a Democrat.
But over the next decade, as he embarked on his militant reform
crusades in Massachusetts, Brandeis could muster only random,
ineffective support from his own party. And his causes in state
politics were mainly negative battles of protest. He could fight to
prevent things from happening (as in the case of his franchise
quarrels with Boston traction interests, or his celebrated war
against the merger of the New Haven Railroad with the Boston
and Maine), but because of the bankrupt condition of his own
party he was rarely in a position to initiate positive or corrective
reforms without substantial Republican support. It was not
until Brandeis escaped from the political matrix of Massachusetts and could identify himself with the regenerated national
Democratic party after 1910 that his Progressivism bloomed in
full creative fashion.[15]

For many Massachusetts families the first Bryan campaign
forced a permanent switch of party affiliations. Thus the Salton-
stalls, whose traditional Democratic affiliations had been recognized by President Cleveland in the naming of Leverett Saltonstall to the Collectorship of the Port of Boston, crossed party lines
in 1896. The Collector's son, Richard M. Saltonstall, who had
been a member of the Young Men's Democratic Club, left the
party after Bryan's nomination, and his son, the Leverett Saltonstall who has served as Republican Governor and United States
Senator for Massachusetts, cast his first vote for President Taft
in 1912. Meanwhile a village blacksmith in North Attleboro
named Joseph W. Martin abandoned his Democratic loyalties
for Republicanism in 1896. So fervent a party man had he been
before the advent of Bryan that he had wanted to name his son,
born on the eve of the 1884 election, Grover Cleveland Martin.
At the mother's insistence the boy took his father's name instead,
and grew up to become Republican speaker of the United States
House of Representatives.[16]

Other Cleveland Democrats dropped out of politics altogether
after 1896. One instance was the gentleman farmer John E.
Russell, who had led the van of Democratic tariff reformers as a

congressman in the 1880's, who had befriended Grover Cleveland and been offered high office in Cleveland's second administration, and who ran for governor of Massachusetts in the depression years 1893 and 1894. Russell now retired to his farm at Leicester and resumed his experiments in stockbreeding. In 1898 he renewed his old acquaintance with Cleveland's former party lieutenant, William C. Whitney of New York, but now their letters were more concerned with race horses than politics. When Russell broke up his library he sent Whitney his studbooks. He lived on till 1903, genial, wise, and politically ignored. "Until 1896," he wistfully told a friend the year before he died, "I knew every active young Democrat in the Commonwealth." [17]

The year 1896 made an old-fashioned young man of Charles S. Hamlin. Returning to Boston from his position in the Treasury Department after Grover Cleveland left the White House in the spring of 1897, Hamlin was much sought after as a corporation lawyer. But his bolt to the Gold Democratic ticket the previous summer was a kiss of death to his continuing political ambitions. ("Hamlin shall never return to the Democratic party. I shall not permit it," George Fred Williams was heard to say.) Hamlin's intellectual growth seemed arrested too. Thereafter his political utterances had an odd mustiness about them. He could locate new problems, but he could not respond to them with any but the old formulas of tariff reform and self-reliance. Thus in 1899 he addressed himself to the trust problem:

Another most important domestic issue is the proper regulation of the so-called trusts, or to put it in another form, and the really practicable form, of opening our markets to foreign competition where domestic combinations, assisted by the tariff, have stifled internal competition.

And in 1902, answering the socialist complaint about the rich and poor:

While undoubtedly the accumulation of wealth in individual hands is greater than at any previous period in our history, yet it must not be forgotten that there is no limitation to wealth except when labor ceases to labor, and that every man if he be given equal opportunity in the world's struggle can support himself comfortably and lay aside something at least for a rainy day.

Time and again Hamlin offered himself as a candidate for the Democratic nomination for governor on these terms, trying to regain a foothold in his party. He never made it. Finally in 1913, when Woodrow Wilson became President, Hamlin went back to Washington to take up his old duties as Assistant Secretary of the Treasury.[18]

A number of important Cleveland Democrats took advantage of the passing political fluidity created by the Spanish American War and its imperial aftermath to slip gently back into Bryan's party. For such political realists as Josiah Quincy and Richard Olney (who was not entirely innocent of presidential ambitions), Bryan's anti-imperialism was an unreckoned opportunity. Neither Quincy nor Olney had associated himself with the anti-imperialist movement in its early phase. In fact neither was in great sympathy with it. In 1898 Josiah Quincy was an avid exponent of American overseas expansion, and in the same year Olney was calling on the nation to pull its head out of the sand and behave like a great world power. Yet by 1900 both men had trimmed their sails. Olney privately professed as deep contempt for the quality of Bryan's anti-imperialist arguments as for his undisciplined talk about trusts: Bryan's notion that the Declaration of Independence justified self-government for the natives of the Philippines was in Olney's estimate "preposterous." Yet in September 1900 Olney announced his support for Bryan, largely on the issue of McKinley's Philippine policy, which, he said, "leaves millions of human beings outside the pale of any recognized code of law, and signifies for our new possessions for an indefinite period militarism of the most unadulterated sort." Similarly, Josiah Quincy attempted to make up for 1896 in 1900. Admitting that he had been "at first a little dazzled by our new possessions," he declared that the Philippine question had placed the issue of human liberty above that of currency. While he still believed in expansion, he did not believe in force. He was, therefore, Bryan's man.[19]

The great majority of regular Democratic leaders in Massa-

chusetts supported Bryan in 1900. Having done so, they forth-
with set about with other eastern party leaders to exorcise
Bryanism from the party by the next presidential contest. In
Massachusetts this entailed getting rid of George Fred Williams.
Williams was a stubborn antagonist. After 1897 he never again
ran for public office, but for years thereafter he came to do battle
at party conventions and add the heat of 1896 to the proceedings. It was not until 1902 that his enemies decisively wrested
control of the party from him. At the annual state convention
that year Williams presented for the delegates' approval a
flaming manifesto announcing that "a heartless capitalism, born
of greed and nourished by law, is perverting our institutions and
morals, invading press, pulpit, and college, and oppressing labor
and trade." In an act of conscious emancipation from Bryanite
radicalism the convention voted down Williams' platform, substituted in its place a properly evasive document, and proceeded
to nominate for governor William A. Gaston, the free-spending
president of the Boston Elevated Railroad Company and a
trusted lieutenant of the Elevated's owner, J. P. Morgan. "The
Massachusetts Democracy is now at last free from the terrible
incubus which has weighed it down since 1896," the *Boston
Transcript* announced.[20]

Faced with the choice between Gaston and the Williams
faction, established Yankee Democrats like Josiah Quincy and
Charles S. Hamlin lined up reluctantly with Gaston. Irish leaders
also supported Gaston, and with this semblance of unity the
Democratic minority in the state seemed to show signs of emer-
gence from the depths of 1896. In the presidential year 1904
party leaders launched a trial balloon for Richard Olney, and
when it subsided they agreeably supported the choice of the
conservative New York Judge Alton B. Parker as a national candidate. Parker was a passable heir to the Grover Cleveland tradition, but in 1904, placed against Theodore Roosevelt, he was a
pale gold brick. His sober conservative appeal, calculated to
attract those put off both by Bryan's supposed radicalism and
Roosevelt's bullish energy, was offset in many minds by the
recent record of the Democratic party. In Massachusetts the

party's internal quarrels had irreparably damaged its reputation among those who had supported it in the Cleveland years. When Hamlin appealed to Charles Francis Adams for a party contribution in 1904, Adams—conveniently forgetting his membership in the Young Men's Democratic Club in the 1890's—replied coolly that he was not and never had been a Democrat. Then he relieved himself of pent-up irritation at the party's demonstrated incompetence in the role of responsible opposition: "Why the Democratic managers, as such, should, during recent years, have made it a part of their political wisdom to drag their organization through all the dirt, filth and mire anywhere to be found, and absolutely prevent the possibility of its appearing as a legitimate, recognized and respectable party of the 'Outs,' has been unto me a mystery." On the other hand, to younger middle-class Progressive reformers like Edwin D. Mead the substitution of Parker for Bryan robbed the Democratic party of its one vital force. Mead wrote to Moorfield Storey just before the 1904 election:

> The movement represented most conspicuously by Bryan, however crude in much (although the judgment of it merely as a "free silver" movement is vastly cruder and more superficial), is to me the only hopeful or prophetic thing in the Democratic party today. The scramble to throttle and get rid of it, to make the party "solid" with Wall Street and earn a reputation for being "safer" and "more conservative" than Roosevelt, to men of radical social and economic views, like myself, who have a sincere and high admiration for Roosevelt for the courageous and progressive position he has taken on many industrial problems, is a discouraging spectacle.[21]

Although Roosevelt drubbed Parker at the polls, a popular shoe manufacturer named William L. Douglas managed to be elected as Democratic Governor of Massachusetts in 1904. While he lasted in office only one year, his tenure aided the task of knitting the Democrats of the state back together again. Meanwhile George Fred Williams was coming to be regarded as an eccentric relic of the unhappy past. His personal following dwindled rapidly after 1900. Bryanism sunk no deep roots in the thin soil of Massachusetts, and the eclectic band of radicals who had gathered in 1896 scattered in random directions. Some, like the corporation lawyer Harry Jaquith, dropped politics as quickly as he had taken it up. Robert Treat Paine III eventually went over to Roosevelt. The volatile Tim Coakley turned Republican in 1903. Of the trade-unionists, Frank Foster returned to his union work, finally disenchanted with the ways of two-party politics; Harry Lloyd and George E. McNeill embraced the Socialist party in 1902. In 1903 Williams tried to pool his remaining political strength in a new, nonpartisan organization called the People's Rule, the aim of which, he said, was to restore popular sovereignty to Massachusetts despite its corrupt party system by vesting the people with the right to veto acts of state legislation at the polls. The People's Rule was stillborn. The following year, grasping for a fresh hope, Williams came out in favor of William Randolph Hearst for President.[22]

By associating his distrust of the power of corporate monopoly with Bryanism, free silver, and direct democracy, Williams had cast a superficial aura of radicalism over the reform wing of the Democratic party in Massachusetts. And by identfying reform with resentment against the Boston Irish, he had snapped the taut bond of cooperation between urban Irish and suburban Yankee Democrat. Thus he helped to deliver the party over to his worst enemies—in Boston, the Lomasneys and Curleys of the wards; in state politics, the Gastons and Whitneys of the corporations; in national politics, the Alton B. Parkers. Such personal influence as he could muster in the party remained negative and unsettling. The conservative, corporate faction of the Democratic party proved scarcely more successful than the Bryanites at attracting consistent majorities in Massachusetts—or at securing permanent control of the party. Possession of the nominating machinery passed back and forth almost yearly between the party's far extremes as faction-ridden Democrats tried to patch together a winning coalition. In 1907 when Henry M. Whitney lumbered openly into the political arena to secure a Democratic nomination for governor, Williams helped to organize a bolt which ensured Whitney's burial at the polls.[23]

This was the Dedham lawyer's last public service to Massachu-

setts. After serving briefly a few years later as Minister to Greece
(a post with which Woodrow Wilson's Secretary of State William Jennings Bryan rewarded him in 1913), Williams returned
to finish his career in the relative obscurity of the Boston legal
profession. His long flirtation with destiny, which had begun
in 1884 with his bolt to Grover Cleveland, was over. Like so
many of his young contemporaries who took up the cause of
Cleveland Democracy back in the 1880's, he had thought to
carve a place for himself in the history of his times. He had clung
to the dream of greatness longer than most. Now there was
nothing left but the practice of law. Williams lived on till 1932,
when he died almost unnoticed in a Boston nursing home. The
monument on the Williams family burial plot in Dedham's Old
Village Cemetery is a broken mast. It commemorates Williams'
father, who perished in 1861 while trying to bring his ship into
Boston in a storm. It could as well commemorate the son.[24]

In 1910 the Democrats of Massachusetts put the bitter quarrels of the past behind them, elected a governor (a former Republican named Eugene Foss who was unmarked in any way by
the grim legacy of 1896), and won more seats in the General
Court than in any year since 1890. Two years later the electoral
votes of the Bay State went to Woodrow Wilson. In Massachusetts and across the nation, a new era had dawned for the
Democratic party.

In the decades since, the Cleveland Democrat has steadily
slipped into the limbo for discarded archetypes. Even the fusty
frock-coat, beaded-curtain propriety one once learned to associate with him has lost its clutch on the imagination. He is hard
to remember, much less surround with accurate meaning. In
Massachusetts, and especially in Boston, he diminished in importance even more swiftly than his numbers thinned out. Implacable fortune rudely deprived him of even a semblance of the
control over his environment he so deeply longed for. Those
who did not share his aims found it easy to slough them off
whenever other purposes rose to be served. This was hard for
men whose fathers and professors had held up to them for
emulation the memory of an early, finer Boston, the Yankee Hub,

the American Athens, the City on a Hill, the extended blur of former greatness.

Back in 1880 the Harvard philosopher and sometime Mugwump William James acknowledged that the older Boston was a thing of the past. But in the course of a celebrated assault in the *Atlantic Monthly* upon the determinism of Herbert Spencer he speculated confidently that the chance birth of a few great men in Boston would restore the city to its former glory. His optimism was robust: "Would a Spencerian evolutionist pretend that such an event is *incompatible* with the sociological condition of Boston at the present day? Surely not." In the same article James prophesied the certain triumph of Mugwump reform in America.[25] His faith in the Boston of 1880 contrasted vividly with the somber reflections of his brother a quarter century later. In *The American Scene* Henry James told of returning to Boston, where he had lived for a time as a young man, and observing the immigrants on the Common near the State House:

> The people before me were gross aliens to a man, and they were in serene and triumphant possession . . . They gave the measure of the distance by which the general movement was *away*—away, always and everywhere, from the old presumptions and conceivabilities . . . Therefore had I the vision, as filling the sky, no longer of the great Puritan "whip," the whip for the conscience and the nerves, of the local legend, but that of a huge applied sponge, a sponge saturated with the foreign mixture and passed over almost everything I remembered and might still have recovered.[26]

The sensitive intuitions of the James brothers shed bright if refracted light on the problems of their contemporaries in the city who had entered politics to avert the disappearance of the older Boston. The hopeful efforts of the Cleveland Democrats had been repeatedly rewarded with bitter results. They had sought to elevate the tone of politics by personal example, by party action, by passing laws. Yet in the minds of most of them, the tone of the Democratic party and American politics in general was distressingly dismal after 1896. They had sought to contain, control, and guide the headlong course of popular democracy. Yet their efforts at containment and guidance ended in what they took to be a blind, undisciplined escape by the mass of voters from established, legitimate leadership. They had hoped, particularly in New England, to shake off the fixed domination of Republican party rule. Yet as the century turned the Republican party was more firmly entrenched than ever. If one were to judge the Cleveland Democrats solely by their effort to adjust their elitist instincts to the task of maintaining political control in an age of mass democracy, one might be moved to count their movement as an unqualified and unlamented failure.

But the meaning of their experience had relevance beyond their time and place. Theirs was not the only group movement in American politics motivated by a desire to control the present by restoring the past. Nor was it the only one to fall short of the aspirations that launched it. Nor was it barren of important results, though some of these were unintended. The ill-fated drive of the Cleveland Democrats for tariff reform, by which they had sought to make their reform impact in national politics, ended in disaster. Their insistence upon low tariffs and sound currency as party priorities in the 1890's ultimately lost them their party. In fact the challenge of Bryanism so vividly dramatized their distrust of broad federal initiative toward economic and social reform that the Cleveland Democrats have come to wear the label Bourbon, and to be remembered as a stodgy, standpat, backward-looking breed of men.

If their record in Massachusetts is any indication, however, the image of obscurantism may be questioned by weighing their behavior in national politics against their more lively and imaginative response to the problems of industrial society at the level of state action. Led by Governor Russell and Josiah Quincy, the young Democrats of Massachusetts emphatically demonstrated that their conservatism in national politics was balanced by an earnest sense of social responsibility in state government. The importance of the distinction between national and state behavior becomes clear when one remembers that across the nineteenth century the state governments bore a much more intimate and functional relation to the people, and carried under prevailing constitutional assumptions a greater responsibility for the social welfare of the people, than did the government in Washington.

Bay State Democrats worked hard to impose their will at the State House on such issues as administrative reform, the amelioration of factory conditions, metropolitan planning, and improvement in electoral machinery. Their efforts were partly blunted by an antique state constitution, public apathy, and their own political inhibitions. Such reforms as they achieved, moreover, were dwarfed by those in other states a decade later in the rush of Progressivism. Nevertheless, they contributed importantly to the fact that at the outset of the Progressive Era, Massachusetts stood above most other states in the public protection it provided its citizenry against industrial barbarism and special privilege. Indeed it can be argued that in an important sense Massachusetts had already passed through its reform era by the time the general Progressive movement got underway.[27]

It was in the city of Boston itself, in the hectic combat of urban affairs, that the gentle reformers met perhaps their sternest test. Under the stress of ethnic tensions and intraparty strife the ethic of Cleveland Democracy was subjected to wide extremes of interpretation, ranging from the prudent businesslike vigor of Nathan Matthews' mayoralty to the quasi-socialist experimentalism of Josiah Quincy. But neither version of the ideal was to prove viable in the Boston of the new century. The failure of Yankee Democrats in the city to work out a modus vivendi with the growing Irish majority left a heritage of durable embitterment which would last for decades to come.

Perhaps in America as much can be learned of the past through the pathology of defeat as by the measurement of success. In the last analysis the Cleveland Democrats are important because at no level of government—national, state, or local —did their claim to leadership prevail. Time and again, aware of their minority status, they had tried to make up what they lacked in numbers through the influence of their ideas. Products of the best homes, education, and professional grounding their community could offer, they had set out with their allies among the Irish to restore to their community the order, harmony, and balance which they had been told existed there before their time. In their work they confronted hard social problems, in the form of economic and ethnic dissidence which challenged their aspiration to leadership and abused their guiding sense of republican equality. Their response to these problems was not irresponsible. It was not neurotic. It cannot be dismissed as merely a passing group adjustment to social cramp. But it was profoundly conservative. Along the way they discovered that their very ideal of community—the value they placed on social balance, ethnic harmony, and ethical propriety—limited their willingness to strike for deep-running changes through public action. In the early 1890's, at the crest of their careers, they found that perpetuation of their community took precedence over its improvement. In a few more years the community as they understood it had vanished. A contentious, changing world had overtaken them, and they were soon forgotten.

SELECTED BIBLIOGRAPHY

MANUSCRIPT AND SCRAPBOOK COLLECTIONS

Brooks Adams Papers. Houghton Library, Harvard University, Cambridge, Massachusetts.

Charles Francis Adams, Jr., Papers. Massachusetts Historical Society, Boston, Massachusetts.

Henry Adams Papers. Massachusetts Historical Society, Boston, Massachusetts.

John Forrester Andrew Papers. Massachusetts Historical Society, Boston, Massachusetts.

Edward Atkinson Papers. Massachusetts Historical Society, Boston, Massachusetts.

Francis W. Bird Papers. Houghton Library, Harvard University, Cambridge, Massachusetts.

Philip Putnam Chase Papers. Massachusetts Historical Society, Boston, Massachusetts.

William W. Clapp Papers. Houghton Library, Harvard University, Cambridge, Massachusetts.

Grover Cleveland Papers. Manuscript Division, Library of Congress, Washington, D.C.

Charles R. Codman Papers. Massachusetts Historical Society, Boston, Massachusetts.

Gaetano Conte, "Societies for the Protection of Italian Immigrants: Documents and Illustrations" (Scrapbook about the work of Reverend Conte in Boston's North End, 1893-1903). Massachusetts Historical Society, Boston, Massachusetts.

Richard Henry Dana III Papers. Massachusetts Historical Society, Boston, Massachusetts.

Henry H. Edes Papers. Massachusetts Historical Society, Boston, Massachusetts.

William C. Endicott Papers. Massachusetts Historical Society, Boston, Massachusetts.

William Everett Papers. Massachusetts Historical Society, Boston, Massachusetts.

Moreton Frewen Papers. Manuscript Division, Library of Congress, Washington, D.C.

Charles F. Gettemy Scrapbooks. Massachusetts State House Library, Boston, Massachusetts.

Mason Green, "Edward Bellamy: A Biography of the Author of Looking Backward" (MS), Houghton Library, Harvard University, Cambridge, Massachusetts.

Charles S. Hamlin Papers. Manuscript Division, Library of Congress, Washington, D.C.

Rutherford B. Hayes Papers. Rutherford B. Hayes Library, Fremont, Ohio.

Thomas Wentworth Higginson Papers. Houghton Library, Harvard University, Cambridge, Massachusetts.

Daniel Lamont Papers. Manuscript Division, Library of Congress, Washington, D.C.

Henry Cabot Lodge Papers. Massachusetts Historical Society, Boston, Massachusetts.

Charles Eliot Norton Papers. Houghton Library, Harvard University, Cambridge, Massachusetts.

Richard Olney Papers. Manuscript Division, Library of Congress, Washington, D.C.

Josiah Quincy Papers. Massachusetts Historical Society, Boston, Massachusetts.

James Ford Rhodes Papers. Massachusetts Historical Society, Boston, Massachusetts.

William E. Russell Papers. Massachusetts Historical Society, Boston, Massachusetts.

Carl Schurz Papers. Manuscript Division, Library of Congress, Washington, D.C.

Frederic J. Stimson Papers. Massachusetts Historical Society, Boston, Massachusetts.

Moorfield Storey Papers. Manuscript Division, Library of Congress, Washington, D.C.

Winslow Warren Scrapbooks. Massachusetts Historical Society, Boston, Massachusetts.

Wheelwright Family Papers. Massachusetts Historical Society, Boston, Massachusetts.

William C. Whitney Papers. Manuscript Division, Library of Congress, Washington, D.C.

Cyrus Field Willard, "Autobiography" (MS), Houghton Library, Harvard University, Cambridge, Massachusetts.

George Fred Williams Diary Notes. Massachusetts Historical Society, Boston, Massachusetts.

NEWSPAPERS AND PERIODICALS

(Consulted for the years covered by this study, except as indicated.)

Boston Daily Advertiser.
Boston Globe.
Boston Herald.
Boston Transcript.
Donahoe's Magazine (Boston), 1889–1893.
Hartford Courant, 1893–1896.
Labor Leader (Boston), 1890, 1894, 1895, 1897.
The Nation (New York).
The Pilot (Boston), 1896.
The Republic (Boston), 1882–1885, 1890–1900.

BOOKS, ARTICLES, AND PUBLIC DOCUMENTS

Abell, Aaron I. "American Catholic Reaction to Industrial Conflict: The Arbitral Process, 1885–1900," *Catholic Historical Review,* 41:4 (January 1956), 385–407.

Abrams, Richard M. *Conservatism in a Progressive Era: Massachusetts Politics, 1900–1912.* Cambridge: Harvard University Press, 1964.

Adams, Charles Francis. *Charles Francis Adams, 1835–1915: An Autobiography.* Boston: Houghton Mifflin, 1916.

Adams, Henry. *The Education of Henry Adams.* New York: Random House, 1931.

Annual Reports of the Massachusetts Bureau of Statistics of Labor, 1885–1895.

Bancroft, Frederic, ed. *Speeches, Correspondence and Political Papers of Carl Schurz.* 6 vols. New York: G. P. Putnam's Sons, 1913.

Barnes, James A. "The Gold Standard Democrats and the Party Conflict," *Mississippi Valley Historical Review,* 17:3 (December 1930), 422–450.

———— *John G. Carlisle, Financial Statesman.* New York: Dodd, Mead, 1931.

———— "Myths of the Bryan Campaign," *Mississippi Valley Historical Review,* 34:3 (December 1947), 367–404.

Baxter, Sylvester. "Boston at the Century's End," *Harper's Monthly,* 99:594 (November 1899), 823–846.

———— "Legislative Degeneracy in Massachusetts," *Arena,* 2:4 (September 1890), 503–506.

Benson, George C. S. *The Administration of the Civil Service in Massachusetts with Special Reference to State Control of City Civil Service.* Cambridge: Harvard University Press, 1935.

Beringause, Arthur F. *Brooks Adams: A Biography.* New York: Alfred A. Knopf, 1955.

Bradford, Gamaliel. "Government by Commissions," *New England Magazine,* 10:4 (June 1894), 453–460.

Bridgman, Raymond L. "Government by Commissions," *New England Magazine*, 10:4 (June 1894), 442–453.

—— *The Independents of Massachusetts in 1884.* Boston: Cupples, Upham, 1885.

—— "Legislatures: A Defense and a Criticism," *American Journal of Politics*, 5:6 (Dec. 1894), 598–607.

—— *Ten Years of Massachusetts.* Boston: D. C. Heath, 1888.

Brooks, John G. "The Question of the Unemployed in Massachusetts," *Economic Journal* (London), 4:14 (June 1894), 361–365.

Brooks, Robert C. "Business Men in Civic Service: The Merchants' Municipal Committee of Boston," *Municipal Affairs*, 1:3 (September 1897), 491–508.

Bryce, James. *The American Commonwealth*, 2nd ed. rev. 2 vols. London: Macmillan, 1891.

Bugbee, James M. *The City Government of Boston.* Johns Hopkins Studies in Historical and Political Science, Third Series. Baltimore: Johns Hopkins University, 1887.

Bushée, Frederick A. "Ethnic Factors in the Population of Boston," *Publications of the American Economic Association*, 3rd series, 4:2 (May 1903), 1–171.

Capen, Samuel B. "The Boston Municipal League," *American Journal of Politics*, 5:1 (July 1894), 1–13.

Carens, Thomas. "Martin Lomasney: The Story of His Life as Related by Him to Thomas Carens," *Boston Herald*, December 2–27, 1925.

Chase, Harvey S. "Municipal Printing in Boston," *Municipal Affairs*, 4:4 (December 1900), 774–777.

Chase, Philip P. "Some Cambridge Reformers of the Eighties; or, Cambridge Contributions to Cleveland Democracy in Massachusetts," *Cambridge Historical Society Proceedings*, 20 (1927–1929), 24–52.

Codman, Charles R. "Memoir of Leverett Saltonstall," *Proceedings of the Massachusetts Historical Society*, 2nd series, 11 (1896, 1897), 337–366.

Coletta, Paolo E. "Bryan, Cleveland, and the Disrupted Democracy, 1890–1896," *Nebraska History*, 41:1 (March 1960), 1–27.

Cullen, James B., ed. *The Story of the Irish in Boston.* Boston: James B. Cullen, 1889.

Curley, James M. *I'd Do It Again: A Record of All My Uproarious Years.* Englewood Cliffs, N.J.: Prentice-Hall, 1957.

Curran, Michael P. *Life of Patrick A. Collins.* Norwood, Mass.: The Norwood Press, 1906.

Cutler, John H., *"Honey Fitz": Three Steps to the White House.* Indianapolis: Bobbs-Merrill, 1962.

Dana, Richard Henry. "The Practical Working of the Australian System of Voting in Massachusetts," *Annals of the American Academy of Political and Social Science*, 2:6 (May 1892), 733–750.

Dinneen, Joseph F. *The Purple Shamrock*. New York: Norton, 1949.

—— *Ward Eight*. New York: Harper, 1936.

Douglas, Francis J. "Municipal Socialism in Boston," *Arena*, 20:5 (November–December, 1898), 545–558.

Ely, Richard T., and L. S. Merriam. "Report on Social Legislation in the United States for 1889 and 1890," *Economic Review* (London), 1:2 (April 1891), 234–256.

Endicott, William C., Jr. "Memoir of William C. Endicott, LL.D.," *Proceedings of the Massachusetts Historical Society*, 2nd series, 15 (1901, 1902), 523–537.

Everett, Charles C. "Memoir of the Hon. William Eustis Russell, LL.D.," *Publications of the Colonial Society of Massachusetts*, 5 (Transactions, 1897, 1898), 83–93.

Feder, Leah H. *Unemployment Relief in Periods of Depression: A Study of Measures Adopted in Certain American Cities, 1857 through 1922*. New York: Russell Sage Foundation, 1936.

Flower, Benjamin O. *Progressive Men, Women and Movements of the Past Twenty-Five Years*. Boston: New Arena, 1914.

Ford, Worthington C., ed. *Letters of Henry Adams, 1892–1918*. Boston: Houghton Mifflin, 1938.

Foster, Frank K. *Evolution of a Trade Unionist*. Boston: Allied Printing Trades Council, 1901.

Francis William Bird: A Biographical Sketch. Boston: privately printed, 1897.

Fuess, Claude M. *Carl Schurz, Reformer*. New York: Dodd, Mead, 1932.

Garland, Hamlin. *A Member of the Third House: A Dramatic Story*. Chicago: F. J. Schulte, 1892.

Garraty, John A. *Henry Cabot Lodge: A Biography*. New York: Alfred A. Knopf, 1953.

Garrison, Lloyd M. "Early Days of Successful Men: William Eustis Russell," *Harper's Round Table*, 17:848 (January 28, 1896), 313–315.

—— *Governor Russell and His Canvass of Cape Cod, November 7, 1892*. New York: Republic Press, 1893.

Gilder, Richard W. *Grover Cleveland: A Record of Friendship*. New York: Century, 1910.

Gilder, Rosamund, ed. *Letters of Richard Watson Gilder*. Boston: Houghton Mifflin, 1916.

Grant, Robert. *Fourscore: An Autobiography*. Boston: Houghton Mifflin, 1934.

Griffin, Solomon B. *People and Politics Observed by a Massachusetts Editor.* Boston: Little, Brown, 1923.

Grimes, Alan P. *The Political Liberalism of the New York Nation, 1865–1932.* James Sprunt Studies in Historical and Political Science, vol. 34. Chapel Hill: University of North Carolina Press, 1953.

Hale, George S. "Memoir of the Hon. Martin Brimmer, A.B.," *Publications of the Colonial Society of Massachusetts,* 3 (Transactions, 1895–1897), 337–347.

Handlin, Oscar. *Boston's Immigrants: A Study in Acculturation,* rev. ed. Cambridge: Harvard University Press, 1959.

——— "The Immigrant and American Politics," in David F. Bowers, ed., *Foreign Influences in American Life: Essays and Critical Bibliographies.* Princeton: Princeton University Press, 1944.

——— *The Uprooted.* Boston: Little, Brown, 1951.

Hart, A. B., ed. *Commonwealth History of Massachusetts,* vols. 4 and 5. New York: States History, 1930.

Hennessy, Michael E. *Twenty-Five Years of Massachusetts Politics from Russell to McCall, 1890–1915.* Boston: Practical Politics, 1917.

Herlihy, Elisabeth M., ed. *Fifty Years of Boston: A Memorial Volume.* Boston: Goodspeed's Bookstore, 1932.

Higginson, Thomas Wentworth. *Cheerful Yesterdays.* Cambridge: Houghton Mifflin, 1898.

Hirsch, Mark D. *William C. Whitney: Modern Warwick.* New York: Dodd, Mead, 1948.

Hoffman, Charles. "The Depression of the Nineties," *Journal of Economic History,* 16:2 (June 1956), 137–164.

Hoogenboom, Ari. *Outlawing the Spoils: A History of the Civil Service Reform Movement 1865–1883.* Urbana: University of Illinois Press, 1961.

——— "The Pendleton Act and the Civil Service," *American Historical Review,* 64:2 (January 1959), 301–318.

Hooker, George E. "Mayor Quincy of Boston," *Review of Reviews,* 19:112 (May 1899), 575–578.

Howe, M. A. DeW. *Barrett Wendell and His Letters.* Boston: Atlantic Monthly Press, 1924.

——— *Portrait of an Independent: Moorfield Storey.* Boston: Houghton Mifflin, 1932.

——— *A Venture in Remembrance.* Boston: Little, Brown, 1941.

Hughes, Sarah Forbes, ed. *Letters and Recollections of John Murray Forbes.* 2 vols. Boston: Houghton Mifflin, 1899.

Inaugural and Annual Addresses of the Mayor of Boston, 1891–1899.

James, Henry. *Richard Olney and His Public Service.* Boston: Houghton Mifflin, 1923.

Jones, Stanley L. *The Presidential Election of 1896.* Madison: University of Wisconsin Press, 1964.

Kellen, William V. "Memoir of Charles Russell Codman," *Proceedings of the Massachusetts Historical Society,* 53 (1919, 1920), 168–176.

Kirkland, Edward C. *Men, Cities and Transportation: A Study in New England History, 1820–1900.* 2 vols. Cambridge: Harvard University Press, 1948.

Knoles, George H. *The Presidential Campaign and Election of 1892.* Stanford University Publications, University Series: History, Economics, and Political Science, vol. 5. Stanford: Stanford University Press, 1942.

Lambert, John R. *Arthur Pue Gorman.* Baton Rouge: Louisiana State University Press, 1953.

Lawson, Thomas W. *Frenzied Finance.* New York: Ridgway-Thayer, 1906.

Lord, Robert H., John E. Sexton, and Edward T. Harrington. *History of the Archdiocese of Boston in the Various Stages of its Development, 1604 to 1943,* vol. 3. New York: Sheed and Ward, 1944.

Luce, Robert. *Legislative Assemblies: Their Framework, Make-up, Character, Characteristics, Habits, and Manners.* Boston: Houghton Mifflin, 1924.

Mann, Arthur. *Yankee Reformers in the Urban Age.* Cambridge: Harvard University Press, 1954.

Mason, Alpheus T. *Brandeis: A Free Man's Life.* New York: Viking, 1946.

Matthews, Nathan. *The City Government of Boston: A Valedictory Address to the Members of the City Council, January 5, 1895.* Boston: Rockwell and Churchill, 1895.

Merk, Lois B. "Boston's Historic Public School Crisis," *New England Quarterly,* 31:2 (June 1958), 172–199.

Merrill, Horace S. *Bourbon Democracy of the Middle West, 1865–1896.* Baton Rouge: Louisiana State University Press, 1953.

——— *Bourbon Leader: Grover Cleveland and the Democratic Party.* Boston: Little, Brown, 1957.

Mills, Roger Q. "New England and the New Tariff Bill," *Forum,* 9:4 (June 1890), 361–370.

Milne, Gordon. *George William Curtis and the Genteel Tradition.* Bloomington: Indiana University Press, 1956.

Mitchell, Broadus. *The Rise of Cotton Mills in the South.* Johns Hopkins University Studies in Historical and Political Science, 39:2. Baltimore: The Johns Hopkins Press, 1921.

Morgan, Arthur E. *Edward Bellamy.* New York: Columbia University Press, 1944.

Morgan, James. *Charles H. Taylor, Builder of the Boston Globe.* Boston: 1923.

―――― *The Life Work of Edward A. Moseley in the Service of Humanity.* New York: Macmillan, 1913.

Morison, Elting E., ed. *The Letters of Theodore Roosevelt,* vols. 1 and 2: *The Years of Preparation, 1868–1900.* Cambridge: Harvard University Press, 1951.

Morse, John T., Jr. *Memoir of Colonel Henry Lee, with Selections from His Writings and Speeches.* Boston: Little, Brown, 1905.

Neilson, William A., ed. *Charles W. Eliot: The Man and His Beliefs.* 2 vols. New York: Harper, 1926.

Nevins, Allan. *Grover Cleveland: A Study in Courage.* New York: Dodd, Mead, 1934.

―――― ed. *Letters of Grover Cleveland, 1850–1908.* Boston: Houghton Mifflin, 1933.

Nixon, Raymond B. *Henry W. Grady: Spokesman of the New South.* New York: Alfred A. Knopf, 1943.

North, S. N. D. *Factory Legislation in New England: Its Tendencies and Effects, Its Legal and Economic Aspects.* Boston: Arkwright Club, 1895.

Norton, Charles Eliot. "The Public Life and Services of William E. Russell," *Harvard Graduates' Magazine,* 5:18 (December 1896), 177–194.

Norton, Sarah, and M. A. DeW. Howe, eds. *Letters of Charles Eliot Norton.* 2 vols. Boston: Houghton Mifflin, 1913.

Parker, George F. *Recollections of Grover Cleveland.* New York: Century, 1911.

Parsons, Frank. *The City for the People,* rev. ed. Philadelphia: C. F. Taylor, 1901.

Paul, Arnold. *Conservative Crisis and the Rule of Law: Attitudes of Bar and Bench, 1887–1895.* Ithaca: Cornell University Press, 1960.

Perry, Bliss. *Life and Letters of Henry Lee Higginson.* 2 vols. Boston: Atlantic Monthly Press, 1921.

―――― *Richard Henry Dana, 1851–1931.* Boston: Houghton Mifflin, 1933.

Pope, Jesse E. *The Clothing Industries in New York.* Columbia, Mo.: University of Missouri Press, 1905.

Powers, Samuel L. *Portraits of a Half-Century.* Boston: Little, Brown, 1925.

Quincy, Josiah. "The Development of American Cities," *Arena,* 17:88 (March 1897), 529–537.

―――― "Governor Russell and the Young Democracy of Massachusetts," *Belford's Magazine,* 8:39 (August 1891), 394–402.

―――― "Issues and Prospects of the Campaign," *North American Review,* 163:2 (August 1896), 182–194.

────── "Municipal Progress in Boston," *Independent,* 52:2672 (February 15, 1900), 424–426.

────── "Regulation of the Lobby in Massachusetts," *Forum,* 12:3 (November 1891), 346–357.

────── "Working of the Massachusetts Corrupt Practices Law," *Forum,* 15:2 (April 1893), 142–147.

Reno, Conrad. *Memoirs of the Judiciary and the Bar of New England for the Nineteenth Century.* 2 vols. Boston: Century Memorial Publishing Company, 1900.

"Report of Committee to Investigate Methods for and Against Legislation Concerning Elevated Railroads and to Inquire into the Conduct of Members of the House in Connection therewith," *Massachusetts House Document No. 585* (1890), pp. i–xxviii, 1–594.

"Report of the Committee on Manufactures on the Sweating System," *U.S. House Report,* 52 Cong., 2 sess., no. 2309 (1893), pp. i–xxix, 1–265.

"Report of the Joint Special Committee Appointed by the General Court of 1891 to Consider the Subject of Changing, Consolidating or Abolishing the Various State Commissions," *Massachusetts Senate Document No. 73* (1892), pp. 1–76.

"Report of the Massachusetts Board to Investigate the Subject of the Unemployed," *Massachusetts House Document No. 50* (1895), parts I–V.

Rezneck, Samuel. "Patterns of Thought and Action in an American Depression, 1882–1886," *American Historical Review,* 61:2 (January 1956), 284–307.

────── "Unemployment, Unrest, and Relief in the United States during the Depression of 1893–97," *Journal of Political Economy,* 61:4 (August 1953), 324–345.

Roche, James J. *Life of John Boyle O'Reilly.* New York: Cassell Publishing Co., 1891.

Russell, Charles T., Jr., ed. *Speeches and Addresses of William E. Russell.* Boston: Little, Brown, 1894.

Russell, William E. "The Issues of 1896: A Democratic View," *Century Magazine,* 51:1 (November 1895), 73–77.

────── "Jefferson and His Party Today," *Forum,* 21:5 (July 1896), 513–524.

────── "Political Causes of the Business Depression," *North American Review,* 157:6 (December 1893), 641–652.

────── *The Proper Province and Office of Constitutional Law.* New Haven: Hoggson and Robinson, 1894.

────── "Significance of the Massachusetts Election," *Forum,* 12:4 (December 1891), 433–440.

────── "The Tariff Question from a Democratic Standpoint," *A*

Practical Book for Practical People. Springfield, Mass.: King-Richardson, 1896.

────── "A Year of Democratic Administration," *Forum*, 17:3 (May 1894), 254–267.

Sageser, Adelbert B. *The First Two Decades of the Pendleton Act: A Study of Civil Service Reform.* Lincoln, Neb.: University of Nebraska, 1935.

Shaler, Nathaniel S. "The Economic Future of the New South," *Arena*, 2:3 (August 1890), 257–268.

Shannon, David A., ed. *Beatrice Webb's American Diary, 1898.* Madison: University of Wisconsin Press, 1963.

Solomon, Barbara M. *Ancestors and Immigrants: A Changing New England Tradition.* Cambridge: Harvard University Press, 1956.

Speed, J. G. "A Possible Presidential Candidate: Hon. William E. Russell and His Public Career," *Leslie's Weekly* (May 28, 1896), 371–372.

Stimson, Frederic J. "Democracy and the Laboring Man." *Journal of Social Science*, 35 (December 1897), 167–192.

────── "The Ethics of Democracy," *Scribner's Magazine*, 1:6 (June 1887), 661–671.

────── *My United States.* New York: Scribner's, 1931.

Storey, Moorfield. "The American Legislature," *Report of the Seventeenth Annual Meeting of the American Bar Association Held at Saratoga Springs, New York, August 22, 23, and 24, 1894* 245–272. Philadelphia: 1894.

────── "Municipal Government of Boston," *Proceedings of the National Conference for Good City Government Held at Philadelphia, January 25 and 26, 1894,* 61–71. Philadelphia: National Municipal League, 1894.

────── *Politics As a Duty and As a Career.* New York: G. P. Putnam's Sons, 1889.

Summers, Festus P., ed. *The Cabinet Diary of William L. Wilson, 1896–1897.* Chapel Hill: North Carolina University Press, 1957.

Summers, Festus P. *William L. Wilson and Tariff Reform.* New Brunswick, N.J.: Rutgers University Press, 1953.

Thomas, Harrison C. *The Return of the Democratic Party to Power in 1884.* New York: Columbia University Press, 1919.

Tributes of the Bar and of the Circuit Court of the United States to the Memory of Sherman Hoar. Boston: G. H. Ellis, 1899.

Van Nostrand, A. D. "The Lomasney Legend," *New England Quarterly*, 21:4 (December 1948), 435–458.

Wadlin, Horace G. "The Growth of Cities in Massachusetts," *American Statistical Association Publications,* new series, 13 (March 1891), 159–173.

———— "The Sweating System in Massachusetts," *Journal of Social Science*, 30 (October 1892), 86–102.

Ware, Edith Ellen. "Political Opinion in Massachusetts During Civil War and Reconstruction," *Studies in History, Economics and Public Law*, vol. 74, 197–415. New York: Columbia University Press, 1917.

Warner, Sam B. *Streetcar Suburbs: The Process of Growth in Boston, 1870–1900*. Cambridge: Harvard University Press and the M.I.T. Press, 1962.

Warren, Charles. "A Manufacturer of History: A Story of Newspaper and Political Life," *McClure's Magazine*, 14:6 (April 1900), 525–537.

Wayman, Dorothy G. *Cardinal O'Connell of Boston: A Biography of William Henry O'Connell, 1859–1944*. New York: Farrar, Straus, and Young, 1955.

Wheelwright, Edmund M. "Memoir of the Hon. John Forrester Andrew, LL.B.," *Publications of the Colonial Society of Massachusetts*, 3 (Transactions, 1895–1897), 351–374.

White, Henry. "The Sweating System," *Bulletin of the Department of Labor*, 1 (November 1895-November 1896), 360–379.

Whittelsey, Sarah S. *Massachusetts Labor Legislation: An Historical and Critical Study*. Philadelphia: American Academy of Political and Social Science, 1901.

Whitten, Robert H. *Public Administration in Massachusetts: The Relation of Central to Local Authority*. New York: Columbia University Press, 1898.

Williams, George Fred. "Imminent Danger from the Silver-Purchase Act," *Forum*, 14:6 (February 1893), 789–796.

———— "The Way Upward," *Arena*, 19:101 (April 1898), 439–463.

Williamson, Harold F. *Edward Atkinson: The Biography of an American Liberal, 1827–1905*. Boston: Old Corner Book Store, 1934.

Willoughby, William F. *Regulation of the Sweating System*. Herbert B. Adams, ed., Monographs on American Social Economics, vol. 9. Boston: Wright and Potter, 1900.

Wood, Gordon. "The Massachusetts Mugwumps," *New England Quarterly*, 33:4 (December 1960), 435–451.

Woods, Eleanor H. *Robert A. Woods: Champion of Democracy*. Boston: Houghton Mifflin Co., 1929.

Woods, Robert A., ed. *Americans in Process: A Settlement Study*. Boston. Houghton Mifflin Co., 1902.

———— *The City Wilderness: A Settlement Study*. Boston: Houghton Mifflin Co., 1898.

Woods, Robert A. "Settlement Houses and City Politics," *Municipal Affairs*, 4:2 (June 1900), 395–398.

NOTES

CHAPTER ONE · 1884

1. *Boston Advertiser*, June 7, 1884; Richard Henry Dana, Journal, II, 569, Dana Papers; Moorfield Storey, Scrapbook, 1876–1885, Storey Papers.

2. Information gleaned from James L. Harrison, comp., *Biographical Directory of the American Congress, 1774–1949* (Washington, 1950).

3. F. B. Patton to William Everett, July 20, 1882, Everett Papers. For the phrase "Snivel Service Reform," see Boston *Republic*, May 24, 1884.

4. Dana, Journal, II, 558, Dana Papers; Moorfield Storey, Scrapbook, 1876–1885, Storey Papers; Ari Hoogenboom, *Outlawing the Spoils: A History of the Civil Service Reform Movement, 1865–1883* (Urbana, 1961), pp. 194, 215–252.

5. Dana, Journal, II, 567, Josiah Quincy to R. H. Dana, May 30, 1884, Dana Papers; Massachusetts General Court, *Journal of the House of Representatives*, 1884, p. 716.

6. Philip P. Chase, "Some Cambridge Reformers of the Eighties," *Cambridge Historical Society Proceedings*, 20:26 (1927–1929); H. L. Trefousse, *Ben Butler: The South Called Him Beast!* (New York, 1957), pp. 240–245; M. A. DeWolfe Howe, *Portrait of an Independent: Moorfield Storey* (Boston, 1932), pp. 102, 103; Moorfield Storey to H. C. Lodge, June 14, 1883, and Aug. 9, 1883, Lodge Papers.

7. Josiah Quincy to H. C. Lodge, Sept. 12, 1883, C. R. Codman to H. C. Lodge, July 25, 1883, Lodge Papers; Winslow Warren to William Everett, Sept. 13, 1883, Everett Papers.

8. John A. Garraty, *Henry Cabot Lodge* (New York, 1953), p. 73; the quotation may be found in Winslow Warren to William Everett, Sept. 20, 1883, Everett Papers.

9. Winslow Warren to William Everett, Sept. 20, 1883, Everett Papers.

10. George Putnam to J. F. Andrew, May 21, 1884, Andrew Papers.

11. Carl Schurz to G. F. Edmunds, draft, March 9, 1884, J. P. Butler to Carl Schurz, May 11, 1884, Schurz Papers.

12. Moorfield Storey, Scrapbook, 1876–1885, *passim*, Storey Papers; G. F. Williams to Carl Schurz, Oct. 30, 1884, Schurz Papers. See Raymond L. Bridgman, *The Independents of Massachusetts in 1884* (Boston, 1885), p. 10, for the membership of the Committee of One Hundred. For the tale of the Mulligan Letters, see Allan Nevins, *Grover Cleveland: A Study in Courage* (New York, 1934), pp. 160–162.

13. *Boston Traveller*, Aug. 11, 1884.

14. Forty-two years after the event, the Mugwump Moorfield Storey wrote to an inquiring historian, "I had been opposed to Mr. Blaine for some

time having discovered what his character was. I was at the meeting of the Reform Club where Mr. Cleveland was nominated for the Presidency on Saturday, and I was at the meeting on Monday when President Eliot spoke and the Mugwump movement was launched. I wrote the address of Massachusetts, I prepared the record of Mr. Blaine to which I devoted a large part of the summer, and I know the whole history of the movement." Moorfield Storey to Philip P. Chase, Boston, July 2, 1926, Chase Papers.

15. Robert Grant, *Fourscore: An Autobiography* (Boston, 1934), p. 189; Winslow Warren to William Everett, July 28, 1884, Everett Papers. See Bridgman, *Independents*, p. 9, for Eliot's speech.

16. *Boston Advertiser*, Oct. 2, 1884.

17. Bridgman, *Independents*, p. 29. See *Boston Advertiser*, June 9, 1884, for Adams' warning.

18. Nevins, *Grover Cleveland*, pp. 163–169; James Freeman Clarke to Grover Cleveland, Sept. 15, 1884, Brooks Adams to Grover Cleveland, Oct. 28, 1884, Cleveland Papers.

19. See Bridgman, *Independents*, pp. 7, 8, and 45, respectively, for the opinions of Codman, Higginson, and Forbes.

20. For Peter Butler, see *Boston Transcript*, July 2, 1894; for F. O. Prince, see *Boston Herald*, Oct. 26, 1896; for C. T. Russell, see S. L. Powers, *Portraits of a Half Century* (Boston, 1925), p. 135; for Richard Olney, see Henry James, *Richard Olney and His Public Service* (Boston, 1923), p. 10; for Henry M. Whitney, see *Boston Transcript*, Jan. 26, 1923.

21. For James S. Whitney, see *Boston Advertiser*, Oct. 25, 1878.

22. Elizabeth Stevenson, *Henry Adams* (New York, 1955), p. 66; Leverett Saltonstall to W. C. Endicott, June 4, 1885, Endicott Papers; *Francis William Bird: A Biographical Sketch* (Boston, 1897), pp. 77, 78; *Boston Advertiser*, Sept. 7, 1876.

23. *Boston Advertiser*, Sept. 18, 1878; Trefousse, *Butler*, p. 242.

24. W. E. Russell to C. T. Russell, Sept. 11, 1882, Russell Papers.

25. James J. Roche, *Life of John Boyle O'Reilly* (New York, 1891), p. 239; M. P. Curran, *Life of Patrick A. Collins* (Norwood, Mass., 1906), pp. 90–94.

26. An undated 1883 campaign handbill in the Endicott Papers lists the prominent Democratic bolters of 1883.

27. Roche, *O'Reilly*, p. 240. See Boston *Republic*, Aug. 16, 1884, for the Boston district leader's remark.

28. Curran, *Collins*, pp. 83–90; *Boston Herald*, Sept. 4, 1887; Boston *Republic*, July 19, July 26, and Aug. 16, 1884.

29. Boston *Republic*, June 14, 1884; Bridgman, *Independents*, p. 21.

30. Richard Olney to W. C. Endicott, Sept. 14, 1884, Endicott Papers; Brooks Adams to Carl Schurz, Oct. 2, 1884, Schurz Papers. See Endicott Papers, Sept. 1884, for telegrams urging Endicott to run and a rough draft of his final reply.

31. Brooks Adams to Carl Schurz, Oct. 24, 1884, Schurz Papers; Henrietta Dana to R. H. Dana, Nov. 8, 1884, Dana Papers.

32. *Boston Advertiser*, Nov. 5, 1884; S. B. Griffin, *People and Politics*

Observed By a Massachusetts Editor (Boston, 1923), p. 295; Bridgman, *Independents*, p. 13; Boston *Republic*, Nov. 8, 1884.

33. G. F. Williams to Carl Schurz, Nov. 10, 1884, Schurz Papers.

CHAPTER TWO · THE MUGWUMP MIND

1. Important interpretations of the generation to which the Mugwumps belonged are to be found in Richard Hofstadter, *The Age of Reform* (New York, 1955), pp. 135–143, and Barbara M. Solomon, *Ancestors and Immigrants: A Changing New England Tradition* (Cambridge, 1956), pp. 1–58. For a striking description of the Boston temper in the 1880's, see Frederic J. Stimson, *My United States* (New York, 1931), chap. 8.

2. See Raymond L. Bridgman, *The Independents of Massachusetts in 1884* (Boston, 1885), p. 10, for a listing of the more prominent Mugwumps.

3. For Eliot, see Philip P. Chase, "Some Cambridge Reformers of the Eighties," *Cambridge Historical Society Proceedings*, 20:31–33 (1927–1929); for Norton, see Solomon, *Ancestors and Immigrants*, pp. 10–16, 20, 21, and Kermit Vanderbilt, *Charles Eliot Norton: Apostle of Culture in a Democracy* (Cambridge, Mass., 1959), chap. 7.

4. Charles Francis Adams, *Charles Francis Adams, 1835–1915: An Autobiography* (Boston, 1916), pp. 170–198; Solomon, *Ancestors and Immigrants*, pp. 25–30; Brooks Adams to Henry Adams, Jan. 8, 1897, Brooks Adams Papers.

5. Charles R. Codman, Notes and Reminiscences, II, 4, 5, 54, 69, Codman Papers; J. T. Morse, Jr., "Colonel Charles Russell Codman," *Massachusetts Historical Society Proceedings*, 52:87–95 (1918–1919); Charles R. Codman to Silas Burt, Sept. 12, 1885, Cleveland Papers.

6. Thomas Wentworth Higginson, *Cheerful Yesterdays* (Cambridge, Mass., 1898), pp. 26, 44, 98, 344, 350, 363; Edward Bellamy to T. W. Higginson, Dec. 21, 1890, T. W. Higginson Papers; Chase, *Cambridge Historical Society Proceedings*, 20:28–30 (1927–1929).

7. Harold F. Williamson, *Edward Atkinson: The Biography of an American Liberal, 1827–1905* (Boston, 1934), pp. vii, 2, 3, 99; Edward Atkinson to J. W. Carter, March 7, 1884, Edes Papers. Atkinson's self-characterization is quoted from Edward Atkinson to C. P. Wormely, Dec. 1, 1890, Atkinson Papers. His advice to the governor may be found in Edward Atkinson to W. E. Russell, Jan. 16, 1891, Russell Papers.

8. M. A. DeWolfe Howe, *Portrait of an Independent: Moorfield Storey* (Boston, 1932), pp. 9, 11, 22, 139–177. Adams' comment is on p. 9; Storey's on p. 172.

9. *Boston Herald*, Oct. 30, 1892; William Everett to Henry H. Edes, Nov. 2, 1885, July 27, 1887 (containing his boast about his lack of convention), and Dec. 22, 1889, Edes Papers; Winslow Warren to William Everett, Oct. 17, 1886, Josiah Quincy to William Everett, Sept. 19, 1892, Moorfield Storey to William Everett, July 5, 1894, Everett Papers; William Everett to W. E. Russell, Feb. 21, 1893, Russell Papers.

10. E. M. Wheelwright, "Memoir of the Hon. John Forrester Andrew, LL.B.," *Publications of the Colonial Society of Massachusetts*, 3:351–374

(1895–1897); B. Kimball to J. F. Andrew, Oct. 14, 1884, F. L. Higginson to J. F. Andrew, Sept. 29, 1886, G. W. Curtis to J. F. Andrew, Oct. 7, 1886, Andrew Papers; J. F. Andrew to W. W. Clapp, July 14, 1884, Clapp Papers; Theodore Roosevelt to Edmund Wheelwright, Oct. 23, 1895, Wheelwright Papers. The letters from Kimball and Higginson, respectively, contain the quoted passages.

11. Richard Henry Dana, Journal, II, 567–609 (quotation from p. 609), Dana Papers; Bliss Perry, *Richard Henry Dana, 1851–1931* (Boston, 1933), p. 158; Elting E. Morison, ed., *Letters of Theodore Roosevelt* (Cambridge, Mass., 1951), I, 122.

12. F. W. Bird to Carl Schurz, April 13, 1888, Schurz Papers; G. F. Williams to W. C. Endicott, April 24, 1885, Endicott Papers; *Boston Transcript,* Nov. 4, 1861; *New York Times,* July 12, 1932; *Dedham Transcript,* July 15, 1932.

13. M. A. DeW. Howe to Edmund Quincy, Dec. 29, 1939, Howe Papers; Josiah Quincy to William Everett, July 29, 1881, Everett Papers; *Harvard College Class of 1880, Secretary's Report, No. 1, 1880,* pp. 16, 22, 24, Harvard Archives; Josiah P. Quincy to Josiah Quincy, Sept. 26 [189?], Quincy Papers; *Boston Herald,* Sept. 9, 1919; *Boston Transcript,* Sept. 8, 1919.

14. Winslow Warren, Scrapbook, Warren Papers; J. W. Carter to Carl Schurz, June 19, 1893, Schurz Papers; Conrad Reno, *Memoirs of the Judiciary and the Bar of New England for the Nineteenth Century* (Boston, 1901), I, 168, 169.

15. Massachusetts Reform Club, *Secretary's Report and Annual Meeting, December, 1889* (Boston, 1890), p. 5; Winslow Warren to William Everett, Dec. 10, 1889, Everett Papers; Carl Schurz to G. F. Williams, Oct. 8, 1886, Russell Papers.

16. Stimson, *My United States,* p. 112. See *The Clubs of Boston* (Boston, 1891), *passim.*

17. Robert Grant, "The Art of Living," *Scribner's Magazine,* 17–18 (Jan.–Nov. 1895); Robert Grant, *Fourscore: An Autobiography* (Boston, 1934), pp. 172–176, 204–208.

18. G. F. Williams to Carl Schurz, Jan. 1, 1885, A. M. Howe to Carl Schurz, June 25, 1885 and Nov. 28, 1888, Schurz Papers.

19. See Stimson, *My United States,* pp. 83–85. For a careful look at the New York Mugwumps, see G. W. McFarland, "The New York Mugwumps of 1884: A Profile," *Political Science Quarterly,* 78:1:40–58 (March 1963). Alexander Johnston to William Everett, Sept. 23, 1887, Everett Papers.

20. G. F. Hoar to H. C. Lodge, Nov. 18, 1884, Lodge Papers; Stimson, *My United States,* pp. 18, 19; Sarah Norton and M. A. DeW. Howe, eds., *Letters of Charles Eliot Norton* (Boston, 1913), II, 254.

21. Adams, *Autobiography,* p. 178; C. F. Adams, *Three Episodes of Massachusetts History,* rev. ed. (Boston, 1896), II, 990; Horace Wadlin, "The Growth of Cities in Massachusetts," *American Statistical Association Publications,* n.s., 13:162, 172 (March 1891).

22. Norton and Howe, eds., *Letters,* II, 166. See F. J. Stimson, "The Ethics of Democracy," *Scribner's Magazine,* 1:6:671 (June 1887).

23. Carl Schurz to Grover Cleveland, rough, undated draft of letter written after 1884 election, probably not sent, Schurz Papers; Solomon, *Ancestors and Immigrants*, pp. 50–53; Norton and Howe, eds., *Letters,* II, 309; Edward Atkinson to A. J. Scott, Nov. 24, 1890, Atkinson Papers; Moorfield Storey to W. E. Russell, Nov. 7, 1890, Russell Papers.

24. Dana, *Journal,* II, 571, Dana Papers; Edward Atkinson to A. J. Scott, March 13, 1890, Atkinson Papers.

25. Winslow Warren to William Everett, Nov. 5, 1886, A. A. Ross to William Everett, Nov. 10, 1886, G. F. Williams to William Everett, Nov. 15, 1886, Everett Papers.

26. Winslow Warren to William Everett, Nov. 5, 1886, Everett Papers; Arthur Mann, *Yankee Reformers in the Urban Age* (Cambridge, Mass., 1954), pp. 182–184; Edward Atkinson, *The Margin of Profits: An Address Delivered Before the Central Labor Lyceum of Boston on Sunday Evening, May 1, 1887* (New York, 1887), p. 50.

27. Moorfield Storey, "The American Legislature," *Report of the Seventeenth Annual Meeting of the American Bar Association* (Philadelphia, 1894), p. 246; Atkinson, *Margin of Profits,* p. 45; C. W. Eliot, *American Contributions to Civilization* (New York, 1898), pp. 12, 13.

28. Codman, Notes and Reminiscences, III, 16–18, Codman Papers.

29. Williamson, *Atkinson,* p. 271; "Reply to Edward Atkinson by R. M. Chamberlin," in Atkinson, *Margin of Profits,* p. 57.

30. Moorfield Storey, *Politics as a Duty and as a Career* (New York, 1889), p. 29; Stimson, *Scribner's,* 1:6:671 (June 1887), James Bryce, *The American Commonwealth,* 2nd ed. rev. (London, 1891), I, 495, 496n; W. D. Howells, *The Rise of Silas Lapham* (Boston, 1885), p. 60; C. W. Eliot to T. W. Higginson, March 31, 1896, Higginson Papers; Edward Atkinson to R. S. Howland, Oct. 8, 1890, Atkinson Papers.

31. Atkinson, *Margin of Profits,* p. 12.

32. Grant, *Fourscore,* pp. 372, 373.

33. C. H. Shepard to W. E. Russell, Nov. 14, 1892, Russell Papers; Dana, *Journal,* II, 736, Dana Papers; Perry, *Dana,* p. 132; Stimson, *My United States,* p. 112.

34. E. B. Haskell to H. C. Lodge, Oct. 23, 1886, Lodge Papers; Howe, *Storey,* p. 156; Curtis Guild to H. C. Lodge, July 11, 1890, Lodge Papers.

35. For the quotation on the Committee of One Hundred, see G. F. Williams to William Everett, Sept. 16, 1884, Everett Papers; for Everett's remark, see M. A. DeW. Howe, *A Venture in Remembrance* (Boston, 1941), p. 194; for the complaint of the Dedham Mugwump, see G. F. Williams to Grover Cleveland, Jan. 1, 1885, Cleveland Papers; for his comment on his defeat, see G. F. Williams to Carl Schurz [Nov. 1892], Schurz Papers.

36. James Russell Lowell, *Political Essays* (Boston, 1888), p. 306; G. F. Williams, *Oration Delivered Before the City Council and Citizens of Boston . . . July 5, 1886* (Boston, 1886), pp. 12–20; L. W. Bacon, *The Defeat of Party Despotism By a Re-enfranchisement of the Individual Citizen* (Boston, 1886), pp. 1–16; G. F. Williams to Grover Cleveland, Jan. 1, 1885, Cleveland Papers; Storey, *Politics as a Duty,* pp. 7–10.

37. Winslow Warren to William Everett, Sept. 27 [1886] Everett Papers.

38. Winslow Warren to William Everett, July 23, 1885, Everett Papers.

39. *Boston Transcript,* July 23, 1896.

40. Perry, *Dana,* 53.

CHAPTER THREE · THE VICTORS AND THE SPOILS

1. Allan Nevins, *Grover Cleveland: A Study in Courage* (New York, 1934), p. 199; A. B. Sageser, *Two Decades of the Pendleton Act* (Lincoln, Neb., 1935), p. 68; Bliss Perry, *Richard Henry Dana, 1851–1931* (Boston, 1933), p. 151; James Bryce, *The American Commonwealth,* 2nd ed. rev. (London, 1891), I, 76; C. R. Codman to W. C. Endicott, Nov. 13, 1885, Endicott Papers. See also Ari Hoogenboom, "The Pendleton Act and the Civil Service," *American Historical Review,* 64:2:301–318 (Jan. 1959).

2. H. F. Williamson, *Edward Atkinson: The Biography of an American Liberal, 1827–1905* (Boston, 1934), p. 267n; G. F. Williams to Carl Schurz, Nov. 19, 1884, Schurz Papers; *Nation,* 39:1011:413 (Nov. 13, 1884), and 39:1013:452–453 (Nov. 27, 1884).

3. *Nation,* 39:1013:452 (Nov. 27, 1884); G. F. Williams to Carl Schurz, Nov. 19, 1884, and Nov. 24, 1884, Schurz Papers. The self-restraint of Massachusetts Mugwumps did not last. By 1887 even the president of Harvard was recommending local businessmen for federal office. See C. W. Eliot to Grover Cleveland, Jan. 27, 1887, Cleveland Papers.

4. Grover Cleveland, *Letters of Grover Cleveland, 1850–1908,* Allan Nevins, ed. (Boston, 1933), pp. 52, 53.

5. Carl Schurz to R. B. Hayes, Sept. 6, 1885, G. W. Curtis to R. B. Hayes, June 3, 1892, Hayes Papers; G. W. Curtis to Carl Schurz, Aug. 12, 1887, Jabez Fox to Carl Schurz, July 31, 1885, C. R. Codman to Carl Schurz, Jan. 31, 1887, Carl Schurz to C. R. Codman, draft, Feb. 3, 1887, Schurz Papers; C. R. Codman, Notes and Reminiscences, II, 56–66, Codman Papers; Carl Schurz, *The Reminiscences of Carl Schurz* (New York, 1908), III, 414; Gordon Milne, *George William Curtis and the Genteel Tradition* (Bloomington, Ind., 1956), p. 182; Winslow Warren to William Everett, Nov. 24, 1888, Everett Papers.

6. G. F. Williams to W. C. Endicott, April 24, 1885, and April 27, 1885, Endicott Papers; R. H. Dana to Grover Cleveland, Sept. 25, 1886, Dana Papers.

7. A. J. Carswell to Grover Cleveland, Feb. 13, 1885, Cleveland Papers; Carl Schurz to G. F. Williams, Nov. 16, 1884, Russell Papers; *Boston Republic,* Jan. 3, 1885, Feb. 28, 1885, and March 21, 1885; William Everett to W. C. Endicott, March 16, 1885, Endicott Papers. The phrase, "Irish or Dynamite wing," is from Carswell's letter to Cleveland.

8. *Boston Herald,* Sept. 15, 1905; M. P. Curran, *Life of Patrick A. Collins* (Norwood, Mass., 1906), pp. 1–45; S. B. Griffin, *People and Politics Observed by a Massachusetts Editor* (Boston, 1923), 299–301.

9. Boston *Republic,* Feb. 14, 1885, and March 7, 1885; J. B. O'Reilly to Daniel Manning, Nov. 15, 1884, T. F. Meehan to Daniel Manning, Jan. 22, 1885, S. B. Griffin to F. L. Stetson, Feb. 11, 1885, W. C. Endicott to

Grover Cleveland, telegrams, Feb. 23, 1885, and Feb. 26, 1885, Cleveland Papers; Curran, *Collins*, pp. 100–103; Griffin, *People and Politics*, pp. 280–282; W. C. Endicott, Jr., "Memoir of William C. Endicott, LL.D.," *Massachusetts Historical Society Proceedings*, 2nd ser., 15:523–537 (1901, 1902). For the quoted comment on Endicott, see A. M. Howe to Carl Schurz, March 19, 1885, Schurz Papers. Endicott's grandfather, Jacob Crowninshield, was appointed Secretary of the Navy by Jefferson, but never served.

10. Boston *Republic*, April 25, 1885, and May 9, 1885; *Boston Record*, April 22, 1885; G. F. Williams to W. C. Endicott, April 22, 1885, April 23, 1885, April 15, 1886, and April 26, 1886, Endicott Papers; G. F. Williams *et al.* to Grover Cleveland, May 12, 1885, Cleveland Papers.

11. Winslow Warren, Scrapbook, *passim*, Warren Papers; F. M. Forbes to R. B. Hayes, April 28, 1877, Hayes Papers; Ari Hoogenboom, *Outlawing the Spoils: A History of the Civil Service Reform Movement, 1865–1883* (Urbana, 1961), 130, 131; Bernard O'Kane to W. E. Russell, Feb. 13, 1892, Russell Papers.

12. C. H. Taylor to W. C. Endicott, March 9, 1885, Leverett Saltonstall to W. C. Endicott, March 9, 1885, March 16, 1885, and April 6, 1885, Endicott Papers; Boston *Republic*, March 14, 1885; Mark D. Hirsch, *William C. Whitney: Modern Warwick* (New York, 1948), p. 351; Patrick Collins to Grover Cleveland, June 22, 1885, Cleveland Papers. Peter Butler and Benjamin F. Butler were not related to each other.

13. C. R. Codman, "Memoir of Leverett Saltonstall," *Massachusetts Historical Society Proceedings*, 2nd ser., 11:340–354 (1896, 1897); Leverett Saltonstall to W. C. Endicott, March 16, 1885, H. L. Higginson to W. C. Endicott, March 10, 1885, Endicott Papers; C. R. Codman to Grover Cleveland, May 30, 1885, Cleveland Papers. The quotation is from Codman's "Memoir," p. 341.

14. C. A. Prince to W. C. Endicott, Oct. 14, 1885, G. F. Williams to W. C. Endicott, May 14, 1885, N. S. Shaler to Grover Cleveland, June 2, 1885, Endicott Papers.

15. For Williams' remark, see G. F. Williams to Grover Cleveland, Sept. 22, 1887, Cleveland Papers. For Maguire's role in the collectorship fight, see Leverett Saltonstall to W. C. Endicott, Oct. 13, 1885, C. A. Prince to W. C. Endicott, Oct. 14, 1885, Endicott Papers; Boston *Republic*, June 13, 1885, *Boston Herald*, Sept. 4, 1887. For further details on Maguire's career, see Chapter Six.

16. Patrick Collins to Grover Cleveland, Nov. 7, 1885, and Oct. 4, 1886, John E. Fitzgerald to Grover Cleveland, Nov. 11, 1885, Cleveland Papers; Leverett Saltonstall to W. C. Endicott, Nov. 14, 1885, G. F. Williams to W. C. Endicott, Nov. 20, 1885, Endicott Papers; Cleveland, *Letters*, p. 89; Curran, *Collins*, pp. 104–107.

17. J. M. Curley, *I'd Do it Again* (Englewood Cliffs, N.J., 1957), p. 3; J. H. Cutler, *"Honey Fitz": Three Steps to the White House* (Indianapolis, 1962), p. 24; Boston *Republic*, Aug. 10, 1895; *Boston Herald*, Dec. 14, 1885; D. P. Toomey and T. C. Quinn, eds., *Massachusetts of Today*

(Boston, 1892), p. 272; A. J. Carswell to Grover Cleveland, Feb. 13, 1885, Cleveland Papers.

18. Boston *Republic,* July 18, 1885, Aug. 15, 1885, and Nov. 7, 1885; *Boston Transcript,* July 11, 1885; *Boston Herald,* Nov. 17, 1885; J. M. Bugbee, *The City Government of Boston* (Baltimore, 1887), p. 42; Leverett Saltonstall to W. C. Endicott, Dec. 20, 1855, Endicott Papers.

19. Nevins, *Cleveland,* pp. 246–248; G. F. Williams to W. C. Endicott, March 23, 1886, April 16, 1886, May 13, 1886, and Feb. 14, 1887, Endicott Papers; G. M. Stearns to Grover Cleveland, Feb. 10, 1886, Leverett Saltonstall to Grover Cleveland, April 13, 1886, Cleveland Papers.

20. G. F. Williams to W. C. Endicott, March 31, 1886, and April 5, 1886, Endicott Papers.

21. Winslow Warren to J. F. Andrew, Oct. 4, 1886, Andrew Papers; G. F. Williams to Carl Schurz, Oct. 9, 1886, Winslow Warren to Carl Schurz, Oct. 9, 1886, Schurz Papers.

22. G. G. Crocker to J. F. Andrew, Oct. 15, 1886, Francis O'Doherty to J. F. Andrew, Nov. 1, 1886, Andrew Papers; Winslow Warren to William Everett, Nov. 5, 1886, Everett Papers; *Boston Globe,* Oct. 1, 1886; *Boston Transcript,* Nov. 3, 1886; Josiah Quincy, "Governor Russell and the Young Democracy of Massachusetts," *Belford's Magazine,* 8:39:395, 396 (Aug. 1891).

23. R. H. Dana, Journal, II, 567, 580, 590, Dana Papers; R. H. Whitten, *Public Administration in Massachusetts: The Relation of Central to Local Authority* (New York, 1898), pp. 140–144.

24. Boston *Republic,* Dec. 27, 1884, and Jan. 17, 1885.

25. *Boston Herald,* Dec. 11, 1925; Jabez Fox to J. F. Andrew, May 20, 1885, Andrew Papers; J. P. Tolman to William Everett, Feb. 26, 1886, Everett Papers; *Massachusetts Acts and Resolves 1887,* chap. 437; W. E. Russell to W. F. Kennedy, June 1, 1892, Russell Papers. The quotation is from Fox to Andrew.

26. H. F. Swift to J. F. Andrew, Sept. 17, 1887, Andrew Papers; Winslow Warren to J. M. Corse, Sept. 21, 1887, J. M. Corse to W. C. Endicott, Sept. 22, 1887, Endicott Papers; G. F. Williams to Grover Cleveland, Sept. 22, 1887, Patrick Collins to Daniel Lamont, Sept. 29, 1887, Cleveland Papers. Maguire's report is quoted in the *Boston Herald,* Sept. 20, 1887.

27. Moorfield Storey to J. F. Andrew, Aug. 7, 1887, and Sept. 8, 1887, Andrew Papers.

28. *Boston Herald,* Sept. 21, 1887; G. M. Stearns to G. F. Williams, Sept. 19, 1887, Cleveland Papers.

29. *Boston Herald,* Sept. 21, 1887; Sylvester Baxter to G. F. Williams, April 16, 1886, Endicott Papers; R. H. Dana to Grover Cleveland, Nov. 19, 1887, Dana Papers.

CHAPTER FOUR · THE TARIFF AND THE YOUNG DEMOCRATS

1. Theodore Gerrish, *Life in the World's Wonderland* (Biddeford, Me., 1887), p. 86.

2. G. F. Williams to F. W. Bird, Jan. 4, 1887, Bird Papers.

3. G. F. Williams to W. C. Endicott, April 15, 1886, and May 6, 1886, Endicott Papers; Winslow Warren to William Everett, April 22 [188?], Everett Papers.

4. T. B. Reed to H. C. Lodge, Sept. 19, 1887, Lodge Papers.

5. James Bryce to T. W. Higginson, Feb. 2, 1887, T. W. Higginson Papers.

6. Boston Herald, Feb. 9 to Feb. 23, 1887; W. E. Russell, Scrapbook, 1886–1887, passim, Russell Papers.

7. Hamilton A. Hill, Boston's Trade and Commerce for Forty Years, 1844–1884 (Boston, 1884); Festus P. Summers, William L. Wilson and Tariff Reform (New Brunswick, N.J., 1953), pp. 67, 68; E. C. Kirkland, Men, Cities, and Transportation: A Study in New England History, 1820–1900 (Cambridge, 1948), I, 96, 148–157, 363–386, 398–400, 430–432; F. J. Stimson, My United States (New York, 1931), pp. 72, 73. The phrase quoted is on p. 72.

8. Roger Q. Mills, "New England and the New Tariff Bill," Forum, 9:4:361–370 (June 1890); Peleg McFarlin, New England's Lost Supremacy —Shall It Be Regained? An Address Delivered at Brockton, Mass., October 28, 1890 (Boston, 1891), pp. 5–14; John E. Russell, Address of Hon. John E. Russell, President of Democratic State Convention, Worcester, Sept. 18, 1890 (Boston, 1890), pp. 7ff; Arthur H. Cole, The American Wool Manufacture (Cambridge, Mass., 1926), II, 22.

9. Joseph Dorfman, The Economic Mind in American Civilization (New York, 1949), III, 49–69, 80; J. A. Garraty, Henry Cabot Lodge (New York, 1953), p. 113; F. B. Joyner, David Ames Wells: Champion of Free Trade (Cedar Rapids, Ia., 1939), pp. 25–222; Summers, Wilson, pp. 49, 50; W. C. Endicott to J. H. French, Sept. 27, 1884, Endicott Papers; Gamaliel Bradford to Carl Schurz, Nov. 20, 1884, Schurz Papers; H. F. Williamson, Edward Atkinson: The Biography of an American Liberal, 1827–1905 (Boston, 1934), p. 135; Josiah Quincy to J. F. Andrew, Jan. 31, 1885, Andrew Papers.

10. Boston Transcript, Nov. 3, 1886; G. F. Williams to Grover Cleveland, Nov. 3, 1886, Cleveland Papers; Boston Herald, Oct. 29, 1903; F. P. Rice, Time Notes (Worcester, Mass., 1915), p. 363; S. B. Griffin, People and Politics Observed by a Massachusetts Editor (Boston, 1923), p. 248; J. E. Russell to W. C. Whitney, Nov. 25, 1898, Whitney Papers.

11. C. R. Codman to Grover Cleveland, Oct. 16, 1885, Cleveland Papers; C. R. Codman to William Everett, June 1, 1886, Everett Papers; R. H. Dana to C. W. Eliot, Oct. 20, 1887, Dana Papers.

12. R. W. Gilder, Grover Cleveland: A Record of Friendship (New York, 1910), p. 13; Williamson, Atkinson, p. 148; J. F. Clarke to Grover Cleveland, Dec. 10, 1887, Leverett Saltonstall to Grover Cleveland, Dec. 7, 1887, Cleveland Papers; Josiah Quincy to Carl Schurz, Dec. 16, 1887, G. F. Williams to Carl Schurz, Dec. 19, 1887, Schurz Papers; L. M. Sargent to H. C. Lodge, Dec. 9, 1887, and Dec. 14, 1887, Lodge Papers; Boston Herald, Dec. 30, 1887.

13. F. W. Taussig to H. C. Lodge, March 14, 1888, J. T. Morse to H. C. Lodge, March 15, 1890, Lodge Papers; F. W. Taussig to Edward Atkinson, Jan. 7, 1890, Atkinson Papers; Report of the Committee on Political Science

for 1888–89, Harvard Archives; "Political Economy as Taught at Harvard," *American Economist,* 5:6:91 (Feb. 7, 1890).

14. Leverett Saltonstall to W. C. Endicott, April 6, 1885, Endicott Papers; F. A. Claflin to William Everett, Oct. 21, 1889, James Means to William Everett, Nov. 25, 1891, Everett Papers.

15. *Boston Herald,* Oct. 9, 1898; Sherman Hoar to W. E. Russell, Sept. 6, 1886, and Oct. 25, 1886, W. E. Russell to N. S. Shaler, April 10, 1893, Russell Papers; J. E. Russell to Richard Olney, Nov. 19, 1894, Olney Papers; *Tributes of the Bar and of the Circuit Court of the United States to the Memory of Sherman Hoar* (Boston, 1899), pp. 24–26, 39, and *passim; Harvard College Class of 1882, Sixth Report of the Secretary, 1907,* pp. 93–96, Harvard Archives.

16. C. S. Hamlin, Scrapbook, I, 13, 44; C. S. Hamlin, Diary Index-Digest, I, 380; C. S. Hamlin, Diary, I, 44, 46, 56–57, Hamlin Papers.

17. D. P. Toomey and T. C. Quinn, eds., *Massachusetts of Today* (Boston, 1892), p. 83; Boston *Republic,* March 8, 1890, and Dec. 6, 1890; *Boston Transcript,* Dec. 12, 1927.

18. T. J. Coolidge, Jr., to J. F. Andrew, Dec. 29, 1887, Andrew Papers; *Constitution, By-Laws, and Declaration of Principles of the Young Men's Democratic Club of Massachusetts* (Boston, March 1888, and Feb. 1, 1889), *passim.* A series of these handbooks, hereafter cited as *Y.M.D.C. Handbook,* covering the years from 1888 to the turn of the century, are in the Russell Papers.

19. J. M. Corse to W. C. Endicott, Aug. 3, 1888, Endicott Papers; G. F. Williams to F. W. Bird [Spring 1888], Bird Papers; *Y.M.D.C. Handbook* (Boston, March 1888), 3.

20. *Y.M.D.C. Handbook* (Boston, Oct. 1894), *passim;* W. E. Russell to W. L. Wilson, Feb. 10, 1891, Russell Papers.

21. C. C. Everett, "Memoir of William Eustis Russell," *Publications of the Colonial Society of Massachusetts,* 5:83 (1897, 1898); W. E. Russell, *Speeches and Addresses of William E. Russell,* C. T. Russell, Jr., ed. (Boston, 1894), p. xii; S. L. Powers, *Portraits of a Half Century* (Boston, 1925), p. 135.

22. L. M. Garrison, "Early Days of Successful Men: William Eustis Russell," *Harper's Round Table,* 17:848:313–315 (Jan. 28, 1896); Samuel Williston, *Life and Law: An Autobiography* (Boston, 1940), pp. 26, 27; Stimson, *My United States,* p. 52; Harvard *Crimson,* Dec. 4, 1876, June 15, 1877, and July 3, 1877. The quoted phrases about Russell at Harvard may be found in the *Boston Transcript,* July 23, 1896, and July 16, 1896, respectively.

23. Russell, *Speeches,* p. xii; Philip P. Chase, "Some Cambridge Reformers of the Eighties," *Cambridge Historical Society Proceedings,* 20:28, 42–48, (1927–1929); C. E. Norton, "The Public Life and Services of William Eustis Russell," *Harvard Graduates' Magazine,* 5:18:178–180 (Dec. 1896); Everett, *Publications of the Colonial Society of Massachusetts,* 5:84, 85 (1897, 1898); C. W. Eliot to W. E. Russell, Dec. 10, 1887, Russell Papers; W. E. Russell, Scrapbooks, *passim,* Russell Papers.

24. Physical description taken from W. E. Russell passport dated July 20, 1889, Russell Papers.

25. Chase, *Cambridge Historical Society Proceedings*, 20:42 (1927–1929); Arthur Gilman, ed., *The Cambridge of Eighteen Hundred and Ninety-Six* (Cambridge, Mass., 1896), pp. 82–86, 374, 375; J. A. Grant to W. E. Russell, Nov. 7, 1890, Jabez Fox to J. Underwood, Oct. 11, 1886, Jabez Fox to W. E. Russell, Oct. 12, 1886, F. S. Mosely to Babbitt, Oct. 25, 1888, Russell Papers. The quotation is from Mosely to Babbitt.

26. J. B. O'Brien to G. F. Williams, Oct. 6, 1890, Russell Papers; Robert Grant, *Fourscore: An Autobiography* (Boston, 1934), pp. 188–190; Russell, *Speeches*, pp. 84, 85.

27. Russell, *Speeches*, pp. 23, 233. The Macaulay quotation is from his speech on parliamentary reform, delivered to the House of Commons, March 2, 1831.

28. For Russell's gubernatorial races, see *Boston Herald*, Sept. 20, 1887; H. G. Alvord to W. E. Russell, Oct. 12, 1887, and J. E. Russell to W. E. Russell, Sept. 2, 1888, Russell Papers. Russell and the "Cambridge Idea" are discussed in Gilman, ed., *Cambridge*, pp. 82–100, and Chase, *Cambridge Historical Society Proceedings*, 20:48 (1927–1929). The liquor issue and behavior of "Saloon Democrats" are discussed in R. L. Bridgman, *Ten Years of Massachusetts* (Boston, 1888), pp. 109–116; J. A. Titus to W. E. Russell, Oct. 3, 1889, and Nov. 7, 1889, Winslow Warren to W. E. Russell, Nov. 6, 1889, Russell Papers.

29. C. F. Gettemy, Scrapbook, VII, 97, Gettemy Collection; M. M. Cunniff to W. E. Russell, Aug. 18, 1886, J. B. O'Reilly to W. E. Russell, July 5, 1890, Russell Papers.

30. The reports referred to are in the Russell Papers for 1888.

31. Grover Cleveland, *Letters of Grover Cleveland, 1850–1908*, Allan Nevins, ed. (Boston, 1933), pp. 221, 222; Massachusetts General Court, *Journal of the House of Representatives*, 1890, pp. 553–557, 596–602, 604–610; Boston *Republic*, March 29, 1890; Mills, *Forum*, 9:4:362–370 (June 1890); Ida M. Tarbell, *The Tariff in our Times* (New York, 1911), pp. 190–202.

32. Boston *Republic*, Jan. 11, 1890; W. C. Endicott to Grover Cleveland, Nov. 7, 1890, Cleveland Papers; Nathan Matthews to William Everett, Feb. 3, 1890, Everett Papers; Charles Warren to G. F. Williams, Oct. 15, 1890, Edward Atkinson to G. F. Williams, Oct. 16, 1890, Russell Papers; Everett, *Publications of the Colonial Society of Massachusetts*, 5:90 (1897, 1898); T. W. Higginson, *Cheerful Yesterdays* (Cambridge, 1898), p. 353; Norton, *Harvard Graduates' Magazine*, 5:18:182 (Dec. 1896).

33. Russell, *Speeches*, pp. 252, 332, 336.

34. Russell, *Speeches*, pp. 27, 236, 275, 316, 350.

35. Boston *Republic*, May 31, 1884, Nov. 1, 1884, Jan. 4, 1890, Jan. 11, 1890, May 24, 1890, Sept. 27, 1890, Oct. 18, 1890; Michael E. Hennessy, *Twenty-Five Years of Massachusetts Politics* (Boston, 1917), pp. 1–9. *Boston Herald*, Nov. 6, 1890, quotes the Worcester Republican, Congressman J. H. Walker.

36. T. H. Reilly to Josiah Quincy, Nov. 8, 1890, Russell Papers.

CHAPTER FIVE · THE STATE: EFFORTS AT REFORM

1. H. C. Lodge, ed., *Selections from the Correspondence of Theodore Roosevelt and Henry Cabot Lodge, 1884–1918* (New York, 1925), I, 92, 98, 125, 128, 130; John A. Garraty, *Henry Cabot Lodge* (New York, 1953), p. 129; W. E. Russell, "Significance of the Massachusetts Election," *Forum*, 12:4:435–438 (Dec. 1891). Lodge's comment on the Boston Democratic majority is taken from an undated typewritten interview in File PQ (1890), Lodge Papers.

2. Lloyd M. Garrison, *Governor Russell and His Canvass of Cape Cod* (New York, 1893), pp. 7–18.

3. W. E. Russell to A. P. Putnam, March 24, 1891, W. E. Russell to Charles Parkhurst, July 27, 1891, W. E. Russell to J. E. Russell, Feb. 1, 1893, Russell Papers. The quotation is from R. L. Bridgman, "Government By Commissions," *New England Magazine*, 10:4:445 (June 1894).

4. Bridgman, *New England Magazine*, 10:4:448; W. E. Russell, *Speeches and Addresses of William E. Russell*, C. T. Russell, Jr., ed. (Boston, 1894), pp. 136, 137, 148–150; Gamaliel Bradford, "Government by Commissions," *New England Magazine*, 10:4:454, 455n. (June 1894).

5. Russell, *Speeches*, p. 151; Bradford, *New England Magazine*, 10:4:455; Bridgman, *New England Magazine*, 10:4:446. Ben Butler's chosen title is cited in Bridgman's article, p. 446.

6. Seth Low, *The Problem of Municipal Government in the United States: An Address Given Before the Historical and Political Association of Cornell University, March 16, 1887* (Ithaca, 1887), pp. 14–18; Russell, *Speeches*, pp. 136–138, 148–168, 191–193; W. E. Russell to Gamaliel Bradford, Aug. 31, 1891, W. E. Russell to F. L. Young, April 10, 1893, Gamaliel Bradford to W. E. Russell, Jan. 8, 1892, Russell Papers.

7. W. E. Russell to F. A. Walker, Feb. 18, 1891, Russell Papers; "Report of the Joint Special Committee Appointed By the General Court of 1891 to Consider the Subject of Changing, Consolidating, or Abolishing the Various State Commissions," *Massachusetts Senate Document No. 73* (1892), p. 64, and *passim; New York Times,* June 21, 1961.

8. James Bryce, *The American Commonwealth,* 2nd ed. rev. (London, 1891), pp. 451, 515; Charles W. Eliot, *American Contributions to Civilization* (New York, 1898), pp. 85, 86; *Practical Politics,* 2:11:214 (Dec. 1, 1900); R. H. Dana, Journal, II, 559, Dana Papers; C. S. Hamlin, Diary, I, 103–105, Hamlin Papers; L. M. S. to H. C. Lodge, n.d., probably 1892, T. J. Coolidge to H. C. Lodge, May 21, 1892, R. A. Southworth to H. C. Lodge, Dec. 11, 1896, Lodge Papers; "Report of the Special Committee to Investigate Attempts at Bribery, etc.," *U.S. Senate Report,* 53 Cong., 2 sess., no. 606 (Aug. 2, 1894), pp. 351, 352.

9. Moorfield Storey, "The American Legislature," *Report of the Seventeenth Annual Meeting of the American Bar Association* (Philadelphia, 1894), pp. 252–256.

10. Richard Olney to J. W. Sanborn, Jan. 23, 1893, Olney Papers; A. T. Mason, *Brandeis: A Free Man's Life* (New York, 1946), p. 89. See also Thomas W. Lawson, *Frenzied Finance* (New York, 1905), I, 138–141, 149–161.

11. Sylvester Baxter, "Legislative Degeneracy in Massachusetts," *Arena*, 2:4:503–506 (Sept. 1890); R. L. Bridgman, "Legislatures: A Defense and a Criticism," *American Journal of Politics*, 5:6:598–602 (Dec. 1894); *Practical Politics*, 2:11:214 (Dec. 1, 1900); Robert Luce, *Legislative Assemblies* (Boston, 1924), p. 390.

12. *Boston Herald*, June 11, 1890; Boston *Republic*, March 1, 1890, and April 19, 1890; *Hartford Courant*, Sept. 16, 1893; H. M. Whitney to W. W. Clapp, Jan. 17, 1887, and Jan. 22, 1887, Clapp Papers; E. H. Clement, "Nineteenth Century Boston Journalism," *New England Magazine*, 37:1:93–96 (Sept. 1907); Boston Elevated Railroad Company, *Fifty Years of Unified Transportation in Metropolitan Boston* (Boston, 1938), 25ff. For summaries of Whitney's career, see S. L. Powers, *Portraits of a Half Century* (Boston, 1925), pp. 197–203; *Boston Transcript*, Jan. 26, 1923.

13. *Boston Herald*, June 11, 1890; Winslow Warren to G. F. Williams, June 12, 1890, Russell Papers; "Report of Committee to Investigate Methods Used For and Against Legislation Concerning Elevated Railroads . . . ," *Massachusetts House Document No. 585* (1890), pp. xi, 310, 411, 500, and *passim*. Whitney's counsel is quoted in *Boston Herald*, June 17, 1890.

14. Boston *Republic*, July 5, 1890; *Boston Herald*, June 17, 1890, and June 18, 1890; Moorfield Storey to G. F. Williams, June 12, 1890, Russell Papers; G. F. Williams, Diary Notes, Sept. 3, 1895; typewritten record of interview of George Fred Williams by Prof. Philip Putnam Chase, Oct. 1, 1926, Russell Papers. Quincy's report was published in *Boston Herald*, July 1, 1890.

15. *Boston Herald*, July 1, 1890, and July 2, 1890; *Nation*, 51:1306:22 (July 10, 1890); Josiah Quincy, "Regulation of the Lobby in Massachusetts," *Forum*, 12:3:346–357 (Nov. 1891).

16. G. F. Williams, Diary Notes, Sept. 10, 1895; undated typewritten memorandum on lobby issue, signed by "N.M. Jr.," Nathan Matthews to G. F. Williams, Sept. 27, 1890, W. E. Russell to G. F. Williams, Dec. 4, 1890, W. E. Russell to J. H. Bishop, Feb. 10, 1891, Russell Papers; Russell, *Speeches*, pp. 129–136, 202, 308–311; *Nation*, 52:1333:42–43 (Jan. 15, 1891).

17. For evidence suggesting Whitney's role in Massachusetts politics, see G. A. Perkins to W. E. Russell, Jan. 11, 1892, Francis Peabody, Jr., to W. E. Russell, Nov. 10, 1892, Russell Papers; T. J. Coolidge to H. C. Lodge, May 21, 1892, Lodge Papers.

18. R. H. Dana, "The Practical Working of the Australian System of Voting in Massachusetts," *Annals of the American Academy of Political and Social Science*, 2:6:734 (May 1892); R. H. Dana to William Everett, March 29, 1888, Everett Papers.

19. Dana, *Annals of the American Academy . . .* , 2:6:734–739 (May 1892); Bliss Perry, *Richard Henry Dana, 1851–1931* (Boston, 1933), p. 134; R. H. Dana, Journal, II, 575, 581, 591, 592, 612, Dana Papers. The quotation is from Dana's Journal. See also T. H. Russell to Grover Cleveland, Jan. 6, 1885, Cleveland Papers.

20. For various views on the secret ballot, see *Nation*, 52:1335:82 (Jan.

29, 1891), and 56:1448:226 (March 30, 1893); W. E. Russell to C. S. Connerat, Jan. 16, 1891, J. W. Carter to G. F. Williams, June 21, 1892, Russell Papers; P. O. Larkin to H. C. Lodge, Oct. 16, 1891, Lodge Papers; J. E. Russell to W. C. Whitney, Aug. 6, 1892, Whitney Papers; J. M. Curley, *I'd Do It Again* (Englewood Cliffs, N.J., 1957), pp. 18, 19; Boston *Republic,* Jan. 25, 1890, and Sept. 6, 1890; Robert A. Woods, ed., *Americans in Process* (Boston, 1902), p. 165.

21. Josiah Quincy, "Working of the Massachusetts Corrupt Practices Law," *Forum,* 15:2:142–147 (April 1893); Dana, Journal, II, 617, Dana Papers; *Nation,* 54:1403:369 (May 19, 1892), and 55:1433:442 (Dec. 15, 1892); George Lyman to H. C. Lodge, Oct. 18, 1893, Lodge Papers.

22. *Nation,* 53:1377:381 (Nov. 19, 1891); *Boston Herald,* April 17, 1891; C. S. Hamlin, Diary, I, 26, Hamlin Papers; Grover Cleveland to D. S. Lamont, Oct. 13, 1891, Josiah Quincy to Grover Cleveland, Oct. 22, 1891, Nathan Matthews to Grover Cleveland, Nov. 5, 1891, Cleveland Papers; Josiah Quincy, "Governor Russell and the Young Democracy of Massachusetts," *Belford's Magazine,* 8:39:397 (Aug. 1891); Russell, *Speeches,* pp. 122–127.

23. N. S. Shaler, "Memorandum Concerning the Province and Effect of Local Government in Massachusetts," typewritten undated memorandum in Russell Papers.

24. Harold F. Wilson, *The Hill Country of Northern New England* (New York, 1936), pp. 97–155; W. M. Cook, "Murders in Massachusetts," *American Statistical Association Publications,* n.s., 23:377 (Sept. 1893); R. H. Whitten, *Public Administration in Massachusetts: The Relation of Central to Local Authority* (New York, 1898), p. 96. See R. L. Bridgman, *Ten Years in Massachusetts* (Boston, 1888), pp. 121–122, for a striking statement about the rural-urban clash.

25. Horace Wadlin, "The Growth of Cities in Massachusetts," *American Statistical Association Publications,* n.s., 13:162–172 (March 1891).

26. Whitten, *Public Administration,* p. 81.

27. Bridgman, *Ten Years,* pp. 19, 20; *Nation,* 52:1343:251 (March 26, 1891); H. H. Pratt to William Everett, May 14, 1885, Everett Papers; Boston *Republic,* April 25, 1885, and June 9, 1894; Russell, *Speeches,* pp. 199–201; typewritten draft of speech delivered at Ashfield Academy dinner, Aug. 22, 1895, Russell Papers.

28. Henry W. Putnam, *Oration Delivered Before the City Council and Citizens of Boston . . . July 4, 1893* (Boston, 1893), pp. 27, 28.

29. *Boston Transcript,* Jan. 26, 1923; Boston *Republic,* April 19, 1890; L. P. Hager, ed., *History of the West End Street Railway* (Boston, 1892), pp. 11ff; W. E. Russell to Spencer Borden, Feb. 11, 1891, Russell Papers; S. M. Crothers, "Reminiscences of Cambridge," *Cambridge Historical Society Publications,* 31:7, 8 (1945); Ephraim Emerton, "Recollections of Sixty Years in Cambridge," *Cambridge Historical Society Publications,* 20:54, 55 (1927–1929); Sam B. Warner, *Streetcar Suburbs: The Process of Growth in Boston, 1870–1900* (Cambridge, Mass., 1962), pp. 25–29.

30. H. L. Higginson to W. E. Russell, Dec. 13, 1892, Russell Papers;

Edward Atkinson to H. M. Whitney, April 12, 1892, Atkinson Papers; Russell, *Speeches*, p. 206.

31. W. S. Bigelow to H. C. Lodge, April 20, 1895, Lodge Papers; Nathan Matthews, Jr., *Argument of Mayor Matthews Before the Committee on Transit of the Massachusetts Legislature, April 4, 1894* (Boston, 1894), pp. 7–11; Mason, *Brandeis*, pp. 106–117.

32. W. S. Allen, *Development of Street Railways in the Commonwealth of Massachusetts* [1898], p. 22; Charles W. Eliot, *Charles Eliot, Landscape Architect* (Cambridge, Mass., 1903), I, 316–338, II, 354–357.

33. Sylvester Baxter to W. E. Russell, June 14, 1892, C. F. Adams to W. E. Russell, Dec. 19, 1892, Russell Papers; C. F. Adams, *Charles Francis Adams, 1835–1915: An Autobiography* (Boston, 1916), p. 185; Sylvester Baxter, "Seaside Pleasure-Grounds for Cities," *Scribner's Magazine*, 23:6:681–684 (June 1898).

34. Today the suburban cities connected to downtown Boston by rapid transit contain some of the most dismal and depressing residential districts in New England. Meanwhile, the North End, commonly regarded in the 1890's as Boston's worst slum concentration, has become recognized as one of the city's most vital and attractive areas. A plausible explanation, together with a stinging indictment of the "Garden City" ideal of metropolitan planners, is found in Jane Jacobs, *The Death and Life of Great American Cities* (New York, 1961), pp. 8–11, 33, and *passim*.

35. Hannah Josephson, *The Golden Threads: New England's Mill Girls and Magnates* (New York, 1949), pp. 228–285; J. R. Commons *et al.*, *History of Labour in the United States* (New York, 1921), II, 138–144; Susan M. Kingsbury, ed., *Labor Laws and Their Enforcement, with Special Reference to Massachusetts* (New York, 1911), chap. 1; Sarah S. Whittelsey, *Massachusetts Labor Legislation: An Historical and Critical Study* (Philadelphia, 1900), pp. 12–14; M. C. Cahill, *Shorter Hours: A Study of the Movement Since the Civil War* (New York, 1932), pp. 106–110.

36. For strikes, see "Nineteenth Annual Report of the Bureau of Statistics of Labor," *Massachusetts Public Document No. 15* (1886), p. 46. Analysis of legislative party divisions is based on scattered newspaper evidence. The legislative journals do not indicate party affiliations. Newspapers occasionally printed party breakdowns in their editorial columns. For examples, see *Boston Herald*, April 15, 1891, and April 26, 1892. See also Russell, *Speeches*, pp. 320–323. For textile manufacturers' attitude toward labor legislation, see Whittelsey, *Massachusetts Labor Legislation*, p. 69, and S. N. D. North, *Factory Legislation in New England: Its Tendencies and Effects, Its Legal and Economic Aspects* (Boston, 1895), *passim*.

37. For McEttrick, see D. P. Toomey and T. C. Quinn, eds., *Massachusetts of Today* (Boston, 1892), p. 221; Michael McEttrick to G. F. Williams, Oct. 23, 1891, Russell Papers. For Mellen, see Edwin M. Bacon and Richard Herndon, eds., *Men of Progress* (Boston, 1896), pp. 326, 327. For Howard, see Boston *Republic*, Jan. 12, 1884, and Sept. 29, 1894. For Moseley, see James Morgan, *The Life Work of Edward A. Moseley in the Service of Humanity* (New York, 1913), pp. 23, 24. For Quincy's role in

labor legislation, see Bridgman, *Ten Years*, p. 74; Boston *Republic*, Dec. 7, 1895.

38. For the arbitration law, see Bridgman, *Ten Years*, p. 81, and *Massachusetts Public Document No. 15* (1888), p. 116. For weekly payments, see Whittelsey, *Massachusetts Labor Legislation*, pp. 32, 76; William Hooper to J. F. Andrew, Jan. 22, 1884, Andrew Papers; Boston *Republic*, Feb. 14, 1885.

39. Massachusetts General Court, *Journal of the House of Representatives*, 1887, p. 108; Boston *Republic*, Dec. 7, 1895; Bridgman, *Ten Years*, p. 81; Whittelsey, *Massachusetts Labor Legislation*, pp. 19, 28–30; M. E. Hennessy, *Twenty-Five Years of Massachusetts Politics* (Boston, 1917), p. 25.

40. R. T. Ely and L. S. Merriam, "Report on Social Legislation in the United States for 1889 and 1890," *Economic Review* (London), 1:2:238 (April 1891); Whittelsey, *Massachusetts Labor Legislation*, pp. 60, 72, 77; Russell, *Speeches*, pp. 142, 143.

41. Massachusetts General Court, *Journal of the House of Representatives*, 1892, p. 1105; *Boston Herald*, April 26, 1892; W. E. Russell to Robert Howard, July 6, 1892, and Nov. 28, 1892, Robert Howard to W. E. Russell, Nov. 12, 1892, Russell Papers. The quotation is from Howard to Russell.

42. Oscar Handlin, *Boston's Immigrants*, rev. ed. (Cambridge, Mass., 1959), pp. 75–77, 81; *Massachusetts House Document No. 255* (1891), p. 8; Theodore Roosevelt, *An Autobiography* (New York, 1913), pp. 88–90.

43. "Report of the Committee on Manufactures on the Sweating System," *U.S. House Report*, 52 Cong., 2 sess., no. 2309 (1893), p. 98; *Boston Herald*, Oct. 4, 1890, and Oct. 5, 1890.

44. *Massachusetts House Document No. 149 (1891)*, pp. 8–14; *Massachusetts House Document No. 255* (1891), pp. 2–11; W. F. Willoughby, *Regulation of the Sweating System* (Boston, 1900), pp. 4–10.

45. *Massachusetts House Document No. 149* (1891), p. 1; Wadlin's words are quoted from *Massachusetts House Document No. 255* (1891), p. 10. See also W. E. Russell to H. G. Wadlin, March 5, 1891, W. E. Russell to John Crowly, Nov. 17, 1891, W. E. Russell to E. J. Haynes, Feb. 5, 1892, Russell Papers.

46. *Massachusetts Acts and Resolves 1891*, chap. 357; Willoughby, *Regulation of the Sweating System*, p. 8; J. E. Pope, *The Clothing Industries in New York* (Columbia, Mo., 1905), pp. 191, 192; H. Marot and C. L. Pratt, *The Makers of Men's Clothing: Report of an Investigation Made in Philadelphia* [n.d., n.p.], p. 23; W. E. Russell to Edwin Bacon, June 1, 1892, Russell Papers; *U.S. House Report*, 52 Cong., 2 sess., no. 2309 (1893), pp. 112–114, 126; Woods, ed., *Americans in Process*, pp. 8, 48, 125, 129. The words of the Philadelphia social worker are quoted from Marot and Pratt's report.

47. *U.S. House Report*, 52 Cong., 2 sess., no. 2309 (1893), p. xxviii.

48. George W. Parker to W. E. Russell, Nov. 26, 1892, Russell Papers.

49. Ely and Merriam, *Economic Review*, 1:2:236 (April 1891); W. E. Russell, "Individualism in Government: A Plea for Liberty," typewritten

draft of address given at Ann Arbor, Michigan, Jan. 18, 1895, Russell Papers.

CHAPTER SIX · THE CITY: EFFORTS AT COOPERATION

1. The best descriptions of Irish political life in Boston are in Joseph Dinneen, *The Purple Shamrock* (New York, 1949), pp. 15–38, and Dinneen, *Ward Eight* (New York, 1936), *passim.* For a contemporary appraisal, see Boston *Republic,* April 28, 1894.

2. The best biographical sources for Maguire are *Boston Record,* June 15, 1895; *Boston Globe,* Nov. 29, 1896; Boston *Pilot,* Dec. 5, 1896; Boston *Republic,* Dec. 5, 1896; and J. B. Cullen, ed., *The Story of the Irish in Boston* (Boston, 1889), p. 412. For Doherty, see *Boston Transcript,* May 17, 1883.

3. Boston *Republic,* Dec. 20, 1884 (quoting the New York *Irish-American*); *Boston Herald,* Sept. 4, 1887. Information about Maguire's real-estate ventures was received from Sam B. Warner, Jr., author of *Streetcar Suburbs: the Process of Growth in Boston, 1870–1900* (Cambridge, Mass., 1962).

4. Boston *Record,* June 15, 1895; *Nation,* 45:1161:241 (Sept. 29, 1887). For Maguire's warning about "internecine strife," see Boston *Republic,* Aug. 2, 1890. For Maguire's attitude toward Godkin, see Boston *Republic,* May 3, 1890. For Maguire's relations with Grover Cleveland, see Boston *Republic,* Aug. 1, 1891; C. S. Hamlin, Diary, I, 25, 37, Hamlin Papers.

5. For Gargan, see Edwin Bacon and Richard Herndon, eds., *Men of Progress* (Boston, 1896), p. 479; T. J. Gargan to W. E. Russell, Dec. 9, 1891, and Dec. 24, 1893, Russell Papers; T. J. Gargan, *Oration Delivered Before the City Council and Citizens of Boston . . . July 4, 1885* (Boston, 1885), pp. 29–35.

6. D. P. Toomey and T. C. Quinn, eds., *Massachusetts of Today* (Boston, 1892), p. 49; *Boston Herald,* Oct. 7, 1886; G. F. Williams, Diary Notes, Sept. 3, 1895; Theodore Roosevelt to R. H. Dana, Feb. 14, 1891, Dana Papers; J. H. O'Neil to W. E. Russell, April 10, 1892, Russell Papers; J. H. O'Neil to Richard Olney, April 27, 1896, Olney Papers. O'Neil's comment on the McKinley bill is quoted in *Boston Herald,* Oct. 9, 1890.

7. For Donahoe, see Cullen, ed. *Irish in Boston,* pp. 227–230; *Donahoe's Magazine,* 23:5:442–446 (May 1890). For O'Reilly, see Arthur Mann, *Yankee Reformers in the Urban Age* (Cambridge, Mass., 1954), pp. 27–44; J. J. Roche, *Life of John Boyle O'Reilly* (New York, 1891), pp. 240, 333, 347; F. J. Stimson, *My United States* (New York, 1931), pp. 116–119; J. B. O'Reilly to D. S. Lamont, June 20, 1888, Cleveland Papers.

8. Boston *Republic,* May 3, 1890; *Boston Herald,* April 14, 1892.

9. J. H. O'Neil, *Oration Delivered Before the City Council and Citizens of Boston . . . July 4, 1894* (Boston, 1894), pp. 28–30; *Donahoe's Magazine,* 22:5:472 (Nov. 1889).

10. F. A. Bushée, *Ethnic Factors in the Population of Boston* (New York, 1903), pp. 62, 66, 75, quotation from 113, 114; Boston *Republic,* Feb. 22, 1896.

11. Bushée, *Ethnic Factors,* pp. 10, 33, 73, 74; Robert H. Lord *et al., History of the Archdiocese of Boston in the Various Stages of Its Development, 1604 to 1943* (New York, 1944), III, 100–125; *Boston Herald,* Dec. 12, 1888 and Dec. 11, 1889; Lois B. Merk, "Boston's Historic Public School Crisis," *New England Quarterly,* 31:2:179–199 (June 1958).

12. The extended quotation is from *Boston Record,* Nov. 27, 1894. The phrase "entente cordiale" is from G. H. Lyman to H. C. Lodge, Oct. 25, 1895, Lodge Papers. See Lord, *Boston Archdiocese,* III, 146–156; Donald L. Kinzer, *An Episode in Anti-Catholicism: The American Protective Association* (Seattle, 1964), pp. 26–28, 186–188.

13. Bushée, *Ethnic Factors,* pp. 5, 6; *Boston Advertiser,* March 21, 1894; R. A. Woods, ed., *Americans in Process: A Settlement Study* (Boston, 1902), pp. 273, 274; Boston *Republic,* May 10, 1890.

14. *Boston Advertiser,* Oct. 18, 1895. Quotation from Gaetano Conte, "Societies For the Protection of Italian Immigrants: Documents and Illustrations," a scrapbook of Reverend Conte's activities in the North End, 1893 to 1903, p. 21.

15. Boston *Republic,* Jan. 11, 1890, and April 19, 1890.

16. K. E. Conway and M. W. Cameron, *Charles Francis Donnelly: A Memoir, With an Account of the Hearings on a Bill for the Inspection of Private Schools in Massachusetts in 1888–1889* (New York, 1909), pp. 31, 32, 34–39, 49–51, 64–66, 148, 149, 183–185; G. F. Williams, Diary Notes, Sept. 11, 1895.

17. J. B. O'Reilly to J. F. Andrew, Jan. 31, 1887, J. E. Killian to J. F. Andrew, Oct. 16, 1888, H. W. Swift to J. F. Andrew, Nov. 7, 1888, Andrew Papers; Boston *Republic,* Aug. 2, 1890, Oct. 4, 1890, and Oct. 18, 1890; J. H. O'Neil to W. E. Russell, Feb. 2, 1892, W. E. Russell to J. H. O'Neil, Feb. 4, 1892, Patrick Maguire to W. E. Russell, June 30, 1892, and Aug. 2, 1893, W. E. Russell to Spencer Borden, Feb. 1, 1893, Russell Papers; Sherman Hoar to Richard Olney, July 17, 1894, Olney Papers.

18. Rerum Novarum was published in *Donahoe's Magazine,* 26:1:97–112 (July 1891).

19. *Donahoe's Magazine,* 23:5:461 (May 1890); Merk, *New England Quarterly,* 31:2:195 (June 1958); *First Annual Report of the Massachusetts Association Opposed to the Extension of Suffrage to Women* (Boston, 1896), pp. 6–8; Stimson, *My United States,* p. 111; Robert Grant, *Fourscore: An Autobiography* (Boston, 1934), p. 127; W. E. Russell, "The Suffrage a Burden, Which Women Don't Want," undated draft of speech in Russell Papers; C. R. Codman, Notes and Reminiscences, II, 9, Codman Papers; Roche, *O'Reilly,* p. 227; F. J. Stimson, "The Ethics of Democracy," *Scribner's Magazine,* 1:6:671 (June 1887); Boston *Republic,* Sept. 21, 1895; Charles F. Gettemy, Scrapbooks, II, 31, Gettemy Collection; *Boston Advertiser,* Jan. 30, 1894, quoting Donovan; Nathan Matthews, Jr., *The City Government of Boston* (Boston, 1895), p. 176, n. 4; W. B. Lawrence to H. C. Lodge, April 3, 1894, Lodge Papers.

20. For the prohibition issue, see R. A. Woods, ed., *The City Wilderness: A Settlement Study* (Boston, 1898), p. 118; Woods, ed., *Americans in*

Process, pp. 106, 107; C. S. Hamlin to W. E. Russell, Dec. 5, 1892, Russell Papers; W. E. Russell, *Speeches and Addresses of William E. Russell*, C. T. Russell, Jr., ed. (Boston, 1894), pp. 10–15, 144, 300. For the naturalization issue, see W. E. Russell to Sherman Hoar, March 22, 1892, Russell Papers; Boston *Republic*, Oct. 10, 1896.

21. Boston *Republic*, May 10, 1890, Dec. 6, 1890, and Dec. 13, 1890. For Taylor, see James Morgan, *Charles H. Taylor, Builder of the Boston Globe* (Boston, 1923), pp. 3, 85, 123; C. H. Taylor to Grover Cleveland, Nov. 14, 1884; G. F. Williams, Diary Notes, Sept. 3, 1895.

22. J. M. Bugbee, *The City Government of Boston* (Baltimore, 1887), p. 45; *Hartford Courant*, July 29, 1893; A. B. Hart, ed., *Commonwealth History of Massachusetts* (New York, 1930), V, 71–92; Nathan Matthews, Jr., *Argument of Mayor Matthews Before the Committee on Transit of the Massachusetts Legislature, April 4, 1894* (Boston, 1894), *passim;* G. F. Williams, Diary Notes, Sept. 10, 1895; T. W. Lawson, *Frenzied Finance* (New York, 1906), I, 100–109; Nathan Matthews to W. E. Russell, March 16, 1893, Charles Goodwin to W. E. Russell, March 18, 1893, Russell Papers; Matthews, *City Government*, pp. 12, 31, 58, 59, 95, 99, 112–115, 131, 168–185; S. B. Capen, "The Boston Municipal League," *American Journal of Politics*, 5:1:7 (July 1894); Edward Atkinson to Henry Lee, Sept. 2, 1891, Atkinson Papers; Moorfield Storey, "Municipal Government of Boston," *Proceedings of the National Conference For Good City Government Held at Philadelphia January 25 and 26, 1894* (Philadelphia, 1894), p. 61.

23. Matthews, *City Government*, pp. 174–180; Moorfield Storey, *The Government of Cities: The Need of a Divorce of Municipal Business from Politics* [Buffalo, 1891], p. 7.

24. *Hartford Courant*, Dec. 9, 1893; L. H. Feder, *Unemployment Relief in Periods of Depression: A Study of Measures Adopted in Certain Cities, 1857 through 1922* (New York, 1936), p. 83; "Report of the Massachusetts Board to Investigate the Subject of the Unemployed," *Massachusetts House Document No. 50* (1895), IV, v–lxiii.

25. *Massachusetts House Document No. 50* (1895), III, 109–111; R. H. Dana, Journal, II, 685, 686. Dana Papers; *Boston Advertiser*, Jan. 5, 1894, and March 8, 1894. See J. G. Brooks, "The Question of the Unemployed in Massachusetts," *Economic Journal*, 4:14:361–365 (June 1894).

26. *Boston Common Council Proceedings, 1894*, p. 4; *Massachusetts House Document No. 50* (1895), I, xxv, 12, 33, 34; "Twenty-Fourth Annual Report of the Bureau of Statistics of Labor," *Massachusetts Public Document No. 15* (1893), pp. 141, 142, 169; *Report of the Citizen's Relief Committee, Boston, 1893–1894* (Boston, n.d.), p. 35 for quotation from committee member, and *passim; Harper's Weekly*, 38:1941:197, 198 (March 3, 1894).

27. *Boston Advertiser*, Feb. 14, 1894, March 1, 1894, March 6, 1894, and Nov. 13, 1894; Boston *Republic*, May 26, 1894; *Boston Herald*, Feb. 21, 1894, and March 12, 1894; *Boston Globe*, Oct. 8, 1894; Mann, *Yankee Reformers*, pp. 194–197; *Massachusetts House Document No. 50* (1895), III, 5–12; Woods, ed., *Americans in Process*, pp. 121, 130, 134.

28. *Boston Common Council Proceedings, 1894*, pp. 4, 1050; Matthews, *City Government*, pp. 104–107, 175, 182.

29. Conrad Reno, *Memoirs of the Judiciary and the Bar of New England For the Nineteenth Century* (Boston, 1900), I, 65, 66; C. S. Hamlin, Scrapbook, XXXIV, 125, Hamlin Papers; *Boston Advertiser*, Nov. 12–17, 1894, Dec. 5, 1894; *Boston Record*, Dec. 7, 1894, and Dec. 12, 1894. The two quotations are from *Boston Advertiser*, Nov. 15, 1894, and the Hamlin Scrapbook, respectively.

30. M. P. Curran, *Life of Patrick A. Collins* (Norwood, Mass., 1906), p. 128; Woods, ed., *Americans in Process*, pp. 4–6.

31. Bacon and Herndon, eds., *Men of Progress*, p. 867; *Practical Politics*, 2:11:224–225 (Dec. 1, 1900); Woods, ed., *City Wilderness*, pp. 31, 39, and *passim*. The South End boss sketched in *City Wilderness*, pp. 123–129, is almost certainly Donovan.

32. *Boston Herald*, Dec. 2–Dec. 27, 1925; Woods, ed., *Americans in Process*, pp. 43, 63, 64, 183–189; C. F. Gettemy, Scrapbook, V, 113, Gettemy Collection; D. G. Wayman, *Cardinal O'Connell of Boston* (New York, 1955), pp. 47–52. The phrase "six o'clock Democrat" is from the installment of Lomasney's biography in *Boston Herald*, Dec. 10, 1925.

33. Bacon and Herndon, eds., *Men of Progress*, pp. 475, 476; Woods, ed., *Americans in Process*, pp. 180–183, 269, 270; *Boston Advertiser*, March 21, 1894, June 11, 1894, Sept. 21, 1894, and Sept. 22, 1894; Cyrus Willard, "Autobiography," chap. 10, p. 21, and chap. 12, p. 2; J. H. Cutler, *"Honey Fitz"*: . . . *The Life and Times of John F. (Honey Fitz) Fitzgerald* (Indianapolis, 1962), pp. 15–68.

34. Woods, ed., *Americans in Process*, pp. 159, 180, 184; A. D. Van Nostrand, "The Lomasney Legend," *New England Quarterly*, 21:4:441 (Dec., 1948); J. F. Fitzgerald, *Oration Delivered Before the City Council and Citizens of Boston . . . July 4, 1896* (Boston, 1897), pp. 12, 17, 22.

35. *Boston Advertiser*, June 6, 1896.

CHAPTER SEVEN · THE NATION: EFFORTS AT CONTROL

1. Raymond B. Nixon, *Henry W. Grady, Spokesman of the New South* (New York, 1943), p. 345. See C. Vann Woodward, *Origins of the New South, 1877–1913* (Baton Rouge, 1951), pp. 114–141.

2. Harold F. Williamson, *Edward Atkinson: The Biography of an American Liberal, 1827–1905* (Boston, 1934), pp. 166–175; Broadus Mitchell, *The Rise of Cotton Mills in The South* (Baltimore, 1921), pp. 117–123, 237, 238; A. B. Hart, ed., *Commonwealth History of Massachusetts* (New York, 1930), V, 375; J. C. Calhoun to Edward Atkinson, April 15, 1890, Atkinson Papers; N. S. Shaler, "The Economic Future of the New South," *Arena*, 2:3:267, 268 (Aug. 1890).

3. Merrill D. Peterson, *The Jeffersonian Image in the American Mind* (New York, 1960), pp. 250–265; Edward Atkinson to John Ott, Nov. 12, 1892, W. E. Russell to Edward Atkinson, March 17, 1890, Atkinson Papers; Nixon, *Grady*, p. 347; W. E. Russell, Scrapbook, V, 13, Russell Papers; W. E. Russell, *Speeches and Addresses of William E. Russell*, C. T. Russell,

ed. (Boston, 1894), pp. 16–28. See J. A. Barnes, *John G. Carlisle, Financial Statesman* (New York, 1931), pp. 187, 188.

4. *Boston Transcript,* June 9, 1884, containing the Kidder quotation; G. F. Williams to Carl Schurz, Feb. 10, 1885, Schurz Papers; Richard Olney to W. C. Endicott, May 27, 1886, Endicott Papers; F. J. Stimson, *My United States* (New York, 1931), p. 83; R. E. Riegel, *The Story of the Western Railroads* (New York, 1926), p. 286; J. D. Hicks, *The Populist Revolt* (Minneapolis, 1931), p. 31; C. R. Codman, *Notes and Reminiscences,* II, 129–134, Codman Papers.

5. H. S. Merrill, *Bourbon Democracy of the Middle West, 1865–1896* (Baton Rouge, 1953), pp. 205, 206, 210; Hicks, *Populist Revolt,* pp. 179–181; H. U. Faulkner, *Politics, Reform and Expansion, 1890–1900* (New York, 1959), pp. 114–118.

6. Edward Atkinson to William Fowler, Nov. 4, 1890, Atkinson Papers; Winslow Warren to William Everett, Nov. 17, 1890, Everett Papers; F. P. Summers, *William L. Wilson and Tariff Reform* (New Brunswick, N.J., 1953), pp. 113–117.

7. T. J. Coolidge to H. C. Lodge, April 26, 1890, H. L. Higginson to H. C. Lodge, Nov. 17, 1890, Lodge Papers. See C. F. Adams to Carl Schurz, Sept. 10, 1896, Schurz Papers.

8. H. L. Higginson to H. C. Lodge, Nov. 17, 1890, Lodge Papers. See Charles Hoffman, "The Depression of the Nineties," *Journal of Economic History,* 16:2:152 (June 1956).

9. Edward Atkinson to Grover Cleveland, Jan. 9, 1891, Edward Atkinson to Edmund Howland, Jan. 3, 1891, Atkinson Papers.

10. Higginson's speech is quoted in *Boston Herald,* Jan. 21, 1891; Atkinson's warning about investments may be found in Edward Atkinson to W. P. Parrish, Jan. 23, 1891, Atkinson Papers; Russell's anxieties are expressed in W. E. Russell to W. L. Wilson, Feb. 10, 1891, Russell Papers.

11. Grover Cleveland, *Letters of Grover Cleveland, 1850–1908,* Allan Nevins, ed. (Boston, 1933), pp. 245, 246; W. E. Russell to Grover Cleveland, Feb. 14, 1891, W. E. Russell to W. H. Page, March 28, 1891, Russell Papers; Edward Atkinson to Edmund Howland, Jan. 3, 1891, Edward Atkinson to Charles Nordhoff, March 20, 1891, Atkinson Papers.

12. W. L. Wilson to Carl Schurz, March 16, 1892, Schurz Papers.

13. Undated memorandum, Box 19, Russell Papers.

14. R. Q. Mills to G. F. Williams, Nov. 18, 1891 (copy), Russell Papers; C. C. Jackson to J. F. Andrew, Nov. 19 [1891], Andrew Papers; W. L. Wilson to Carl Schurz, March 16, 1892, Schurz Papers; G. F. Williams, Diary Notes, Sept. 3, 1895.

15. J. R. Lambert, *Arthur Pue Gorman* (Baton Rouge, 1953), p. 175; J. H. O'Neil to W. E. Russell, Jan. 13, 1892, J. H. O'Neil to W. E. Russell, Jan. 28, 1892, Russell Papers.

16. Russell, *Speeches,* pp. 37, 38, 307, 343–347; Cleveland, *Letters,* p. 221; W. E. Russell to J. H. O'Neil, Jan. 15, 1892, Russell Papers.

17. Sherman Hoar to W. E. Russell, Jan. 24, 1892, W. E. Russell to G. F. Parker, Feb. 16, 1892, Russell Papers; A. M. Howe, "Tribute of Archibald Murray Howe to John Forrester Andrew," *Colonial Society of*

Massachusetts Publications, 3:152 (Transactions, 1895–1897); G. F. Williams to Edward Atkinson, Feb. 16, 1892, Atkinson Papers; "Free Coinage of Gold and Silver," *U.S. House Report,* 52 Cong., 1 sess., no. 249 (Feb. 10, 1892), p. 26; *Congressional Record,* 52 Cong., 1 sess., 1892, pp. 2332 and 2518.

18. *Boston Herald,* March 25, 1892; W. E. Russell to Benton McMillan, March 22, 1892, H. P. Tobey to W. E. Russell, April 15, 1892, W. E. Russell to W. L. Wilson, April 20, 1892, W. L. Wilson to W. E. Russell, May 5, 1892, Russell Papers; C. S. Hamlin, Diary, I, 18–21, Hamlin Papers; Summers, *Wilson,* pp. 130, 131.

19. Allan Nevins, *Grover Cleveland: A Study in Courage* (New York, 1934), pp. 480, 481; C. S. Hamlin, Diary, I, 19, Hamlin Papers; Cleveland *Letters,* pp. 220, 221, 301–304; Winslow Warren to C. F. Adams, Dec. 11, 1891, Adams Papers. The phrase "lunacy of poverty" is from W. L. Wilson to Carl Schurz, July 29, 1892, Schurz Papers.

20. *Boston Herald,* April 9, 1892, and April 15, 1892 (quoting Lomasney); Nevins, *Cleveland,* p. 486; C. S. Hamlin to G. F. Williams, March 1, 1892 (copy), W. E. Russell to Grover Cleveland, March 16, 1892, Russell Papers; C. S. Hamlin to Grover Cleveland, Feb. 29, 1892, March 5, 1892, March 7, 1892, and March 25, 1892, Cleveland Papers; J. E. Russell to W. C. Whitney, March 11, 1892, March 27, 1892, April 9, 1892, and June 29, 1892, copy of circular letter sent by W. C. Whitney, June 3, 1892, Whitney Papers; W. C. Whitney to Carl Schurz, July 8, 1892, Schurz Papers. Russell's phrase about Whitney's "final dividend" is from Russell to Whitney, June 29, 1892.

21. Nevins, *Cleveland,* pp. 498, 499; G. H. Knoles, *The Presidential Campaign and Election of 1892* (Stanford, 1942), pp. 83, 247; G. F. Williams to W. E. Russell, July 27, 1892, Russell Papers; *To the Voters of Massachusetts,* undated campaign pamphlet issued by "Independent Cleveland Headquarters," 1892, in Widener Library, Harvard University; Edward Atkinson to G. F. Williams, Oct. 5, 1892, Atkinson Papers; *Boston Transcript,* Nov. 2, 1892; C. S. Hamlin, Diary, I, 32, 38, Hamlin Papers.

22. Cleveland, *Letters,* p. 304; *Boston Transcript,* Nov. 9, 1892, and Nov. 10, 1892; E. M. Wheelwright, "Memoir of John Forrester Andrew," *Colonial Society of Massachusetts Publications,* 3:369 (Transactions, 1895–1897); *Boston Herald,* June 12, 1891; H. P. Tobey to W. E. Russell, March 18, 1892, Russell Papers; *Nation,* 55:1428:343 (Nov. 10, 1892); G. F. Williams to Carl Schurz, Dec. 14, 1892, Schurz Papers; Winslow Warren to C. F. Adams, Nov. 11, 1892, Adams Papers; J. E. Russell to W. C. Whitney, Nov. 10, 1892, Whitney Papers.

23. Woodward, *New South,* p. 271.

24. Richard Olney to W. E. Russell, March 7, 1891, and June 13, 1891, Russell Papers; Richard Olney to J. M. Forbes, Nov. 1, 1892, G. G. Haven (director of the Boston & Maine) to Richard Olney, Feb. 23, 1893, C. E. Perkins (president of the Chicago, Burlington, & Quincy) to Richard Olney, Feb. 23, 1893, Olney Papers; D. S. Lamont, Memoranda, "Concerning the Appointment of the Cabinet, Second Cleveland Administration," Jan. 4, 1893, and Feb. 22, 1893, Grover Cleveland to D. S. Lamont, Feb. 19, 1893, Lamont Papers.

25. Barnes, *Carlisle*, pp. 233, 234, 251–254; G. F. Williams to Carl Schurz, Dec. 14, 1892, and Jan. 20, 1893, Schurz Papers; Circular letter signed by A. L. Lowell and seven others, Jan. 4, 1893, Atkinson Papers; Nevins, *Cleveland*, pp. 523, 524. See G. F. Williams, "Imminent Danger From the Silver-Purchase Act," *Forum*, 14:6:789–796 (Feb. 1893).

26. H. L. Higginson to Richard Olney, April 19, 1893, Olney Papers; H. L. Higginson to C. S. Hamlin, May 5, 1893, and June 2, 1893, Hamlin Papers.

27. Nevins, *Cleveland*, p. 526; H. L. Higginson to Richard Olney, April 19, 1893, C. C. Jackson to Richard Olney, May 10, 1893, Olney Papers.

28. Sigourney Butler to Richard Olney, July 5, 1893, Olney Papers; R. Q. Mills to Edward Atkinson, Sept. 2, 1893, Atkinson Papers; Josiah Quincy to D. S. Lamont, Oct. 17, 1893, Lamont Papers; Nevins, *Cleveland*, pp. 546–548.

29. Lee's letter appears in *Speeches by Leading Business Men at the Dinner of the New England Tariff Reform League, January 18, 1894*, pamphlet issued by New England Tariff Reform League (Boston, 1894), p. 34. See also Winslow Warren to William Everett, Jan. 15, 1894, Everett Papers.

30. Winslow Warren to William Everett, May 15, 1894, Phineas Pierce to William Everett, Aug. 1, 1894, Everett Papers. For views on income tax, see *Labor Leader*, Jan. 20, 1894; Boston *Republic*, Feb. 3, 1894; Richard Olney to Ellen Hammond, May 22, 1894, Olney Papers; J. H. O'Neil to J. F. Andrew, Jan. 10, 1894, Andrew Papers; Patrick Collins to W. E. Russell, Jan. 16, 1894, Russell Papers; H. L. Pierce to William Everett, Jan. 29, 1894, Everett Papers.

31. Boston *Republic*, April 28, 1894, and May 19, 1894.

32. Boston *Republic*, Oct. 5, 1895; W. L. Wilson to William Everett, Nov. 30, 1895, Everett Papers.

33. "The New Party," undated brochure in Box 19, Russell Papers; R. H. Dana, Journal, II, 649, Dana Papers; Edward Atkinson to W. H. Brawley, March 1, 1892, Edward Atkinson to Sherman Hoar, March 23, 1892, Atkinson Papers.

34. C. F. Adams, "Mr. Cleveland's Tasks and Opportunities," *Forum*, 15:3:298–303 (May 1893).

35. Moorfield Storey to Carl Schurz, Oct. 24, 1893, Schurz Papers.

36. M. D. Hirsch, *William C. Whitney, Modern Warwick* (New York, 1948), p. 407; A. M. Howe to Carl Schurz, Dec. 21, 1892, Schurz Papers.

37. Nevins, *Cleveland*, p. 517; Josiah Quincy to D. S. Lamont, Nov. 18, 1895, Lamont Papers; John A. Garraty, *Henry Cabot Lodge* (New York, 1953), p. 104; William Slade, "Attractions and Abuses of our Consular Service," *Forum*, 15:2:163–166 (April 1893); L. W. Bacon, *The Defeat of Party Despotism By the Re-enfranchisement of the Individual* (Boston, 1886), p. 7; F. H. Underwood (consul in Glasgow) to F. W. Bird, Aug. 25, 1885, Bird Papers; Josiah Quincy to C. E. Norton, Jan. 4, 1893, Norton Papers; W. E. Russell to Sigourney Butler, April 10, 1893, Russell Papers.

38. R. W. Gilder, *Grover Cleveland: A Record of Friendship* (New York, 1910), pp. 115, 116; Bliss Perry, *Richard Henry Dana, 1851–1931* (Boston, 1933), pp. 156, 157; R. H. Dana, Journal, II, 673, Dana Papers;

R. W. Gilder to Carl Schurz, Jan. 7, 1897, Theodore Roosevelt to Carl Schurz, Aug. 23, 1893, A. M. Howe to Carl Schurz, May 18, 1893 (comparing Quincys and Adamses), Josiah Quincy to Carl Schurz, April 20, 1893, Schurz Papers.

39. M. A. DeW. Howe, *Portrait of an Independent: Moorfield Storey* (Boston, 1932), pp. 181, 182; *Nation*, 57:1466:74 (Aug. 3, 1893), and 57:1478:298 (Oct. 26, 1893); *Good Government*, 8:5:49, 50 (Nov. 15, 1893); G. F. Williams, Diary Notes, Sept. 3, 1895.

40. W. E. Russell to Josiah Quincy, March 10, 1893, Russell Papers; Sigourney Butler to Richard Olney, March 29, 1893, Olney Papers; L. A. Dodge to H. C. Lodge, March 13, 1894, Lodge Papers.

41. R. H. Dana, Journal, II, 671, 672, 677, 678, 703, 704, Dana Papers. Storey is quoted in *Boston Record*, Oct. 26, 1894; Dana is quoted in *Boston Advertiser*, Jan. 13, 1894.

42. C. F. Adams, *Charles Francis Adams, 1835–1915: An Autobiography* (Boston, 1916), p. 200.

43. Moorfield Storey, "The American Legislature," *Report of Seventeenth Annual Meeting of the American Bar Association* (Philadelphia, 1894), pp. 245, 252, 257, 258, 272.

44. C. S. Hamlin, Diary, I, 133, 134, Hamlin Papers.

45. Boston *Republic*, Sept. 21, 1895; C. S. Hamlin, Diary, I, 135, Hamlin Papers; *Boston Globe*, Nov. 2, 1895, for the Williams quotation, and Nov. 6, 1895, for the election results.

CHAPTER EIGHT · 1896.

1. J. K. Jones to Moreton Frewen, Jan. 24, 1898, Frewen Papers. See J. A. Barnes, "Myths of the Bryan Campaign," *Mississippi Valley Historical Review*, 34:3:370–376 (Dec. 1947).

2. F. P. Summers, ed., *The Cabinet Diary of William L. Wilson, 1896–1897* (Chapel Hill, 1957), pp. 27, 28, 44, 51, 67, 83, 84, 94; Allan Nevins, *Grover Cleveland: A Study in Courage* (New York, 1934), pp. 689–698; M. D. Hirsch, *William C. Whitney: Modern Warwick* (New York, 1948), pp. 475–486; J. A. Barnes, *John G. Carlisle: Financial Statesman* (New York, 1931), pp. 453–455; Grover Cleveland, *Letters of Grover Cleveland, 1850–1908*, Allan Nevins, ed. (Boston, 1933), p. 430.

3. Adolph S. Ochs to James Swann, Oct. 17, 1894, Henry Watterson to W. E. Russell, Dec. 22, 1893, Walter Hines Page to W. E. Russell, March 2, 1894, Richard W. Gilder to W. E. Russell, March 7, 1894, Richard T. Ely to W. E. Russell, Feb. 27, 1892, E. C. Wall to W. E. Russell, Nov. 22, 1892, Tom Taggart to W. E. Russell, May 5, 1892, Orison Swett Marden to W. E. Russell, Dec. 17, 1894, W. E. Russell, Scrapbook, V, 154, Russell Papers; W. A. Robinson, *Thomas B. Reed, Parliamentarian* (New York, 1930), p. 377.

4. For Russell's candidacy in 1892, see James E. Campbell to W. E. Russell, Dec. 26, 1891, F. C. Foster to W. E. Russell, May 20, 1892, W. E. Russell to F. C. Foster, May 29, 1892, J. H. O'Neil to W. E. Russell, Feb. 2, 1892, Russell Papers. For Russell's friendship with Cleveland, see

Richard W. Gilder to W. E. Russell, April 18, 1890, W. E. Russell to Grover Cleveland, June 16, 1891, Russell Papers; R. W. Gilder, *Letters of Richard Watson Gilder*, Rosamond Gilder, ed. (Boston, 1916), p. 462; Grover Cleveland to Richard Olney, Dec. 4, 1897, Olney Papers.

5. Charles S. Hamlin, Diary, I, 72, 154, Hamlin Papers; W. E. Russell, "Political Causes of the Business Depression," *North American Review*, 157:6:641–652 (Dec. 1893); W. E. Russell, "A Year of Democratic Administration," *Forum*, 17:3:257–267 (May 1894); W. E. Russell, "The Issues of 1896: A Democratic View," *Century Magazine*, 51:1:73–77 (Nov. 1895); Edward Atkinson to W. E. Russell, Dec. 20, 1895, T. W. Higginson to W. E. Russell, Dec. 24, 1895, Russell Papers, Nevins, *Cleveland*, p. 695.

6. G. W. Green to W. E. Russell, Feb. 22, 1896, and April 7, 1896, J. E. Russell to W. E. Russell, Feb. 26, 1896, Russell Papers; J. E. Russell to Richard Olney, Feb. 6, 1896, Richard Olney to Josiah Quincy, April 4, 1896, Olney Papers; C. S. Hamlin, Diary, I, 154–160, Hamlin Papers; *Boston Herald*, April 18, 1896, and April 22, 1896. For the Monticello speech, see C. F. Black to W. E. Russell, Feb. 27, 1896, Russell Papers; *Boston Herald*, April 14, 1896; Summers, ed., *Wilson Diary*, p. 64; Merrill D. Peterson, *The Jefferson Image in the American Mind* (New York, 1960), pp. 250–265. The substance of the speech is in W. E. Russell, "Jefferson and His Party Today," *Forum*, 21:5:513–524 (July 1896).

7. J. G. Speed, "A Possible Presidential Candidate: Hon. William E. Russell and His Public Career," *Leslie's Weekly*, May 28, 1896, pp. 371–372; G. H. Lyman to Henry Cabot Lodge, May 9, 1896, Lodge Papers; C. C. Bolton to W. E. Russell, May 5, 1896, Russell Papers. For the character of Russell's national support, see Lynde Harrison to W. E. Russell, April 22, 1896, April 27, 1896, May 26, 1896, June 1, 1896, and June 12, 1896, G. W. Green to W. E. Russell, April 23, 1896, W. H. French to W. E. Russell, April 25, 1896, Russell Papers. For Dickinson's attitude toward Russell, see Summers, ed. *Wilson Diary*, p. 128. See the letters from Lyman to Lodge and from Bolton to Russell for the two quotations.

8. W. C. Whitney to W. E. Russell, June 18, 1896, and June 22, 1896, Russell Papers; W. E. Russell to W. C. Whitney, June 19, 1896, Whitney Papers; Hirsch, *Whitney*, pp. 488–491.

9. Don M. Dickinson to Grover Cleveland, June 20, 1896, Cleveland Papers; C. S. Hamlin, Diary, I, 170, Hamlin Papers; W. C. P. Breckinridge to Daniel Lamont, June 22, 1896, "Memorandum of Suggestions," enclosure to Whitney's circular letter of June 26, 1896, Whitney Papers.

10. *Boston Globe*, July 2, 1896; W. C. Whitney to W. E. Russell, June 29, 1896, Russell Papers; Hirsch, *Whitney*, p. 497.

11. *Official Proceedings of the Democratic National Convention . . . , 1896* (Logansport, Ind., 1896), pp. 192–234; Hirsch, *Whitney*, pp. 502–504; Nevins, *Cleveland*, pp. 701–702.

12. Charles Warren, "The Manufacturer of History," *McClure's Magazine*, 14:6:531–533 (April 1900); S. B. Griffin, *People and Politics Observed by a Massachusetts Editor* (Boston, 1923), pp. 353, 358; *Official Proceedings*, p. 267. Russell's and Bryan's speeches are quoted in *Cleveland Plain Dealer*, July 10, 1896.

13. *Boston Herald,* July 17, 1896; *Boston Transcript,* July 23, 1896. Miss Guiney's poetic tribute to Russell, "The Colors at Cambridge," was published in *Atlantic Monthly,* 106:48–49 (July 1910).

14. *Boston Globe,* July 2, 1896; John Hay to Henry Adams, Aug. 4, 1896, Henry Adams Papers; Carl Schurz to Moorfield Storey, draft, July 4, 1896, Schurz Papers.

15. G. F. Williams, Diary Notes, Sept. 3, 1895.

16. For the Williams quotation, see G. F. Williams to F. W. Bird, Jan. 4, 1887, Bird Papers. For the Everett quotation, see G. F. Williams to W. C. Endicott, July 6, 1886, Endicott Papers. For the Storey quotation, see Moorfield Storey to E. M. Wheelwright, Nov. 15, 1889, Wheelwright Papers. See also *Dedham Transcript,* July 15, 1932; Champ Clark, *My Quarter Century of American Politics* (New York, 1920), II, 393.

17. *Hartford Courant,* July 29, 1893; G. F. Williams to C. F. Adams, [n.d., filed in Dec. 1892, but probably written in 1895], C. F. Adams Papers; R. L. Bridgman to G. F. Williams, Oct. 23 [1890], Russell Papers; G. F. Williams, Diary Notes, Sept. 5, 1895; G. F. Williams to Carl Schurz [Nov. 1892?], Schurz Papers.

18. Henry Austin, *Address of Henry Austin Before the Second Nationalist Club of Boston* (Boston, 1890), p. 16; [B. O. Flower], "Hon. George Fred Williams and Winston Churchill: Two New England Defenders of the People's Cause," *Arena,* 36:203:407 (Oct. 1906); Sylvester Baxter to G. F. Williams, Dec. 26, 1891, April 5, 1892, April 22, 1892, May 24, 1892, and June 25, 1896, Russell Papers. Williams' views on coinage are quoted in L. R. Ehrich to Horace White, July 6, 1896, Schurz Papers. Ehrich is quoting a letter received from Williams. For Williams' influence on Garland, see Donald Pizer, *Hamlin Garland's Early Work and Career* (Berkeley, 1960), pp. 84, 85; Hamlin Garland to G. F. Williams, Oct. 27, 1890, Russell Papers.

19. *Boston Herald,* July 9, 1896.

20. *Boston Globe,* July 15, 1896.

21. *Boston Herald,* July 25, 1896, and July 28, 1896. For Jaquith, see *Boston Herald,* July 15, 1896. For Paine, see *Boston Globe,* July 26, 1896; Barbara M. Solomon, *Ancestors and Immigrants: A Changing New England Tradition* (Cambridge, Mass., 1956), p. 104.

22. For Coakley, see *Boston Advertiser,* Nov. 14, 1893; *Boston Record,* Aug. 21, 1894; *Boston Herald,* Oct. 29, 1896; *Harper's Weekly,* 40:2082:1118, 1119 (Nov. 14, 1896). For Keenan, see E. M. Bacon, ed. *Men of Progress* (Boston, 1896), p. 888; S. B. Anthony and I. H. Harper, *History of Woman Suffrage* (New York, 1902), IV, 740.

23. Arthur Mann, *Yankee Reformers in an Urban Age* (Cambridge, Mass., 1954), pp. 188–200; Frank Foster to W. E. Russell, Jan. 4, 1892, Russell Papers; *Labor Leader,* Feb. 24, 1894, and March 17, 1894; *Boston Globe,* July 15, 1896. The *Globe* quotes Foster's Faneuil Hall speech.

24. *Boston Globe,* July 26, 1896; Frank Foster to G. F. Williams, Sept. 17, 1896, Russell Papers. For Lloyd, see *Boston Record,* Oct. 28, 1896. For McNeill, see *Boston Globe,* July 14, 1896. For Mellen, see *Boston Globe,* July 26, 1896.

25. *Boston Globe,* Aug. 4, 1896; Brooks Adams to W. E. Russell, Nov. 10, 1892, Brooks Adams to G. F. Williams, June 22, 1896, Russell Papers; *Boston Advertiser,* Sept. 28, 1893; C. F. Gettemy, Scrapbook, II, 145 and 164, Gettemy Collection; Brooks Adams to H. C. Lodge, Nov. 24, 1893, Jan. 13, 1894, and April 23, 1894 (the letter of April 23, 1894 commenting on the Boston banker), Lodge Papers; C. F. Adams to Evelyn [Mrs. Brooks] Adams, Jan. 7, 1895, C. F. Adams Papers; Brooks Adams to Henry Adams, April 6, 1896, June 29, 1896, and July 12, 1896 (the letter of July 12, 1896 describing the Chicago Convention), Brooks Adams Papers.

26. For Adams' feeling that he had to speak for the silver cause, his delight that "not a mouse has squeaked," and his protestation against office or responsibility, see Brooks Adams to Henry Adams, Aug. 17, 1896, Brooks Adams Papers; for Adams' statement that he would be out of the country on election day, see *Boston Globe,* Oct. 8, 1896; for his remarks on the campaign, see Brooks Adams to Henry Adams, Oct. 28, 1896, Brooks Adams Papers. See also Brooks Adams to G. F. Williams, Sept. 23, 1896, and Oct. 5, 1896, Russell Papers.

27. C. W. Eliot to T. W. Higginson, Aug. 31, 1896, T. W. Higginson Papers; C. S. Hamlin, Diary, I, 166, Hamlin Papers; Moorfield Storey to Carl Schurz, July 8, 1896, Schurz Papers; *Boston Transcript,* July 10, 1896, for Warren's view.

28. *Boston Globe,* July 26, 1896, for Matthew's remark; Young Men's Democratic Club, *Democratic Notes,* 1:3:3 (Oct. 1896); *Boston Herald,* Aug. 1, 1896.

29. A. T. Mason, *Brandeis: A Free Man's Life* (New York, 1946), pp. 63, 88–91, Williams' letter being quoted on p. 89; record of interview by Philip P. Chase of Louis D. Brandeis on June 9, 1927, Russell Papers.

30. For the Gold Democrats' last appeal, see *Boston Herald,* Oct. 22, 1896; for the characterization of the Gold Democrats, see *Boston Herald,* Sept. 6, 1896.

31. J. F. Colby to G. F. Williams, June 26, 1896, Russell Papers.

32. Winslow Warren to Carl Schurz, April 16, 1896, Carl Schurz to Winslow Warren, draft, April 21, 1896, Moorfield Storey to Carl Schurz, June 10, 1896, A. M. Howe to Carl Schurz, July 7, 1896, Schurz Papers. The quotation is from Howe to Schurz.

33. James Loeb to Carl Schurz, July 18, 1896, July 22, 1896, Aug. 5, 1896, and Aug. 8, 1896, Schurz Papers. The quotation is from Loeb's letter of Aug. 8, 1896.

34. C. F. Adams to Carl Schurz, Sept. 10, 1896, C. R. Codman to Carl Schurz, Sept. 13, 1896, Schurz Papers; C. V. Holman to William Everett, Oct. 16, 1896, Claude G. Bowers to William Everett, Oct. 30, 1896, Everett Papers; T. W. Higginson to G. F. Williams, July 17, 1896, Record of interview by Philip P. Chase of Eugene Waumbaugh on Feb. 1, 1927, Russell Papers. See also M. A. DeW. Howe, *Barrett Wendell and His Letters* (Boston, 1924), pp. 109n, 114, 115.

35. *Boston Herald,* July 10, 1896; *Boston Transcript,* July 10, 1896; *Boston Republic,* July 18, 1896, Sept. 5, 1896, and Oct. 17, 1896.

36. *Boston Herald,* July 12, 1896, and July 14, 1896; *Boston Globe,* July 16, 1896, quoting the Irish leader, Joseph Corbett.

37. *Boston Herald,* July 23, 1896, July 25, 1896, and Aug. 5, 1896, respectively, for the three quotations.

38. *Boston Herald,* Aug. 14, 1896.

39. *Boston Herald,* Sept. 9, 1896, and Sept. 10, 1896.

40. *Boston Herald,* Aug. 23, 1896, quoting Williams, Sept. 1, 1896, and Sept. 12, 1896; *Boston Record,* Sept. 12, 1896; Timothy Coakley to G. F. Williams, telegram, Sept. 12, 1896, Russell Papers.

41. W. J. Bryan to G. F. Williams, telegram, Sept. 1, 1896, Arthur Sewall to G. F. Williams, Sept. 19, 1896, Russell Papers.

42. *Boston Herald,* Sept. 26, 1896, and Sept. 27, 1896; *Boston Transcript,* Sept. 26, 1896; W. J. Bryan, *The First Battle* (Chicago, 1896), pp. 493–497.

43. G. H. Lyman to H. C. Lodge, Sept. 26, 1896, Lodge Papers; H. J. Jaquith to G. F. Williams, Oct. 23, 1896, Russell Papers; *Boston Globe,* Oct. 26, 1896, for Williams' telegram; *Boston Herald,* Oct. 31, 1896, for the state committee chairman's comment.

44. L. S. Pratt to G. F. Williams, Oct. 21, 1896, and Oct. 22, 1896, Russell Papers; *Boston Herald,* Oct. 24, 1896, and Oct. 29, 1896.

45. J. W. Sharkey to G. F. Williams, Aug. 27, 1896, W. T. Way to G. F. Williams, Oct. 29, 1896, F. A. Hobart to G. F. Williams, Oct. 5, 1896, Oct. 6, 1896, and Oct. 8, 1896, Russell Papers. The quotation is from Sharkey to Williams.

46. Josephus Daniels, *Editor in Politics* (Chapel Hill, 1941), p. 196; G. H. Lyman to H. C. Lodge, Oct. 29, 1897, Lodge Papers; Mary Gunning to G. F. Williams, Nov. 5, 1896, Russell Papers; *Boston Transcript,* Sept. 28, 1896, for Bryan's Lynn speech; S. Kasinski to G. F. Williams, Sept. 30, 1896, Russell Papers.

47. Annie T. Auerbach to G. F. Williams, Sept. 28, 1896, and Dec. 8, 1896, B. O. Flower to G. F. Williams, Aug. 6, 1896, and Oct. 28, 1896, Russell Papers; Boston *Pilot,* May 16, 1896, July 18, 1896, July 25, 1896, Aug. 1, 1896, Sept. 19, 1896, and Oct. 31, 1896.

48. *Boston Globe,* Nov. 4, 1896. The voting returns of 1896, nationally and in Massachusetts, have been subjected to close scrutiny and various interpretations. Bryan, as would be expected of any Democrat, ran much better in Massachusetts cities than in rural areas. William Diamond has shown that Massachusetts led the nation in the ratio of urban to rural support for Bryan. Nevertheless, as he notes, Bryan received only 32.6 percent of the state's "urban" vote. See William Diamond, "Urban and Rural Voting in 1896," *American Historical Review,* 46:2:281–305 (Jan. 1941). V. O. Key has commented on Diamond's findings as follows: "To the extent that urban-rural tension played a part in Massachusetts in 1896 it was evidently no more salient than it had been in 1892; Democratic candidates did relatively better in the cities than in the country at both elections. Between 1892 and 1896 Democratic strength declined in both rural and urban population and to about the same extent." V. O. Key, "A Theory of Critical Elections," *Journal of Politics,* 17:1:3–18 (Feb. 1955).

It seems worth while to stress that of those Massachusetts voters who supported Bryan, many did so out of party regularity. The regular Democratic organization opposed neither Bryan nor Williams at the polls. Rather they opposed Williams' efforts to seize control of the party before the election.

CHAPTER NINE · MAYOR QUINCY'S BOSTON

1. *Boston Globe*, Nov. 4, 1896.
2. Boston *Republic*, Oct. 31, 1896.
3. *Boston Transcript*, Nov. 30, 1896, and Dec. 1, 1896.
4. C. F. Gettemy, Scrapbook, VII, 90, 93, 155, Gettemy Collection.
5. G. F. Williams, Diary Notes, Sept. 3, 1895; W. E. Russell to Josiah Quincy, March 10, 1893, Russell Papers; *Nation*, 57:1476:261 (Oct. 12, 1893); Boston *Republic*, Aug. 25, 1894, and Dec. 14, 1895; *Labor Leader*, Dec. 14, 1895.
6. Josiah Quincy, "Issues and Prospects of the Campaign," *North American Review*, 163:2:182–194 (Aug. 1896); C. S. Hamlin to Josiah Quincy, Aug. 27, 1896, as quoted in *Practical Politics*, Aug. 16, 1902; Brooks Adams to Henry Adams, Sept. 12, 1896, Brooks Adams Papers; Josiah Quincy to G. F. Williams, Sept. 24, 1896, Russell Papers; *Boston Transcript*, Sept. 26, 1896.
7. David A. Shannon, ed., *Beatrice Webb's American Diary, 1898* (Madison, 1963), p. 75; M. A. DeW. Howe, *A Venture in Remembrance* (Boston, 1941), p. 139; Henry Adams, *Letters of Henry Adams, 1892–1918*, W. C. Ford, ed. (Boston, 1938), p. 52; R. H. Dana, Journal, II, 681, Dana Papers.
8. Josiah P. Quincy to Josiah Quincy, Oct. 15 [189?], Quincy Papers; E. C. Kirkland, *Men, Cities, and Transportation: A Study in New England History, 1820–1900* (Cambridge, Mass., 1948), II, 294, 295.
9. Josiah Quincy, "The Orator in a Modern Democracy," Commencement Parts 1880, Harvard Archives.
10. William C. Edwards, *Historic Quincy Massachusetts* (Quincy, 1957), pp. 76, 77.
11. K. E. Conway and M. W. Cameron, *Charles Francis Donnelly: A Memoir* (New York, 1909), p. 50.
12. *Boston Globe*, Oct. 24, 1901; Josiah Quincy, "The Development of American Cities," *Arena*, 17:88:529 (March 1897).
13. R. C. Brooks, "Business Men in Civic Service: The Merchants' Municipal Committee of Boston," *Municipal Affairs*, 1:3:491–508 (Sept. 1897); Dorman B. Eaton, *The Government of Municipalities* (New York, 1899), p. 302.
14. *Boston Herald*, Nov. 19, 1899.
15. T. A. Whalen, "Boston's Municipal Printing Plant," *City Government*, 8:4:88 (April 1900); H. S. Chase, "Municipal Printing in Boston," *Municipal Affairs*, 4:4:774–777 (Dec. 1900); G. E. Hooker, "Mayor Quincy of Boston," *Review of Reviews*, 19:112:577 (May 1899); Josiah Quincy, *Address of Josiah Quincy, Mayor of Boston, to the City Council*,

January 4, 1897 (Boston, 1897), pp. 35–38; Quincy, *Arena,* 17:88:532–533 (March 1897).

16. Robert A. Woods, "Settlement Houses and City Politics," *Municipal Affairs,* 4:2:395–398 (June 1900). See also Arthur Mann, *Yankee Reformers in the Urban Age* (Cambridge, Mass., 1954), pp. 115–123, and Robert A. Woods, *The Neighborhood in Nation-Building* (Boston, 1923), *passim.*

17. Eleanor H. Woods, *Robert A. Woods: Champion of Democracy* (Boston, 1929), pp. 120–126, 148, the Woods quotation appearing on p. 148; Josiah Quincy, "Municipal Progress in Boston," *Independent,* 52:2672:424–426 (Feb. 15, 1900), Quincy's words about public bathing appearing on p. 424; Josiah Quincy, *Inaugural Address of Josiah Quincy, Mayor of Boston, to the City Council, January 6, 1896* (Boston, 1896), p. 36; E. M. Herlihy, ed., *Fifty Years of Boston: A Memorial Volume* (Boston, 1932), pp. 677–679, the Lee comment appearing on p. 678.

18. The Lee quotation is from Herlihy, ed., *Fifty Years,* p. 677; Quincy's words may be found in Josiah Quincy, *Address of Josiah Quincy, Mayor of Boston, to the City Council, January 2, 1899* (Boston, 1899), p. 56. See Hooker, *Review of Reviews,* 19:112:577 (May 1899); F. J. Douglas, "Municipal Socialism in Boston," *Arena,* 20:5:550–552 (Nov.–Dec. 1898). For Joseph Lee's interest in playgrounds, see B. M. Solomon, *Ancestors and Immigrants: A Changing New England Tradition* (Cambridge, Mass., 1956), pp. 138–140.

19. *Boston Traveller,* Oct. 29, 1901; Quincy, *Address, 1897,* pp. 63, 64; Robert A. Woods, ed., *Americans in Process: A Settlement Study* (Boston, 1902), pp. 87–89.

20. Quincy, *Address, 1899,* pp. 43–51; Twentieth Century Club, *A Survey of Twenty Years, 1894–1914* (Boston, 1914), pp. 12, 14; *The Twentieth Century Club of Boston, 1894–1904* [Boston, 1904], pp. 20, 21; W. I. Cole, "Free Public Organ Recitals in Boston," *Review of Reviews,* 16:94:579–581 (Nov. 1897); C. B. Ware to William Everett, Dec. 15, 1898, Everett Papers; *Boston Herald,* May 9, 1896; *Boston Traveller,* Oct. 12, 1901; Sylvester Baxter, "Boston at the Century's End," *Harper's New Monthly Magazine,* 99:594:834 (Nov. 1899).

21. Quincy, *Arena,* 17:88:536 (March 1897).

22. Hooker, *Review of Reviews,* 19:112:575, 576, 578 (May 1899); R. W. Gilder to Carl Schurz, Jan. 7, 1897, Schurz Papers; Brooks Adams to Henry Adams, Sept. 12, 1896, Brooks Adams Papers; Shannon, ed., *Webb's Diary,* pp. 74, 76, 85, quoting Charles Francis Adams, on p. 74; G. H. Lyman to Henry Cabot Lodge, Dec. 23, 1897, Lodge Papers.

23. Baxter, *Harper's,* 99:594:833 (Nov. 1899); Shannon, ed., *Webb's Diary,* p. 74n, quoting Mead; C. R. Woodruff, ed., *Proceedings of the Columbus Conference For Good City Government . . . 1899* (Philadelphia, 1899), p. 178; *Review of Reviews,* 19:112:515 (May 1899).

24. Shannon, ed., *Webb's Diary,* pp. 74–87. See also Mark Howe, ed., *Holmes-Laski Letters: The Correspondence of Mr. Justice Holmes and Harold J. Laski, 1916–1935* (Cambridge, Mass., 1953), p. 521.

25. The quotation from the Republican strategist may be found in G. H. Lyman to H. C. Lodge, Nov. 29, 1897, Lodge Papers. Riley's attack on

Quincy is quoted in *Boston Herald*, Dec. 6, 1897. For biographical information on Riley, see *Boston Transcript*, Dec. 14, 1897.

26. *Boston Herald*, Dec. 22, 1897; G. H. Lyman to H. C. Lodge, Dec. 23, 1897, Lodge Papers.

27. *Boston Herald*, Jan. 4, 1898, May 16, 1899, May 31, 1899; Quincy, *Address, 1899*, pp. 15–19, 25, 29.

28. Lomasney's opinion of Quincy's ideas is quoted from *Boston Herald*, Dec. 13, 1925. See also *Boston Herald*, Dec. 11, 1925; *Boston Transcript*, Dec. 1, 1899, and Dec. 30, 1899; *Practical Politics*, Aug. 16, 1902; Woods, ed., *Americans in Process*, p. 188; *Proceedings of the City Council of Boston, 1899* (Boston, 1900), pp. 31–34, 38–40, 73, 74, 92. For Quincy's opinion of the City Council, see Josiah Quincy, *Address of Josiah Quincy, Mayor of Boston, to the City Council, January 2, 1899* (Boston, 1899), p. 26. For a suggestion of Quincy's difficulties with the Republican-controlled legislature, see F. W. Dallinger, *Recollections of an Old-Fashioned New Englander* (New York, 1941), pp. 88, 89. Quincy's most comprehensive reply to critics of his mayoralty is his *Valedictory Message of Josiah Quincy, Mayor of Boston, 1896–1899* (Boston, 1900), pp. 19–48.

29. G. A. Copeland, "An Insolvent Utopia," *Harper's Weekly*, 44:2269:549 (June 16, 1900); Josiah Quincy to C. E. Norton, June 29, 1900, and July 2, 1900, Norton Papers; Joseph F. Wall, *Henry Watterson: Reconstructed Rebel* (New York, 1956), pp. 269–270; *Debates in the Massachusetts Constitutional Convention, 1917–1918* (Boston, 1920), III, 887–930.

30. A. B. Hart, ed., *Commonwealth History of Massachusetts* (New York, 1930), V, 77.

31. Shannon, ed., *Webb's Diary*, p. 78; "Fruits of the Feudalism of Privilege," *Arena*, 36:203:418 (Oct. 1906); "The Battle Between Plutocracy and Popular Rule in Various Commonwealths," *Arena*, 36:204:548 (Nov. 1906).

CHAPTER TEN · AFTERMATH

1. See E. E. Schattschneider, *The Semi-Sovereign People* (New York, 1960), pp. 78–85.

2. R. H. Dana, Journal, II, 776, Dana Papers; Bliss Perry, *Richard Henry Dana, 1851–1931* (Boston, 1933), pp. 158, 192; Charles Warren, "Secretary's Annual Report for the Year 1896," *Massachusetts Reform Club Report and List of Members . . . December 5, 1896* (Boston, 1897), p. 6.

3. C. F. Adams to H. C. Lodge, Feb. 18, 1897, Lodge Papers; C. R. Codman, Notes and Reminiscences, III, 7, Codman Papers. For an interesting exchange on the tariff question, see C. F. Adams to Mark Hanna, Nov. 28, 1896, and Mark Hanna to C. F. Adams, Dec. 22, 1896, Charles Francis Adams Papers.

4. Charles Warren, "Secretary's Annual Report for the Year 1900," *Massachusetts Reform Club Report and List of Members . . . December 1, 1900* (Boston, 1901), p. 11.

5. C. C. Jackson to W. E. Russell, March 27, 1896, Russell Papers. See

Walter Lafeber, "The American Business Community and Cleveland's Venezuelan Message," *Business History Review*, 34:4:393–402 (Winter 1960), for a reassessment of the business response. Lafeber carefully notes opinions on both sides among Bostonians. My own reading of the evidence convinces me that the weight of politically important State Street sentiment was against Cleveland's policy.

6. C. F. Adams to H. C. Lodge, Feb. 18, 1897, G. H. Lyman to H. C. Lodge, June 9, 1898, Lodge Papers.

7. *Boston Herald*, Dec. 4, 1898, quoting Charles Francis Adams; Sarah Norton and M. A. DeWolfe Howe, eds., *Letters of Charles Eliot Norton* (Boston, 1913), II, 270; Winslow Warren to William Everett, May 25, 1899, Everett Papers; Fred H. Harrington, "The Anti-Imperialist Movement in the United States, 1898–1900," *Mississippi Valley Historical Review*, 22:2:211–230 (Sept. 1935).

8. Harrington, *M.V.H.R.*, 22:2:216–220, 230 (Sept. 1935).

9. M. A. DeW. Howe, *Portrait of an Independent: Moorfield Storey* (Boston, 1932), pp. 198–207, 224–229.

10. Schurz is quoted in C. M. Fuess, *Carl Schurz, Reformer* (New York, 1932), p. 366; Adams' letter to Schurz is published in *Boston Herald*, Oct. 31, 1900. See also *Boston Herald*, Oct. 29, 1900, and Edward Atkinson to Moorfield Storey, June 20, 1899, Atkinson Papers.

11. Charles Warren, "Secretary's Annual Report for the year 1901," *Massachusetts Reform Club Report and List of Members . . . December 7, 1901* (Boston, 1902), p. 6; Julian Codman, "Secretary's Annual Report for the Year 1902," *Massachusetts Reform Club Report and List of Members . . . December 6, 1902* (Boston, 1903), p. 9; Moorfield Storey to C. E. Norton, Sept. 8, 1907, Norton Papers, quoted in text; Howe, *Storey*, pp. 280–289; W. D. Howells, *Poems* (Cambridge, Mass., 1885), p. 83.

12. M. A. DeW. Howe, *Barrett Wendell and His Letters* (Boston, 1924), pp. 108, 109. See Henry F. May, *The End of American Innocence* (New York, 1959), pp. 33, 54, 62.

13. G. F. Williams to Moreton Frewen, Dec. 5, 1896, Frewen Papers; G. H. Lyman to H. C. Lodge, June 30, 1897, Lodge Papers.

14. C. S. Hamlin, Diary, I, 316, Hamlin Papers.

15. C. F. Gettemy, Scrapbook, VII, 92, Gettemy Collection; Alpheus T. Mason, *Brandeis: A Free Man's Life* (New York, 1946), pp. 106–241.

16. Leverett Saltonstall to author, April 9, 1962; Joseph W. Martin, Jr., *My First Fifty Years in Politics* (New York, 1960), p. 20.

17. J. E. Russell to C. S. Hamlin, Aug. 29, 1896, Hamlin Papers; J. E. Russell to W. C. Whitney, Nov. 25, 1898, Whitney Papers; J. E. Russell to Mr. Hall, Aug. 6, 1902, inserted in C. S. Hamlin, Scrapbook, XXV, 1, Hamlin Papers.

18. C. S. Hamlin, Diary, I, 179, 227, 228, Hamlin Papers; *Boston Globe*, Aug. 27, 1899; *Springfield Republican*, Sept. 3, 1902. Williams' remark is quoted in Hamlin's Diary, I, 179.

19. See Richard Olney, "International Isolation of the United States," *Atlantic Monthly*, 81:487:587 (May 1898), and *passim* for his early view. His caustic opinion of Bryan's stance is expressed in Richard Olney to S. B.

Griffin, Feb. 5, 1900, Olney Papers. His public support of Bryan is quoted from *Boston Herald,* Sept. 6, 1900. Quincy's early view is reported in *Boston Globe,* Dec. 20, 1898. His later view is quoted in *Boston Herald,* Oct. 20, 1900.

20. *Boston Herald,* Sept. 17, 1902; *Boston Transcript,* Sept. 18, 1902.

21. *Boston Herald,* Jan. 10, 1904; George E. Mowry, *The Era of Theodore Roosevelt,* (New York, 1958), pp. 176–178; C. F. Adams to C. S. Hamlin, April 1, 1904, Hamlin Papers; E. D. Mead to Moorfield Storey, Oct. 20, 1904, Storey Papers.

22. On Douglas, see Michael E. Hennessy, *Twenty-Five Years of Massachusetts Politics* (Boston, 1917), pp. 128–132. For Paine, see *Harvard College Class of 1888, Secretary's Report, No. VII* (Boston, 1913), p. 122. For Coakley, see *Springfield Republican,* Sept. 28, 1903. For Lloyd and McNeill, see *Springfield Republican,* Sept. 21, 1902. For Foster, see his highly autobiographical novel, *The Evolution of a Trade Unionist* (Boston, 1901), especially pp. 111 and 116. On Williams, see *Boston Globe,* Jan. 11, 1903; *Boston Herald,* March 21, 1904, and March 22, 1904.

23. Hennessy, *Twenty-Five Years of Massachusetts Politics* is a superficial but convenient chronicle of these years, as well as the entire period from 1890 to 1915. The reader should consult Richard M. Abrams' fine study, *Conservatism in a Progressive Era: Massachusetts Politics, 1900–1912* (Cambridge, Mass., 1964).

24. *New York Times,* Oct. 19, 1913, Nov. 16, 1914, and July 12, 1932.

25. William James, "Great Men, Great Thoughts, and the Environment," *Atlantic Monthly,* 46:276:454–455 (Oct. 1880).

26. Henry James, *The American Scene* (New York, 1907), p. 231.

27. See the perceptive remarks of Richard M. Abrams, in his "A Paradox of Progressivism: Massachusetts on the Eve of Insurgency," *Political Science Quarterly,* 75:3:379–399 (Sept. 1960).

INDEX

Adams, Brooks: and 1884 campaign, 17; and Young Men's Democratic Club, 86; and 1896 campaign, 221–224, 244; mentioned, 22

Adams, Charles Francis (1807–1886), 12, 13, 54

Adams, Charles Francis (1835–1915): sketch, 21–22; and Mugwumps, 5–6, 10; and Storey, 24; and Quincy, Mass., 33; and tariff reform, 76, 195–196, 264; and Young Men's Democratic Club, 86; and civil service reform, 196; and depression, 201; and Brooks Adams, 222; and 1896 campaign, 229; and imperialism, 266–267; supports McKinley, 269; on Democratic party, 277; mentioned 216, 270

Adams, Charles Francis (1866–1954), 254

Adams, Henry, 22, 24, 215, 223, 244, 245

Adams, John Quincy, 12, 14, 33, 55

Allen, Isaac, 241–242

Altgeld, John Peter, 230

American Federation of Labor, 220

American Protective Association, in Massachusetts, 151–153

Ames, James Barr, 20

Ames, Oliver, 6, 38, 64, 65, 67

Andrew, John F.: sketch, 25–26; as Mugwump, 23; candidate for governor, 64–65; and Young Men's Democratic Club, 84; runs for Congress, 95, 99, 154; as Congressman, 180, 184, 190; defeated, 187; death, 272; mentioned, 35, 67, 146, 189

Anti-Catholicism, in Boston, 150–153

Anti-imperialism, ix, 265–269, 275

Anti-Imperialist League, 268

Arena, 238, 246, 260

Arkwright Club, and tariff reform, 78

Arthur, Chester, 4, 7

Atkinson, Edward: sketch, 22–23; on Irish nationalism, 34; on democracy, 34–35; on labor, 36, 37; as inventor, 38; on the rich, 39; on functions of government, 50; as tariff reformer, 75, 76, 95, 177; and Young Men's Democratic Club, 86; on rapid transit, 124; on Mayor Matthews, 160; and the New South, 173–175; on silver, 178–180, 191; hope for a new party, 195; as anti-imperialist, 267; mentioned, 21, 198

Bancroft, George, 57

Baring Brothers, failure in 1890, 178

Baxter, Sylvester, 125–126, 217, 254

Bayard, Thomas F., 11

Bellamy, Edward, 125, 140, 162, 217, 255

Bennett, J. Q., 89

Bird, Francis W., 13, 14, 27

Blaine, James G., viii, 1, 7, 15, 18, 24, 25

Bland, Richard P., 183, 184

Board of Strategy (Boston), 248, 256, 257, 259

Boston: heterogeneous population, xi; and Mugwumps, 20; political clubs, 29; port, 57; North End, 34, 54, 63, 134, 152, 168–170; South End, 167, 170, 250–251, 260; West End, 134, 168; charter of 1885, 62, 159; O'Brien's may-